FROM HOPE TO HARRIS

The Reshaping of Ontario's Schools

Ontario's schools are currently in turmoil. Under the Harris government, sweeping changes in governance, finance, and curriculum have produced unprecedented conflict and deep divisions. *From Hope to Harris* sets these developments in a broad historical context.

Beginning with a portrait of the school system in 1950, the year the Hope Commission offered its own blueprint for Ontario's schools, Gidney describes the expansion of the system, changing purposes, conflicts over curriculum and pedagogy, reorganization of governance and finance, and new departures in provision for Roman Catholic and francophone education. He highlights the struggles over other forms of equitable treatment for children and young people, and the impact of larger social changes on the schools. The politics of education under successive Ontario governments is a major theme, and includes an extended discussion of the origins, events, and immediate aftermath of the Harris government's 'common sense' revolution in education.

From Hope to Harris charts the major landmarks, the paths taken or not taken, and the debates that have washed over the Ontario educational landscape from the 1950s to the end of the century. Given the current unrest over educational issues, this book will be of interest to teachers and parents alike, and to all those concerned about the future of public education in Ontario.

R.D. GIDNEY is Professor Emeritus, Faculty of Education, University of Western Ontario.

FROM HOPE TO HARRIS

The Reshaping of Ontario's Schools

R.D. GIDNEY

UNIVERSITY OF TORONTO PRESS
Toronto Buffalo London

© University of Toronto Press Incorporated 1999
Toronto Buffalo London
Printed in Canada

ISBN 0-8020-4292-9 (cloth)
ISBN 0-8020-8125-8 (paper)

Printed on acid-free paper

Canadian Cataloguing in Publication Data

Gidney, R.D. (Robert Douglas), 1940–
From Hope to Harris: the reshaping of Ontario's schools

Includes bibliographical references and index.
ISBN 0-8020-4292-9 (bound)   ISBN 0-8020-8125-8 (pbk.)

1. Education – Ontario – History – 20th century.   I. Title.

LA418.O6G524 1999   370'.9713'09045   C99-930719-3

University of Toronto Press acknowledges the financial assistance to its
publishing program of the Canada Council for the Arts and
the Ontario Arts Council.

This book has been published with the help of a grant from the Humanities
and Social Sciences Federation of Canada, using funds provided by the
Social Sciences and Humanities Research Council of Canada.

University of Toronto Press acknowledges the financial support for its publishing
activities of the Government of Canada through the Book Publishing Industry
Development Program(BPIDP).

Canadä

Contents

Acknowledgments

This book is the product of a career spent teaching and learning at the Faculty of Education, University of Western Ontario. Many of my colleagues at Western have read and critiqued bits and pieces of my work, willingly shared their own research with me, and set me straight on issues I had yet to understand. Forced to read earlier drafts of this manuscript, my graduate students offered helpful commentary and insights drawn from their own extensive experience in the schools. Two deans of the faculty, B.B. Kymlicka and Allen Pearson, gave me the kind of moral and material support that only good deans know how to provide. From the time I first proposed the project, Gerry Hallowell, at the University of Toronto Press, offered encouragement and maintained his own enthusiasm even when mine flagged. Paul Axelrod and Elizabeth Smyth were kind enough to read the entire manuscript and give me the benefit of their comments and criticism. To all these people, my thanks. For the graphics, my thanks to Jim Thomson, as well as to Wendy Saby and her colleagues in the Media Production Centre at the Faculty of Education.

I owe a special debt of gratitude to a handful of people who have gone to unusual lengths to ensure this book would be better than I could have done by myself. During the later stages of the project, Jennifer and Allan Brooks were relentless in helping me gather together essential sources. Two long-standing colleagues, Jerry Paquette and Don Gutteridge, put their academic expertise, their experience in Ontario's schools, and their remarkable grasp of educational issues at my disposal without stint or hope of reward. They read and reread successive drafts, and offered me indispensable advice all along the way. In addition, Jerry generously allowed me to use the fruits of his own hard work on educational finance, while Don struggled, against the odds, to improve my prose. My heartfelt appreciation. Then there is Wyn Millar. Without her this book would never have been started or finished; without her, in any case, there are no books worth writing.

FROM HOPE TO HARRIS

The Reshaping of Ontario's Schools

1

Introduction

The title of this book is not as ironic as it might seem. I begin at mid-century, the year in which a royal commission, chaired by Justice John Andrew Hope, offered its post-war blueprint for Ontario's schools. I conclude with an account of the major changes introduced by the Harris government in 1997–8, the apogee of its attempt to fundamentally refashion the province's education system. The intervening decades have been years of rapid change, sharp shifts in direction, and, at times, tumultuous conflict. My purpose is to chart these developments – to provide a historical map of the major landmarks, the paths taken or not taken, the debates that have washed across the educational landscape.

While the book addresses a broad range of issues, it does not pretend to be comprehensive, something that would have required a much longer, more unwieldly text. I have very little to say about the special character or distinctive developments of Ontario's regions, such as the north, or the province's large urban communities. While I hope my account helps illuminate their past, they need their own historians. For the same reason, some important topics are given only the briefest treatment or left out altogether. To cite only some examples: the Canadian studies movement of the late 1960s and 1970s, the origins and rise of instruction in French as a second language and French-immersion education, the use of computers and other technology in the schools, the changing place of religious observance and instruction, private schools,[1] and though in many ways inextricably interlinked, the massive changes in post-secondary education that have taken place over the last five decades. I have also attempted to avoid, where possible, excessive documentation; I explain in the bibliographic note how I have proceeded in that respect.

THERE ARE CERTAIN fundamental structural features of Ontario's school system, most of which have been in place for a century or more. Since all the chapters that follow assume a working knowledge of these features, an elementary introduction may be helpful to those unfamiliar with them. One premise is that public education will be paid for by public funds. The detailed provisions for financing elementary and secondary education have long been complex, but the principles are simple. The money to pay for schools comes from a combination of local property taxes and grants from the provincial government. The Ontario Ministry of Revenue places a dollar value (or an assessed value) on each piece of property in the province and then each municipality charges the owner a certain percentage of that value. This is what is meant by a property tax, and such taxes are paid by the owners of almost all property in the province, residential, commercial, and industrial alike. The money raised is spent by the municipalities on local services ranging from roads and sewers to police and firemen, and by school boards to finance the elementary and secondary schools. Government grants, the second source of financial support for the schools, come from a variety of sources including provincial sales tax, levies on items like gasoline and liquor, and provincial income tax (which we all pay even though we first pay it to the federal government, which then gives it back to the province).

Government grants are intended to help localities meet the costs of providing education at a standard determined by provincial policies. They can be crudely divided into three types. One, commonly called a 'foundation grant,' provides all localities with a set per-pupil amount designed to pay for basic classroom services ranging from teacher's salaries and textbooks to classroom supplies and custodial services. Another is the 'categorical grant,' intended either to compensate for special costs and needs (for example, heating in northern Ontario, rural transportation, or English as a second language) or to encourage boards to pursue policies or innovations that the government has identified as worthwhile. The third is an equalization adjustment. The total value of property in different localities can vary enormously depending on the wealth of their residents or the size and number of their businesses and industries. In order to ensure that each locality has at least the minimum amount of money to maintain the educational services required of it, government compensates poorer communities by means of larger grants or by some equivalent transfer of funds.

A SECOND PREMISE is the principle of public control. That principle exists for two reasons. One is that public education is designed to serve public purposes and must, therefore, be amenable to public control. The second, though obviously overlapping, is that there must be public accountability for the raising and spending of taxes. Unlike the case in many other countries, however, in Canada public control of education is exercised not by the national government but by the government of each province. Section 93 of the British North America Act – the legislation that, in 1867, gave birth to this country – began with the words: 'In and for each province the Legislature may exclusively make Laws in relation to education.' And Section 93 is now incorporated into the Constitution Act of 1982. As a result, the federal or Canadian government has no control over education in Canada.

Immediately some qualifications must be made to that blunt generalization, because the federal government does indeed have certain limited constitutional responsibilities for education, and some influence in shaping educational policy. For example, the constitution gives the federal government responsibility for status Indians living on reserves, and it either pays for the maintenance of schools on reserves or purchases educational services from a nearby school board. Ottawa also bears broad responsibilities for national economic development and the country's general welfare, and that often has educational implications. In many areas of Canadian life, such as the promotion of research and development or the production of a skilled workforce, educational and economic policy can hardly be divorced or even tidily divided into federal and provincial jurisdictions. Thus over the course of this century the federal government has sporadically tried to influence educational policy on a number of fronts. It can do so by throwing money at the provinces in the hope that they will adopt this or that educational initiative, or by inviting provincial participants to co-operate through some other means. But it *cannot* intervene against a provincial government's will. To reiterate, education in this country is exclusively a provincial jurisdiction, and thus each province makes its own rules and can create the kind of system it wishes.

Or almost. Though they are relatively few, there are some things a province cannot do. The Canadian Charter of Rights and Freedoms contains protections relating to education for individuals and minority groups which cannot be abridged by any provincial government. Ontario, moreover, cannot limit the legal rights granted to Roman Catholic separate schools: the existence of the Catholic school system is guaranteed in the Canadian constitution and cannot be abolished or even much changed by the provincial government alone.

The separate schools, however, are also *public* schools in the sense that they are financed by grants and local taxes like other public schools, and in all but their religious policies are administered just like the rest of the public system. Whatever else they are, they are not 'private schools.' Many of the latter exist in Ontario, and always have. Though section 93 gives the province jurisdiction over these schools as it does over nearly all our educational institutions, including the universities, private schools operate relatively independently of public control and receive no public funding. Parents who choose to send their children to private schools must pay the tuition fees such schools charge, and pay their public school taxes as well.

THE PROVINCIAL LEGISLATURE exercises its control over public education by passing laws that specify how the system is to be organized and administered. Most of the pertinent legislation affecting schools is gathered together in the Education Act. Along with the regulations made under that act (which equally have the force of law), it provides the legal authority for the governance of public education.[2] For decades, governance has been divided into two distinct parts: on the one hand, the minister of education and his or her ministry,* responsible for education throughout the province, and, on the other, elected trustees responsible for operating the schools in particular localities.

The minister is a politician, an elected member of the legislature, a member of the party in power and of the cabinet. While the premier acting alone, or the cabinet as a whole, may decide on major initiatives, in most circumstances it is the minister who sets policy and priorities. The political tasks of the minister are to persuade cabinet colleagues to support recommended policies financially or otherwise, defend those policies in the legislature, shepherd new legislation through the House, and persuade the public to support government policy and the educational system generally. The minister, however, is also the political head of the Ministry of Education, the group of civil servants who advise the minister on virtually all matters connected with public education and who administer the system. The ranking permanent officer in the ministry is normally designated the deputy minister, but he or she is a civil servant, not a politician, and is responsible to the minister for its general operation. Though most of the real work of policy-making and administration is done

---

*In the early chapters of this book I will refer to the 'Department of Education.' That traditional name was changed to the 'Ministry of Education' in 1972. As of 1993 the formal title was changed to the 'Ministry of Education and Training.' I will use the abbreviated terminology throughout.

by civil servants, it is, according to law and constitutional convention, the minister who exercises power and who bears responsibility for the operation of the ministry.

In recent decades the span of control exercised by the minister has ranged from the elementary and secondary schools alone to the universities, colleges, and other forms of educational provision. But traditionally the primary responsibility was the school system. Within that sphere, the powers of the minister have been extensive. There is, indeed, hardly any aspect of the system that is outside his or her jurisdiction. The minister, for example, controls what is to be taught in the schools, who will be allowed to teach it, and the books or other materials it will be taught from. Most of the minister's powers, it is perhaps worth emphasizing, apply equally to all government-funded schools; thus when I write about educational policy in Ontario I am referring, in the main, to policies that directed the activities of public and separate, French and English, schools alike, and not, simply, to one or another part of the system.

Public control at the local level is exercised by school trustees elected by the voters in each municipal unit. Collectively the trustees form a 'board of education,' and have a variety of duties: to build and maintain schools, hire teachers and support staff, and generally oversee the provision of education within their jurisdiction. Trustees have, and have always had, a good deal of latitude in some matters relating to both the quality and quantity of education offered in their communities. But this latitude does not extend to essentials. Boards *must* provide school facilities, hire licensed teachers, enforce the attendance laws, and so forth. School boards, in other words, are responsible for carrying out provincial policy and cannot opt out of Ontario's school system.

In 1998 the provincial government assumed the power to set the amount to be raised by school boards from local property taxes. But that was *not* the case before 1998, and it is crucial the reader understand the difference: otherwise entire tracts of what follows will be rendered unintelligible. Traditionally in Ontario, indeed for a century and a half before 1998, school boards themselves decided, without restriction, how much money to spend on local schools and determined how much money to raise from property taxes to pay the bills. To put it another way, while the provincial government controlled the size of its own grants to schools, local school boards were free to raise any additional amounts they wished to, and largely free to decide how that money was spent.

HOWEVER BARE BONES this account of the structure of the school system, it does direct attention to two of the three motifs that run through the text from beginning to end. One of these is governance: that is, the relative roles of province and locality in providing direction for the schools, and the changing structure of local administration. The second is educational finance. Though rarely considered a compelling subject, finance is central to nearly all debates about educational quality and equity, and deserves more serious attention than it often gets. Finally, there is the third motif: the curriculum, or what I will sometimes call the program of studies. What gets taught, who decides what gets taught, how it gets taught, and how we assess what gets learned are issues that go to the heart of the educational enterprise. Though there are exceptions, one or another of these motifs provides the focus for distinct chapters throughout the book.

I begin my account with an overview of the school system in the years around mid-century. That provides a kind of 'baseline' designed to set the stage for the decades that followed. Chapters 3 and 4 recount the remarkable developments of the 1960s; 5 and 6 are devoted to the period 1971–85, when a very different temper prevailed. I then double back over these years, in chapters 7 and 8, to examine the separate school system, Franco-Ontarian education, and several other issues relating to a broadening mandate for the schools. Beginning with chapter 9, I provide an account of the last fifteen years of the twentieth century – an era which had its own coherence and which ended with the turbulent first three years of the 'Mike Harris government.'

2

The Education System at Mid-Century, 1945–1960

By 1945 or 1950 Ontario already exhibited many of the features we usually associate with a modern urban industrial society. Two-thirds of its people lived in towns and cities and worked at urban occupations. Large numbers were engaged in plants and factories manufacturing everything from iron and steel to precision machine tools, automobiles, and consumer electronic products. The province had completed the building of its first superhighway, the Queen Elizabeth Way, and most of its larger communities were knit together not just by ribbons of rail but by paved highways as well. Even in isolated parts of the province many homes now had electricity, and localism everywhere was in retreat before the intrusive presence of the radio, imposing its cosmopolitan and homogenizing influence on town and country alike.

Yet in many respects mid-century Ontario was also a dramatically different kind of society than it would be fifty years later. By modern standards, Ontario's urban communities were of modest size. Even the greater Toronto area, with just over a million people, was much smaller than it is now, and the extent of suburbanization was still limited: though the city had been spreading outwards for decades, its nearest neighbours, North York, Scarborough, and Etobicoke, remained predominantly rural townships dotted by farms, hamlets, and villages. Hamilton had 208,000 people, nearly all living beneath the escarpment; at just under 100,000, London's population was less than a third of the size it is now; and most of Ontario's urbanites lived in towns that were half or less their present size. Just over 25 per cent of the province's inhabitants still lived in rural areas – on farms or in communities with fewer than a thousand people. If a growing number of men and women worked in 'white-collar' occupations, a substantial majority were still employed in either primary industry – agriculture, forestry, or mining – or in factories. Ontario might already have one superhighway, but the building of the 400 or the 401 had hardly been thought of, and the tracery of narrow, two-lane highways that criss-crossed the province still followed routes carved out of the wilderness a century ago or more. If radio had penetrated everywhere, only a handful of Canadian children had ever watched television, the icebox was more common than the fridge, the automobile remained the preserve of the better-off, and electric trolleys not only trundled along the streets of the larger towns and cities but offered the most accessible link between many communities.

It was also a society just beginning to emerge from fifteen years of wrenching dislocation and haunting insecurity. The depression of the 1930s had brought massive unemployment, industrial stagnation, municipal bankruptcy, and spiritual demoralization. The Second World War, which began for Canada in 1939, solved some of these problems. Building an army and meeting the industrial and agricultural demands created by the war fuelled economic growth, put people back to work, and restored a sense of common purpose. Yet the war bred its own dislocations, of people and resources, and the dominant mood of the immediate post-war years was a deep yearning for normality, security, and stability.

BY 1950, ONTARIO's school system was the product of a century of accretions. Decades of piecemeal innovation designed to accommodate it to a changing social and economic order had not yet entirely erased its origins in an agrarian society hardly more than a step removed from first settlement. Nowhere was this legacy revealed more plainly than in the organization of local school administration. As I write, Ontario has seventy-two school boards, and most share the same structure and function: a dozen or more elected trustees exercise jurisdiction over an extensive geographic unit, often the size of several counties. That unit will contain many schools, both elementary and secondary, and the board will employ a large number of teachers, supervisory officers, and various other personnel. In the late 1940s, by contrast, Ontario had over 4000 school boards. A few of these, located in the larger towns and cities, were responsible for all the public elementary and secondary schools within their boundaries, and employed not only teachers and principals but a director of education and other supervisory officers. There were, however, other boards responsible for high schools or elementary schools alone, as well as boards responsible for only a village, for a single township, or indeed a single school. Aside from perhaps a janitor or two, who might be part-time in any case, most of these boards employed only teachers or, where there was more than one, a 'head teacher' or principal. By far the most common form of local governance was the board of trustees of a rural 'school section.' In such cases three elected trustees presided over the affairs of a single school, which usually had one classroom and one teacher, and drew its pupils from a geographical area approximately six miles square. A township that was largely rural might contain as many as fifteen of these sections, and in Ontario as a whole there were about 2300 of them in 1950.

Except for the most isolated parts of northern Ontario, the entire province was divided into elementary school units of one kind or another. That was not the case, however, for secondary education. The development of the secondary schools had been largely distinct from the elementary schools. Thus they had had their own school boards, some of which still survived in 1950. Because they had been exclusively urban institutions, the boundaries of a high school board's jurisdiction rarely extended beyond the incorporated urban area where the school was situated. But that meant that large parts of rural Ontario lay outside the purview of any high school board, and special provision had to be made to ensure access for 'county pupils,' as they were called, to the high schools in the towns and villages.*

LIKE THE BOARDS, the schools were also smaller and more diverse. In 1948, for example, Ontario had some 6800 elementary schools, nearly twice as many as there are today, and that despite a population a third the size. Forty-four hundred of them, or 71 per cent, had one teacher and a single classroom. Another 600 had but two of each. Only 853 had six classrooms or more, and there were just 150 elementary schools which, in the modern mode, had twenty or more classrooms. Transported back by the proverbial time-machine, modern teachers or pupils might not feel much out of place in some of the recently built, multi-classroom elementary schools of 1950, though they might be struck by the fact that even when the desks were movable, children still sat (and were expected to sit quietly) in tidy rows. To enter the door of the typical Ontario rural school, however, was a different matter. Here one might find a one-room schoolhouse containing twenty or thirty pupils aged six to fourteen and fifteen, and spanning grades 1 to 8, all taught by one female teacher, the oldest boys and girls sitting in a row on one side of the room, the youngest on the other, and the

*For a vivid illustration of the degree of diversity of local administration, the sheer jumble, indeed, of different boards and overlapping jurisdictions, see the map of an imaginary Ontario county on page 236 of the *Report of the Royal Commission on Education in Ontario, 1950* (Hope Report).

rest in between. During the course of the school day each grade might be taught a lesson or two and in some cases taught jointly. But for much of the time, pupils, young or old, were expected to get on with their seat work while the teacher moved sequentially through the grades. The pedagogical arrangements might seem quaint; the physical facilities in many one-room schools were downright primitive. In 1950, 40 per cent of them still lacked inside toilets; 15 per cent lacked a 'safe water supply'; about a third of the rural public schools and half the separate schools did not yet even have hydro.[1]

Many of Ontario's schools might be ill equipped for the task at hand, but at least provision was made for the basic education of the vast majority of youngsters. Not so in the case of children with special needs. There had long been educational institutions run by the province for the profoundly deaf and the blind. But for most others, provision was meagre and haphazard. It was entirely limited to the elementary schools in urban communities, and even then was far from extensive. Ontario had several thousand elementary school classes in 1950–1; yet the total number of special-education classes, of all kinds, was hardly more than six hundred. Children with special needs were not the only ones to be ill served by the schools, however. Even setting aside the vast disparities in facilities characteristic of town and country, or between the settled south and the thinly populated north, children attending Roman Catholic schools were disadvantaged compared to their public school counterparts, Franco-Ontarian children faced even more formidable obstacles to obtaining an education, and large numbers of aboriginal youngsters were not served at all.

AS IS THE CASE today, the secondary schools at mid-century tended to be substantially larger than most elementary schools; still, by current standards, they were of modest size. In 1948, 28 per cent of the high schools had five classrooms or fewer, and an equivalent number of teachers; only 17 per cent had more than twenty rooms. The average attendance across the province was 328 and the average staff size was fifteen. While nearly all urban communities had a high school, there were also more than a hundred 'continuation schools' located where a village and nearby townships generated some demand for secondary education but not enough to sustain a full-fledged secondary school. Most commonly they offered only grades 9 to 11; students then had to transfer to the nearest high school – and often board away from home – to finish their secondary education.

In Ontario, as elsewhere, it had long been the conviction of many leading educators that the single most urgent issue confronting education in the countryside was consolidation: larger administrative units and larger schools, they believed, would bring economies of scale, the pedagogical benefits of a greater division of labour, and more varied and improved educational opportunities. By 1950 some progress had been made, resulting in the establishment of over five hundred 'township boards' absorbing myriad school sections; still, most townships remained organized by section. In urban areas there had been a significant increase in the number of amalgamated high and elementary school boards. Yet consolidation proceeded slowly and erratically. Local people remained jealous of local control and the closing of a schoolhouse might deprive a small community of its only public institution. Rural Ontario was still a powerful force in provincial politics, and even those politicians who favoured consolidation were not prepared to impose it. But the constraints were not only political. The effects of depression and war had meant that there was no money to build the new schools that consolidation required and, equally, local municipalities lacked the funds to create or maintain the all-weather roads, or to purchase the buses, that would enable pupils to travel beyond the boundaries of their school section.

JUST AS THE SCHOOLS at mid-century were substantially different from those of the 1990s, so was the pattern of school attendance. Since 1919, school attendance had been compulsory between ages eight and sixteen. By 1950, most children were enrolled in grade 1 before they reached the age of eight; but they were nearly evenly divided between ages six and seven, with rural children starting later than their urban counterparts. Few five-year-olds were enrolled in grade 1, and kindergarten was not available except in the larger urban areas – by 1950 only some six hundred classes were in operation. Thus the majority of children started school in grade 1, at the age of either six or seven.

Once in school, nearly all pupils stayed into their fourteenth year. But the law provided that parents who could demonstrate financial need could apply for an 'exemption certificate' permitting a child to leave school and enter the workforce at age fourteen. In the late 1940s large numbers of parents were still exercising that option and five or six thousand exemptions were granted each year, though mostly for those aged fifteen. After that, the retention rate dropped precipitously. In 1948 it was estimated that 54 per cent of all students who entered elementary school had dropped out by age sixteen. Of the entire 15–19 age group, fewer than 40 per cent were in school. In the late 1940s, these patterns held true for boys and girls alike.

Even these figures gloss over some of the more striking differences between schooling in the 1990s and at mid-century. Because high schools were less accessible, rural children in particular often completed all the formal education they would ever receive in the elementary school. In that, however, they were not alone. Of all those who left school in 1948, only 67 per cent completed grade 8 and only 61 per cent actually entered grade 9. After that, the dropout rate was staggering (see figure 1*). Very large numbers of Ontario youngsters, in other words, never reached high school, only a minority proceeded beyond grade 10, and 80 per cent failed to complete grade 12. The significance of these last figures can perhaps best be grasped by two simple comparisons. Twenty years later, in 1970–1, 80 per cent of those who had begun grade 9 three years earlier would be enrolled in grade 12, and 65 per cent would receive a grade 12 graduation diploma. Whether we measure by age or by grade, the average levels of schooling in mid-twentieth-century Ontario were substantially below what they are today.

Though some secondary schools offered a vocational program and many more had commercial departments, what all high schools offered, and what the vast majority of students actually enrolled in, was the academic or 'general course.' It consisted of a core of English, physical education, history, geography, mathematics, science, Latin, French, and, if facilities allowed, home economics, commercial subjects, or shop.[2] One would normally take a total of six or seven subjects, but since most high schools were small and could offer relatively few courses, a student's options were limited. Most subjects were organized in a sequential manner, with each year's work prerequisite to the next. The program of studies, moreover, was not 'streamed.' In grade 10 or 11, for example, some students might take Latin and others shop, but in both cases the vast bulk of their time would be spent in *common* courses in other academic subjects. Everyone, that is to say, took the same content in most subjects and wrote the same examinations, moving in lockstep through each course and grade until one of three things happened: they failed (which significant numbers did); they opted to leave school; or they completed grade 12 or 13.

There were reasons for the academic bias of the high school, the proportionately enormous enrolments in the general program, and the high attrition rates. Vocational programs were unavailable to large num-

*The figures are collected in an appendix at the back of the book.

bers of students,* in part because they were expensive; commercial programs were more common, in part because they were cheaper; but neither was as low-cost as a Latin or English teacher standing with textbook in hand at the front of a class. In this respect the depression and then the diversion of resources to wartime purposes played their parts in shaping the character of the mid-twentieth-century high school.

But there was more to it than that. Even where vocational training existed, far larger numbers chose to enrol in the general program of the high schools and to leave school at the end of grade 9 or 10. Why? Today we take it for granted that the high school constitutes one part of a continuum intended to provide a basic education for all young people. As late as mid-century, however, that notion was only beginning to take hold. The Adolescent School Attendance Act of 1919 had asserted the principle of compulsory education to age sixteen; changes first introduced in the late 1930s and gradually implemented thereafter shifted the curriculum in grades 9 and 10 towards a program more suited to the majority of students, pushing academic specialization into the senior grades. But even these innovations still accorded with the view that the appropriate period for universal education extended to grades 9 or 10, corresponding to the age group six to sixteen. The educational mandate for those ten years was to ensure that the next generation achieved literacy and numeracy, acquired an elementary familiarity with their rights and duties as citizens, and were exposed to a modicum of the common culture. That accomplished, parents and teachers alike took it for granted that most students would enter the workforce. To do so, moreover, was an entirely practical proposition in an age when the economy could still soak up large amounts of relatively uneducated labour, when technical training was commonly acquired on the job, and when even most clerical jobs required only grade 9 or 10.

The senior high school had an essentially different purpose: to select and prepare a minority of students for the universities and professions, for teaching, and for a small number of other white-collar occupations that required an education beyond the norm. And it accomplished this task in a particular way. The education it offered that minority was an induction

*In 1948 Ontario had 239 high schools, 114 continuation schools, and some 60 vocational schools (a few of these were free-standing; the rest were housed in a wing of the local high school). In the light of more recent usage it is perhaps worth emphasizing that at mid-century the term 'vocational' school referred to one that taught craft skills to quite advanced levels and required a mix in each grade of shops and conventional academic courses. It was not a euphemism for a school serving 'slow learners.'

into a group of academic subjects, the unique cultural value of which was not seriously challenged, and which, it was believed, trained the mind as no other program of studies could do. Put another way, the senior high school was one of the key gatekeepers of the social system and, at the same time, a guardian of the cultural order. It identified those destined for leadership, broadly construed, and inculcated the values and knowledge that constituted the good and the true. At mid-century this relatively limited but sharply focused and morally ambitious mandate had a large degree of legitimacy in Ontario. The fact that both the role of the Ontario high school and the certainties that underpinned its mandate would undergo so dramatic a transformation in the succeeding fifty years must obviously preoccupy us in the chapters that follow.

AND SO MUST THE CHANGING character of the separate school system, which was also substantially different at mid-century than it is today. Catholic schools were supported by public funds to grade 10 only. Grades 11, 12, and 13 received no funding at all, nor were they subject to the authority of the ministry. These grades in the Catholic school were private schools, supported by tuition fees, subsidies provided by parishes, and other private benefactions. Moreover, grades 9 and 10 received elementary school grants rather than the larger secondary school grants given to the same grades in the public high schools. And while the public schools received a significant portion of their local receipts from the property taxes paid to municipalities by large business and industrial corporations, the separate schools had no access to these funds. Indeed they laboured under other significant disadvantages as well. At least two questions thus present themselves: Why separate schools at all? And why, if they were going to exist, were they subject to these disabilities?

That first question is *not* the same as, Why *Catholic* schools? The Church, and many lay Catholics throughout the world, have for centuries been committed to the principle that Catholic schools are an essential institution, one leg of the tripod which bears responsibility for raising the young in Christian holiness, the others being the family and the Church itself. Catholics have never been, nor are they now, alone in this conviction. It has meant, however, that everywhere, in the old world and the new, Catholics have worked diligently and with great devotion to establish schools for their own children. In some places, the United States being one good example, the structure of Catholic education is maintained by entirely voluntary means, since no denominational education of any kind receives public money. There are provinces of Canada, like British Columbia, where this was traditionally true as well. In Ontario, however, some types of Catholic schools have received public funding for well over a century, a circumstance that can only be explained by reaching back before Confederation to the early history of the province, when it was still known as Upper Canada.

In the middle decades of the nineteenth century, Upper Canada was overwhelmingly Protestant and often violently anti-Catholic. Indeed, if most Upper Canadians had had their way, there would have been no separate schools – the Protestant majority simply would not have allowed it. Between 1840 and 1867, however, Upper Canada was locked in a legislative union with Lower Canada (Quebec). There was a single legislature in which each section had an equal number of seats. And because of that, Roman Catholics in Lower Canada, who constituted the vast majority of its population, had considerable influence over school legislation in Upper Canada *and* vice versa. The result was a series of compromises in both sections that provided for the public funding of two sorts of minority religious schools, and two sorts only – Roman Catholic in Ontario and Protestant in Quebec.[3]

The old legislative union ended with Confederation in 1867 and jurisdiction over education was given to the provinces. But the rights of minority religious schools *already enshrined in law* were guaranteed in the Confederation agreement itself – the British North America Act. In some cases these legal rights were clear and undisputed – the right to establish elementary schools, for example, to receive government grants to support them, to offer denominational religious instruction in them, or to elect their own trustees. But there were other issues where the pre-Confederation legislation was ambiguous or its interpretation disputed. One of these was the vexed question of public funding for Catholic secondary education. The lineage of the Ontario high school springs most directly from the Upper Canadian grammar school, and there was no such thing as a denominational grammar school funded under any of the pre-Confederation grammar school acts. But the program of studies in a few elementary schools, including some separate schools, overlapped that of the early years of the grammar school. Thus after 1867 the government concluded that separate schools did have the right to public funding for grades 9 and 10. Since these grades had been taught only in the separate elementary schools, however, the government also decided that they should be eligible only for elementary grants, instead of the larger amounts received by secondary schools.

In the late nineteenth and early twentieth centuries this settlement was

increasingly challenged, and during the 1920s Catholics began a prolonged legal campaign to reverse it. But the courts decided that Catholics
had no right to public funds beyond what they already had. While the
Ontario government could not abridge legal rights that existed at Confederation (as interpreted by the courts), it was assumed, on the other hand,
that it could, of its own accord, extend them. But a large and often vocal
opposition to any extension of funding for separate schools made the issue
one that politicians wanted to avoid like the plague.

Catholic schools suffered one other important financial burden as well.
Local property taxation raised revenues from assessing residential, commercial, and industrial properties. Some of the most lucrative of the latter
two were owned by large corporations. Only individual Catholic property
owners, however, could direct their taxes to the separate schools. So long
as one could identify the owners of businesses and industries, no problem
arose. But with the rise of the modern public corporation in the twentieth
century, the situation changed dramatically: 'ownership' was diffused
amongst a large number of stockholders and turnover was high. How,
then, was one to identify the number of Catholic owners so that a corporation could direct a proportionate share of its property taxes to the separate
schools? The answer was that it was impossible to tell, and thus corporate
property taxes went, by default, to the public system. The Catholic schools,
in sum, were poor cousins not only because of the elementary grant to
grades 9 and 10 but, far more important, because they had no access to a
significant portion of the total property assessment in municipalities all
over Ontario. Catholic ratepayers, moreover, had no obligation to direct
their property taxes to these schools, and for a variety of reasons many
parents opted to support the public schools, further depriving the separate system of tax support.

Given that situation, there were only two options. Individual Catholic
separate school supporters could be taxed substantially more than their
next-door neighbours who supported the public schools, or the schools
had to be operated with far lower per-pupil expenditure. But early on,
Catholic leaders discovered that they could not solve the problem by
raising their rates – faced with substantially heavier taxation, too many
Catholic parents voted with their children's feet and switched their tax
dollars to the public schools. Thus the only viable alternative was to run a
cheaper system. And for nearly a hundred years after Confederation, that
is exactly what Catholics did. The key to a cheaper system was cheap
labour, and the separate school system survived largely because it could
depend on the devoted commitment of the religious orders – nuns and

teaching brothers. At mid-century something like 46 per cent of separate school teachers came from this source. But even their large contribution hardly eliminated the disparity in resources between the separate and public schools.[4]

THOUGH THE PROVINCE'S boards of education and its schools were a numerous and diverse lot, they were knit together into a system by the Ontario Department of Education, which not only played a central role in policy-making but exercised its supervisory responsibilities directly and emphatically. In the first place, it set out what was to be taught in the schools in an unequivocal manner. Every elementary teacher, for example, possessed a copy of what two or three generations would nickname, because of the colour of its cover, the 'little grey book,' a volume that provided an outline of topics and subjects to be covered in the first six grades of elementary school.[5] High school teachers had subject outlines that provided them with the same information. One did not opt out or select topics from this or that portion of the guide; one taught the prescribed content, and taught it in the sequence indicated, organizing one's daily lessons and weekly units of work accordingly.

Having prescribed what teachers were to teach, and pupils to learn, the department then sent out inspectors to see that it was done. A corps of public (or separate) school inspectors visited the elementary schools on a regular basis, advising and supervising trustees, principals, and teachers alike.* They were there to help trustees, and especially those in very small units who lacked other sources of advice, on all manner of issues ranging from boundary disputes and the filing of annual reports to the esoterica of local finance. They spent a half-day or more in the classroom observing teaching techniques, sometimes criticizing or demonstrating better ways to do things. They checked the 'day-book,' which contained an on-going record of the work covered each school day, and confirmed the attendance rolls. At the high school level the inspectorate was organized by region, and also by subject, with one or two inspectors responsible for supervising the teaching of history or English or mathematics across the whole province. As well, teams of subject inspectors would periodically descend upon particular schools to examine their overall operation.

The third means of control, and of ensuring public accountability, was

---

*Only a handful of cities with their own supervisory officers were exempt from this requirement, and even then local inspectors were expected to fulfil the public school inspector's mandate.

through province-wide examinations. Earlier in the twentieth century
these had been used to determine promotion standards at various points
in the system. Generations of grade 8 pupils, for example, had written the
'high school entrance examination,' the admission ticket to high school.
Gradually, however, promotion decisions were turned over to teachers,
principals, and boards, and by 1950 only the 'grade 13 departmentals'
remained. The departmentals were a set of province-wide, subject-by-
subject, centrally set and marked examinations written at the end of the
grade 13 school year. The results, for each student, were published in the
local newspaper, and the marks awarded were uncontaminated by any
mitigating influence: teachers' evaluations or term marks played no part
in determining the outcome. A year's work, indeed the fruits of five years'
study, depended on a series of three-hour ordeals in a stuffy classroom
during a sultry week or so in June.

The results were of critical importance to anyone wishing to go on to
post-secondary education, but they were no less so to teachers and principals, for the quality of instruction was judged and ranked by the number
of 'passes' and the percentage of 'firsts.' Justifiably or not, the grade 13
departmentals served as an unusually public measure of accountability,
reassuring the community that its high schools were providing the quality
of education expected of them, or alerting trustees, principals, and parents alike that changes were called for.

ONTARIO'S SCHOOL TEACHERS shared the characteristics of the education
system itself. The workforce was much smaller than it is today, comprising
only about 25,000 elementary and secondary school teachers (about 22
per cent of its present size), and of that number, secondary school teachers represented a much smaller proportion of the whole – no more than
16 per cent (compared to 38 per cent today). Teachers at mid-century
were also a more diverse lot, divided by education, salary, and gender to a
much greater extent than now. Perhaps the most striking difference was
the long-standing gap between the status of the secondary and the elementary school teacher, based in part on the simple fact that the former made
substantially more money than the latter. But that in turn only reflected
more deeply rooted distinctions. First, at a time when a far smaller percentage of the population ever entered the halls of a university, and a
degree conferred far greater prestige than it does now, secondary school
teachers were, in the main, university graduates. With few exceptions,
elementary school teachers had completed high school only: at mid-
century, no more than 5 or 6 per cent had graduated from university. High

school teachers gained status as well from the peculiar role of the selective secondary school. They were not only the gatekeepers to the higher reaches of the social order, but, in the senior grades especially, were also specialists in that group of subjects deemed of unique worth in conferring culture and mental discipline. While the professional training of both secondary and elementary school teachers occupied a period of only nine or ten months, they were trained in different institutions with different orientations. Candidates for high school certificates received their professional education at the Ontario College of Education, which was linked to the University of Toronto. Elementary school teachers went directly from high school to small 'normal schools'* staffed by civil servants appointed by, and usually drawn from, the Department of Education.

Beyond the fundamental status distinctions between secondary and elementary school teachers, there were other divisions. Regardless of qualifications, women teachers were almost universally paid less than men, and that applied to both the secondary and elementary schools. In the latter, women constituted more than 80 per cent of the workforce but men held most (but far from all) of the administrative positions,[6] from principal to public school inspector, and tended to dominate teaching in the senior grades. Moreover, when province-wide voluntary associations of teachers began to develop in the period immediately after the First World War, all of these differences were embedded deeply enough to result in the creation of three separate organizations – the Ontario Secondary School Teachers' Federation, the Ontario Public School Men Teachers' Federation, and the Federation of Women Teachers' Associations of Ontario (which however represented only elementary school women teachers).[7] Language and religion were no less divisive in this respect, eventually throwing up two more organizations, L'Association des enseignantes et des enseignants franco-ontariens, founded in 1939, and the Ontario English Catholic Teachers' Association, founded in 1944.

Before 1944, the three senior associations achieved some degree of success in improving the lot of teachers, but their effectiveness was limited by the voluntary nature of their membership and by the lack of any real bargaining power with trustees, who made nearly all the important decisions about hiring and firing, working conditions, and, above all, salaries.

---

*The name 'normal school' usually strikes modern readers as bizarre. It was a literal translation of the French phrase *école normale* and was meant to indicate a school that modelled, or set the norm for, exemplary pedagogical practice. They were renamed 'teachers' colleges' in 1953.

The most significant breakthrough in that respect came in 1944 with the passage of the Teaching Profession Act, a product of agitation by the federations, the example already set in several other provinces, and the concern of a new Conservative government under the leadership of George Drew to consolidate its support as well as to head off a certain amount of radical talk about teacher unionism. The act created the Ontario Teachers' Federation, contained a good deal of high-minded rhetoric about teaching as a profession, and provided for some of its trappings, including the promulgation of a code of ethics and measures regulating internal discipline. But its crucial clauses established compulsory membership: all teachers in government-funded schools had to belong, and pay dues, to one or another of the five 'affiliated' federations. It was this provision above all that created strong teachers' organizations in Ontario and laid the groundwork for collective solidarity in pursuit of improved salaries and working conditions in the years to come.

The act of 1944, however, also perpetuated divisions by making OTF little more than an umbrella organization and leaving most of the real power in the hands of the five affiliates, which occasionally worked in concert but mostly as separate entities. Because it began in a stronger position, with over 90 per cent of secondary school teachers already members before 1944, and because it had more social and geographical cohesiveness, OSSTF tended from the beginning to be the most aggressive and innovative affiliate. Still, common agendas and tactics quickly emerged, above all about the improvement of salaries and the establishment of public salary schedules based on qualifications and experience to replace bargaining between trustees and individuals alone.

On the face of it, the Teaching Profession Act provided few tools to achieve such ends. The employment relationship was governed solely by the 'standard contract' each individual teacher signed with his or her board. OTF and its affiliates were not legal unions, and before 1975 teachers had no right to strike or even to engage in collective bargaining. In 1947, nonetheless, the leadership of OSSTF invented the 'pink letter,' a device subsequently adopted (with suitable colour modifications) by the other affiliates as well. In substance this was nothing more than a warning to all other teachers in the province that a 'disagreement' had arisen between board X and its teachers, and that any individual member of the affiliate who accepted a job with board X would not receive any future support, in salary negotiations or other difficulties, from the federation. A weak reed indeed, the reader might think; but given the high level of solidarity within OSSTF, it discouraged most teachers from applying for jobs to the recalcitrant board. It was given additional clout in 1950 when coupled with the threat of 'coincidental' resignations submitted by all of a board's teachers, to take effect on one of the two dates allowed in the standard contract. In another era, when larger numbers of teachers were looking for jobs, such tactics might have had little impact. But in the years around mid-century there was already a shortage of teachers, one that would become more severe over the next two decades. And thus the 'pink letter' and its variants would become powerful tools in extracting salary concessions from school boards. Teachers might still be divided in many ways; but the Teaching Profession Act had provided them with collective voices, if not *a* collective voice, and a certain ingenuity in putting the act to work provided them with the power to control the conditions of their labour in ways that had never been possible before.

IN THE CLOSING YEARS of the Second World War, Canadians had begun to turn their attention to the kind of nation they wanted to build in the post-war era. Both economic and social policy became the focus of much debate, and education received its fair share of attention. In Ontario the government appointed a royal commission with a broad mandate to review the existing system of elementary and secondary education and to recommend any changes that would better equip the province's young people for the modern world. The commission, consisting of twenty individuals and chaired by John Andrew Hope, got down to work in 1945, found its task more difficult than expected, and didn't submit a final report until 1950.

The recommendations of the Hope Report were broad-ranging and on some issues quite radical. It argued, for example, that all children should be in school for a full ten years, and thus that compulsory education should extend from six to sixteen without exception. It advocated that all boards establish kindergarten programs and that elementary school teachers receive a far more extended education than was currently the case. It attacked what it considered to be the stultifying effects of system-wide uniform examinations and called for the abolition of grade 13. Health services should be extended to all students, the report maintained, and there should be a massive expansion of special-education programs to serve all children with learning disabilities. For a variety of reasons it proposed to reorganize the structure of schooling into a system consisting of six years of elementary school, four years of high school, and a three-year junior college, the latter to provide both vocational courses and university preparation. Finally, the existing system of local administration was to be replaced by large regional boards and consolidated schools, to increase both the economic and educational efficacy of the schools.

Much of this would come to constitute a program of reform for Ontario education, and one that would be largely implemented over the next thirty or forty years. In that respect the Hope Commission was far from irrelevant. Yet it had only a limited impact on provincial educational policy in the 1950s.[8] In the first place, the commission's proposals flew in the face of the politics of consolidation. Individual politicians might well favour larger units and the government might consider encouraging voluntary amalgamations, but no one was prepared to impose consolidation on rural Ontario. The plan to reorganize the structure of the schools was also deemed too expensive and unnecessary. More important, the report provoked a storm. The 6-4-3 pattern, along with related recommendations made by the majority of the commissioners, would have restricted the existing rights of the Roman Catholic schools. A lengthy minority report argued the injustice and illegality of all such proposals, and the entire report suffered as this particular part of it became a political hot potato: none of the three parties had any stake in pursuing an issue that, over three or four generations, had been one of the most divisive in Ontario. Weighed down by such hefty baggage, the Hope Report sank from sight, leaving hardly a ripple of memory behind it. And even when some of its other recommendations were implemented, no one was eager to recall their origins or attribute them to the political orphan Hope had become.

II

Whatever the value of this baseline portrait of the schools at mid-century, it masks the dynamism of the post-war era. The Second World War was followed by some of the best times this country has ever known. Despite conversion to a peacetime economy and demobilization of the armed forces, Canadians suffered no major post-war recession. European industry and agriculture had been badly disrupted, and the nation's wheat and industrial products were in great demand. American business, looking for new fields of investment, found Canada a safe and promising haven. From 1950 to 1953 the Korean War gave another boost to the country's manufacturing and resource industries. The discovery of oil and natural gas in the West and the subsequent building of the pipelines from west to east not only created a major refinery capacity at Sarnia but also provided a continuing source of cheap fuel for southern Ontario's manufacturers.

The result was an unprecedented economic boom, and one that, with only a few downturns, would last until the early 1970s. For most of that period Canadians experienced low unemployment, low inflation, rapidly rising productivity, and rapidly rising incomes. In Ontario, personal real income per capita tripled between 1939 and 1975 – tripled in less than a generation. By any standard it was a period of quite remarkable economic growth.

The boom had both private and public consequences. Rising incomes enabled large numbers of families, for the first time, to buy a decent house, purchase a car or consumer durables like refrigerators and television sets, take an annual holiday, or afford better preventive dental and health care. At the same time, economic growth enlarged the tax base to provide for the expansion of public services. Improvements in the province's economic and social infrastructure, long neglected or postponed because of depression and war, could now be pressed forward. County and township roads were macadamized or paved. During the late 1940s and 1950s rural electrification was completed. The system of divided highways was extended north from Toronto and the 401 was begun, superimposing a new and different transportation grid on the old. Indeed, between 1950 and 1957 the highway department was the government's biggest spender, though by the latter year education and other public services were beginning to compete with it. In the late 1940s government spending accounted for just over 4 per cent of the gross provincial product; by 1960 that portion was 7 per cent and by 1972–3 it stood at 16 per cent. Yet the sheer magnitude of the economic boom meant that increasing personal wealth generated growing tax revenues without severe tax increases *and* without an accumulating government debt.

Along with rapid economic growth, there was also a major shift in the occupational structure. New technologies were introduced that were more dependent on specialist knowledge and research; business firms grew larger and more complex; and because people were better off they had more money to pay for all kinds of personal and social services. The result was a massive expansion in the availability of, and demand for, white-collar work. From 1951 onwards, each successive census recorded a rapid decline in the percentage of the workforce employed in farming, forestry, and fishing; a roughly stable proportion of blue-collar jobs in the 1950s and then a period of significant decline; and large increases in all forms of white-collar work.[9] 'White collar' is a crude occupational category, encompassing managers and professionals as well as technical, clerical, and sales people. But the trend was important for this reason: access to virtually all forms of white-collar work tended to be tied to higher levels of schooling than was the case with jobs in either of the other categories.

The post-war years also witnessed the continuing shift of Ontario's population from rural to urban communities. By 1961 nearly 80 per cent of the province's people lived in incorporated urban areas. Virtually all towns and cities increased their size, but perhaps the most dramatic growth took place in those rural areas located next to towns and cities. The extreme example is to be found in Etobicoke, Scarborough, and North York, the three townships bordering the city of Toronto. In 1941 Scarborough, for example, had a population of just over 24,000; by 1971, the figure was 343,000. For all three areas, the corresponding figures are 66,000 and 1,121,000. In effect, these three townships were transformed over the course of a mere twenty or thirty years from a mix of villages, small towns, and farms into large cities. And, on a more modest scale, the same thing was happening elsewhere. Between 1951 and 1961 alone, London grew from 95,000 to 170,000; Welland from 15,000 to 36,000; Sudbury from 42,000 to 80,000; Kingston from 33,000 to 54,000.

Ontarians not only moved from country to city but their absolute numbers increased as well. In 1941 the province had some 3,700,000 people. By 1971 the figure had grown to 7,600,000, and by the mid-1990s to over 11,000,000. In the three decades between 1941 and 1971, in other words, the province's population *doubled*; over the course of the last fifty years, it *tripled*. Immigration to Ontario accounted for much of that growth: there was substantial migration from other parts of Canada, but immigrants from outside the country also came to the province in large numbers – during the 1950s, for example, at an annual rate of 50,000 or more. And typically, both kinds of migrants tended to be not only young but also in the first stages of family formation. That is to say, they were producing, or soon would produce, a considerable number of school-age children.

Perhaps the most familiar demographic shift in the post-war era was the 'baby boom.' Before 1945, birth rates had been declining for decades in Canada as in much of the rest of the industrialized world. Because the economic pressures of the depression militated against marriages or having children, the number of births reached a historic low during the 1930s. In the first half of the 1940s, however, the birth rate began to increase, and it rose more rapidly once the troops came home. In 1936 the fertility rate for Ontario women was 2.2 – that is, on average, 2.2 children per woman of child-bearing age, which demographers usually consider equivalent to zero population growth. By 1961, the figure stood at nearly four children for each woman of child-bearing years! (See figures 2 and 3.)

THE COMBINED IMPACT of these economic and demographic developments on the schools was dramatic. Every year from the late 1940s until 1965 an ever-larger cohort of children started school, adding their own numbers to the already swollen classes ahead of them (see figure 4). Thirteen or fourteen years after they were born they entered high school. Had nothing else changed, the schools would have been stretched to the limit just to accommodate them.

But unlike their parents or grandparents, those who grew up in the 1950s and the baby boomers who followed them began to stay in school, in ever-increasing numbers, until they were seventeen or eighteen. Because of good times, parents could afford the luxury of keeping their children in school longer; because many of them valued education they pushed their youngsters to stay in school in order to 'have a chance we never had.' No adult refrain was more familiar to a generation of post-war young people, especially to those from working-class families. Youngsters who followed that advice commonly became the first member of their extended family to complete high school and go on to become elementary school teachers or university graduates. It was not just a matter of parental pressure, however; there were also enormous incentives for students to stay in school. While blue-collar jobs were plentiful enough in the decade before 1957, the real growth areas, and some of the most attractive jobs, lay in the white-collar sector, where the demand for engineers, teachers, technicians, public servants, and clerical workers seemed to be expanding endlessly. Because these were also jobs that required more formal education, young people stayed in school longer to qualify for them. In 1946 only 38 per cent of those aged fifteen to nineteen had been in school. By 1955, 51 per cent were in school, and by 1960, 63 per cent. By the late 1950s, then, the high schools were under pressure from two sources – the sheer volume of enrolments as the leading edge of the baby boom began to reach high school age, and a rapidly increasing participation rate for those aged fifteen to nineteen.

The result was helter-skelter expansion, first at the elementary and then at the secondary level. Between 1946 and 1961, while the total population increased by 50 per cent, elementary enrolment jumped 116 per cent and secondary enrolment 141 per cent. Expansionary pressures were sharp everywhere; at the extreme, in the new suburbs being carved out of the townships surrounding the larger cities, they were horrendous. In 1951 Scarborough had about twenty elementary schools, some of them still one-room rural schools, and one high school, situated in the extreme south-west of the township nearest Toronto, where most residents lived. By the mid-1960s it had some eighty multi-class elementary schools and sixteen high schools.

In the years 1946 to 1961 alone, the number of Ontario classrooms doubled; but the total number of schools hardly increased at all. There were two reasons for this. First, many old, small schools were simply torn down and replaced by buildings with more classrooms. In other cases, large new wings were added to existing buildings. Second, good times made possible a massive upgrading of local roads, while a growing number of larger boards meant more of them had the resources to pay for school consolidation and pupil transportation. In 1950–1, for example, some 50,000 pupils were transported by bus; a decade later the figure had tripled to 161,000. Most of this busing was in rural areas and thus was associated with a decline in the number of one-room schools.

At the same time, rebuilding invited innovation. Since they were starting from scratch, and since there was money to spare, trustees incorporated in their architectural plans all the characteristic features of what we now think of as the modern school plant. For the elementary school that meant a brightly lit, single-story building with space for manual training and domestic science, facilities for art and music, movable desks, and all the other accoutrements thought necessary for a high-quality education. For the high schools it meant gymnasiums, laboratories, libraries, and audio-visual facilities. During the 1950s, in sum, local trustees throughout the province, assisted by the Ontario government, embarked on a vast pro-gram of renewing the physical infrastructure of education.

Teacher supply was less easily managed. The small number of young adults born in the 1930s or early 1940s and coming of age in the post-war years inevitably meant there would be a shortage of entrants into teaching. That in turn meant a sharp cutback in entrance standards in order to scoop up anyone remotely qualified. School boards also launched ener-getic recruiting drives in other parts of Canada and more especially in Britain, and were rewarded by a considerable inflow of well-qualified but badly paid teachers from England and other parts of the United Kingdom. The one bright spot lay in steadily rising salaries through the 1950s and early 1960s.[10] The teachers' federations certainly had a hand in this; but their job was made easy by the shortage of teachers itself, as well as by the pliability of trustees eagerly committed to making their schools suitable vessels for the education of their post-war wards. Rising salaries, in any case, were to make teaching a much more attractive option than it had been at the end of the war. The result was an expanding workforce sufficient to meet the pressures of the enrolment boom. Sufficient, indeed, that the elementary schools managed to maintain a roughly stable ratio of pupils to teachers from 1945 to 1961, while in the secondary schools there was even a modest decline over the same years.

BY 1960 ONTARIO EDUCATION was a much larger enterprise than it had been a short fifteen years before. But was it a *different* sort of enterprise? In some respects, yes. Following the recommendations of the Hope Commission, the law had been changed in 1954 to make school attendance compulsory at age six rather than eight, and the province's school attendance officers became ever more reluctant to issue work-exemption certificates. Thus nearly all children aged six to sixteen were now in school. Government stimulation grants had made kindergarten a far more common experience, in urban areas at least, though total enrolments were still substantially below those in grade 1. There had been a steady expansion of rural high school districts and more busing, which meant fewer fourteen- and fifteen-year-olds finishing their education in the higher grades of the rural elementary schools. Though largely confined to urban areas, the number of special-education classes had doubled during the decade of the 1950s and health services had become more common. Other school resources multiplied as well.

Yet the degree of change should not be overdrawn. The Hope Commission (among many other voices) had proposed administrative reorganization to overcome the effects of geography and financial resources on the quality of education. Ten years later the disparity between going to school in city, town, or countryside was still great. Large urban areas with mixed residential and business assessments could afford the newest buildings, the best equipment, the best-qualified teachers, a richer mix of academic and vocational programs, and more special services. Small towns and rural areas often had no such resources. The number of school boards had fallen since 1950 from 4200 to 3700 in 1961; but that still left a very large number of small, poor boards. Though the number of one-room schools had declined by a third, there were still 3000 of them in 1961, and there were many small urban communities with no secondary facilities for vocational or commercial training. If these sorts of measures constitute the criteria for assessing access to a quality education, then regional differences in equality of educational opportunity were at least as great in 1960 as they had been a decade or more earlier.

Though over 60 per cent of the 15–19 age group was now in school, the attrition rate remained high. Consider the fate of the grade 9 class of 1958. Of the more than 74,000 youngsters who started high school that year, 20 per cent left before entering grade 10. That grade coincides with the point when most young people turn sixteen, and as had long been the case, a large number left school at the end of grade 10, only 58 per cent continuing on to enrol in grade 11. Fifty-one per cent entered grade 12; 43 per cent received their graduation diplomas. Twenty-nine per cent entered grade 13; 16 per cent graduated. The vast majority of secondary school students continued to enrol in the general or academic course – 76 per cent in 1961 – with access to much the same limited range of academic subjects as they had a decade earlier. In most subjects there remained a single guideline, defined by the Department of Education and closely followed by most teachers, which determined the success or failure of all children regardless of aptitude or interest. In many respects, the high school experience of 1959 remained like that of 1945, or indeed, as I have argued elsewhere, not entirely unlike that of 1890.[11]

YET THERE WAS NO SHORTAGE of proposals for change. Right from the beginning of the twentieth century an emerging critique of existing school systems across North America had coalesced fairly rapidly into a substantive program of educational reform. That program was rooted in three central ideas. First, urbanization and industrialization demanded a new sort of curriculum more relevant to the modern world and to a more complex economy. Second, the emergence of the discipline of psychology as an experimental science generated new theories about children's mental and physical development that challenged the traditional organization and pedagogy of the classroom. And third, the widening of democracy in society at large prompted calls for parallel progress in education, especially with respect to a more extended education for all young people and the democratization of the school itself.

Singularly or in conjunction these ideas gave rise to a multitude of innovations such as the expansion of vocational education, the introduction of new subjects like domestic science and manual training, and the extension of the school-leaving age. They also contributed a new impetus to older reform initiatives such as school consolidation. But more important, they constituted the intellectual underpinnings of a movement known in North America as 'educational progressivism.' By the 1920s and 1930s this reform program was enormously influential in the United States, and it aroused considerable enthusiasm amongst many Canadian educators.

Progressivism has provoked much controversy over the past few decades, but some of the innovations pioneered by those who considered themselves progressives are now so universally accepted that few would challenge them – vocational education, kindergarten, or the provision of school health services, for example. There is, however, a more contentious set of core doctrines. At its heart, progressivism was a movement devoted to the wholesale reform of public education, including classroom practices. This meant, in the first place, the reform of the program of studies to give less emphasis to the traditional academic subjects, which progressives saw as primarily intended to cater to a minority of able students pursuing university preparatory studies, and which were of limited use to the vast majority of students. What was needed, they maintained, was a more practical and relevant bias: more vocational education, for example, more concern with contemporary problems and issues, more education in life skills, all of which would better prepare young people for the 'real world.' Progressives also pointed out that 'the whole child goes to school' – that is to say, the school must take responsibility for not just the child's intellectual development but his or her social, emotional, and physical growth as well. Learning to read mattered; but so did the cultivation of good health habits, the ability to get along with others, and the child's self-esteem. Changes had to be made, moreover, not only in the curriculum – *what* was taught – but also in *how* it was taught. Learning theory, progressives claimed, tells us that the school must be 'child-centred.' The curriculum must focus on the interests, needs, and abilities of children; must actively engage them in the learning experience; must provide for individual differences in learning styles and the pace at which learning takes place. Self-directed learning was critical as well: students would learn best if they had opportunities to select their own learning experiences, or plan them in concert with peers and teachers, rather than have content and sequence simply imposed by adults.

I will have occasion to explore these ideas further in other chapters, but this brief summary should indicate the scope of the progressive assault on the traditional school: the attack on the privileged place of a small group of academic subjects and on a program of studies arbitrarily imposed by adults, the cry for more relevance to the demands of modern society and the broad needs of children who must adapt to them, the denigration of 'passive' learning in all its forms, the demand for individualization, and, concomitantly, an end to the lock-step nature of schools organized by grades and around examinations as tests of progress.

From the 1920s onwards, progressivism proved attractive to many Ontario educators. As was the case elsewhere, it had particular appeal to elementary school teachers and administrators, in part because its doctrines were especially applicable to the education of young children – often offering much better or more effective methods of teaching than the conventional routines of the time. Its appeal, however, also lay in the fact that it constituted a distinctive ideology that gave elementary teachers a role independent of the academic secondary school and the university, and of the traditional status hierarchy that entailed. Its impact, in any case, can be measured in a variety of ways. At the local level, innovative school superintendents pressed for the establishment of school health services or the introduction of domestic science and manual training. In the normal schools, instructors incorporated some of progressivism's pedagogical methods into their lessons and preached the virtues of its key doctrines. By the late 1930s it had received the cautious approval of the Department of Education itself. Nowadays the 'little grey book' – the revised program of studies for the elementary schools, introduced in 1937 – may seem utterly conventional; yet at the time it was considered innovative, and in some quarters even radical, for its emphasis on the importance of play in the primary grades, its promotion of group work through the 'project method,' and its introduction of 'integrated studies' – social studies, for example, in place of the separate subjects of history and geography. There were other signs of the influence of progressives in the 1930s, and again in the postwar years. For example, in 1949 the minister of education, Dana Porter, introduced 'divisions' in the school curriculum: primary (grades 1–3), junior (4–6), intermediate (7–10), and senior (11–13). More than just a change in nomenclature, the 'Porter Plan,' as it was called, was intended to replace lock-step grades, in the primary years especially, with multi-age grouping, while the introduction of the intermediate level was to provide a smoother transition from elementary to high school and to create a special and coherent curriculum for an age group that, according to the educational psychologists, had its own distinctive characteristics.[12]

THE FACT REMAINS, nonetheless, that until the mid-1960s progressivism had a very limited influence in Ontario: the rhetoric of reform far outran actual changes in either the program of studies or the pedagogy of elementary schools, and hardly touched secondary schools at all. There were good reasons for this. Many prized innovations were predicated on large investments in physical plant: domestic-science or manual-training rooms, let alone vocational schools, cost money, and during the years of depression and war there was little to spare. In the 1950s great progress was made in incorporating these and other facilities into the fabric of the new schools being built to meet the needs of the baby boom. But rapid expansion gave priority to the construction of ordinary classrooms over things still often considered 'frills.' Similarly, much pedagogical innovation hinged on consolidation. In the one- or two-room rural school there was a good deal of de facto 'multi-age grading,' group work, and individualization; but there were also limits to what teachers could accomplish.

There was also the sheer weight of the academic tradition at work. To large numbers of people, professionals and laity alike, the job of the high school was, pre-eminently, preparation for higher education, not mass education; indeed, as late as 1949 there were cries of outrage when, under the Porter Plan, introductory Latin was ousted from grade 9 in order to make room for a 'common year' that allowed students to explore options before choosing a course of studies in grade 10. The universities had a powerful influence over the high school curriculum and, no less critical, over the loyalties of high school teachers, who were, in the main, deeply committed to the subject specialties they had studied in those universities and now taught in the high schools. And that leverage extended down into the senior grades of the elementary schools as well, where teachers were expected to prepare their students carefully to meet the expectations of high school teachers.

The academic tradition was also a dominant influence within the Department of Education itself. The power to appoint public school inspectors, traditionally in the hands of the county councils, had been transferred to the minister of education in 1930, and from that point on the elementary inspectorate began to develop a cohesion and influence within the department that it had never had before. But the high school inspectorate, always appointed by the minister, was also a powerful influence in policy-making and provided the pool from which senior bureaucrats were usually drawn. The department, moreover, was organized to reinforce the barriers and status distinctions that separated the secondary from the elementary schools: control over the program of studies as well as inspection and administration was sharply divided into secondary and elementary sections, each staffed by those qualified to teach one or the other. Even where there was a single board of education responsible for both elementary and secondary education, supervisory officers were, by regulation, qualified only for responsibilities in one or the other panel. And despite the notion

of an 'intermediate division' with a coherent curriculum across grades 7 to
10, the reality was that, with only a handful of exceptions,[13] the schools,
physically and otherwise, were either elementary or secondary, and their
teachers had little or no contact with each other. Even in the late 1950s,
the 'learning continuum K–12,' like the idea of secondary education for
all or the unified administration of the schools, still seemed an alien
notion. The particular traditions, assumptions, and practices of the Ontario high schools were, in sum, shielded from attack from below. Both the
organizational structures and the intellectual tradition would have to be
undermined before that could be changed.

The strength of the academic tradition lay primarily in the rich legacy of
Anglo-American thought, stretching back into the nineteenth century and
beyond, about the nature and meaning of a liberal education.[14] In the
twentieth century, the tradition was also being re-articulated by a disparate
group of critics who considered educational progressivism a hazard to the
intellectual health of the young. Though pejoratively labelled 'conservatives' or 'traditionalists' by progressives wishing to disparage them, neither
term really fits them well; but because such terminology is not only
conventional but also serves as a convenient shorthand, I will adopt that
usage too.

Educational conservatives tended to believe that the schools should
focus first on cultivating literacy and numeracy and then on teaching the
core academic subjects of English, mathematics, science, modern languages, history, and perhaps geography or a related social science. Most
would not argue that this should be the exclusive preoccupation of the
schools, for there might well be room for other subjects and activities. But
they generally asserted that these were the most worthwhile or essential
studies because they were doubly useful. They constituted the basics for
practical life: students had to master the skills associated with literacy and
numeracy to cope with daily life, or learn history, for example, to function
as effective citizens. And these were also the most useful subjects because
they constituted the essential ways in which humans conceptualize, and
imagine, the world. Mathematics, for example, was not simply one subject
amongst others, which might or might not be selected as students saw fit; it
was a fundamental way of organizing human experience, and there was no
substitute for it. Because of that, it necessarily had a claim to a privileged
place in the school curriculum. Similarly with both English composition
and literature, the former because it was deemed essential to our ability to
communicate effectively, and the latter because it exposed students to
some of the classic texts that encompass the work of the human imagina-

tion and serve as the best exemplars of coherent exposition or analysis. While some conservatives questioned the principle of secondary education for all, believing that the unmotivated would do better beyond the confines of the school, most believed that the core curriculum should be taught to all because to do otherwise is to rob them of the critical skills and knowledge that all people in a democracy have a right to inherit.

Generally, conservatives were less interested in pedagogical issues than were progressives, but they tended to believe in the traditional authority of the teacher, the necessity for the teacher to define what is to be learned and to teach it through structured lessons and direct instruction. Motivating the pupil – ensuring the child is interested – was to be encouraged but was secondary since pupils had to learn certain things whether they liked it or not. Similarly, learning was seen as necessarily orderly and sequential. Better a handful of subjects taken each year, in orderly progression, the conservative might say, than a supermarket where students pick and choose according to their 'interests' and where teachers must pander to their whims.

From the 1930s onwards the success of progressivism in the United States provoked a succession of 'conservative' critics to attack both its principles and its pedagogy, a reaction that reached a crescendo in the early 1950s and left the progressive movement in tattered (though only temporary) retreat. Progressivism made far less headway in Canada, and especially in Ontario; still, it provoked equally fierce opposition in newspapers, magazines, and speeches from both educators and the laity. Many examples might be cited but by far the most influential was Hilda Neatby's *So Little for the Mind: An Indictment of Canadian Education*, first published in 1953. Indictment it was, condemning progressivism, in blunt terms, as 'anti-intellectual, anti-cultural, and amoral.'[15] A professor of history at the University of Saskatchewan, Neatby mounted a robust defence of traditionalist values in Canadian education, poured ridicule on the mindless clichés progressives substituted for coherent analysis, and scorched the educational bureaucrats and the 'experts' ensconced in the teachers' colleges who wrote the policy documents or promoted the ideas which, she believed, were undermining Canada's education systems. To the extent that Neatby suggested that progressivism had run rampant in the schools, she was patently off-target: anyone who actually attended Ontario's elementary and high schools in the 1940s or 1950s knows better.[16] But that the language of progressivism was creeping into policy documents and pedagogical treatises is undeniable, and more than anyone else, Neatby sounded the alarm. During the rest of the 1950s and early 1960s, advocates of progressivism remained on the defensive; much of the curriculum change that did take place was carried out by academics and teachers who, while pioneering some exciting innovations in both programs and pedagogy, did so within the context of traditional assumptions. The best-known example was a co-operative effort carried out jointly by the University of Toronto and the Toronto Board of Education, and summarized in an influential report published in 1962. Its title was *Design for Learning*, and it opened with an incisive essay by one of Canada's most distinguished scholars, Northrop Frye, whose views on education were perceptive, always sensitive to the broad purposes of the schools rather than narrowly academic, but hardly sympathetic to what he condemned as the excesses of progressive education. 'It was the confusion,' he wrote, 'of educational and social functions, implicit in the motto, "The whole child goes to school," that made "progressive" theories so fatuous.'[17]

Despite the importance of the conservative voice in countering the influence of progressivism, the chief bulwark throughout the 1950s was probably the minister of education himself. Called out of retirement by Premier Frost in 1951, W.J. Dunlop had had a long career as a school teacher, principal, and university administrator before entering politics. An enthusiast, par excellence, for all the virtues of the little red schoolhouse, Dunlop was adamantly opposed to the core doctrines of progressivism, suspicious of 'frills' in education, and even reluctant to press forward with school or board consolidation. Thus he presided, until 1959, over a department where change was not prized, and those bureaucrats sympathetic to progressivism could only keep their heads down and bide their time.

For good reasons, then, the dynamism of the 1950s was largely confined to the physical expansion of the system and did not extend to substantial in-school change. In the latter domain a moderate conservatism and the academic tradition continued to be predominant, as they had for decades. It was only in the 1960s that the conservative grip over the tenor of educational policy would be broken, to be gradually replaced by a refurbished progressivism as the new orthodoxy in Ontario education.

3

Restructuring and Refinancing Education in the Sixties

Though it is now sometimes treated as such, the explosive growth in enrolments which began early in the post-war years was no short-term phenomenon that 'happened' in the 1950s and then disappeared. It constituted, rather, a critical *continuing* problem from the early 1950s through to the mid-1970s, a period of more than two decades. The peak year for elementary enrolments didn't occur until 1970; for the high school, not until 1976. Thus one dominant theme of the entire period was the scramble to find enough money and enough teachers just to accommodate the baby boom and rising participation rates in the high school. Indeed, during the 1960s and early 1970s it would have been a substantial achievement if government had accomplished nothing more than that.

What is most remarkable about the 1960s, however, is that, in the name of providing a better and more extended education for all Ontario's young people, public policy became aggressively interventionist on a wide variety of fronts. Confronting one set of stresses, government took on an even greater challenge – to rewrite the province's educational purposes and restructure its educational system in ways that led to far greater expansion, and a far greater financial commitment, than anything demanded by demographic pressures alone.

In this chapter, and the one that follows, I propose to explore the disparate changes in structure and classroom practice that, taken altogether, amounted to a massive reshaping of Ontario's education system. I begin, nonetheless, with a 'preface' designed to situate both chapters in a larger context. What ideas and interests coalesced to produce circumstances that not only allowed but promoted rapid change? What was it that gave the sixties its peculiar dynamism, in education as in so many other things?*

I

The impetus for innovation arose in part from the challenge of sustaining economic growth. Even in the mid-1950s there were already Canadians, in Ontario as elsewhere, complaining that the education system was failing to produce either the quality or quantity of professional and technical skills the country needed to promote its competitive position in the international economy. Their voices swelled after 1957 as the country slid into its first short, sharp post-war recession. The bulk of the newly unemployed were unskilled labourers with low levels of education. That was the case, the critics contended, because a changing economy had less and less work to offer the unskilled. White-collar work, on the other hand, constituted a rapidly growing sector. Much of it required advanced levels of education and specialist qualifications: the economy of the future, it was said, would be dominated by 'knowledge industries.' Yet the demand for skilled labour outpaced the supply from Ontario's schools and colleges. Canada had prospered during the post-war years, so the argument went, but that was because the country had taken in large numbers of highly skilled immigrants. With European economic recovery now nearly complete, that flow was bound to diminish and Canada would have to depend on its own resources. What was needed, then, was a substantial expansion and reorientation of the education system to reflect the needs of the new economy.

At about the same time, a number of economists began to flesh out in more sophisticated form an old idea – that investment in education could create 'human capital,' which, they argued, was as important to economic growth as other forms of capital, or even more so. Though this thesis became very influential during the 1960s, it was the subject of considerable debate and growing scepticism within the discipline of economics itself. As K.J. Rea remarks, however, 'The concept of human capital was quickly picked up by the media, politicians, and other opinion-makers' and its implications seemed clear: 'greater emphasis should be placed on expanding investment in education relative to investment in other assets ... The importance of the new "scientific" knowledge lay in the effect it had in

---

*I use 'the sixties,' however, as a bit of shorthand for an era that lasted from the late 1950s to the early 1970s, a 'long decade' with its own coherence and character.

transforming governments, certainly in the case of Ontario, from agencies forced to accommodate such an expansion into agencies enthusiastically promoting it.'[1]

In part at least, the conviction that education must be democratized flowed from the same premise. Students who dropped out of school at fifteen or sixteen, or took an academic program only for lack of an alternative, represented a tragic waste of human capital – a waste for individuals themselves because they failed to acquire the skills that would earn them better incomes, but also a waste of the nation's pool of potential talent. Raising high school participation rates, along with increasing access to vocational programs and to post-secondary education, was thus an imperative goal of public policy. For economic reasons alone young people had to be encouraged to stay in school.

But there was more to the democratization argument than that. Many students dropped out of school, critics contended, because the high school program was rigorously academic and highly selective. Having failed to do well in the existing program, students had no option but to leave. By the late 1950s or early 1960s, moreover, it was well established that a majority of those who left school early were working-class or minority young people, many of whom were entirely capable of doing more advanced work. They left school, nonetheless, some because of financial necessity, others because a program of studies primarily designed to prepare students for university seemed irrelevant to their own future. The result was a dropout rate heavily differentiated by social class, a phenomenon that in the post-war era had come to be seen by many as inherently unjust. The evidence of class bias in educational systems came from many sources within Canada and beyond its borders. In Ontario it was already well documented by the late 1950s, a result of a series of studies funded by the Atkinson Foundation that were widely read among a small but powerful group of educational administrators and policy-planners.[2] But if one Canadian contributor deserves to be singled out it is Carleton University sociologist John Porter, author first of a series of articles on the subject and then of an enormously influential book, published in 1965, *The Vertical Mosaic: An Analysis of Social Class and Power in Canada.* Among other things, Porter documented the relationship between social class and educational opportunity, and made the case, in the name of both social justice and economic advantage, that the goal of equality of educational opportunity must be vigorously pursued.

The long era of post-war prosperity helped reinforce such arguments as well. It encouraged the belief that social goods like health care or education need not, and should not, be rationed on the basis of wealth. Education was a good in itself and thus advocates of a more inclusive educational system insisted that every child should have the chance to develop his or her capacities to the fullest extent. But that was only possible if an extended education was within reach of all. There were, moreover, no financial barriers to dampen the enthusiasm for such an innovation. 'When Ontario voters demanded new hospitals, instant universities, multi-lane highways, a network of community colleges and universal medicare,' writes Desmond Morton of the 1960s, 'the province could afford them with little threat to its triple-A credit rating.'[3]

The context of international relations also mattered. Neither the call for democratization nor the demand for greater investment in knowledge and skills was simply the product of the Cold War; but both were reinforced by the conviction that they were key components in the political and military defence of the West. An informed and committed people was less likely to become the dupe of tyranny; economic growth was a critical vindication of the market economy; science and engineering skills were essential to victory, however the war, cold or hot, was won. The erudite arguments of economists and sociologists were undoubtedly having an impact on public opinion in the late 1950s and early 1960s; but for many, policy-makers and ordinary citizens alike, nothing made the case for greater investment in science and engineering more urgently than the unremitting ping, ping, ping of Sputnik making its way across the heavens in that memorable October of 1957.*

It mattered too that such ideas held out the promise of greater access and opportunity at a moment when the sidewalks and side streets of urban and suburban Ontario were jammed with baby carriages and tricycles. By the early 1960s most of the baby boomers had been born, and their parents had generous hopes for their future. Those parents were also voters – voters who now had a tangible personal stake in the province's schools and colleges. In theory at least there had always been one cheap and easy solution to the crush of numbers caused by the baby boom: allow pupil-teacher ratios to double or triple, stiffen examination requirements in the high schools to keep numbers the same as in earlier decades, and increase entry standards to higher education proportionately. Outside of any other consideration, that course of action was never in the political cards in an era when some 20 per cent of the Ontario population, most of

---

*The first satellite to orbit the earth, Sputnik was launched by the Soviet Union at the height of the Cold War.

whom were too young to vote themselves, had a phalanx of doting parents to promote their interests at the polls.

From the late 1950s, moreover, young people were beginning to acquire a voice of their own. Though there were subtle (and sometimes not so subtle) differences in the attitudes and outlook of various age cohorts throughout the period, the post-war generation can be crudely divided into two groups. One consisted of those born just before or during the war, who grew up in the prosperous 1950s, came of age in the early 1960s, and were the generation that pioneered everything from raising the participation rates in secondary and post-secondary education to adopting rock and roll as their international anthem. Following them were the baby boomers, a younger group, born after the war, who flooded into the high schools and then the universities during the later 1960s, absorbing the new youth culture like fish in water, and pushing it in new directions. The two groups shared much in common, however, including a set of values that placed an emphasis on individual fulfilment as defined by individuals themselves, a conviction that a new world was aborning with little to learn from the past, a suspicion of existing structures, imposed rules, and traditional authority of all kinds, and an intense romanticism characterized by the belief that if only such fetters could be broken, they would be free to create a brave new world.

Though it was by no means exclusively theirs, this ideology was the particular property of the able young. That they should find it attractive is not surprising, since it had long had a powerful hold on other generations making the transition from adolescence to adulthood. But in the 1960s it had a special impact. Because of their sheer numbers, young people could make their voices heard. And a series of political and social developments enhanced the degree of their bitterness and disillusionment with all constituted authority and traditional wisdom. Those who came of age in the late 1950s and 1960s were first shaken by the assassination of President Kennedy and the violence meted out to the idealists of the civil-rights movement. By the mid-1960s the conflict in Vietnam held centre stage. Amongst a growing number of North American young people, the animating impulses of idealism were channelled into new levels of political activism in pursuit of their own versions of democratization, into outright rebellion against the existing political order, or into the building of a counterculture that, at best, turned its face against the world and, at worst, degenerated into a drug-induced miasma of mindless disaffection. Though the defining moments of the 1960s mostly occurred outside of Canada, young people in Ontario absorbed the messages, shared the sentiments,

and made the causes their own. The schools and universities, now shelter-
ing such large concentrations of the young, were particularly exposed, and
would bear the brunt of both their anger and their idealism.

Where education was concerned, disaffection found expression in another way as well. Beginning in the early 1960s, a spate of sometimes
intelligent and always angry books began to appear, condemning warp
and woof the effects of the public education system in the United States.
Cumulatively, writes Diane Ravitch in her study of American education,

> the indictment of the school was overwhelming. In the eyes of the critics, the
> school destroyed the souls of children, whether black or white, middle-class
> or poor. It coerced unwilling youths to sit through hours of stultifying classes,
> breaking their spirits before turning them out as either rebellious misfits or
> conforming cogs in the great industrial machine. It neglected the needs of
> individuals while slighting the history and culture of diverse minorities. It
> clung to a boring, irrelevant curriculum and to methods that obliterated
> whatever curiosity children brought with them. It drove away creative teach-
> ers and gave tenure to petty martinets. For those who agreed with the critics,
> there was no alternative other than to change the schools or to abandon
> them.[4]

Read perhaps by only a small minority of Ontarians, such accounts were
nonetheless lapped up by radicalized university students, committed young
teachers and professors, and others convinced of the need for fundamental educational change. Well before such voices reached a crescendo,
Ontario had its own vigorous radical voice, *This Magazine Is About Schools*,
founded in 1966 by Bob Davis and a group of like-minded colleagues who,
in Ravitch's formulation, saw 'no alternative other than to change the
schools or to abandon them.' Davis, indeed, had (temporarily) done the
latter: a high school history teacher, he created 'Everdale Place' in 1966,
one of the best known of the 'free schools' that would be founded all over
North America by those who had lost faith in the ability of the existing
school system to reform itself. *This Magazine*, however, never entirely gave
up the good fight, and quickly became a rallying point for all those, radical
and moderate alike, who believed the public school system, while salvage-
able, was in need of a thoroughgoing renovation.

Neither the American critics nor the contributors to *This Magazine* were
representative of their generation. Throughout the decade of the 1960s
the voice of the young was no more unanimous about the extent or
direction of educational change than was that of their elders. But alto-

gether, the effect was to add yet another element to a climate conducive to educational change by raising expectations, publicizing alternatives, articulating forceful critiques, and, cumulatively, de-legitimizing the status quo.

Finally, that climate was fostered by the fact that both notions, democratization and education for economic productivity, were sufficiently broad (or perhaps the right word is fuzzy) to appeal to a very diverse audience. Unrepentant elitists could support democratization if they believed that national economic growth was at stake. Convinced ideologues of left and right might both be committed to promoting greater equality of educational opportunity. Academics and schoolteachers had no difficulty persuading themselves, or, in the 1960s, even persuading others, that the schools and universities were essential services: investment in human capital also meant, for them, jobs, money, and prestige. And politicians had an obvious stake in anything that promised increases in employment and individual incomes. Thus potent ideas had the power to mobilize potent interests.

IN ONTARIO THESE BROAD interests and ideas were transformed into specific policy initiatives by the provincial Progressive Conservative party. Though there are several good accounts of provincial politics from the mid-1940s to the mid-1970s, a skeletal introduction may be helpful. In 1943 Ontario's voters had put the Conservatives in power, and, in a fit of absent-mindedness, left them there for just over forty years. Throughout the 1950s the premier was Leslie Frost, a sober-sided Lindsay lawyer, who proceeded with caution on all matters and always with a sharp eye to a balanced budget. In 1959 the venerable William Dunlop was succeeded as minister of education by a London lawyer named John Robarts, who almost immediately began to breathe new life into what was by then widely regarded as a moribund department of government. And in 1962, the year after Robarts became premier,[5] he appointed William Davis, yet another lawyer, as his minister of education, a post Davis would hold until 1971, when he himself replaced Robarts as premier of the province. The fact that two successive ministers of education went on to become premiers is important: this was an era when the education portfolio was in the hands of prominent and powerful men within the Conservative caucus and the cabinet, something that helped to ensure priority treatment for education issues and education spending. We are also dealing with *young* men in power. Throughout his decade as minister, Davis was in his thirties; he was only 41 when he became premier. Though born before the war, in some of his most formative experiences he belonged to the post-war generation; his intuitive empathies lay with the present rather than the past and left him open to new ideas and opinions. And that was even more true of the young executive assistants and political advisers with whom he surrounded himself.

These were also men willing to invest in the public sector and accept, with some equanimity, an expanding role for government. Neither Robarts nor Davis, it hardly needs saying, were socialist revolutionaries. In principle they were committed to the supremacy of the private sector and to efficient management – it was said of John Robarts that he saw himself as the chairman of the board of Ontario Limited. Yet Conservative politics had long been the politics of pragmatism and the name 'Progressive Conservative' aptly illustrates the ideological ambiguity that characterized party policy. Though the Tories were usually less enthusiastic about investing in social policy than in economic development, education had always been something of an exception, and during the 1960s and 1970s so was social policy generally. Indeed it was the Conservative party itself that presided over the construction of Ontario's modern 'service state.'[6]

II

Given the concerns about the dropout rate, and the conviction that vocational education needed more emphasis, it is plausible to think that, under any circumstances, the secondary schools would have been one of the first targets for reform, and certainly as early as 1960 Robarts and his advisers had begun to formulate ideas about curriculum change. But plans already afoot were entirely overtaken by a chain of events that followed from a policy initiative of the federal rather than the provincial government.

By 1960, Canada was still mired in recession, and unemployment had risen to 8 per cent, the highest it had been since the end of the war. The leading edge of the baby boom was now in high school and drawing ever closer to entering a labour market already glutted with unskilled workers. Convinced that Canada had to make greater provision for vocational training of all kinds, the federal government hatched a plan to promote skill training both for adults who were out of work and for those not yet in the workforce. The plan was set out in the Technical and Vocational Training Assistance Act of 1960 (TVTAA), in which the federal government proposed to pay 75 per cent of the capital costs for the expansion of technical and vocational education, along with a significant proportion of operating costs for programs where at least 50 per cent of school time was devoted to vocational subjects. Initially the program was to run for only three years, though it was later extended to six.

The act was intended to encourage the provinces to establish institutions that were 'tertiary' in nature, such as trades schools and colleges of technology. The original aim, in other words, was the creation or extension of a sector distinct from the secondary schools. But by spring 1961 the Ontario government had persuaded Ottawa to allow the money to be spent by local boards of education to build vocational schools, or vocational wings of composite schools, and to subsidize the operating costs of related vocational programs. There was a good reason for the Ontario government to want TVTAA extended to secondary education. Millions of dollars were at stake: spreading the money as widely as possible would have a broad effect on stimulating employment in the construction trades and related businesses throughout the province. As an additional incentive, the provincial government announced that for the first three years of the agreement it would pay an additional 25 per cent of capital expenditure. School boards were told, in effect, they could construct whole new buildings without assuming any of the capital costs whatsoever, and operate schools where a large part of the running costs were covered besides.

There was just one problem. Vocational studies played only a modest role in secondary education: most students, including the vast majority of those who stayed beyond age sixteen, were enrolled in the academic program. To take advantage of the TVTAA money, that had to be changed, and changed fast. It was. The agreement between Ottawa and Queen's Park had been struck in March of 1961; by the following September Robarts was able to announce a full-scale rewrite of the course of studies. Formally known as 'the Reorganized Program of Studies,' it was almost immediately, and universally, dubbed 'the Robarts Plan.' Introduced for incoming grade 9 students in September 1962, it spread upwards with them through the grades and was fully in place in 1966.

The reorganized program was much more complex than any of its predecessors. First, the old general course was divided into three distinct '5-Year branches': Arts and Science; Business and Commerce; and Science, Technology, and Trades. Despite the titles of the latter two, all of these were academically oriented. That is, '5-year Business and Commerce' students took a secretarial option consisting of two or three courses a year but also enough academic subjects to allow them to proceed to grade 13 and then to post-secondary education. A similar mix characterized the '5-year Science, Technology, and Trades.' In other words, while these programs provided vocational training, they also kept other options open, allowing a student at the end of grade 12 to choose between the job market or preparation in grade 13 for higher education. The intent was to capture those students able enough to carry a full slate of university preparatory subjects who might otherwise select (and had often selected in the past) a terminal vocational course at some earlier point in their careers. The three branches were assumed to be for the academically able, assessed at 20 or 30 per cent of the student population.

There was nothing very new about the five-year branches; they were mainly variants of alternatives available within the old general course, in which students could select shops or commerce as options to be taken along with their academic work. The really innovative part of the Robarts Plan was the construction of three parallel 'four-year' branches: 4-year Arts and Science, Business and Commerce, and Science, Technology, and Trades.* Each of these was intended to be terminal at grade 12; courses were to be designed for those of average ability, and to lead directly to the labour market or, after 1966, into the newly established Colleges of Arts and Applied Technology. Students could opt for the 4-year Arts and Science branch, though it was rather assumed that most of them would not. However, along with their vocational training all four-year students would also take a traditional list of academic courses such as English, history, or mathematics. But these were to be different from the five-year courses, with a more practical or relevant bias. Finally, there was also to be a two-year course with a predominantly practical bias for those of low ability, to prepare them directly for jobs. Students in this category were 'transferred' to the high school rather than 'promoted,' and their program of studies was predominantly non-academic.

What effects did the Robarts Plan have on the Ontario secondary school? 'A principal purpose of the reorganization,' Robarts had written in late 1961, 'is to retain in school until at least the end of the Grade 12 year a much higher proportion of pupils who enrol in Grade 9.' Certainly, that goal was achieved: between 1960 and 1971 the proportion of the age group fifteen to nineteen that remained in school rose from 62 to 77 per cent. By the latter year, 80 per cent of those who entered grade 9 three years earlier were enrolled in grade 12 and 65 per cent of them received their grade 12 graduation diploma. Undoubtedly some of that increase

---

*Even this idea wasn't entirely new. The vocational and commercial schools had divided their students into matriculation classes, 4-year classes preparing for employment, and 2-year terminal programs. What was new was the extension of the model to all of Ontario's high schools.

was due to long-term trends at work since the end of the war. But the new opportunities to acquire vocational skills, and the establishment of high school programs for those of average ability, mattered as well. Moreover, the infusion of federal money enabled school boards across the province to complete the renewal of the physical infrastructure. Though that had been going on since the immediate post-war years as boards built modern new schools to accommodate the first wave of the baby boom, TVTAA generated a building spree. Between 1961 and 1966 alone, 278 new vocational or composite schools were built, and 55 additions completed. Most of the baby boom, along with the generation that taught it, learned and worked in new high schools, and it was those buildings which, in the main, would constitute the store of facilities at the end of the century, and probably for years thereafter.

In assessing the consequences of the Robarts Plan, many people have been critical of the rigorous 'streaming' involved, and perhaps rightly so. It organized students' programs of study around tight packages of sub-jects, with a particularly sharp segregation between five-year and four-year programs: once a student had been slotted into a four-year package in grade 9 or 10, it was very difficult to change. Nor was there any room to take individual courses at different levels of difficulty. One consequence was that the various streams almost immediately reflected the social hierar-chy itself, with a disproportionate number of students from middle- and upper-income families in the five-year programs and an equally dispropor-tionate number of students from lower-income or immigrant families in the four- or two-year programs. In the larger cities that social segregation was amplified: in some cases special 'vocational' schools were built exclu-sively to house the two-year programs; in others, the academic high schools maintained a student population predominantly enrolled in the five-year arts and commercial programs while the old technical school inherited the four- and two-year programs with only a modest, mostly commercial and technical five-year stream, or none at all. It needs to be reiterated, however, that the intent of the Robarts Plan was not to disenfranchise students by restricting access to the senior high school, but to make it more inclusive: by widening career options through the creation of two new five-year streams, and above all, by attempting to attract and hold a new clientele – one that had traditionally left school early – with courses in the four- and two-year branches that were supposed to appeal more to the interests and needs of the average student.

Whatever the immediate impact of the Robarts Plan, it has a larger historic significance. Over the three or four decades before 1961, more and more young people attended high school and completed grades 9 and 10; indeed by 1960 there was already something like universal education to age 16. Yet the Ontario high school remained, in many respects, much as it had been for nearly a century: rigorously academic and highly selective, in the senior grades especially, and focused primarily on preparation for post-secondary education. The Robarts Plan had a quite different premise, that of secondary education for all. A century or so earlier, the vessel for universal education had been the common or public school; the grammar or high school had purposes that were distinct, and far more limited. Though compromised in many respects, that dualism remained in place until 1961. With the introduction of the Robarts Plan, however, universal education was extended upwards to grade 12 and the high school became a mass institution designed to cater to all young people. For good or ill, we live with the consequences of that decision still.

III

Ontario, as we've already seen, entered the second half of the twentieth century with many small administrative units, each responsible for the maintenance of a handful of schools or, often enough, only one. Yet opinion among most people who paid attention to such matters was nearly unanimous: consolidation was the essential prerequisite for virtually all other reforms envisaged in the period. The small elementary school or the district high school with modest enrolments lacked the specialist teachers, the program variety, the options, and the equipment to educate children of different interests and abilities or to prepare young people properly for jobs. Indeed it was impossible even to dream of implementing the Robarts Plan in many of Ontario's small high schools. Equally, no small school board had the tax base to build schools with adequate facilities or to exploit the economies of scale or levels of efficiency to be gained in large units of administration.

As late as 1963, Premier Robarts was still promising that consolidation would only be encouraged, not imposed. A year later, he and the cabinet had changed course. A successful election may have helped to persuade the reluctant that they could take the risk early in a new term; it probably mattered too that the pace of urbanization was reducing dependence on the voters of rural Ontario. The critical factor, however, seems to have been the implications of the Ontario Foundation Tax Plan, the name for a new method of distributing provincial grants that was formulated in the early 1960s and put in place in 1964. Even at that point Ontario still had

3472 administrative units. Two hundred and two of them had an average daily attendance of 1000 pupils or more; 1121 school boards had an average daily attendance of 30 or fewer! To be effective, on the other hand, the Foundation Tax Plan required both large units and, in terms of their tax base, comparable ones. That reality seems to have been decisive in pushing the government from voluntarism to compulsion. Coincident with the introduction of the plan, in early 1964, William Davis brought legislation before the House that made the township the administrative unit for the public schools in rural areas. In one fell swoop, writes David Cameron, 'one of the oldest public institutions in Ontario, the three-member board of trustees of the rural public school section, was eliminated.'[7]

At the same time, legislation was also put in place to pave the way for the voluntary creation of even larger units, this time at the county level. But in following years little progress was made. Thus, perhaps emboldened by the relative absence of public opposition to township boards and by another successful election result, Robarts announced that the basic unit would become the county (or in northern Ontario, the district). Passed in 1968, the act took effect 1 January 1969. This was an equally radical measure – moving from boards representing townships, villages, towns, and cities, to boards for entire counties, and in many cases from boards responsible only for high schools or elementary schools to boards responsible for both. The combined result of the legislation of 1964 and 1968, in any case, was to reduce the total number of administrative units in Ontario from something like 3500 to 230. Even that latter figure disguises the significance of the change, for it included a number of small boards which were either special-purpose or responsible for isolated areas. The vast majority of Ontario's schools and students were now under the jurisdiction of 126 boards, most of which were county- (or district-) wide though some Roman Catholic jurisdictions covered two counties or more.[8] Only the very largest urban municipalities were left with their own public boards: Windsor, London, Hamilton, Ottawa, and Toronto, the last a unique 'federated' structure with powers divided between the Metropolitan Toronto School Board and six city boards.[9]

Over the two or three years that followed, the new educational structure began to take shape. Trustees hired directors and superintendents, often drawn from the pool of senior ministry officials attracted by the higher salaries the boards were willing to offer. They recruited additional staff ranging from subject consultants and psychologists to full-time secretaries, accountants, and supervisors. They rented, or, more often, built central offices to house them. Working together, trustees and administrators began the task of establishing system-wide policies for the large body of employees they now directed, eliminating the diverse, ad hoc, or customary arrangements common among the now-extinct small boards, and replacing them with routinized procedures relating to lines of authority, promotion and hiring, salary negotiations, and the multitude of other rules and regulations that typically constitute the personnel policies in large organizations. With that came the standardization and co-ordination of school routines, ranging from bus schedules, the supervision of teachers, and curriculum planning, to policies about who paid for coffee in the staff rooms. This kind of bureaucratization had long been in place in Ontario amongst large urban school boards responsible for the work of many schools and hundreds of employees. But extended now to rural and small-town communities used to doing things differently, it homogenized educational administration according to big-city models.

In the name of efficiency and equity, the county boards also completed the process of school consolidation. In Kent County, for example, the new Merlin Area Public School replaced eleven small elementary schools, some of them with just one classroom. The last of the small high schools were closed, replaced by composite schools large enough to offer a full range of academic and vocational facilities. And when new schools were built, in urban and rural areas alike, they incorporated all the latest educational fashions, from expensive audiovisual resource centres to open-concept classrooms.

In many small communities, consolidation caused a good deal of grief. There were protest meetings and sometimes bitter confrontations over the closing of schools that had been valued centres of community life and had fulfilled the aspirations of generations of parents and students.[10] Trustees and administrators, on the other hand, focused on the achievements of the new boards. With more than $50 million already spent since amalgamation, what had the Carleton County Board to show for it two years later, asked one reporter? 'Equalized services and opportunities across the county, say trustees, including French instruction and kindergarten for everyone ... teacher interchanges, consultative and psychological services, special classes for the emotionally and physically handicapped and the gifted, standardized salaries for teachers, and less competition among the various areas to get good teachers.'[11] Whatever the losses, there were large gains in providing rural and small-town children with the educational services and opportunities long available only in the cities and large towns. Or so, at least, it seemed to many at the time; the educational virtues of big schools, by contrast, would continue to be debated, and sometimes bitterly, long after they had become a fait accompli.[12]

THE ADVENT OF THE LARGE school board was accompanied by a major change in the regulatory role of the Department of Education. That was not simply an accidental outcome of consolidation but an integral part of the plan. Given their new financial and human resources, large school boards were expected to operate with a high degree of independence, taking over the department's routine supervisory roles such as inspecting and then recommending new teachers for certification, or supervising the operation of the schools. The boards were also expected to provide leadership in program planning and educational innovation: they could now take on such tasks effectively, while those close to the scene would be more responsive to local conditions than departmental officials located in faraway Toronto. Thus provincial inspection was abandoned at the end of 1968. For the first time since the system was founded in the mid-nineteenth century, the Department of Education ceased to have direct contact with the schools. Departmental officials, including those in a series of regional offices, existed to advise, support, and explain provincial policy, but it was now the job of board officials to implement it and to enforce the rules and regulations.

The department also withdrew on other fronts. In 1960 it still specified, in great detail, what was to be taught in the schools. That too was gone by the early 1970s. Similarly, it abandoned the direct evaluation of student achievement: in 1967, the grade 13 examinations were abolished. These are both issues I will return to. My point here is simply that each was part of a larger retreat by the department from its traditional regulatory role.

A RETREAT INDEED, but far from an abdication of provincial authority. In some areas the degree of delegation was substantial. Yet local boards had to draw their directors and other supervisory officers from a pool of candidates who met ministry qualifications and who remained responsible for implementing ministry policy. Indeed, when the Toronto board tried to hire a prominent American school administrator with a reputation for radical innovation, the men from the ministry objected and William Davis flatly refused permission, offering as his only reason that the individual in question did not hold Ontario qualifications.[13] In the early 1970s the ministry would impose new program requirements on Ontario's high schools regardless of local wishes, and place sharp restrictions on the right of trustees to raise money they considered necessary to fund their schools. By 1971 or 1972, not surprisingly, trustees were already bemoaning their lack of autonomy and wondering aloud just what decentralization actually meant.[14]

One can equally ask, however, what was 'local' about the new county boards? The trustees themselves now represented a large geographical area, compared at least to patterns in the past, and their interests tended to be system-wide rather than focused on a handful of schools or, indeed, on a single one. Inevitably the new boards of trustees tended to be distanced from parents and the communities they were elected to represent. And the same might be said of the new bureaucracies the trustees employed. 'While the school inspector of the past was a representative of the central authority,' Derek Allison and Allen Wells have argued,

> he often worked personally with the many neighbourhood trustees and was often a well-known public figure. Now, however, directors [of education] administered their generally large and complex organizations from positions at the apex of formal hierarchies that placed them beyond the reach of most parents and taxpayers. From the perspective of the local community, then, the movement of the board and central office to some distant county seat had a centralizing effect. By these tokens, Ontario's modern system of school administration and supervision might best be described as regionally centralized rather than decentralized.[15]

The same kind of distancing, Peter Hennessy has suggested, occurred between teachers, on the one hand, and trustees and senior board officials, on the other. The teacher in a large urban school board might never have had much contact with either. But in smaller communities, contact was frequent and often face-to-face, and carried beyond school affairs to churches, social clubs, and other community institutions. After 1969, that level of intimacy was lost even in rural Ontario, and one consequence was to widen the gap between 'them and us,' and thus contribute to the growing teacher militancy of the 1970s.[16]

From a decade of school and board consolidation, in any case, Ontarians inherited three things. First, there was the large school. Whether we are talking about the township elementary school or the suburban composite high school, the scale of operation grew massively, owing to the conviction that sheer size was a precondition of both quality and equality of opportunity. Second, there was the large administrative unit, responsible for a substantial number of schools scattered across a relatively extensive geographical area, with huge pools of students and teachers, and run by numbers of supervisory officers. And finally, there was a significant devolution of control from the Department of Education to local boards.

IV

Teacher education underwent its own revolution during the 1960s and early 1970s. The shortage of teachers in the post-war era had substantially compromised academic and professional standards of training. Though grade 13 remained the preferred standard, candidates for elementary school teaching could enter the teachers' colleges directly from grade 12, or complete their training in summer sessions, measures abandoned only in the early 1960s when the supply of teachers began to match the demand. By mid-decade, summer sessions became the norm for entry to secondary school teaching: in 1963 the dean of the Ontario College of Education estimated that 8000 of the 14,500 teachers then employed had been trained through summer courses only. Of *new* entrants, the vast majority opted for the summer rather than the full-year program. The former remained in place until 1967, when William Davis announced that the last entry class would be admitted the following year. That decision required some courage because secondary enrolments were still rising; it was taken, nonetheless, apparently because of the conviction that, once the worst of the shortages were over, the drawbacks of the summer program would far outweigh its advantages. Its most serious defect was the lack of any provision for practice-teaching: students began teaching, at the end of the first summer, with hardly a period's worth of experience in practising their craft.

A review of secondary school teacher training was carried out in 1961–2 by a committee appointed by the minister, but it recommended only very modest changes in the existing 'consecutive' program (teacher training following the completion of the university degree), which, it thought, was overall the best possible model available. It did, however, endorse a decision to expand, beyond Toronto, the number of institutions offering the program. Summer schools, introduced in London and Kingston in 1960, were the first steps in establishing Althouse College of Education, opened in 1965, and McArthur College of Education (1968), institutions affiliated respectively with the University of Western Ontario and Queen's.

Much more radical changes in teacher education took place at the elementary school level. There had been a long-term tendency, especially in the United States, to extend the length of training for elementary

school teachers, increase the academic requirements, and link professional training more closely to the university. In the post-war era the same
trend manifested itself in various parts of Canada, but in Ontario at least,
the desperate shortage of teachers and the establishment of the emergency program of teacher training muted any talk during the 1950s of
raising standards. There was, however, increasing criticism of the province's provision for the academic and professional training of its elementary school teachers, and in 1964, Davis established the Minister's
Committee on the Training of Elementary School Teachers, chaired by
C.R. MacLeod, the director of education for Windsor. Armed with a broad
mandate, the committee received briefs from across the province, investi-
gated programs elsewhere, and submitted its report in 1966. Though it
devoted a good deal of attention to the content of professional training
itself, the report's key recommendations were as follows. First, all new
elementary school teachers should possess a university degree, on the
grounds that 'the major deficiencies in elementary school teacher education in Ontario are related to insufficient maturity and inadequate academic education on the part of the student teacher and that a teacher at
any level, by the very nature of his task, should be a scholar and an
educated person.'[17] Second, a teacher's academic and professional education should be more closely linked, and the appropriate environment to
accomplish that was within the university; thus all teacher-training programs should be turned over to the universities. Finally, in order to put an
end to the wall of separation between elementary and secondary school
teachers, they should be trained together in the same institutions. Davis
expressed unequivocal support for the MacLeod Report's main recommendations, and planning for the transition began almost immediately
after it was released.

It took far longer than expected to implement it, in large part because
negotiations with the universities proved difficult and protracted. Differences over control of program content had to be ironed out, and the
universities balked at the department's insistence on providing jobs for,
and giving tenure to, the staffs of the teachers' colleges. That problem was
finally resolved by an agreement guaranteeing them term appointments
only, along with the opportunity to qualify themselves for tenure-track
positions if they chose to do so. During the late 1960s and early 1970s, in
any case, most universities established new faculties of education and,
where secondary teacher-training facilities already existed, arranged for
the merger of the teachers' colleges with them. Over the same period,
successive universities agreed to award the 'BEd.' for completion of profes-

sional training. That too was something new in Ontario: traditionally the only qualification awarded was a ministry certificate.[18]

The transition to a fully graduate occupation would take decades to accomplish because those already in the occupation in 1973 remained in possession of valid teaching certificates. But because these practitioners traditionally had only high school education and were trained in institutions outside the university, the changes were crucial in reducing the stigma attached to elementary school teaching. At the same time, the Ministry of Education, long the arbiter of elementary schoolteacher training, had largely withdrawn from that role, giving up one more aspect of program control, this time to the universities and their faculties of education.

ONE RELATED DEVELOPMENT deserves attention here. In the early 1960s John Robarts and William Davis were both concerned about the absence of a research capacity within the Department of Education. Its research budget for education was minuscule compared with some other government departments, large changes were being implemented without preliminary testing, and Davis in particular was eager to promote the infusion of new ideas into the system. The promotion of research, then, was part of the overall plan for the reform of education in the 1960s, and the result was the creation of the Ontario Institute for Studies in Education. Established by legislation in 1965, OISE was a 'stand-alone' institution, a college in its own right, responsible for basic and applied research, development and dissemination, and graduate teaching, in education.* There were some serious teething problems as well as some long-term difficulties in fulfilling its admittedly broad mandate. There were also some major drawbacks in separating it from initial teacher training, and from a more organic connection with both the universities and the school system. But guaranteed an ample annual income, it quickly became a key centre for research on many vital aspects of education (as well as many that were not), and for educating a significant proportion of the graduate students who would be appointed to Ontario's new faculties of education.

V

It goes almost without saying that the price of educational expansion and change was high.[19] In 1945 provincial and local spending on elementary

---

*'Stand-alone' until the mid-1990s, when it was fully integrated into the University of Toronto and amalgamated with that university's faculty of education.

and secondary education had amounted to $62 million; by 1960 that figure was close to half a billion dollars, and by 1970, $1.6 billion. A graphic portrait, both literally and figuratively speaking, is provided in figures 5 and 6. While expenditure rose steadily in the 1950s, it climbed at precipitous rates in the decade that followed. During the 1960s, wrote one observer, 'population grew from 6.1 million to 7.4 million (20.8%), and Gross Provincial Product from $14.6 billion to $32.5 billion (122%); educational expenditures jumped from $234 million to $1.3 billion (454%).'[20] Those latter figures, it must be added, represent provincial spending alone and don't include the spiralling amounts raised by local school boards.

Growing enrolments were one obvious cause of these increases. The baby boom had to be taught, and that in itself would have required greater expenditures for teachers and schools. But what mattered far more was the matrix of decision-making – by individuals to stay in school longer and then to pursue post-secondary education; by local communities and boards of trustees with a new enthusiasm for investing in education; and by a provincial government that was introducing a wide variety of changes. Rising adolescent participation rates meant the rapid expansion of secondary schools, which had always been more expensive to operate, and had always received larger government grants, than elementary schools. The number of schoolteachers rose from 25,000 in 1950 to over 93,000 in 1970; but secondary school teachers, always better paid than their elementary school counterparts, increased disproportionately, from fewer than 5000 in 1950 to over 33,000 in 1970. The shortage of new teachers, and the willingness to pay them better, brought substantial gains in salaries over the two and a half decades after 1945. The conviction that smaller classes would improve the quality of instruction led to progressive improvements in the pupil-teacher ratio (PTR) but also to the employment of many more teachers than would have been necessary otherwise. There were large capital costs entailed in the expansion of the physical plant to accommodate enrolment growth. There were ever-increasing expenditures as well to pay for the variety of new programs being introduced, ranging from kindergartens, special education, and vocational options, to rural school consolidation. Added to all of this was the effect of modest inflation for most of the post-war period: a steady decline in the purchasing power of the Canadian dollar brought an increase in the costs of buying all sorts of goods and services.

While total expenditure on education rose dramatically, there were also important shifts in the pattern of educational spending. First, there was a major reordering of provincial budget priorities. In 1950 education accounted for 16 per cent of the government's budget, a significant proportion perhaps, but one not wildly incongruent with the amounts spent to meet its other responsibilities; by 1970 spending on the schools *and* post-secondary education accounted for 32.5 per cent of that budget – one in three of all tax dollars the province raised. At the local level the same trend was at work. In 1945 only 29 per cent of property taxes went to finance elementary and secondary education; the rest paid for streets and sewers, firefighters, police, and all the other services provided by the municipality. By 1969, 59 per cent was spent on schools alone. Education, then, was absorbing an enormously increased proportion of Ontario's tax dollars at both the provincial and local levels.

At the same time, the government was also assuming an ever-higher proportion of the costs of funding the schools. In part this was due to its own policy initiatives on education, such as secondary education for all or school and board consolidation. In order to ensure that such initiatives were implemented it had to make greater resources available to local boards. However, in order to cope with the enrolment boom *and* innovation, boards also had to raise ever-greater amounts from the only source available to them – property taxation. But as they did so they inevitably met resistance from property owners, and all the more so since the modernization of Ontario's municipal services was also pushing up local taxes at the same time. For these reasons alone the government was forced to increase its share of the burden of education (and other municipal costs). It was also pressed in the same direction by arguments about fairness. The property tax was (and remains) a regressive one, hitting hard at large numbers of those who could ill afford it. The revenues of the provincial government, on the other hand, came from taxes on income and from other sources that more accurately reflected the ability to pay. The result of the transfer from locality to province, in any case, was substantial. In 1950 the province paid about 36 per cent of school operating costs; by 1967 this had risen to 47 per cent, and by the early 1970s would reach 60 per cent. Thus the province increasingly carried more and more of the burden of paying for the schools.

It was not only education costs that were rising during the 1950s and 1960s, however. Indeed, they have to be set within the context of Ontario's burgeoning 'service state': the introduction of expensive new welfare schemes, the investment in highways and other improvements in the physical infrastructure of the province, growing subsidies to municipalities, and, though still a relatively modest proportion of the budget for most

of the 1960s, the provision of health care. Until the mid-sixties, the
prosperity of the post-war era had underwritten all these developments
without need to resort to large tax increases or deficit financing. But at
that point the provincial government's fiscal commitments began to out-
run its budgeting resources. As a result, in 1967 and 1968 it stepped up its
effort to find additional sources of revenue and began an attempt to
introduce restraints on public expenditure.

The costs of elementary and secondary education, meanwhile, had
begun to escalate at an unprecedented rate. The annual increase in
spending had long been high: from 1950 to the mid-1960s it typically grew
by 10 to 15 per cent a year. But in 1967 it hit 19 per cent and in 1968, 20 per
cent. Some of the reasons were simply an acceleration of earlier trends.
These were the peak years of elementary school enrolment, the PTR was
declining at a rate unmatched in more than twenty-five years, and the rate
of inflation had turned sharply upwards after 1965, driving the price of
goods and services up with it, and encouraging teachers to press for larger
salary increases just to maintain their standard of living. Given the government's worsening financial position, all of this was worrying enough.* But
the real crunch came early in 1969, when education costs suddenly became an explosive political issue.

ACROSS ONTARIO THAT SPRING, the first tax notices were mailed out by the
new county boards. Many communities found themselves faced with a
25 per cent increase in property taxes, in some it was more like 50 per cent,
and in a few, higher than that. Because of rising land values during the
1960s, farm property was particularly hard hit: at a time when farmers
believed they were receiving a diminishing portion of the provincial pie,
they were suddenly faced as well with a steep increase in property taxes
that seemed out of all proportion to the costs incurred by their urban
neighbours. In many parts of Ontario there were noisy protest meetings
and in some cases rural municipalities threatened to withhold their portion of the education taxes until something was done.[21]

The government reacted almost immediately, promising increased grants
for 1969 to subsidize local rates in many small communities. In order to
counteract the more general complaints about soaring property
taxes, moreover, Davis announced that provincial funding would be raised

---

*Worrying enough, at the time; but the late 1960s or early 1970s was not the 1990s or even
the mid-1970s. The issue was not how to *reduce* the deficit or curb the debt but how to avoid
going into debt in the first place.

to 60 per cent of total costs over a period of three years, and for those boards hardest hit, raised to that level in 1970. By the end of 1969 these measures had, temporarily at least, taken the edge off the protests, but that and a lost by-election in Middlesex South – in Premier Robarts' political backyard – where high education taxes were one of the key issues exploited by the opposition, alerted party leaders to ominous rumblings in the constituencies.

The promise of additional grants, however, had also blown a large hole in the government's restraint program and made a direct attack on educational spending a cabinet priority. Indeed the issue was considered so urgent that in September 1969, Davis and Charles MacNaughton, the provincial treasurer, convened a special meeting of the province's directors of education and chairs of boards, and proceeded to read them the riot act.* Ontario, MacNaughton declared, continued to face 'a formidable task in preventing our chronic shortage of revenue from resulting in massive and mounting deficits ... If education costs were allowed to increase at their present rate, there would be no new revenue left for the maintenance of all other public programs.' Davis was blunter still, asserting that there had been excessive and unnecessary expenditures by some school boards and that if they '"failed to put their own houses in order" pressure would mount for the Department of Education to do it.'[22]

Just to show the government meant business, Davis introduced an amendment to the Education Act in November 1969 allowing him to impose maximum spending limits on local boards. Though only a few brief words, it represented a major departure in the relationship between central and local authorities. Traditionally, boards had been free to raise property taxes as they saw fit and the government's grant rose accordingly as it met 'approved' costs stipulated in the grant regulations. But if the government was now to pick up 60 per cent of the costs, it wanted to be sure that it had some control over what those dollar amounts were. The amendment, which challenged cherished notions about the autonomy of local boards and the rhetoric of decentralized decision-making, was vigorously attacked by board representatives and other stakeholders. Davis smoothed the waters in his inimitable way, replying that his new weapon was there to be used only if, at some indeterminate point in the future, boards failed to act responsibly and the public weal was thereby threatened.

---

*An unprecedented meeting as a *Globe* reporter noted: 'Until the County School Boards were established ... there were simply too many for anywhere but Maple Leaf Gardens.' *Globe*, 16 Sept. 1969.

Hoping perhaps that tough talk alone would do the trick, the government did little more for most of 1970 beyond imposing limits, early in the year, on the growth of government grants to the schools. In the meantime, the situation deteriorated. In 1969 education costs had risen 16 per cent, and in 1970 would rise another 15 per cent. Throughout 1970, moreover, warfare between boards and their teachers intensified. The Ontario Federation of Agriculture was promoting a farm tax strike and the province's municipalities were demanding a freeze in education spending. By fall it was apparent to Davis and his cabinet colleagues that much more drastic action to control education expenditure had to be taken. The result was two initiatives, announced in late October and November.

The first was intended to address the conflicts between boards and teachers. A three-man committee of inquiry was established, eventually chaired by Judge R.W. Reville,[23] to review the process of teacher-board bargaining and make recommendations that might improve it. The second initiative was the invocation of Davis's new powers under the 1969 amendment to the Education Act. Grant regulations would be forthcoming in early 1971, he declared, that would impose ceilings on the total amount each board could spend.* The ceilings would be set at levels consonant with average spending so that most boards would have little difficulty in conforming to them and at worst would have to make only modest reductions in their estimates. But a few big-spending urban boards, Davis warned, would be hard hit, required in the first year to cut estimated over-expenditures by half in 1971 and to fall within the limits of the ceilings by 1972.

The timing of the fall 1970 initiatives was not fortuitous, coming as they did amongst rumours that John Robarts was about to resign as leader of the Conservative party, something he actually did in early December. During the 1960s, Davis had gradually established himself as one of the leading figures in the party. By 1967 or 1968 he had become heir apparent to the throne, and when Robarts retired the Davis forces assumed an easy victory. Yet as the leadership race began, several contenders built their platforms around an attack on Davis and his big education budgets as a threat to Ontario's welfare. In part for that reason, Davis squeaked into the leadership, in January 1971, by 44 votes – a very close call. That lesson was

*Given the account that follows in this and succeeding chapters, it is important to note the difference between these 'expenditure ceilings' restricting the *total* amount a board could spend, and 'grant ceilings,' which limited only the amount the government awarded to boards as its share of total spending.

not lost. The tax revolt in the rural constituencies, combined with the discovery that there was political mileage to be made by attacking educational spending generally, confirmed the new Davis government in its conviction that the ceilings were not only necessary but would prove politically palatable in the provincial election to come.

BECAUSE THE ESTABLISHMENT of the expenditure ceilings was announced so late in the year, and because the grant regulations were not issued until February 1971, there was a good deal of chaos and confusion as boards scrambled to trim projected spending to their reduced circumstances. And thus the ceilings were almost immediately dubbed 'the cutbacks.' That, however, is a misnomer of no small proportion. The ceilings did indeed impose a reduction in the rate of growth of school-board expenditure. In understanding their intent, however, the critical word is *rate*. Dollar amounts would increase in 1971. But the rate of increase in school-board spending, which in the late sixties had run from 15 to 20 per cent a year, was to be brought down to something more like 7 or 8 per cent. Boards would have more money, not less, but a good deal less than trustees and their employees expected.

The introduction of the ceilings provoked dismay among high-spending trustees, especially those in Ottawa and Metro Toronto, and a good deal of political pressure on the Davis government. To some extent it worked. Those boards hit the hardest were offered extensions, and provisions were made in the regulations to meet their special circumstances. The government, nonetheless, stood by the principle of the spending ceilings, and insisted they would be applied more rigorously in the following year.

The only other concession it made (if indeed a concession it could be called) to the storm of criticism the ceilings provoked was the appointment, in April 1971, of a 'Committee on the Costs of Education.' Chaired by T.A. McEwan, its membership was made up of businessmen, accountants, and educational administrators. It was charged with the task of reviewing all aspects of expenditure on the schools, including the implications of the ceilings. Whatever the long-term contributions of the committee, its establishment found immediate use in the election campaign of 1971, allowing the Tories to deflect criticism of high spending by replying that the entire matter was under study by an independent group.

Education spending, in any case, played only a limited role in that campaign. In some constituencies there were loud complaints about property taxes and both the Liberals and the NDP offered to provide relief by raising the provincial share to 80 per cent or more. The Conservatives stuck to their commitment of 60 per cent. Though school finance was important to the outcome in some ridings, other issues dominated the election campaign and the result was a solid majority for the Davis government.

EVEN AS LATE AS 1968, William Davis could still declare that 'education for years to come has to be the No. 1 priority in government spending.'[24] Scant years later, in 1971, John White would deliver a very different message. And though White was speaking as minister of university affairs, his phraseology applied every bit as much to the schools as to postsecondary education. 'There will be cries of alarm from here and there when the first step makes it clear to the university community and everyone in Ontario that we insist on more scholar per dollar from this point on.'[25] To juxtapose these two quotations is to capture the essence of the shift taking place as the 1960s gave way to the 1970s, and the long post-war era of good times and heady optimism receded in the face of new and troubling circumstances.

4

The Reorientation of Curriculum and Pedagogy

During the 1960s significant changes in structure reshaped the school system in many ways. But no less important were policy initiatives in curriculum and pedagogy that, once launched, took on a momentum of their own, and cumulatively resulted in substantive and far-reaching changes in Ontario's classrooms.

They began, in part, with the unintended consequences of the Robarts Plan. Increasingly after 1962, most young people, not just the intellectually able or the more bookish, stayed in school to grade 12. But stayed to learn what? From the beginning, the five-year and four-year courses were supposed to be different, the latter geared to the aptitudes and interests of the average student. Yet whatever branch they enrolled in, students were still required to take a substantial core of academic subjects. Inevitably it took time for many teachers to acclimatize themselves to the presence of the new clientele, and to rethink the content of their courses and their pedagogy. A whole new program of studies had to be conceptualized, and then translated into the units and lessons that constitute the guts of daily classroom teaching. Teachers, however, had been given months, not years, to do that, and sometimes the initial responses were uncertain or, occasionally, even bizarre. Because much of the content of the five- and four-year courses was overlapping, for example, there was a tendency to teach the same content and use the same methods but, in the four-year classes, teach it at a slower pace. In other cases large amounts of content, including some of the more challenging ideas, were jettisoned from the four-year courses, leaving them bereft of the intellectual and pedagogical values that justified them in the first place. Inevitably these sorts of adjustments bred discontent and frustration amongst students, multiplied discipline problems, and led to demands for new approaches to the curriculum from students and teachers alike.

Though a relatively modest program in terms of its total enrolment, the four-year Arts and Science branch was the focus of one major curriculum initiative from 1962 to 1965. Because it was a program of general education that did not lead on to university, the department decided to enrich students' options in the senior years, not simply to sustain their interest but to offer them a range of subject matter traditionally available only at the post-secondary level. Thus courses were developed in theatre arts, politics, economics, 'Man in Society' (sociology and social issues), biology, and geology. For all the four-year branches, compulsory academic courses were modified as well. In grade 11 and 12 history, for example, five-year students continued to pursue the established course on the development of Western civilization, which took two years to complete; in an attempt to preserve what was considered valuable and at the same time clear the ground for new options, a rewritten version for four-year students covered the same ground, caveman to Sputnik, in one year. While the revision of the five-year English program, completed in 1964, made only modest changes in the traditional content, its equivalent for four-year students placed much greater emphasis on the practical uses of English composition. In literature, breadth rather than depth of reading was stressed: dozens of paperback novels and modern plays were suggested, in the hope that they would prove relevant to students' lives and encourage the habit of reading. Similar adjustments were made in other subjects.

Some of this worked and some of it didn't. More 'relevance' did not always reduce classroom tensions, nor did offering 'four-year grade 11 tech boys' (as staffroom shorthand had it) the compacted version of Western civilization. But the new options in four-year Arts and Science did raise some provocative questions. The vast majority of high school students did not go on to university; why then should politics, economics, or sociology be available only to those in four-year A and S? Why not also to those in four- or five-year B and C or ST and T, branches that still required large dollops of compulsory subjects even in grades 11 and 12? And if, at the high school level, these were as legitimate as traditional subjects, why not allow all students more choice in the subjects they took?

As teachers and principals gained experience with the Robarts Plan, moreover, some of its rigidities became apparent. Students who caught fire academically in grade 11 or 12, for example, could not easily move laterally from four-year to five-year streams. Equally, the program labelled all students as either good at, or not so good at, everything from physics and mathematics to Latin and English literature. All students, in other words, were defined as either five-year or four-year types, locked exclusively into a full set of either advanced or general courses. Traditional promotion policies contributed to the problems as well. Most students who had two or more failures were doomed to repeat their entire year, regardless of the fact that they received a passing grade in most of their subjects.

By the mid-1960s, there was enough dissatisfaction to encourage principals and teachers in a number of high schools to begin to grope their way towards new methods of organizing the program of studies, experimenting with subject promotion, semestering, and individualized timetables to enable students to take subjects at different levels of difficulty or allow them access to a wider variety of options. For some, the impetus for innovation grew out of nothing more than the concrete situation confronting them. Others, however, were influenced by a movement known as 'ungrading' or 'open education,' a new version of some old progressive ideas, and by projects designed to implement it in the United States and other parts of Canada.

In both its American and British guises, ungrading had begun as a pedagogy applied to young children and the elementary school. Its most ardent advocates, in Ontario as elsewhere, tended to come from elementary school backgrounds – teachers who had become principals, superintendents, or civil servants in the Department of Education. The essential message was that children learn at different rates and have different interests, yet schools were organized around lock-step grades that required them to learn the same amount of material at the same rate; those who didn't, failed at the end of a year and were made to repeat it. Schooling needed to be reconstructed to provide for 'continuous progress,' to make sure that all students learned at their own rates. Applied to the Ontario high school, these notions meant, at the very least, an end to rigid distinctions between four- and five-year students, a recognition that any given student might be 'advanced' in some subjects and have more difficulty with others (which meant timetables must be organized to take account of such individual differences), and an acknowledgment that no student should be held back a whole year or grade because he or she failed this subject or that (which meant abandoning existing promotion practices). The idea of ungrading, in sum, had potentially large consequences for the high schools.

Implementing any of these innovative ideas, however, brought principals face to face with 'HS1,' the Department of Education circular that set out the basic rules for the award of Ontario secondary school graduation diplomas. Commonly known as the principal's bible, HS1 required the high schools to be organized around the Robarts Plan, specified the compulsory and optional subjects in each branch, and provided that different subjects would be allotted different amounts of teaching time. English, for example, was to receive eight periods a week; most subjects had to make do with five or fewer. Large numbers of compulsory subjects, differential time allocations, and five or six distinctive branches made it almost impossible to open up the program of studies. The question thus became, Would the department encourage or discountenance the experiments beginning to emerge in a few Ontario high schools?

Like John Robarts before him, from the time he became minister William Davis had thrown open the doors to new people and new ideas (or refurbished old ones), and made it clear that change was the order of the day. There was not only a massive amount of curricular revision under way in the department, but pedagogical fads and fashions of every stripe were getting a hearing; 'team teaching' was hot, for example, as was interdisciplinary work, and educational technology ranging from programmed learning to educational television. Similarly, 'ungrading' was being advocated by progressives old and new, including senior civil servants whose long-time sympathies with progressivism had been curbed during Dunlop's reign as minister of education, and who were now prepared not just to tolerate but to promote such experiments.

Undoubtedly the most influential figure among them was J.R. McCarthy, an ex–elementary school teacher and inspector. Predisposed from his teaching experience to favour the new ideas in education, he went on to do graduate work at Teachers' College, Columbia University, the pre-eminent centre for the formulation and dissemination of progressivism during the first half of the twentieth century. He then joined the department, where in 1956 he was appointed assistant superintendent of curriculum, and rose rapidly in the hierarchy. Strongly committed to decentralization and to the reform of both curriculum and conventional pedagogy, he would also recruit a bevy of younger men sympathetic to his own views.[1]

McCarthy would exercise enormous influence within the department during the 1960s, increasingly so, indeed, as Davis withdrew from detailed oversight of its affairs in the second half of the decade. And so it was with the future of HS1. In the summer of 1966, McCarthy, then deputy minister of university affairs, told the Ontario Secondary Headmasters Association, 'The flexibility which I believe the secondary school can now adopt leads me to one concept that I think worthy of thorough study by everyone engaged in the educational enterprise. I refer to the possibility of initiating, on an experimental basis, the concept of the non-graded secondary school.'[2] Transferred to education in late 1966, McCarthy was as good as his word: in May the following year, five secondary schools were given formal permission 'to experiment with a different method of student scheduling which will provide greater flexibility and assist with individualized student programs.'[3] The result, filtered through the systematizing efforts of a supervisory committee, was the prototype of the credit system. The recommendation of the committee, however, was that a substantial core of compulsory subjects be maintained: 13 out of 27 credits for graduation, including 4 credits of English, and 3 each for social science, natural sciences and mathematics, and physical education. If implemented, the result would have been a good deal of 'ungrading,' *and* a good deal of adherence to traditional notions that some subjects were more equal than others and thus must be taught to all students.

THE ROBARTS PLAN WAS NOT the only emergent problem in the early 1960s. Both on academic and administrative grounds, the grade 13 year and the examinations crowning it had come under increasing attack for a decade or more. In response, Davis appointed in 1964 the 'Grade 13 Study Committee,' which included university and secondary school representatives, prominent local school administrators, and senior members of the department. 'Very early on the morning of ... [its] first meeting,' wrote its chair, 'the opinion was expressed that not only was there a great deal to be said in favour of the Grade 13 year and a great deal to be said against it, but that everything that could be said – both pro and con – had already been stated over and over again. The merits of Grade 13, and equally its defects, had in the past several years been exhaustively delineated in a variety of official reports, public addresses, and muttered curses.' Given that conclusion, the committee wrapped up its deliberations quickly and submitted a report of only thirty-five pages that recommended, over the long haul, the abolition of both the fifth year and the departmental examinations. Preparation for university entrance would be completed through a special course in grade 12. As for the abolition of the 'departmentals,' the committee expressed concern about both uniformity and the maintenance of academic standards, and it assumed that some alternative system of accreditation would be put in place: 'when proper safeguards are developed,' the report said, 'external examinations, which circumscribe the teaching and encourage the cramming of factual information, should be eliminated.'[4]

Both the universities and secondary school teachers had reservations about eliminating grade 13 and since it was a long-term proposal in any case, that recommendation was apparently shelved by either Davis or his senior advisers. But in March 1966, Davis announced that the departmen-

tal examinations would be abandoned altogether after 1967; the responsibility for conducting the school-leaving exams would be turned over to the
schools themselves. He justified the move in the name of greater flexibility,
teacher responsibility, the decentralization of control over the curriculum,
and the alienation of students caused by the unproductive stress of the
examinations. But he was also blunt about the practical reasons. The rising
number of candidates had made it almost impossible to complete marking
in time for the universities to assess admission applications adequately.
Though the system had been streamlined in recent years, he added, it was
no longer possible, on a purely physical basis, for the department to
continue with the existing practices. Davis intimated, however, that a new
set of aptitude and achievement tests would be introduced to supplement
school records as the basis for university admissions.

   That latter alternative was already being developed in the mid-sixties:
tests modelled on the Scholastic Aptitude Tests widely used for university
admissions in the United States and, because they were administered by a
Canada-wide organization named the Service for Admission to Colleges
and Universities, conventionally referred to as the SACU. Their use spread
quickly in Ontario, and by 1970 all but one of the province's universities
included them as part of the admissions process. Their fate, however, is
succinctly summarized by Alan King. The tests were

> discontinued in 1972, in part because the expansion of the university system
> and the consequent need for students made fine decisions related to admis-
> sions less important. Also, research conducted at the time showed that the
> Ontario Scholastic Aptitude Test scores, both verbal and mathematical, had a
> very low correlation with first-year university average marks and that grade 13
> average marks were much more powerful predictors of university marks.
> Given these results, combined with the financial difficulties of funding large-
> scale testing, it is not surprising that this scheme of standardized examina-
> tions failed to become established as a standard admission criterion. Instead,
> final school marks on grade 13 courses plus final marks obtained on selected
> high school courses in prior grades became the basis for admission into
> university.[5]

PARALLELING THE PROGRAMMATIC innovations just beginning in the secondary schools was another initiative, begun in the early 1960s when
McCarthy was still superintendent of curriculum, to rewrite the curriculum of the primary and junior divisions (grades 1 through 6). It was to be
the first major revision since the 'little grey book' of 1937, and this project

too reflected the 'breath of fresh air' wafting through the corridors of the Department of Education. The result was a series of pamphlets, published between 1966 and 1970 and collectively entitled *Interim Revisions,* for each of the subjects of the Primary/Junior curriculum.* They were accompanied by a more general statement of aims and objectives, *Interim Revision Introduction and Guide,* published in 1967.[6]

Though compromised by the conservative pedagogical mood of the post-war years, and by the hostility of the minister of education himself, the 1937 program of studies had incorporated a substantial element of progressive theory to which the authors of the *Interim Revision Guide* paid full homage, quoting at length its statement of aims, objectives, and pedagogical prescriptions. But the *Interim Revisions* did more than reaffirm the progressive impulse of 1937: they pushed it harder and further. What had originally been a moderate attempt to counterbalance traditional pedagogical formulas by an emphasis on 'activity, interest and social participation' now became a much more forceful assertion of the superiority of 'child-centred' techniques. The *Guide* proselytized for the virtues of individualization, ungrading, flexible timetables that allowed large blocks of time for activities, and classrooms organized to promote a variety of simultaneous group and individual pursuits. As for teachers, they were to become facilitators rather than directors, and formal didactic teaching was discouraged. The pervasive tone is caught in the following paragraph.

> Within each classroom there should be provision for a wide range of experiences and activities in order that children may take an active part in their own learning. Rich and varied materials stimulate curiosity, experiment and discovery. Children should do as much as possible by themselves since the more they learn through their own experiences and discoveries, the more meaningful and lasting their learning will be. An ancient Chinese maxim strikes one as very appropriate:
>
> > *I hear and I forget;*
> > *I see and I remember;*
> > *I do and I understand.*[7]

---

*Just as 'HS1' (High School 1) was the departmental circular that laid out requirements for the high school program, P1J1 (Primary 1/Junior 1) was the basic circular for the organization and program in grades 1 to 6. The 'little grey book,' the *Interim Revisions,* and *The Formative Years* were successive P1J1 documents. These basic documents and their successors such as *OSIS* (*Ontario Schools, Intermediate and Senior*) and the new curriculum documents of the late 1990s have the force of law behind them.

Inevitably, subject content received less emphasis, or was interpreted merely as a vehicle for the acquisition of skills. English itself was reinterpreted to include, in equal portions, the 'communication skills' of listening, speaking, reading, and writing. The 1937 program of studies had never mentioned the first one, and had introduced the section on English with this well-crafted opening paragraph: 'English rightly occupies first place among the intellectual exercises of the elementary school. It is of prime importance that children learn to speak and write their mother tongue clearly, accurately, and gracefully, and to use good books as a source of information and pleasure.'[8] While hardly disavowing such goals, the authors of the *Interim Revisions* stressed the importance of an 'integrated language program,' and discountenanced formal instruction in grammar or using direct instruction to correct spoken or written usage. The emphasis now fell on helping each child 'to read critically, and write creatively.'[9]

The 'little grey book,' moreover, had outlined, in fairly concrete fashion, the kind of English or mathematical skills students might reasonably be expected to demonstrate grade by grade. Though the exact time allocations were not dictated, teachers were given a clear guide to follow but were also given limits to the tasks they were expected to complete in each grade. The little grey book, in other words, provided direction without regimenting either content or pedagogical technique. With the new emphasis on decentralization, however, much of this went by the board. The *Interim Revisions* stressed 'approaches' and 'philosophies,' and gave examples; teachers were expected to flesh out not simply the details but much more ambitious aspects of curriculum design. Equally, achievement levels were far more loosely defined. Bar graphs indicated what skills might be taught and when, but expected attainments were blurred across both divisions, and, in the case of mathematics, the graph was accompanied by an italicized injunction warning that 'any exactness in relating the above interpretation of the dots, lines and dashes to grade levels is to be avoided.'[10]

BUT WHY, THE READER may ask, were they called '*Interim* Revisions' in the first place? Thereby hangs a tale. When the project was first conceived, the revision of the program was intended to be a thoroughgoing and carefully organized sequence of four successive stages: a small group within the department would prepare the ground by assembling pertinent information, research, and curricula from other jurisdictions; a provincial committee would then be appointed 'to establish the Aims and Objectives for the education of all children in Kindergarten and Grades 1–6'; that done, professional educators would translate aims into curricular materials and course outlines; concurrently, teachers would be involved in examining current ideas and practices, and assessing the proposals put forward by the committee.

At some point during 1964 or early 1965, however, the modest Provincial Committee on Aims and Objectives, K to grade 6, metamorphosed into a very different beast.[11] 'Since the publication of the Hope Report ... in 1950,' the minister's *Annual Report for 1965* explained, 'no thoroughgoing study of the purpose and direction in the education system of the Province has been undertaken. In the intervening 15 years, the social, economic and technical changes sweeping the world have affected the whole structure of education everywhere. For these reasons, the Provincial Committee on Aims and Objectives came into existence at an opportune time.'[12] Another explanation is that the committee had discovered early on that it was impossible to define aims for K–6 without considering the larger aims of the system as a whole. Whatever the reasons, in any case, this new version of the committee was to 'set forth the aims of education' for the entire system, K–13. Its other terms of reference, though, seemed to indicate that its main work would still focus on K–6: the committee was directed to 'identify the needs of the child as a person and as a member of society, to outline objectives of the curriculum' for children in kindergarten to grade 6, and 'to prepare means by which these aims and objectives may be achieved.' Thus the overall emphasis of the committee's mandate reflected its origins, and so did its membership. Of the twenty-four appointees, no more than four had any contact with the secondary schools and none were at that moment directly connected with secondary education either as teachers or as administrators. Seven, on the other hand, were ex–elementary school teachers serving in various administrative posts. Eleven were drawn from outside the world of professional education, though many of them had served as members of boards of education. There were two university representatives, the presidents of York and Windsor. The committee was chaired by the Hon. Justice E.M. Hall, a distinguished Canadian jurist.[13] It began work in April 1965, and a Scarborough elementary school principal, Lloyd A. Dennis, was appointed its 'Secretary and Research Director.' Because of the weight of other responsibilities Hall was carrying, Dennis was elevated to co–chairman in 1967. Meanwhile the work of revising the elementary curriculum went on, but was labelled 'interim' so as not to anticipate the committee's conclusions.

Published in May 1968, the committee's work bore the title *Living and*

Learning. But it would almost universally be referred to, then and after, as the 'Hall-Dennis Report.' The contrast with the Hope Report (and indeed with most other similar documents) couldn't have been greater. Hope had been some nine hundred pages long, bound in civil-service blue, graced with not so much as a single photograph to break the flow of its spartan prose, and weighed down by a politically explosive dissenting opinion on the separate school question. *Living and Learning* ducked most of the difficult issues relating to separate schools, and no other subject divided the committee enough to provoke a minority report. The entire document was hardly more than two hundred pages long, it was lavishly illustrated with coloured and black and white photographs, drawings, and children's artwork, with points of emphasis printed in blue or red ink, and its large rectangular shape and bright cover suggested it belonged on a coffee-table rather than a bookshelf. Indisputably, it was an attractive volume.

The report offered 258 recommendations ranging from proposed changes in teacher-education programs to the role and structure of the ministry, minority and special education, educational TV, and the abolition of grade 13. Much of the report was uncontroversial in the sense that most people committed to the school system would have welcomed many of its recommendations or at least agreed that implementation of them might well constitute improvements. Some of these I will return to in later chapters. But it is the heart of the report, its central thrust, that demands elucidation here. It was, in the first place, much more wide-ranging than its mandate suggested, reaching far beyond K–6 and making recommendations for the high schools that extended well beyond 'aims.' It was, as well, very much the child of its age. While never denying the value of preparation for employment, the uses of career training, or the role of the school in promoting economic efficiency, the emphasis of the report fell almost exclusively on education for personal fulfilment. Education was about 'self-realization' and not about fitting individuals for predetermined economic or social roles. In this respect, Hall-Dennis reflected the anti-technocratic, anti-traditionalist, romantic impulses of the 1960s. Nor should the report be singled out for criticism on this score: similar impulses were reshaping practices and policies within the universities and were the particular property not just of university students but of a professoriate gripped by the same mood.

Not surprisingly, then, the report was fiercely critical of what it called traditionalist or conservative educational thought and practice. 'The school's learning experiences are imposed, involuntary, and structured'; pupils were a 'captive audience,' their bodies and minds fettered by a multitude of rules and regulations.[14] The pedagogy of the past (and too often the present) was simply to stuff students with the content of arbitrarily defined subjects through methods emphasizing mindless rote. But a new age was upon us, characterized by rapid economic, technological, and social change. What counted, in this new age, was the ability to find and organize knowledge rather than the acquisition of particular bodies of content. Thus the fundamental purpose of schooling was 'to learn to learn.' Since children learn at different speeds and have different interests, 'the modern curriculum must be flexible, not only by providing options for pupils with different interests at more senior levels, but by providing learning experiences to meet the needs of individual young people at every level ... The obvious corollary is that the curriculum must provide for the individual progress of pupils. To make this possible, two major innovations are indicated: complete abolition of the graded system throughout the school; and the use of individual timetables at the senior level.' To increase variety, vocational, commercial, and academic subjects were to be open to all without restriction, and courses offered at two or more levels of difficulty, allowing students to find their own level in the courses they chose to take.

The learning experience was not, however, to be organized around conventional subjects, which were described as arbitrary assemblages of 'knowledge, skills, and ideas in a particular field,' created primarily for instructional purposes. Schooling that was content-oriented 'seems to be based on the premise that unless subject matter is presented to a pupil in a logical sequence, or an organized pattern, he will never organize it for himself. But schooling that takes into account both the learner as an integrating organism and the subject matter pertinent to the dynamic interests of the learner cannot be organized around subjects which are patterns of the logic of other people.' On the other hand, 'the study of man, or a curriculum embracing all of life, is too formidable a sea for students to navigate without charts of some sort.' Thus Hall-Dennis suggested that the curriculum be organized into three broad areas. The first was communications, 'embracing all aspects of learning that relate to man's interchange of thought,' including the ability 'to speak and listen, to read and write, to record and to film, to paint, to dance. It also involves aspects of social studies, mathematics, business and commerce, manual arts, and almost all of man's activities in which ideas are transmitted and received.' The second area was 'man and his environment,' which included the sciences but also aspects of geography, applied mathematics, 'the practical aspects of agriculture, of manual arts, of home and consumer economics, and much of what is called vocational training.' Finally, there was the 'Humanities,' embracing studies related to human aspirations, ideals, and values – the fine and practical arts, philosophy and religion, and aspects of physical education.

There is, the reader will note, a good deal of overlap in these lists. That was deliberate because the committee was determined to resist 'the temptation to list the traditional subjects that might appear in each. To do so would defeat the purpose of such a thematic approach. The approach is intended to free teachers and pupils from the confines of structured, isolated subjects, to encourage a wider exploration of knowledge relative to each theme, and to emphasize the embracing nature of the learning experience.'

That experience, moreover, had to include the active involvement of the learner in defining what is to be learned and how. Children, within very broad limits, had to have the freedom to choose what they would learn, when and how, and at what speed, because willing involvement, or intrinsic motivation, is crucial if real learning is to take place. And that, in turn, indicated a new role for the teacher – as guide, adviser, and facilitator, rather than authoritarian leader. Because interest and active involvement is crucial to learning, such pedagogical techniques as projects, discovery methods, group work, individual research, and joint teacher-student planning were all appropriate. Meaningless exercises from textbooks, conventional drills, memory work, and other forms of rote were to be avoided, as were prerequisites or other imposed sequences: guidance, yes, direction, no.

Since children learn at different rates, the report continued, failure was a meaningless concept: indeed, 'a child who is learning cannot fail.' Not only do year-end examinations and other similar methods of evaluation emphasize rote learning and test the trivial, but failure to pass them 'can be demoralizing' and destroy rather than encourage an interest in learning. Systems of individualized and continuous assessment needed to be put in place. Similarly, report cards that emphasized marks and rankings had to be replaced with richer and more probing 'learning profiles.' '"Ungrading,"' the report added, 'could be quite disappointing if year-end examinations and competitive report cards were not abolished at the same time.'

According to their own lights at least, the committee did not abandon the cause of literacy and numeracy. Language was 'the *sine qua non* of education in civilized society' and thus 'the school must teach accepted usage of language and a discriminating vocabulary if pupils are to understand what they hear and read ... and if they are to be able to think and express their thoughts ... Comprehension of English (or French ...) and ability to use it must therefore be achieved by all ... Together with simple mathematics, they constitute the one skill which must be measured and brought to an acceptable standard in keeping with the pupil's ability.' On the other hand, the committee considered it 'imperative to abandon in all teaching or directed learning, except for senior students in academic courses, what strikes most pupils as useless and repulsive – dreary drill on spelling, for example, or dull expositions of formal grammar. Traditional teaching was designed to elicit a required response. Modern guidance of learning experience must encourage a free and creative response. The teacher must learn to understand and accept the child's manner of thinking, speaking, and writing.'

Living and Learning had a remarkable reception. Critical enough to reflect the extant dissatisfaction with the schools, alert to the disaffection of many young people and to the portents of the cultural upheaval of the late 1960s, the report rode the crest of a wave of enthusiasm for educational reform. Within sixteen months of publication it sold 60,000 copies, something unprecedented in the annals of government reports. It attracted attention across the country and indeed the continent. And it was widely endorsed in the press. There were dissenting voices here and there, and much unease among secondary school teachers who thought its approach suited perhaps to the elementary schools but less so to the high schools.[15] But initially, criticism or thoughtful analysis was swamped by enthusiasm among the public and the profession. Immediately upon its release the government assigned Lloyd Dennis the job of selling the report across the province, but his efforts hardly proved necessary. As he himself remarked, regally, 'We hate to make statements this early, but it seems that the significance of this report has found acceptance across the board.'[16]

OVER THE DECADES that followed, as the memory of the sixties grew dimmer, the Hall-Dennis Report attained almost mythic status, praised or blamed for changing the face of public education in Ontario. That is to give it far too much credit. Its influence, moreover, is often attributed primarily to the larger mood of the late 1960s and the widespread discontent with things as they were. While there is some truth in this, the problem with such an explanation is that the impetus for change was never unidirectional or consensual. Arising from very disparate sources, proposals for change ranged from the most modest sorts of adjustments to the most wild-eyed of educational panaceas. The report responded to this ferment in a highly selective manner. It studiously ignored (though 'contemptuously dismissed' might be a better phrase) the long-standing and well-articulated critique of progressivism that remained influential into the 1960s, and ignored as well such thoughtful work as that in *Design for Learning*, a volume that attempted to rethink curriculum and that, at the same time, maintained traditional notions about the integrity and centrality of subject-oriented teaching. Rather, it largely reiterated views that were already the conventional wisdom amongst the devotees of progressive education: having grazed over these meadows of well-rooted truisms and clichés, the committee threw them back up in codified form, reproducing rather than pioneering a particular vision of Ontario's educational future. The committee, on the other hand, did not declare that 'school is dead': though it contained snippets of the radical rhetoric of the 1960s, it never once broached the notion of abolishing the school system or converting it into myriad free schools.

Not surprisingly. The report was, first and foremost, the product of Ontario's Department of Education itself. The Hall-Dennis committee, as Eric Ricker's research demonstrates, was 'initially structured in a way that was wanted by the department; its agendas and working papers were prepared by the department's staff; almost all of the expert testimony during the early stages of its work was provided by the department; and finally, a number of its members were close associates, or former teachers and professors, or members of the department's curriculum branch.' It was, Ricker adds, 'without question, a Committee that was clearly biased before its work even commenced,' and 'the consensus that emerged in fact reflected a basic view that was wanted.'[17]

The 'view that was wanted' was not J.R. McCarthy's alone. Other members of the department were more directly involved, and the revival of educational progressivism within (and without) the department from at least the early 1960s is apparent in many ways, including the rhetoric of the Interim Revision documents of 1966 and 1967. Indeed, similar views were contained in briefs by all of the leading teachers' organizations (the OSSTF excepted) and in many others besides. Yet McCarthy's influence appears critical, not only because of the ambience he created within the department but because of oft-reiterated, forthright, and forceful expression of his own views. Consider but one example, a brief summary of a presentation he made to the provincial committee in 1965 on 'the aims and objectives of the ungraded elementary school.'

> In describing how a non-graded elementary program could be organized, Dr McCarthy stated that he would eliminate grades, courses divided by grades,

formal examinations, marks, report cards, and promotion as it has been practised, and would substitute a flexible program of continuous pupil progress related to the individual's rate of learning, his readiness, and his mastery of the program, with evaluation shared by the pupils, and with reporting practices which described progress in the program and which involved greater use of parent-teacher interviews.[18]

Such sentiments would echo through page after page of the Hall-Dennis Report. But the effect was simply to *endorse* an extant view of educational reform already well established in influential quarters, and already articulated by the most powerful figure in the ministry aside from William Davis himself, well before the report was produced. A full year before its submission, McCarthy was authorizing the critical experiments in the secondary schools that would lay the groundwork for change. Nor was it the publication of the report alone that was important; the public hearings held in 1965 and 1966 were part of the sales job. As one eager enthusiast of the new order put it, 'It was ... fairly obvious, even before the report was made public, that changes would be recommended by the Provincial Committee ... Many briefs recommended change, *not only in program but also in attitude.* Suffice it to say at this point that change was in the air, and the continuing activities of the committee encouraged those who were seeking to promote it in the schools.'[19]

What purpose, then, did the publication of the Hall-Dennis Report serve in the larger scheme of things? Certainly it provided a 'bully pulpit' from which to preach a particular approach to education to a wider public, and undoubtedly it gave that approach a degree of legitimacy it might not otherwise have had. But it was hardly of decisive importance to the reorientation of pedagogy and the curriculum that was already under way before its publication and that took place after it. J.R. McCarthy, on the other hand, was. However one assesses his influence throughout the period, whether for praise or blame, his place in its history deserves a measure of recognition now too often accorded to the Hall-Dennis Report itself.

MEANWHILE, AS LLOYD DENNIS basked in the acclaim, and used his public platform to condemn Ontario's schools as, among other things, 'pickle factories,'[20] McCarthy and his minions got on with the job of changing them. Beyond the revisions to the primary/junior program of studies, the next big challenge was the secondary schools – a challenge that focused on the rewriting of HS1. That job fell within the purview of the 'program branch,' a relatively new subdivision of the department created as part of a wholesale reorganization carried out in the mid-1960s. Traditionally the responsibility for curriculum and supervision had been rigidly separated into secondary and elementary divisions. 'One of the main functions' of the program branch, however, was 'to put into effect the integration of elementary and secondary education in the Province.' Within the branch was an expanded curriculum section whose purpose was 'to articulate courses of study for Grades 1–13, to provide new courses and programs designed to meet a wide variety of student needs, and to promote the best new teaching methods.'[21] This mandate was, in itself, significant because it was one more not-so-subtle assertion that what counted was the 'K to 12 continuum' rather than any lingering notion about the distinctive purpose of the high school within the system. But the full significance of the reorganization did not become evident until the fall of 1968.

The program branch also included a supervision section, and one of its tasks was the annual preparation of HS1.[22] In a memorandum to the deputy minister, the supervision section argued that it should remain in charge: 'HS1 does not deal with textbooks or course content. It is chiefly concerned with the administration and organization of the school. The supervision section with its staff of former secondary school principals is better equipped than the curriculum section to deal with that aspect.' Dominated by people with elementary school backgrounds, the curriculum section wanted to wrest control over HS1 for itself, and replied that 'curriculum involves the totality of experience that the child has under the aegis of the school, and that textbooks, courses of study, and organization and administration are fringe factors each in its own way affecting that totality.'

The decision about how to proceed rested with McCarthy, and he created a ten-man committee that included only three members of the supervision section. In effect, he gave the curriculum section the power to change the organizational pattern of the secondary schools as its members saw fit, and change it they did, despite the opposition, vocal and otherwise, of the representatives from the supervision section. There was conflict over several points but the key issue was that of compulsory credits. In his persuasive analysis of the development of the new HS1, John Stapleton describes the issue as follows.

Although the Hall-Dennis report publicly supported the areas of study approach, its recommendation was not perceived to represent an accurate reflection of the feeling of secondary school men. The committee thus received no support for the areas of study approach from any group considered to be a reference group for secondary school educators ... The committee was divided into two camps. The curriculum section represented the progressive orientation, the supervision section the traditional orientation. Factors other than ideological aggravated interaction between the two sections. These included the growth of the curriculum section since the 1965 reorganization, the relative decline of the supervision section, the transfer of jurisdictional control of the HS1 document from supervision and curriculum, and the perception that the leadership of the curriculum section had little legitimacy to speak authoritatively about secondary school organization.

Solidly in the majority, the curriculum section easily carried the day. Or as one anonymous member of the committee would crow later, 'We railroaded it through.'[23] Nor was the victory without symbolic significance. Not quite a decade earlier, the secondary schools had been finally transformed from schools with a distinctive mission, especially in the senior grades, to schools like the elementary schools, responsible for the universal education of Ontario's young people. Now, those who traditionally represented the authority and interests of secondary school principals and subject specialists had lost control of those schools, and indeed lost the battle to preserve the sanctity of a curriculum built upon the privileged position of the academic subjects themselves.

HS1 1969–70 CONTAINED two schemes for organizing a high school, the old Robarts Plan and the new credit system. Initially, the intent was to allow principals to organize their schools on either plan. But an off-the-cuff remark by William Davis in March 1969 gave the impression that the latter would quickly become the exclusive standard. His comments sparked more bureaucratic infighting and created the momentum that led to the decision – with, once again, J.R. McCarthy's crucial intervention – to make the credit system mandatory for all high schools in 1972–3.[24]

What were the chief innovations the credit system entailed? Grade 12 graduation requirements were set at a minimum of 27 credits. There was, however, no longer to be a 'grade 12,' since all grades and streams were abolished, along with any distinction between academic, technical, and commercial courses. The value of a credit was set at 110–20 hours of scheduled instructional time, and all subjects given equal weight, with the result (amongst many others) that English lost two-sevenths of its time in the high school curriculum. Subject promotion became the order of the day, as did an emphasis on individualized timetables. Where possible, courses open to all were to be offered at two or three levels of difficulty. As well, there was to be an increase in the number of options, and the new subjects introduced in the first half of the 1960s for four-year Arts and Science alone were now to be available to all students.* Hall-Dennis had recommended that the curriculum be organized around three 'themes'; the committee responsible for rewriting HS1 opted for four: communications, social science, pure and applied science, and arts. Students were required to take one credit from each in grades 9 and 10 and at least one from each during their last two years. Within these groups, however, there was very wide choice. As the department envisioned it, English and French might be slotted under communications but so might shorthand, drafting, and data processing; pure and applied science might include mathematics and chemistry but also business machines and industrial arts. In other words, a student could meet the credit requirements for graduation without ever taking even *one* English or mathematics course![25] Students could attain the graduation diploma, moreover, by taking the requisite number of credits at only grade 9 or 10 level. That indeed was part of the point: for the first time the high school graduation diploma was reconceptualized in such a way that it would be available to all, no longer reflecting 'a fixed level of achievement over which all must jump, whether they have long legs or short,' but rather one 'representing a common amount of educational experience – experience appropriate to the needs and interests and abilities of every student who earns it.'[26]

THE MOMENTUM TO CHANGE the schools did not stop there. By late 1970, a full-scale review of the primary-junior program was under way. The process was complex, involving a series of committees that included representatives from virtually all segments of the educational community. The work was to be completed by 1973 and to be available to the schools that September. In fact, it bogged down badly, in part because the process itself proved to be cumbersome, and because of controversies about both pedagogy and content. By 1974 the document was in its fifth draft and still not ready for publication.[27] Indeed the final version was not issued until early 1975. It replaced the 'interim revisions' as the prescribed program of studies for the primary and junior divisions, and was titled *The Formative Years*.† The document, in a brief twenty-three pages, set out in the tersest of

---

*Among the consequent losses was the coherent program of studies in world and Canadian history that had been virtually compulsory for students, grades 9–12.
†It would remain the official ministry directive for grades 1 to 6 until replaced by *The Common Curriculum* in the mid-1990s.

terms the objectives to be achieved in the various subjects. It was, in this respect, clearly intended to reinforce the decentralizing impulses of the 1960s: the ministry provided the broadest of aims and objectives; the details of what, how, and when were to be left to local people to determine. *The Formative Years* was accompanied by a 'support document,' *Education in the Primary and Junior Divisions,* designed to provide 'an extensive philosophical basis and rationale.'[28] While its discussion of content and pedagogy was more extensive than that contained in the 'interim revisions guide,' its emphases were virtually the same, stressing the virtues of ungrading, individualization, flexibility, informal teaching techniques, and the participation of pupils in shaping their own learning activities. The new P1J1, in other words, was little more than the 'interim revisions' congealed.[29]

Two years after the review of P1J1 was begun, the same process was commenced with the intermediate division. This came to even more grief because of conflicts that proved irreconcilable throughout the 1970s between the views of people with elementary and secondary school backgrounds.[30] As a result, no document giving general direction or focus to these grades was ever released. But the issue here is the intent rather than the outcome. In a remarkable 'position paper' published in September 1972, the ministry outlined its vision for grades 7 to 10.[31] The curriculum was to be divided into 'common' and 'elective' studies. The former would include 'the skills and content usually associated with courses in reading, mathematics, history, physical education, etc.,' which 'might' be taught by individual teachers. But the ministry clearly preferred an integrated approach in which the various disciplines would be subordinated to interdisciplinary themes and activities. The 'electives,' moreover, were to 'go beyond the scope of existing areas of studies,' to

> reflect not only the students' interests but also the areas of competence of teachers, as well as the tremendous variety of resources available in any community. They could encompass poetry, music appreciation, archery, photography, candle-making, Gregg shorthand, astronomy, and film-making, as well as more traditional 'school' subjects. They could be of varying time lengths and different levels of difficulty, but basically they would provide the students with opportunities to make personal choices and to pursue interests in worthwhile learning experiences with varying degrees of intensity.

In the first year (that is, grade 7) the electives might constitute 'approximately one-quarter to one-third of the total program time.' The next three years (grades 8 to 10) 'could consist of lesser times on Common Studies

and up to two-thirds or three-quarters time devoted to electives.' To
achieve this end, a fundamental change in the organization of the intermediate grades was essential. 'The basic characteristic of the program is
flexibility,' the position paper intoned. 'It must enable teachers to provide a
valid educational experience for the students. It is very difficult to provide
for flexibility in a rigid rotary system. It is equally difficult if subject
territoriality is considered ahead of student needs.'

By the early 1970s, in other words, the 'reform' of the program of
studies envisioned by the ministry mandarins reached far beyond the
credit system or the new high school diploma requirements. Extending
from K to 12, it was to remake pedagogical practice, to alter radically the
organization of instruction, and to dethrone the privileged place of the
core academic subjects. However one assesses this ambitious reformula-
tion of aims, pedagogy, and content, which, while drawing on older
strands of progressivism, took its particular shape in the ambience and
enthusiasms of the 1960s, it represented a *programmatic* assault on the
presuppositions and practices of the traditional Ontario school system.

INITIALLY AT LEAST, the principles of ungrading, continuous progress,
integrated studies, and discovery learning spread only slowly in the elementary schools. Though there appears to have been a steady increase
between 1966 and 1972, many schools adopted them partially, or not at
all.[32] In the latter year, for example, only 582 of some 4000 elementary
schools would report that they had 'fully' introduced continuous progress
in the primary division, and 935 would assert that they had done nothing
of the sort. The senior levels of the elementary school, geared as they were
to preparation for high school, remained overwhelmingly organized by
subject, and by clear grade distinctions. Large numbers of elementary
schools, in other words, and perhaps a majority of teachers, continued to
follow the grade and subject organization familiar from the 'little grey
book.' It was only somewhat different in the high schools. With the
introduction of the credit system as an optional organization, more and
more schools moved in that direction, abolishing the streaming built into
the Robarts Plan, opening subject options to all students, and permitting
subject promotion. Still, most boards moved cautiously. When London, for
example, made the shift, at the beginning of the academic year 1971–2, it
retained a substantial compulsory core, including three years of English.[33]

Within the ministry, nonetheless, 'caution' was increasingly discountenanced. Since the early 1960s, innovation had been the order of the day,
and when schools failed to follow suit, innovation was, indeed, *ordered*.
Early in 1972, the minister of education, Robert Welch, gave a keynote

address to the directors and senior program officials of Ontario's school boards as part of a ministry-organized seminar on program development. It was a wide-ranging and remarkable speech, reflecting the determination of key ministry officials both to direct and to force the pace of change. And the real issue at stake was not *what* but *how*, not simply the content of the curriculum, but commitment to the 'approach' or the 'philosophy' of the new pedagogy: as of 1971, Welch declared, the 'interim revisions' had become the 'approved curriculum guideline' for the primary-junior divisions. 'This step means that the Program of Studies for Grades 1 to 6 of the Public and Separate Schools of 1960 – the little grey book, as it was often called – is superseded. It also means that programs in the primary and junior divisions should be made consistent with the *approaches* advocated in the P1J1 documents.'[34]

Welch was even more explicit when he turned to the credit system, which, he reminded his audience, was to become compulsory the following September. 'The superficial features of the new system are relatively easy to implement,' he contended, but 'the philosophy underlying these changes is very different from the one that has been operative in many of our secondary schools in the past.' He reviewed the key emphases of the plan, including the need 'to accommodate the increasing awareness of individuality,' and the forces of change that meant 'we can no longer identify the specific skills and knowledge that all students must possess.' It was critical that parents and 'our communities generally understand not only the changing mechanics but the changing underlying philosophies of educational practice.' Welch then delivered the punch line: 'As the key implementors of provincial policy, I expect you to work as quickly as circumstances allow toward the expression in educational practice of the philosophy expressed in the 1972–73 edition of HS1.'[35]

Over the course of a decade, in sum, the much-contested doctrines of progressivism had not only been adopted as the new orthodoxy by the mandarins in the ministry, but they had also been promoted vigorously in curriculum guidelines, by the Hall-Dennis report, and by all the influence senior ministry officials could exercise within the bureaucracy and without.[36] In 1972 that orthodoxy was elevated to the official 'philosophy' of education in Ontario. Its spirit, not just its mechanics, was to be implemented in the schools, however much local administrators, principals, teachers, or parents believed in it or not, and however much philosophers might carp that it was no 'philosophy' at all.

IN THE LATE 1960s and early 1970s the schools were also being changed by developments that were emphatically *not* part of any agenda promulgated

by the Department of Education, not among the recommendations contained in Hall-Dennis, and not willingly countenanced by the establish-
mentarian version of progressivism so widely admired by the daily press.
Yet the efflorescence of student radicalism washing over secondary and
post-secondary education alike captured far more public attention, and
altered educational institutions in more dramatic ways, and in some respects as fundamental a way, as any of the other changes in the period.[37]

Student radicalism in the universities has not only been the subject of
many retrospective studies, it has remained etched in the memories of
those, on either side of the barricades, who lived through it; the impact on
the secondary schools, however, has been largely forgotten, and
undeservingly so. High school students protested over everything from
the exercise of 'arbitrary authority' to the demand for a more 'relevant'
education, from the imposition of dress codes and rules about hair length,
to the right to smoke on school property, to criticize teachers and principals in school newspapers, and even to influence board and ministry
policies on wider issues. One high point occurred in late 1968 and early
1969, and constituted what R.M. Stamp has described as 'the largest and
loudest student protest in Ontario school history.' It was triggered, he
writes,

> by a routine departmental announcement that in June 1969 classes would
> end five days later than in the previous year. A number of student councils
> labelled the announcement as arbitrary, dictatorial, and showing contempt
> towards students. A threatened walk-out over the issue by Metro Toronto's
> 115,000 students was only averted by ... [the minister of education] in a three-
> hour session with the chairmen of Metro's six inter-school councils. A new
> element had been forcefully introduced into the politics of educational
> decision-making.[38]

But such confrontations were not confined to Toronto. They occurred
in Ottawa and London, and spread out to smaller communities besides. In
Sarnia there was a lengthy campaign for 'high school democracy,' which
meant, as one participant would later describe it, making '"responsible
government" the theme of high school life: i.e., the principal would be
allowed to govern provided he enjoyed the confidence of the student
council.'[39] In Dorchester, a small village outside London, eighty young
women defied a ban on slacks by 'refusing to change into skirts or dresses'
and were banished for the day to the cafeteria.[40] They were backed by the
student council, the principal was forced to retreat, and that in turn led to

a reconsideration of the school's dress code. In some urban communities, reform-minded trustees, themselves members of the post-war generation, abolished dress codes without even a fight, more conservative trustees and administrators reluctantly tagging behind in the hope of defusing a potentially explosive issue. Along with the spreading drug culture in the high schools, something virtually unknown before 1967, the protests and disruptions fed a sense of alarm that the schools, like the universities, were in crisis; indeed at the 1969 convention of the Canadian Education Association, one speaker warned that 'student violence is likely to increase to undreamed of proportions unless educationists take positive steps to change the school system and increase student-teacher communication.'[41] A singularly hysterical reaction? As Christabelle Sethna has recently pointed out, political activism by a small number of Ontario high school students alarmed the RCMP enough to provoke secret surveillance just in case they were contributing to the subversion of the Canadian state.[42] Not surveillance simply of university students or professors, mind, but of adolescents in their mid-teens.

For the high schools the unrest of the late 1960s resulted in a substantial retreat from hitherto unquestioned assumptions about the doctrine of *in loco parentis*. In a remarkably short period of time, dress codes vanished, senior students were put on an 'honour system' for attendance (meaning they could skip school when they liked), and a level of dissent from school policies and practices was tolerated as never before. Surveying the local high school scene in 1972, one London reporter singled out for comment

> the development of a more relaxed and permissive atmosphere which, in turn, reflects similar trends in society ... Standards of behaviour, dress, appearance have virtually disappeared ... These trends are all part of the rapid evolution in recent years of student emancipation, the strident demands for student rights and freedom from what many consider oppressive teacher and administrative authority. This evolution has radically altered the teacher-student relationship in which the teacher now is neither dominant nor all-knowing.[43]

These changes might translate into more respect for the rights of young adults and an end to unnecessary and sometimes mindless regulation; but they could also mean a new degree of tolerance for unbecoming behaviour amongst the young and, more critically, a decline in the ability of teachers to maintain the particular forms of authority requisite to sound learning.

Another reflection of the times was the enthusiasm of some parents for the free-school movement, and a collateral enthusiasm among some big urban boards – again, not just in Metropolitan Toronto – for the creation of alternative schools within the public system for those who found the regular classroom confining, conformist, or not suited to their 'learning styles.' One popular (if pale) variation in conventional high schools was the allocation of days in which students could explore topics of their own choice or even organize their own curriculum. The results could be surprising. 'Revolution was a drag at Forest Hill Collegiate yesterday,' one *Globe* reporter wrote in April 1970.

It had to compete with parapsychology, group dynamics, communism, women's liberation, and blues singing, among other things, and it came out a loser ...

It was also the first anniversary of the suspension of Lee Teperman, a 16-year-old student who had called the principal a paper tiger. He walked along the halls yesterday, handing out a leaflet maintaining that he hasn't changed his mind. It said:

Student week will talk of Revolution.

Don't talk of Revolution,

REVOLT, REVOLT, REVOLT.

But the students were not only not in revolt, they were hardly even talking about revolution.

A seminar on revolution led by Gerry Caplan attracted 10 students. Next door, 125 packed themselves into a classroom built for 35 to hear Dr George Owen explain the mysteries of extrasensory perception, telepathy and clairvoyance.[44]

A New 'Philosophy' or 'Snivelling Drivel'? The Debate over Program Quality, 1973–1984

Almost as soon as the ministry's curriculum and pedagogical innovations had been put in place, they began to provoke controversy. By the early 1980s, the new 'philosophy' was in retreat and its 'mechanisms' were being dismantled. In part, this shift may have arisen from the perceived impact of the changes themselves. But it was also the result of more difficult economic circumstances, which encouraged people to wonder if they were getting their money's worth from the schools; to other new expectations in tough times; and, following the broad educational and social changes of the 1960s, to a more conservative, critical assessment of their consequences.

For whatever mix of reasons, in any case, disaffection spread rapidly and was broadly based. Businessmen began to complain loudly about young employees who didn't know 'the basics' and were undisciplined in the workplace. Parents found the credit system confusing and lacking in focus, and suspected a connection between the extent of curricular freedom and the lack of discipline that seemed to be creeping into the schools. University people argued that their first-year students couldn't read or write, and that the diversity of material taught in the senior grades of the high schools was making it difficult to construct coherent first-year university courses. Following a study in one community college revealing that the average competency of its first-year students 'in vocabulary and reading comprehension was slightly above Grade 10 level,' the board of governors added that lack of competence in English 'inhibits employers from hiring and promoting graduates from business programs.'[1] Both colleges and universities began to introduce courses in remedial English and mathematics to compensate for the failure of high school programs to prepare the students adequately for post-secondary education. In the press, the credit system was commonly referred to as the 'supermarket' or 'cafeteria' approach, or as the 'Do Your Own Thing School System.' By 1975, indeed, an editorial in the *London Free Press* could assert that 'criticism of scholastic standards in Ontario has come from so many quarters – from classroom teachers, universities, businessmen – that defenders of free choice should realize something is wrong. It isn't realistic to dismiss as fiction or exaggeration the continuing horror stories of high school graduates incapable of writing complete sentences or solving simple mathematics problems, of senior high school students without an elementary appreciation of Canadian history, culture and current events.'[2]

If such commentary had come solely from those outside the school system, or merely from a few disgruntled high school teachers, it might have had less influence. But it also represented the voice of the organized profession. Only a matter of months after the imposition of the credit system on the schools, the Ontario Secondary School Teachers' Federation issued a call for a return to compulsory courses 'in the basic skills of reading and writing, Canadian history, geography and politics,' adding that unrestricted optionalization and individualization had 'increased the insecurity of teachers, intensified the loneliness of students, and failed to improve the curriculum.'[3] In the fall of 1973, the effects of the new HS1 were sharply criticized by R.E. Saunders in a 'position paper' in the OSSTF journal. Drawing on the results of research published by Alan King of Queen's University, Saunders lambasted the new high school program, arguing that it served to 'introduce a market system of option choices' that forced teachers to compete against each other for students, failed to require students to take the most essential courses even in the early grades, encouraged them to take easy options in senior high school grades, and actually promoted failures and dropouts rather than discouraging them.[4] Nor was Saunders' article an isolated response. In 1974 the OSSTF commissioned an opinion poll of its members, of parents, and other interested parties, and the results, along with a running commentary, were published in 1976 under the title, *At What Cost? A Study of the Role of the Secondary School in Ontario.* In the minds of many high school teachers, the report revealed, there was too much curricular choice, too much emphasis on individualization (which teachers couldn't cope with in any case), a lack of external standards, too much variation in standards between schools, and a lack of any clear function for the general courses, where the mix of students of different abilities actually encouraged the failure of weaker students because the course content was pitched to those who were more able. More generally, on the central Hall-Dennis notions of choice, individualization, and flexibility, the report had this to say: 'In the cold light of classroom experience, this language seems naive, reflecting the ill-founded hopes of a committee out of touch with the real problems of school and society. The philosophy expressed falls short of present needs in this province.'[5]

In the same year that *At What Cost* appeared, the Ontario Economic Council, a senior advisory body to government, released a position paper on education. Echoing the concerns about inadequate basic skills and preparation in the high schools for post-secondary education, it called for some form of external testing to ensure academic standards and province-wide uniformity in evaluation.[6] The council also commissioned a major study of the schools by two sociologists, Oswald Hall and Richard Carlton, which was published in 1977 under the title *Basic Skills at School and Work: A Study of Albertown*. A lengthy and careful study of one community, canvassing a wide spectrum of views ranging from those of teachers and students to employers and instructors in both the local university and community college, *Basic Skills* reinforced many of the criticisms and pointed to the problems arising from the enthusiasms of the 1960s. In the elementary schools the authors found a good deal of unease about the lack of direction in both content and pedagogy that largely left teachers to construct their own curriculum. Teachers also complained that the emphasis on discovery methods, group work, and continuous progress was hard to interpret or implement. Summing up their reflections on teachers' reactions, Hall and Carlton would write that 'throughout the preceding decades the elementary schools had been buffeted by the forces of expansion, as well as external changes in organization, curricula, pedagogy and objectives. When we arrived on the scene ... we visited an aftermath of uncertainty, conservative reaction, and some discouragement. The gains anticipated earlier had not materialized as expected, and much appeared to have been lost in the way of motivation, sanctions, performance standards, work habits, as well as skill proficiencies.'[7]

There were ironies embedded in the pedagogical enthusiasms of the era as well. Individualization, continuous progress, multi-age groupings, the open-concept classroom, the community school – these were watchwords of a decade that also oversaw the final destruction of the one- or two-room rural school. Yet such schools, out of necessity and custom, had often been prime exemplars of what was now being defined, in very different circumstances, as the 'good' school. As Hall and Carlton wryly remarked, 'Having abolished the old one-room schoolhouse through abrupt consolidation, we have now embraced policies which tend to make a one-room school out of every junior classroom in the Province.'[8]

The effects of 'continuous progress,' social promotion, and curricula that stressed pupil-centred individual and group work over direct instruction in the basic skills of literacy and numeracy, Hall and Carlton continued, were magnified as pupils moved into the senior elementary and then into the high school. For secondary school teachers and administrators alike, 'the overall assessment of skills was consistently negative, indicating a continuing gap between grade-level expectations and performance norms for a large group of new [i.e., grade 9] students.'[9] When they surveyed students and teachers in post-secondary institutions, they discovered that similar views were widely shared: 'There is compelling evidence that many students are poorly prepared to cope with their post-secondary school programs. The deficiencies of students are readily observable to the faculty who teach in the Departments of Mathematics or English. In varying degrees, they are visible to other faculty as well. Students, too, are keenly aware of their shortcomings.'[10]

Of no less concern, however, was the provision made for those students not going on to post-secondary education. In a vein similar to the earlier OSSTF report, Hall and Carlton worried the problem of purpose and focus in the general courses and the high dropout rates that followed, the 'dead-end' nature of a diploma that included only general courses, and the 'covert streaming' that made such courses dumping grounds for the less able or less motivated. It was here that basic skills were most neglected, they concluded. On the other hand, their survey of employment opportunities for such students revealed that few academic skills were required or expected by most employers.

The plight of the 'general students,' indeed, and the high attrition rates among them, provoked yet another study, commissioned by OSSTF, which demonstrated that throughout the 1970s at least two-thirds of students taking general-level courses dropped out before graduating from grade 12. But not even graduation improved their job chances, and large numbers of graduates and dropouts alike faced unemployment. Though the research was less categorical than this, the summary report that appeared in the *Globe and Mail* concluded that general-level courses were of doubtful academic value, offered little job-training, and led mainly to unskilled or semi-skilled labour.[11]

Such conclusions gave extra force to a related argument that was becoming influential in the late seventies and early eighties. Beginning in 1977 and gathering momentum thereafter, there was much hand-wringing about a shortage of skilled tradesmen, the necessity, at a time of substantial unemployment, to import skilled workers from abroad, and the hopeless inadequacies of provision in the education system for job-training. The schools did not take all the blame for this: it fell on business, unions, provincial manpower policies, and even on parents and young people who valued post-secondary education over apprenticeships leading to blue-collar jobs. But the schools were also sharply criticized for encouraging good students to pursue post-secondary preparatory studies rather than job-training. And equally, the credit system was castigated because the degree of optionalization prevented the creation of 'packages' of courses that would lead to more rigorous training for work.[12]

From the early 1970s onwards, virtually all the critics, and all the studies, had remarked on the deleterious consequences of a system with no external performance standards, something of particular concern to the colleges and universities, and to grade 13 teachers as well. In response the Ministry of Education had commissioned a series of 'Interface' studies to explore the state of the linkages between secondary and post-secondary education. And the researchers confirmed some (though not all) of the critics' fears: grade inflation was common in grade 13; there were large variations in grade 13 marks, which benefited students in some schools and disadvantaged those from others when both came to apply to university; failure rates had declined 'substantially' since the elimination of the grade 13 departmentals; though enrolments in senior high school mathematics and English courses remained high, there was a tendency on the part of students to avoid subjects where the risk of failure was high and to opt for low-risk subjects such as home economics and theatre arts. The study also included an opinion poll that generally confirmed Ontarians' scepticism about the efficacy of the program of studies in secondary schools.[13]

That scepticism was shared by opposition politicians. Ever since the election of 1971, the Liberals, under the leadership of Robert Nixon, an ex–high school teacher himself, had called for fewer 'frills' and a return to a core curriculum. Stuart Smith, his successor in the late 1970s, was even more critical than Nixon, speaking and writing about 'the growing loss of faith in Ontario's schools' owing to the 'deteriorating quality of education.'[14] Addressing a group of parents and teachers at one London high school, Stephen Lewis, the recently retired leader of the NDP and Ontario's most prominent social democrat, was quoted as attacking 'the "mediocrity" and "confusion" of the Ontario education system; the "obsession" teachers have with contract demands rather than classroom content and the lack of real teaching excellence in classrooms across the province.' He went on to say that 'he maintains two of his children in private Toronto schools rather than put up with the problems encountered in the public school system.'[15]

BY THE LATE 1970s and early 1980s, then, large numbers of Ontarians seemed notably discontented with the state of the schools, and especially with the state of the secondary schools. Most of the research was (to put the best light on it) less than glowing. Individual assessments ranged from scepticism, moderately expressed, to uninhibited tirade: 'The snivelling drivel,' one county trustee wrote in a letter to the *Globe*, 'that characterizes the utterances of the current mandarins of education is equalled only by the banal content that makes up much of today's school curriculum. Bill Davis, Hall-Dennis and an increasing assortment of high-priced educational quacks continue with their unholy subversion of the education system.'[16] 'Figures no fun,' runs a header for a *Globe* story in 1982; 'Canadian math students so bad some unfit for [university] remedial class.'[17] In one Ontario magazine, it was 'The Trouble in Our Schools: *What* reading, writing, and arithmetic? *What* golden rule?'[18]

II

Whatever the validity of such assessments – and that is a matter I will return to at the end of this chapter – politicians and policy-makers could hardly afford to ignore the insistent, broadly based, and often strident critique being mounted against the province's schools. Though constrained by the limits of their legal powers, some of the more effective responses during the 1970s came from the boards and their personnel, rather than from the ministry itself.[19] Lacking much by way of guidance beyond a 'philosophy' and a handful of highly generalized objectives for the elementary schools, the boards moved in fairly quickly to take over one key programmatic area abandoned by the ministry in the mid-1960s, the task of writing detailed curricular guidelines. Usually working in teams, and led by local curriculum superintendents, principals, or subject consultants, groups of teachers began to construct and field-test their own programs of study, and then to apply them on a board-wide basis.

The process could also be accompanied by the reassertion of other traditional approaches to teaching and learning. A nice illustration is provided by an article in the *Welland Tribune*, featuring an interview with Gerald Blazetich, a local elementary school principal and chairman of the committee responsible for creating a mathematics curriculum for the Niagara South Board of Education. 'The result of their work is a curriculum that Mr Blazetich describes as definitive, sequential and "sometimes that says here's what you teach in Grade 1, here's what you teach in Grade 2!'" It was a style that 'borrows from an old standard, a grey book, used by teachers in the late 1950s and early 1960s.' Blazetich went on to offer a sharp criticism of some of the content in the 'interim revisions,' adding that '"one of its greatest downfalls is that it was too general.'" Indeed 'he does not see much difference between [the board's] new curriculum and that in the grey book. In between the two, however, he said, "I think it's been a disaster."'[20]

Though the degree of prescription varied from board to board, the same process was going on everywhere. In at least some cases, moreover, the new local guidelines were accompanied by benchmark testing, especially in English and mathematics, to ensure that system-wide objectives were being met. Commenting on one such case, London's co-ordinator of mathematics remarked that while he did not personally believe standards had deteriorated in the last few years, 'it will be a lot easier to convince the critics they're wrong with a clearly defined core of skills which all teachers in London will teach and which will be tested across the system.'[21]

Board policies of this sort, however, only reinforced the instincts of a good many teachers, who continued, through the 1970s, to do what they had always done. Despite all the rhetoric about child-centred and informal methods of instruction in the primary grades, teachers adopted the pedagogy embraced by the ministry in *The Formative Years* cautiously or not at all. Large numbers of teachers who had learned their craft in the 1950s or 1960s continued to use traditional methods in organizing their classrooms and teaching the 3 Rs. So much so, indeed, that when the ministry embarked on a provincial review of the primary years in the early 1980s it found that the P1J1 'philosophy,' though prevalent enough in junior kindergarten and kindergarten classes, was not much evident in many primary classrooms.[22] Thus complaints about 'the play school,' which would become so common in the late eighties and early nineties, were rarely heard in the seventies and early eighties.

The one pedagogical issue that did raise the temperature was the open classroom. It was a favourite sixties nostrum and one that the official organ of the ministry would describe in 1971 in sanctimonious terms: 'When new schools are built now, they almost all follow the open-plan concept. School planners and architects regard open schools as a necessary response to less-rigid teaching techniques. Educators have generally approved open-plan schools as providing a better learning environment, and being better suited to the new curricula.'[23] A year later, nonetheless, a ministry poll found that a majority of parents disliked the concept, and only 38 per cent thought the trend towards open classrooms was a good thing.[24] Many teachers hated them, calling them goldfish bowls, and blaming them for contributing to burnout. The protests and controversy they provoked at board meetings and in other forums, in any case, made them flashpoints of public anger. The retreat that followed was archly described by one London reporter: 'Sometimes it has been filing cabinets and bookcases that have been piled up to provide barricades and to delineate one classroom space from another. Sometimes the board has provided portable barriers to do the same job with a touch more elegance. The final solution – and the one reserved for the schools where community clamour has raged the hottest and heaviest – has been the building of complete new walling systems so that all trace of open-area education disappeared forever.'[25]

WILLIAM DAVIS WAS always good at reading the political winds, and so was Thomas Wells, minister of education from 1972 until mid-1978. Hearty, courteous, and conciliatory in public, nearly as adept in circumlocution as Davis himself, good at persuading his opponents that he was always ready to listen and learn (even when he wasn't), Wells was astute enough to recognize that trouble was brewing. A lot of people didn't like the new HS1, and they were making their opinions known. Such views were not welcomed by senior ministry personnel or by the ministry's hired researchers at OISE.[26] As Wells would later say of the bureaucracy, 'The people running the system today were for these changes ... They were not happy to see their handiwork dismantled.'[27] But something had to be done to head off the criticism, and in the autumn of 1973 – only a year after the introduction of the new HS1 – Wells announced that, beginning with the grade 9 class of 1974–5, a compulsory core would be reintroduced, consisting of four credits in English and two in Canadian studies.[28] One of the central principles of the original HS1, in other words, was hardly in place before it was abandoned.

A more significant turnabout took place three years later. During the election campaign of 1975 the Liberals had made hay with charges about lax academic standards, *At What Cost* was released early in 1976, even the Young Progressive Conservatives were demanding changes in the high school curriculum, and the cabinet was now trying to manage the exigencies of minority government. In early October 1976, Wells called a press conference to announce that starting the following September, students in grades 9 and 10 would be required to accumulate a total of seven credits, two in each of English, mathematics, and Canadian history or geography, and one in science. Beginning in 1979, two additional senior credits in English would become mandatory. There would, moreover, be new guidelines issued for these subjects that would stress essential skills and knowledge. It was a classic Wellsian performance, a distillation of style and tone he rarely departed from. Did this represent, a reporter asked, a repudiation of the Davis era in education? 'No, no, not at all,' replied the minister. 'This was not a repudiation, it was just a refinement.'[29]

In mid-November 1976, more followed. The full-scale decentralization of curriculum planning, Wells said, 'was great in theory, but just wasn't working.' The costs had been 'too much in time and money for [local board] curriculum committees all over trying to do the same thing. Why reinvent the wheel 150 times?' Equally, he argued, ministry guidelines had become 'too broad and general. The current guideline for Grade 9 Canadian history, for example, is only 800 words long. "That isn't enough."' As a consequence the government would move towards more detailed guidelines, beginning with the subjects that constituted the new compulsory core. And he promised they would be available for use in September 1977.[30] At the end of the month, moreover, Wells announced that plans were afoot to introduce better testing and evaluation of students in the elementary and high schools.[31]

Here, then, after only six or seven years of the implementation of the innovations of the late sixties, we have the unravelling of some of the central precepts – that young people should be free to choose, in an unlimited way, their own program of studies, and that no one but they and their parents knew what was good for them. It also marks a return to a more centralist policy: government stepped back in to reassert its control over what was happening in the schools. Modest by later standards perhaps – the new core of nine credits consisted of only four subjects in grade 9 and three in grade 10 (or vice versa), plus two senior English credits – it was still a significant retreat, and one that, following so quickly on the heels of the enthusiasms of the late sixties, suggests telling disarray and political back-pedalling rather than coherent program policy-making.

Revised subject guidelines issued in the late 1970s reflected a similar shift. Consider for example those for Intermediate History. In 1973 the key objectives had been that young people 'enjoy the learning experience' and that the needs of the child take precedence over content. The acquisition of basic skills was listed last. In 1977 the new guideline put a good deal more emphasis on basic skills and the first objective had been purged entirely. Similarly with content. In 1973 the guideline had consisted mainly of suggestions to teachers about what they might like to emphasize to their children, along with a broad range of topics they might select to study. The emphasis on studying history itself, moreover, was played down in the name of furthering the development of the child's interest in contemporary Canada. By 1978 history was only somewhat better served, but there was much more specific emphasis on particular topics to be covered and a core of civics that must be taught. The same sorts of shifts were under way in other subjects such as English and science.[32]

An effort was also made to respond to the criticisms about the failure of the schools to prepare young people for work. Several experimental programs were introduced to tighten the linkage between school and employment, but the most important departure was the insertion in the new *HS1 1979–81* of sections encouraging boards to establish 'Cooperative Education' programs.[33] Such courses, which combined in-school and on-site instruction, were not entirely new: some boards had introduced them in the early 1970s. But the formal sanction of the ministry sped their growth and they would gradually become a major feature of high school programs throughout Ontario.

The linkage between senior high school and university proved a more recalcitrant problem. Complaints about grade inflation and the lack of external performance standards had been vociferous and unremitting throughout the middle 1970s. Indeed, pressures from the universities were a key contributory factor leading the government to fund the *Interface* studies published in 1977. But the studies were also an excuse for both the government and the universities to put off action until they were released. Even then, while they confirmed the existence of serious problems, the disagreements about who should administer and pay for testing, and the type of test to be used, persisted. Nor were any individual universities prepared to go it alone, for fear that they would lose students to others. And thus by the early 1980s, the situation was hardly different than it had been a decade earlier. No one was prepared to bite the bullet, and some, within the academy and without, believed it shouldn't be bitten.

The other 'interface' issue was the future of grade 13 itself. The Grade 13 Study Committee of 1964 had recommended its outright abolition, as had the Hope Commission before it and Hall-Dennis after it. 'Before the end of the 1970s,' Thomas Wells told a party conference in 1973, 'Grade 13 will be a thing of the past.'[34] In 1977 a bevy of school boards proposed its abolition as a means of cutting costs.[35] Eternally hopeful, the *Globe* responded to the initiative with a typical editorial, declaring the fifth year of high school pedagogically inexcusable and, in a time of fiscal restraint, 'utterly indefensible.'[36] Not everyone agreed. Grade 13 had its proponents among parents and many university professors who worried that abolition would either unduly compress the program of studies and thus increase the stress on students, or lead to a further decline in the standard of education in the senior high school. But the main opponents of abolition were the high school teachers, many out of conviction, no doubt, but just as many who saw the proposal as a threat to their jobs. And given that reality, Thomas Wells was not about to stick his hand in a hornet's nest. So there it was, at the end of the decade, as at the beginning, clanking its chains, as real and palpable as Marley's ghost.

IN MID-1978, WELLS was replaced as minister of education by Bette Stephenson, a doctor with a wealth of medical and provincial politics behind her, a more determined and assertive personal style, and, occasionally, a tongue sharp enough to raise hackles. Inevitably she inherited the public agenda that Wells had confronted, including the ferment about the program of studies in the high schools. If anything, indeed, the pressures were multiplying at the end of the decade. As part of the routine process of program review, a new HS1 had to be prepared for 1981–3 and serious disagreements were emerging within the HS1 Advisory Committee over a wide variety of issues, including the extension of the compulsory core. The extant HS1, moreover, did nothing to clarify the problems relating to the general courses in the high schools: the ministry had to respond, especially to the complaints about the inadequate preparation the general courses offered for entry either into work or to the community colleges. Finally, there was the particular problem of the 'intermediate years.' For more than two decades the program of studies had been divided into three parts – primary-junior (grades 1–6), intermediate (grades 7–10), and senior (grades 11–13). The curriculum for PJ, such as it was, was laid out in *The Formative Years*, and HS1 covered grades 9–13. But no programmatic prescriptions existed for grades 7 and 8, and no document gave direction or coherence to the notion of the 'intermediate years.' A ministry committee had been at work attempting to provide such direction but was getting nowhere because of wrangling between the secondary and elementary panels.[37]

Though senior ministry officials were aware beforehand of the accumulating bundle of problems, the initiative to confront them came primarily from Stephenson herself.[38] Sympathetic with some of the most frequently aired criticisms of the schools, she was critical as well of the closed planning processes followed by the ministry, and of the undue influence she believed the federations exercised on educational policy-making. And she, above all, provided the impetus for a wide-ranging review of the purposes and program of the intermediate and senior divisions of the schools. She rejected the mechanism of a royal commission, fearing that it would take too long and offer too many unrealistic recommendations. Instead, she initiated the 'Secondary Education Review Project' (SERP), a large-scale and innovative attempt to bring together expertise, experience, and the public voice, and, at the same time, to come up with workable solutions that could be implemented with some despatch. Established in early 1980, the project was the cumulative work of a steering committee consisting of a mix of business and labour leaders, university people, and senior educational administrators drawn from both the ministry and local boards. Several other committees, which included teachers and members of the public, provided reaction, assessment, and proposals for implementation. Before any final decisions were made, a discussion paper was circulated in April 1981, and it provoked something like 2400 submissions from interested parties. A final report was then drafted by the steering committee and released in October 1981.

The tone of the report was a world away from Hall-Dennis. 'Although generalizing about the responses' the project had elicited was

> somewhat perilous, a few broad conclusions can be drawn. The *first* is that people expect the schools to provide students with a *solid, useful, basic education* that prepared them either for direct entry into employment or for post-secondary education. *Second*, while still wanting schools to take into account the variation in students' needs, interests and abilities, most people proposed that the *curriculum be more prescriptive*, particularly in the early grades of secondary school; few if any respondents proposed broadening the students' choice of subjects. *Third*, the feeling is widespread that schools ought to impose much *stricter discipline* than they are imagined to do at present, and finally, the public wants to be assured that standards are being maintained.
>
> What, then, do we want? In general terms, the answers seem to be *coherence and practicality* in school programs, excellence and consistency in standards, a stronger sense of responsibility to the public, and greater quality control in program, instruction, and student achievement.[39]

The ninety-eight recommendations contained in the SERP Report were comprehensive, ranging from finance to special education and Franco-Ontarian education. But the key programmatic proposals can be briefly summarized. First, in the name of economy and common sense, Ontario was to be brought into line with all other jurisdictions in North America: the fifth year of high school was to be abolished and its work compressed into four, with suitable adjustments made in the elementary schools as well. Second, there should be a return to a much larger compulsory core, with more time invested in those subjects already mandated, especially English, mathematics, and Canadian studies. In order to increase province-wide uniformity, the curriculum guidelines in these subjects were to become more prescriptive, and the ministry was to prepare evaluation instruments for the compulsory subjects to ensure provincial objectives were being met. Boards would not be compelled to use them, but would be required at least to review their methods of evaluating students' performance on a regular basis. It took about a year for the ministry to formulate its response, but in November 1982 it replied through *The Renewal of Secondary Education in Ontario*. And *ROSE*, as it came to be known, not only accepted, in whole or in part, nearly all of the main SERP programmatic recommendations, but laid out the implementation process as well.[40]

The keystone was a new document, drafted in 1982–3 and sent to the schools in September 1983, called *Ontario Schools: Intermediate and Senior* (*OSIS*). As its title suggests, it was designed to cover not just grades 9 to 13 but 7 and 8 as well.* It was to begin in September 1984 and, implemented a grade each year, to be fully in place by 1986–7. For the high school it meant an expanded core of sixteen compulsory subjects, which included two senior English and one senior social-science course, along with an increase in the total number of credits required for a graduation diploma – from twenty-seven to thirty. A new set of courses were introduced, known as 'Ontario Academic Courses' (OACs), which might be taken in a fifth year of high school but which students with the appropriate prerequisites could complete during their third or fourth years. Standardized, province-wide levels of difficulty for courses – advanced, general, and basic – were defined, replacing the hodge-podge of local customs about the number and meaning of such levels that had prevailed since 1972. Guidelines were also to be rewritten, especially in compulsory courses, with far more prescription and a sharper differentiation between advanced and general levels.

OSIS not only gave a new direction to the high school but provided new prescriptions for grades 7 and 8 as well. While it specified a considerable list of subjects that were to be taught in those grades, it also identified a particular group – English, mathematics, science, history, and geography – that were to receive higher minimum allocations of teaching time

---

*And for that reason, it replaced the traditional designation for the foundation document, HS1.

than the others. Grades 7 and 8, in other words, were to be organized around a core of key academic subjects, and those subjects were to be privileged in terms of the attention they received.

No less important, *OSIS* de-emphasized the idea of a distinctive period of 'early adolescence,' the crux on which the notion of the 'intermediate' curriculum rested, and stressed instead the 7 to 12 continuum. The organization of the school program, in other words, was conceived in terms of two basic divisions, K–6 and 7–12/OAC. Moreover, *ROSE* had asserted that 'curriculum guidelines will be developed on an intermediate/senior basis. While a separate Senior and Intermediate document might be issued, it would be described as a component of a program which was clearly designed on a Grade 7 to 12/OAC basis.' Over time, moreover, most guidelines were to become intermediate/senior documents, and 'prerequisites would be stated in the guidelines, to ensure provincial consistency.'[41] All of this was not only a long way from Hall-Dennis or the ministry's intermediate-division position paper of 1972, but also a long way from ideas that would dominate the early 1990s. SERP-*OSIS* did not point towards either the intermediate division of the past or 'the transition years' of the future but in another direction entirely.

And what about expectations for assessment and accountability? *OSIS* did not address that issue directly. But it was part of the renewal package. In March of 1984 the Speech from the Throne included a province-wide testing initiative, the question was under consideration by a committee, and the ministry was preparing 'to develop and implement a province-wide testing program that addresses the needs of students, teachers, and various constituent groups.'[42]

Whatever the importance of these various initiatives, it was the proposed abolition of grade 13 that provided a lightning rod, drawing by far the most commentary in the daily press. Editors and columnists loved it, and said so again and again. There were problems nonetheless. While the Council of Ontario Universities approved the proposal, there was talk that individual universities were considering adding a year to the three-year arts program to compensate for it – something that might result in greater public expenditure rather than less.[43] The most formidable opposition, however, came from the federations. OSSTF opposed it outright, predicting that it would cost 3000 jobs at a time when the stresses of declining enrolments were already taking their toll.[44] Elementary teachers objected to any compression of the program of studies that would force secondary work downwards into the elementary school.[45] Thus the original SERP proposal for outright abolition was substantially compromised, the government concluding that it was the better part of political wisdom to allow grade 13 to die by attrition than to kill it outright by regulation. However, the assumption that most students would jump at the chance to shorten their high school studies by one whole year proved false, and grade 13, in its new guise of the OAC courses, continued to thrive. Death by starvation, in other words, didn't work; what grade 13 needed was a stake through the heart.

The new compulsory core in the high schools was also welcomed by the press as a return to common sense and sound academic standards after the long night of permissive education. Once again, however, teachers dissented. Though happy enough with the OAC compromise, OTF (and more strongly, OSSTF) was convinced that a compulsory core of sixteen, primarily academic, subjects, including one credit in French, was unsuitable for general and basic-level students, would seriously reduce enrolments in subjects ranging from music and art to business and vocational options, and hence would substantially increase dropout rates.[46] They also pointed to the irony of reports and policies premised on the need for more and better links between education and work that invited a decline in enrolments in business and technical subjects. Some of this was provoked by fears of yet more job losses, but not all of it. The level of discontent amongst teachers, in any case, rose throughout 1982 and 1983 to culminate in the autumn of 1983 when the OSSTF launched 'an aggressive campaign ... to win the support of parents and school board trustees for a delay of at least one year' in the introduction of *OSIS*.[47] But the government stood its ground, and the document became official policy, as scheduled, in September 1984.

OSIS had plenty of teething problems, all across Ontario.[48] And in some respects the teachers' premonitions about its consequences were dead on. As students were herded into the expanded core of compulsory subjects, enrolments in many electives declined, with vocational subjects especially hard hit. Though the trend had already been under way, the introduction of *OSIS*, and especially the widespread practice of 'front loading'– requiring a large dollop of the compulsory subjects to be taken in grade 9 – resulted in a 30 per cent drop in technical course enrolments in the school year 1984–5.[49]

Yet the introduction of *OSIS* also marks the end of a distinct period in the long debate about the program of studies in the schools. The discontents of the sixties and the reforms they produced had, in turn, generated their own discontents; and though the retreat had been going on since the mid-1970s, its scale was not fully realized until the early 1980s. The trends

toward greater centralization of control in the hands of the ministry, a
substantial core of mandated subjects in the high schools, more prescriptive guidelines, the reassertion of 'the basics' – or at least of the primacy of
traditional academic subjects – and the commitment to accountability
through external appraisal measures all gained impetus between the
creation of the Secondary Education Review Project and the introduction
of *OSIS*. The reaction of one Toronto *Star* columnist to the release of SERP
was not, in this respect, atypical: 'An almost audible sigh of relief swept
across Ontario this week as Education Minister Bette Stephenson formally
buried the permissive era in the province's high schools. "Compulsory
courses are back," she said. "Discipline is in. Experimenting is out. Standards will be tougher."'[50]

III

Audible sighs of relief, as we shall see, turned out to be premature. But at
least one significant question remains to be addressed here: to what extent
did the chorus of criticism directed at the education system represent a
justified or legitimate view of the state of Ontario's elementary and secondary schools?

One thing is certainly clear: not everyone thought it did. The mounting
critique of the 1970s never went uncontested, and while the disgruntled
probably outnumbered them – or were at least more vociferous in making
their views known – there were always those prepared to speak up in
defence of the system, and indeed to launch their own counterattacks in
reply. Some blamed the assault on a corporate agenda designed to roll
back public investment in education. Others asserted that it was nothing
more than self-serving opportunism. 'We have a first-rate education system
in the province of Ontario,' said one president of OSSTF in the mid-1970s.
'Yet that is not the impression we get from the instant commentators of
nightly television, itinerant soothsayers from our universities, or itchy
politicians who seem bent on creating a vote-getting issue for the next
provincial election.'[51]

The facts, the system's proponents declared, pointed in a different
direction. Was the public hopelessly disenchanted with the schools? A
series of reputable public-opinion polls taken across the decade indicated
that the majority of parents, and the public at large, remained highly or
moderately satisfied with the public school system.[52] Despite the vitriol
directed at the 'smorgasbord' curriculum, there had been no significant
decline in high school enrolments in such basic subjects as English and

mathematics.[53] A number of research studies, some quite comprehensive in scope, had revealed that students were, in the main, as well equipped in the basics as they had ever been – or at least were well enough equipped to meet the contemporary demands of the workplace, the universities, and the community colleges.[54] The *Interface* study itself had concluded that there was 'strong evidence that the group of students passing through the interface between secondary and post-secondary studies is as well-educated and well-prepared in basic skills as were similar groups in the past, and as are comparable groups of students in other countries.'[55]

Even those who agreed with conclusions such as these conceded that there was a worrisome gap between public expectations and actual levels of achievement in the high schools. Their most common explanation for the gap was, however, that the critics, and the public at large, had failed to understand how profoundly the institution had changed since the 1950s. 'About half of our current secondary school students would not have been students at all even 15 years ago,' wrote the *Interface* team. 'The schools have been required to cope with increased numbers of the type of students they have traditionally served, as well as to provide service – and perhaps a new kind of service – to as many students again who in the past would not have expected the service at all ... When the general public, or secondary or post-secondary teachers, fail to take into account the rapid and substantial changes in the composition of the student population, there will indeed be expectations of students which are unrealistic.'[56]

Secondary education for all, in other words, had changed the rules of the game, making the clientele of the high school much more diverse, and the institution itself more egalitarian in its purposes. That, as one high school principal argued in 1975, necessarily brought changes in program and pedagogy. 'As soon as these "new students" entered the schools, it was obvious that the traditional patterns of teaching, learning, and curriculum were only of limited use. The average adolescent learner, we found, was unable to mature intellectually within the harsher climate of university-oriented courses, pedagogy, and learning styles. The average learner would not accept the statement that "You must take history because it's good for you." This student needed an entirely different approach.' One response, the author continued, was the introduction of so-called 'Mickey Mouse' courses, a phrase used by the critics 'to describe courses where the learning and teaching is full of excitement, relevance, and enjoyment.' In fact, that sobriquet was nothing more than 'the hang-up of a generation taught to believe that unless education was tough, unpleasant, dull, and even a little boring, it really was not a good education. Now, by offering four years of high school to all its young adolescents rather than an elite of learners, Ontario is hoping that greater benefits may accrue to its society.'[57]

Greater choice, and more flexibility in organizational structures, other proponents contended, encouraged all students to take responsibility for their own learning, a prerequisite to the pleasures, and the necessity, of life-long education. Similarly, a more humane pedagogy in the elementary schools was linked to emphases on problem-solving and self-directed learning. The changes of the 1960s and early 1970s had enriched the educational experience of all students; any retrenchment would result, as one activist told the *Globe*'s Loren Lind, in 'widening the gap between the haves and have-nots in education, intensify school competition, and reduce education to a demeaning process geared to points, marks, credits and increasingly scarce jobs.'[58]

HOW, THEN, DOES ONE assess the legitimacy of these dramatically different perspectives on the state of the school system? Was it as bad as the critics, or as good as its proponents, claimed? Unfortunately, there is no easy answer to these questions, and certainly no clear-cut ones. Consider first the research into levels of achievement in basic skills. It did indeed show that in some respects skill levels in English and mathematics were as good as they had ever been; but the same research also pointed to some worrisome declines, or at least deficits, that demanded more effective instruction.[59] Demonstrating that standards remained as good as in the past, or even better, proved, moreover, to be fraught with difficulties because of the non-compatibility of the tests used, a changing student population, different emphases over time in program and pedagogy, and no reliable baseline data.[60] Researchers were generally forthright in pointing these problems out, and in warning that the results must be used with caution. But they were also prone to view optimistic conclusions in the best light, and to offer quotable generalizations about satisfactory achievement levels that were based on some very shaky evidence.[61] And those publicists eager to rebut the critics were wont to make claims about the definitiveness of the research that reached far beyond the findings themselves, or, when faced with its inadequacies, to fall back upon the argument that, from time immemorial, the schools had always had their critics and in this respect the 1970s were no different than the 1950s or even the fifth century BC.[62] The latter point was true enough; but except as a rhetorical flourish, it did nothing to address the issues at hand; indeed for at least some sceptics it simply drew attention to the holes in both the research and the arguments purveyed by the optimists.

The results of the public-opinion polls are no less problematic. Those commentators or editorial writers who claimed that there was universal disaffection with the schools were clearly wrong: a majority of parents, as well as other members of the public, expressed general approval of the system across the entire decade of the 1970s. Yet the unease is evident as well. There was an overall decline in levels of satisfaction during the decade, and by 1978 those who were dissatisfied to one degree or another with 'school services in general' came alarmingly close to 50 per cent of those polled. There was also a very sharp divergence between the perception of what the schools should be doing and what the public thought they were actually doing, a gap that was widest in such areas as basic literacy and numeracy, job preparation, discipline, and respect for authority.[63] What the polls showed, in other words, was a good deal of faith in public education in principle, and large amounts of dissatisfaction on particular issues. Valued as a public institution, the school was also perceived as failing to meet many objectives the public demanded of it.

Yet this 'expectations gap' also requires interpretation. For many parents, and other adults as well, the yardstick was their own experience and they judged the schools of the 1970s against a narrow range of spelling and computational skills they remembered acquiring in their own youth. As well, they probably overestimated their generation's level of achievement in such skills. They also put inordinate faith in the kind of testing that, while it might validate achievement standards on the part of some youngsters, ruthlessly stigmatized very large numbers as failures, defining them, in effect, as unable to benefit from further education. Indeed, it was precisely that problem which had provoked the search for a broader vision of the meaning of education embodied in the pedagogical and programmatic changes of the post-war era, including the ideal of a full secondary education for all. As good English teachers would reiterate throughout the 1970s, moreover, learning to write demanded a far wider array of skills than simply spelling or instruction in formal grammar. And much of the muddle about levels of achievement in mathematics was due to the difficulties parents (and many teachers) had in understanding the intricacies or purposes of 'the new math.'[64] In a tart response to a newspaper article of 1976 critical of its effects, A.J. Coleman, the chair of the Department of Mathematics at Queen's University and a member of the Science Council of Canada, wrote that

the thoroughgoing reorientation of elementary and secondary school mathematics which began in all civilized countries in the 1960s is good, necessary,

and was long overdue ... the emotional hullabaloo about the 'new math'
stirred up by reactionaries who are mentally too reactionary to change or by
well-intentioned, but misguided, individuals who do not fully understand the
real issues, simply causes confusion which we could well do without; the
'newest' idea in the 'new math,' that of abstract group, was known to Arthur
Cayley 125 years ago.[65]

Equally, the vociferous complaints of some academics about falling
standards need to be approached with scepticism. Whatever else the
Interface study had shown, it nailed down the fact that senior high school
marks in the mid-1970s remained as good a predictor of success in first-
year university as they had in the past – as good as in the golden age of the
much-vaunted grade 13 departmentals.[66] That being the case, if there was
indeed a standards problem, the universities were as complicit in the
process as the high schools. Moreover, if undergraduate work was indeed
being 'dumbed-down' to accommodate the masses of students pressing
into the universities, as some academics claimed, all they had to do was
raise admission standards. But that, as more than one proponent of
pedagogical innovation gleefully pointed out, was something the universities refused to do, given the competition among institutions for students
and for the grants they brought with them. The critique of the high
schools by the academy, in other words, had more than a whiff of hypocrisy
about it (as indeed it does now).

The expectations gap, on the other hand, cannot be explained away –
something the *Interface* team, and others besides, were inclined to do – as a
necessary consequence of the expanded clientele of the high school.
True, a larger percentage of adolescents were now preparing for entry to
post-secondary education than a decade or so earlier. True, secondary
education for all meant that the high school would have to provide an
education for a clientele that would not have darkened its doors thirty
years earlier. And both these developments might have required a modification of traditional pedagogies and different programs of study. But the
problem here is the suitability, or the appropriateness, of the responses
these developments elicited. As English teachers explained over and over
again, the introduction of the credit system had sharply reduced the
number of hours available to teach English.[67] Trained in the university to
value literature over composition, moreover, and freed from any external
stimulus in the form of prescribed guidelines, teachers naturally gave
more attention to the former than the latter, with the result that, in most
schools, the number of weekly composition periods fell from three to

one.[68] Faced with a new clientele, it was also tempting to reorient literature courses to 'relevant' reading or to 'media studies' that might more readily hold the attention of the potentially disaffected. Nor could high school teachers do much about the impact of social promotion in the elementary schools, which left teachers with students who lacked the literacy skills that would enable them to benefit from the intellectual challenges the high school might offer.

In the high schools, subject promotion and the 'smorgasbord curriculum' added their own effects, allowing students to accumulate the requisite credits for graduation by dropping or avoiding subjects they found difficult, regardless of their pertinence to the acquisition of necessary skills or essential knowledge. In the curricular free-for-all that followed the decentralization of program control and the imposition of *HS1 1972–3*, history teachers, protected for generations by requirements that all students take three or four years of Canadian and European history, suddenly had to scramble to maintain their enrolments or lose their jobs. And scramble they did, inventing new, more 'relevant' courses after the models that were infecting university history departments, or moving into the teaching of law, 'Man in Society,' or world politics. Similar developments occurred in other disciplines. The result was the fragmentation of the curriculum documented in Albertown by Hall and Carlton – the loss of a coherent program of studies, the cafeteria high school where students could pick and choose according to their whims and fancies. It was not numbers that created this environment, however; it was *policies* – policies that reflected both the predilections of those responsible for the future of Ontario education and what was happening in the larger society, including the universities.

The proponents of the credit system liked to point out that while it had brought some significant shifts in enrolment patterns in the high school, the vast majority of students continued to select a core of traditional subjects, especially English and mathematics. There was good reason for this; but it hardly offered an exculpation of ministry policy or a resounding defence of its 'philosophy.' The credit system might be largely optionalized in theory but parents, teachers, and guidance councillors tended to be conservative in their advice to students, and most often didn't make fine distinctions between 'advice' and prescription, especially when it came to subjects like English, mathematics, or science. Students were guided by admission requirements for post-secondary education, and principals could (and often had to) manipulate the timetable so that a core of subjects was virtually compulsory in grades 9 and 10. One of the most frequently heard criticisms of ministry diploma requirements, more-over, was that students could graduate from grade 12 with nothing but credits completed in the two lower grades of high school. According to the prescriptions in HS1, that was indeed possible. But any principal who allowed it was 'a jerk,' said one principal: 'We always required 13 senior credits, even when the Ministry said we couldn't make demands of senior students.'[69] A sensible course of action perhaps, but for every administra-tor who engaged in this kind of subversion of Ontario's official 'philoso-phy' of education, there were others who eagerly and enthusiastically promoted in their high schools the spirit as well as the letter of the law.

The outcome, in any case, contained its own ironies. High school retention rates had risen rapidly throughout the 1960s and with them the expectation that a full secondary education for all young people would be achieved in the decade that followed. They had risen, however, within the framework of a highly structured program of studies and one that put great emphasis on a traditional core of academic subjects for both five-year and four-year students, for those in both vocationally oriented and more purely academic streams. At the moment when the credit system was first being introduced, however, retention rates actually began to decline, and they would remain below the peak year of 1969–70 throughout the 1970s.[70] Most of those who left before completing high school, moreover, were students enrolled in the general courses – the new clientele whom the credit system was supposed to be especially designed to serve. Without the focus provided by the external constraints of university or college prepara-tory requirements, without, often enough, the insistent advice of parents attuned to the implications of choices made, confronted too often by teachers uncertain about the value of the general courses, the beneficiar-ies of a ministry no longer committed to any clear conception of what constituted a good education – these young people became the new 'dropout problem' of the late 1970s and 1980s, provoking yet another round of debate about what was wrong with the school system and how to fix it.

It would be silly, and wrong, to insist that the credit system was a sufficient cause for falling retention rates. Employment opportunities were probably more important; indeed as youth unemployment soared in the late 1970s, retention rates began to rise again. As Hall and Carlton had argued, moreover, there were a number of larger changes in society which undercut the holding power of the school and even its ability to impose traditional academic values or standards of discipline.[71] The influence of a non-academic peer culture was immeasurably strengthened as larger cohorts of older adolescents filled the senior grades. Despite their complaints about illiteracy and innumeracy, employers paid little attention to school accomplishments when they hired young people, and were, in any case, adopting technologies that lessened the need for young people to acquire basic skills. The spread of television undermined habits of reading for either pleasure or information. A consumer-oriented culture invited large numbers of young people to work part-time, at the expense of learning in school, and also reinforced the effects of the credit system in making them responsible for the content of their own education. And, as Hall and Carlton emphasized, secondary school teachers, but *also* university and college teachers, colluded with students in modifying instructional practices and course content in ways that accommodated deficits in basic skills. As for one significant source of learning and discipline problems in the senior high schools, one might well point the finger directly at William Davis and a Tory party who, in their eagerness to attract some 412,000 new voters in 1971, lowered the legal drinking age from 21 to 18.[72] It is hardly fair, in sum, and certainly not fruitful for understanding, simply to blame the schools, or even the Ministry of Education, for the malaise about education that struck such deep root in Ontario during the 1970s or early 1980s. What happens in schools is, substantially at least, a reflection of broader currents in society. Any adequate assessment, on the other hand, must also take account of educational policy itself, and address the intellectual underpinnings and educational consequences of the kind of decision-making, at all levels of the educational system, that indubitably contributed to the malaise in the first place.

6

Demography, Economics, and the Revolting Teachers, 1971–1984

If the debate over program quality had been the only issue at stake, the 1970s and early 1980s might not stand out as an era with its own distinctive ambience; one might argue, indeed, that it was little more than a prelude to the much sharper conflicts over quality that would occur in the late 1980s and 1990s. But that debate was accompanied by, and took place in the context of, three other developments which created their own tensions: the spectre of declining enrolments, a much more difficult economic environment, and an unprecedented level of teacher militancy. These too would help mark off the era from the ebullience of the post-war decades.

I

Even in the early 1970s, the full force of the baby boom was still making its impact felt on Ontario's classrooms, crowding the senior grades of the elementary schools and flooding the high schools with unprecedented numbers of young people. Meanwhile, the province's fertility rate had taken a nose-dive. In the late fifties and early sixties, it stood at something like 3.7 births per woman; by 1971 it had declined to 2.2, or what is usually considered to be the level of zero population growth; by the mid-1970s it had fallen to 1.8 (figure 2). And just as the baby boom itself had had an enormous impact on the schools, so indeed would the 'baby bust' of the late 1960s and 1970s. The effects were exacerbated, moreover, by changes in that other engine of enrolment growth, immigration into Ontario, which in 1967 began a long decline that continued through the 1970s.

The consequences made themselves felt unevenly. Though enrolments in the primary grades began to shrink in the early 1970s, the number of secondary school students continued to climb, so that school boards and their administrators faced the phenomenon of expansion and contraction at the same time. By the late 1970s, just as elementary enrolments had begun to stabilize, the problem was deflected into the secondary schools. Across the decade the public schools were hit harder than the separate schools so that the intensity of the problem in the two systems differed substantially. In many rural counties the impact of declining enrolments was magnified by concomitant population loss as people continued to flood into urban communities. In cities and towns, the inner core lost large proportions of its population to the suburbs so that the effects of simultaneous contraction and expansion were felt there as well. The city of Toronto was hard hit, Etobicoke, Scarborough, and North York less so; meanwhile the burgeoning communities on the periphery of Metro experienced absolute growth in both population and school enrolments – Peel didn't suffer its first decline in elementary enrolments until 1978.[1] Yet the impact of declining enrolments eventually struck everywhere (see figure 4). Between 1970 and 1985 the province lost 250,000 students – a quarter of a million in fifteen years! By 1984 there were 2000 fewer teachers than a decade earlier in the public secondary schools, a decline of 6.5 per cent in the size of the workforce; by 1985 there were 7000 fewer jobs in the elementary schools than in 1970 – a loss of 12 per cent.[2]

As the problem spread across Ontario in the early 1970s, and grew more severe in the years that followed, school boards adopted all of the obvious solutions: staff was trimmed, with probationary teachers or would-be new entrants catching the worst of it, while even those with five or ten years' seniority feared for their jobs; early retirement packages were cobbled together to promote the attrition of permanent staff; subject options with small enrolments were slashed; schools – in some cases schools built only a few years before – were closed, the property sold off, and the remaining children bused to schools less visibly hit. Though there was nothing unusual about the following three examples, they help illustrate the extent of the response. In 1980 the Niagara South Board of Education announced that it was proposing to close twenty-two of its eighty-three elementary schools because of declining enrolment and rising costs – that is, a full 26 per cent of its schools.[3] By 1984, the London and Middlesex County separate school board had closed ten schools in six years. The London Board of Education had closed eleven elementary schools and one high school, and was contemplating still more.[4] From 1970, then, the school system began shrinking, and shrinking fast. In a matter of years the imperatives of expansion had given way to the hard realities attendant upon a rapidly declining pool of schoolchildren.[5]

II

The problems of managing system-wide shrinkage would have created considerable stress even if nothing else had changed. The full impact of declining enrolments, however, coincided with a much harsher economic climate than anything the province had experienced since the end of the Second World War.[6] Despite some fluctuations in the rate of growth, the province's economy continued to expand up to 1973 as it had done for more than two decades. Beginning late in that year, however, Ontario, along with the rest of the Western world, entered a period of economic recession that continued through the middle years of the decade, was followed by a few years of sluggish recovery, and then recurred even more sharply in the early 1980s. A sagging economy was accompanied by high rates of inflation, particularly severe in 1974–5, and again in 1979–82, when it reached 11 or 12 per cent annually. The Consumer Price Index, which had stood at 96.1 in January 1970, rose to 195.9 by late 1979. There were particularly sharp increases in energy prices, multiplying fourfold across the decade. Though most Canadians did not actually lose ground, personal incomes from employment failed to increase at the pace they had in the 1960s, and in both the private and the public sector the struggle to match incomes with inflation became fiercer. Unemployment bit harder as well, with young people bearing the brunt of the burden. In part this was because new entrants to the labour force are always at most risk; but it was also because of their sheer numbers, as the bulk of the baby boom began to enter the workforce. In the late 1970s and early 1980s unemployment among the young was running at 15 to 20 per cent, roughly double the rate for the workforce as a whole.

Throughout the period, nonetheless, government expenditures increased inexorably. During the good years the province had committed itself to some very expensive social programs, including a variety of individual and community welfare initiatives, generous subsidies to municipalities to improve services, massive increases in funding for education, and, above all else, health care. Even in the years after 1973, moreover, the Davis government found it difficult to resist the temptation to establish new programs that would ensure victory for the Conservative party at the polls.[7] The result, especially when combined with inflation, was explosive growth in the provincial budget – from $5.2 billion in 1971 to $32 billion in 1985–6. But a decade of recession and slow growth also meant more modest increases in tax revenues. And that in turn meant the government had to raise taxes, or go into debt, or both. Thus, for the first time since the end of the Second World War, the province entered an era of growing government expenditure accompanied by substantially increased taxes, rising government debt, and rising annual deficits.

The recession of the mid-1970s heightened anxieties about the economic consequences of high public spending. In 1975 the federal government introduced legislation designed to curb the wage and price spiral, establishing an 'Anti-Inflation Board' to review wage settlements and roll back those exceeding its guidelines. Already engaged in stiffening its restraint policies, the Ontario government opted into the federal program, applying it to its own public services. The following year the provincial treasurer, Darcy McKeough, announced tough new measures to stabilize government spending over the long haul, and to hold it to an increase of 6.9 per cent in 1977–8. Faced with the recession and runaway inflation of the early 1980s, the provincial government went even further, introducing legislation in the autumn of 1982 that limited wage increases in the public sector to 9 per cent in 1982–3, and 5 per cent in the year after that.[8]

GIVEN THIS ENVIRONMENT, how did those engaged in the educational enterprise, at both the provincial and local level, respond to the economic imperatives of the era? And what patterns of educational spending emerged from those responses? The howls of protest that had greeted the introduction of the expenditure ceilings in late 1970 continued through 1971, the urban school boards especially claiming that the reductions required in their rate of spending would adversely affect the quality of education they offered. Fortified nevertheless by a solid majority in the legislature following the September elections of 1971, the Davis government renewed its commitment to the principle of fiscal restraint, including expenditure ceilings on education. Since the ceilings had been set at a level equivalent to what the average board spent, most boards met them with little grief. But for the urban boards, and above all the Metro Toronto boards, it meant substantial reductions. Admittedly they were in a difficult position. They had the widest (and most expensive) range of services and thus the largest over-expenditure beyond the ceilings. In Ottawa, for example, meeting the ceilings for 1972–3 meant that spending could be increased by only 2 per cent, and when budget talks got under way there were dire warnings about having to lay off almost 10 per cent of staff.[9] Not surprisingly, then, pressures to modify provincial policy were intense. In Metro Toronto, trustees, administrators, and teachers mounted a campaign that included the more conventional forms of lobbying, but also a systematic effort to worry parents about the precarious educational future of their

children and thus to mobilize them to pressure the politicians as well.[10] As
a result, the ceilings were raised modestly above what the government had
intended in 1972, and again in 1973, and extra funds were found for the
high-spending boards.[11]

In 1974, however, inflation drove up the costs of everything from pencils
and paper to fuel bills. Teachers pressed hard to ensure their salaries kept
up with inflation, so that settlements began to exceed what even the
revised ceilings would allow. By the following year, the policy lay in tatters.
The header to a *Globe* story in March 1975 tells it all: 'Major school boards
disregarding provincial budget limits.' The report went on, 'The five-year-
old provincial ceilings on education spending appear on the verge of
collapse as several major school boards disregard them in teacher contract
talks.' In Windsor, the chairman of the board was caustic: 'I don't care
about the ceilings ... I don't need a Big Daddy down in Toronto telling me
how much I can spend. I feel fully responsible to my local taxpayers.' In
Ottawa, the *Globe* report continued, 'the provincial ceilings are being
knowingly ignored by local school trustees, who face a high school teachers' strike entering its third school day today ... the Ottawa trustees' chief
negotiator says his last offer in mediation to the teachers would put his
board $2.2 million over the ceilings.' Much the same thing was the case in
Metropolitan Toronto.[12]

By the spring of 1975, the Tories were also facing an election, and the
Liberals, running a close second in the polls, were calling for the abolition
of the expenditure ceilings.[13] A September election resulted in large gains
by both the Liberals and the NDP, and reduced the Conservatives to a
minority government. Education was only one issue and the deteriorating
state of the economy was probably far more important to the outcome. But
the ceilings had brought down upon the government, and especially upon
Tom Wells, a heap of opprobrium from trustees and teachers, and from
parents who had been persuaded that their children's education was
suffering because of the 'cutbacks.' Thus the question could not help but
arise: Were there more politically palatable methods of achieving the same
ends? And there was also the hope that the new federal anti-inflation
legislation would temper salary settlements and other costs, thus relieving
the provincial government of the burden.

Whatever the exact reasons, the ceilings were abandoned in late 1975,
and the power to raise property taxes to any amount was restored to the
local boards. The government insisted, however, that there would be no
end to restraint policies at the provincial level. The implication was clear:
caps on provincial grants meant that the onus for the control of local

expenditure would fall squarely upon the boards rather than the provincial government. Curbing overall education spending, in other words, would be left to the votes of local ratepayers, or, as Darcy McKeough, the provincial treasurer, would later describe it in a memorable phrase, to 'the discipline of the tax rate.'[14]

And what were the effects of the five-year experiment with expenditure ceilings? Certainly, they played a major role in reducing the rate of increase in educational spending characteristic of the late 1960s. Instead of ranging from 15 to 20 per cent, the annual increase fell to 8.5 per cent in 1972 and less than 5 per cent in 1973.[15] In that respect, the ceilings did the job they were supposed to do. Along with falling enrolments, the exercise in belt-tightening contributed to a significant decline in the number of elementary and secondary school teachers employed in the province's schools, in at least some boards led to modest increases in the pupil-teacher ratio, and probably cut into, or at least restricted the growth of, a range of services such as special education, English as a second language, and French immersion programs. The ceilings also contributed to the escalating conflict between teachers and boards, and between teachers and the provincial government, as we shall see.

Their other most obvious effect was on local tax rates. After the sharp increases of the 1960s, property taxes across Ontario stabilized, and for some boards, including some urban boards, they actually declined.[16] The era of the ceilings also reduced the level of inequity among boards. As Stephen Lawton remarked, 'Many school boards that had previously spent relatively small amounts per pupil were able to catch up with higher spending boards. At this point in time, there was probably greater equity in expenditure per pupil in Ontario than there has ever been – and probably less local autonomy.'[17] That outcome, however, was substantially due to the combination of province-wide ceilings *and* the proportion of total costs borne by the provincial government, which by 1973 had risen to 60 per cent, and which, because of the equalization formulae, worked to the benefit of poorer boards. Summarizing the arguments of a special committee on government spending in late 1975, the provincial auditor would note that 'the province's education grants and unconditional grants have been the major factors ... in restraining property tax increases particularly in the past five years.' With the expenditure ceilings abolished, he added, the committee was very concerned about rapidly rising property taxes in the years to come.[18]

The committee had good cause to worry. What Ontario now had was a vigorous policy of provincial expenditure restraint *and* no direct controls on local taxes. Between 1976 and 1984, government grants to elementary and secondary education sometimes matched inflation or were set slightly above it; just as often, they fell slightly below. So government expenditure rose only modestly. With grants capped in this manner, school boards turned to their only other source of revenue, the local property tax, to meet their obligations and to meet as well what trustees conceived to be the education needs of their communities. The result was a precipitous rise in *total* spending on the schools and a sharp shift in the source of funding (see figures 7 and 8). In the early 1970s, the province had paid 60 per cent of the costs of elementary and secondary education. By the mid-1980s the provincial share had dropped down towards 45 per cent. On the one hand, then, a continuing saga of provincial spending restraints; on the other, rapidly rising property taxes to support the local schools. With increased reliance on the property tax base, moreover, the inequities between assessment-rich and assessment-poor boards once again began to appear and widened inexorably each year.

How does one account for the total increase in educational spending during a period when not only the provincial government but local authorities as well might be expected to exercise restraint? And, more particularly, how does one account for it at a time when the school system *lost* a quarter of a million students? First, these were years when the inflation rate was nearly always high. During the decade 1971–81, dollar amounts spent on education increased by 214 per cent; once inflation is taken into account the increase is a far more modest 24 per cent. Much of that increase, then, was absorbed by rising prices for goods and services, so that boards did not get a lot more for the money they were spending. Energy costs, for example, *quadrupled* between 1970 and 1985. And that hit extra hard in part at least because the great boom in school construction had occurred when energy was dirt cheap and there was limited incentive to invest in energy-efficient buildings.

Boards also had to pay their teachers. As the Committee on the Costs of Education reported, 'While the number of teachers increased by slightly more than 12 percent' between 1972–3 and 1976–7, 'the salary bill rose by $519 million, or 107 percent.'[19] Negotiated settlements accounted for a 'substantial proportion' of this amount, the committee concluded, but the 'other major factor' was the growth in the number of teachers in the higher salary categories. New teachers keep total salary costs down because they start at the bottom of the salary grid; but declining enrolments meant that fewer new teachers were hired, with the result that the entire workforce moved inexorably towards the top of the grid.

Finally, a large number of new programs were introduced, or expanded, during the 1970s and early 1980s, among them provision for special education, heritage language classes, French-language schools, English as a second language, and junior kindergarten, to name only a few. All of these were expensive and some were mandatory provincial policies. In such cases, boards had no choice but to raise the money to pay their share of the funds. Thus, despite declining enrolments, a shaky economy, and government restraint policies, the costs of education continued to escalate throughout the 1970s and early 1980s. An era of restraint it might have been, compared to the 1960s at least, but hardly one of moderating expenditure on Ontario's schools.

III

And, in the midst of all this, there was an unprecedented level of teacher militancy. Teachers had made some solid gains in the two decades before 1970 – for most of the 1960s, salary increases had ranged from 5 to 10 per cent annually. But late in the decade, the gains began to fall behind those won by some other segments of the workforce, and that trend seems to have persisted into the early 1970s.[20] Thus tough bargaining, and salary demands that would at least maintain incomes relative to other comparable workers, and to inflation, were in the cards regardless of any other circumstances. During the 1960s and early 1970s, however, there was also a large influx into teaching of young people who took for granted the gains of the past, who were willing to be much more aggressive than their elders, and who, in many cases, were influenced by the radicalism of the sixties and not afraid to adopt the attitudes and tactics that had hitherto characterized blue-collar unionism. No less important was the influx of British teachers during the previous decades, imbued with a long-established tradition of teacher unionism far more militant than anything Ontarians were used to. By the mid-1970s, moreover, declining enrolments made job security as urgent an issue as salaries. Altogether these circumstances constituted a recipe for confrontation between teachers, their employers, and the government on a scale never experienced before.

The expenditure ceilings were the precipitate cause. At the very moment when teachers began to step up their demands for larger salary increases, the government intervened to restrain them. Thus the teachers' federations fought a war on two fronts: at the local level, board by board, over salary and working conditions; but also against the provincial government, seeking salary increases beyond the limits the ceilings allowed and, more directly, lobbying and demonstrating against the policy of expenditure ceilings itself. 'As a result,' writes Peter Hennessy, 'the Ontario education scene through the years 1971, 1972 and 1973 was spattered with mass resignations, work-to-rule campaigns, one-day strikes ('study sessions'), pink letters, grey letters, hiring embargoes, and boycotts, all related more or less to the question of what was bargainable and at what price.'[21] And spattered by other things as well. In the autumn of 1973, teachers employed by seventeen boards submitted their resignations, to come into effect on 31 December. Facing chaos in the schools, Tom Wells responded with 'Bill 274,' a measure that would have nullified the resignations and forced teachers back to work.

It was a palpable blunder. Traditionally, the Ontario Secondary School Teachers' Federation (OSSTF) had always been more aggressive and confrontational than the other affiliates of the Ontario Teachers' Federation, but Bill 274 brought all of them on-side, and galvanized individual teachers as never before. The proof lay in the remarkable events of 18 December. Taking the day off school, some 20,000 teachers from all over Ontario crowded into Toronto's Maple Leaf Gardens to attend an anti-government rally. Following that, they were joined by another 10,000 in a march on Queen's Park, where they were treated to impassioned speeches by federation leaders and various labour spokesmen, and in the spirit of the season, serenaded the minister of education with 'No Wells, No Wells.' Some 7000 teachers marched on Parliament Hill in Ottawa, and about 2000 attended a rally in sub-zero cold in Sudbury. Another was held in Windsor. Many of those who didn't attend a 'demo' just stayed home. 'At a rough preliminary estimate,' the *Globe* reported next day, 'fewer than 30,000 of the province's 105,000 teachers went to work yesterday.'[22] In effect, the teachers had closed down Ontario's schools.

They were bolstered, moreover, by a wide range of support. Both opposition parties flayed the government, and especially Wells, in and out of the legislature. Backing the teachers was the voice of organized labour, which is perhaps not surprising. But resolute support came from a number of professional organizations too. Why? Teachers had never been governed by the Ontario Labour Relations Act, which defined the terms for collective bargaining and the circumstances under which strikes or lockouts were legal or illegal. Thus teachers had no collective contracts or bargaining rights, nor did they possess the right to strike. Rather, their terms of employment were governed by the individual contracts they each signed with a school board. What Bill 274 did was deny individuals the right to resign – the right to quit a job voluntarily. And that, in turn, raised a frightening spectre for other, similarly situated, occupations. As the dental association put it, the bill was 'a serious infringement of teachers' civil rights which would set a dangerous precedent for other professional and labour groups.'[23]

Confronting this kind of opposition, the government backed down, inventing a face-saving compromise that kept the schools open and the teachers employed. But it wasn't a tidy ending, and the events of December 1973 marked the beginning of a much more serious period of conflict that would persist through the mid-seventies. There are several good accounts of teacher militancy and its consequences during that time and thus I will not reiterate all of the detail here.[24] But it was in this context, and with an election looming, that the government was finally forced to come to grips with the state of teacher-trustee relations and their bargaining procedures.

IN LATE 1970, William Davis had established the Reville Committee to offer advice on exactly those two matters. When finally submitted in 1972, its report largely blamed bargaining problems on teachers, and especially on their federations, which, it claimed, had lost sight of their legitimate professional obligations in the quest for better incomes. It resolutely rejected giving teachers the right to strike as 'inconsistent with the dual status of the teacher as a professional and as a public employee.' Indeed, it went further and, in an unusually aberrant opinion, insisted that 'conflict and strife is not necessary in the process of negotiating salaries and other matters.'[25] The committee's alternative was a system of bargaining at the local level, with the federations largely excluded from participation, and if that failed, compulsory arbitration. Bargaining, moreover, was to be exclusively related to salaries and other issues of compensation; working conditions were to remain management prerogatives.

The Reville Committee, writes Eric Ricker, was 'perhaps the most naively quixotic investigative body ever appointed in the history of Ontario education.'[26] And he is probably right: it ignored the accumulated bargaining experience of both trustees and teachers since the end of the Second World War; it tried to eliminate the influence of teachers' organizations; it tried to eliminate negotiations about working conditions, something teachers considered not only essential but also something already established de facto as a negotiable item; and it flew in the face of the broader history of employee/employer relations in the province. Not even school board trustees were entirely sympathetic to its contents. And thus it met a predictable fate: 'totally discredited,' as Bryan Downie puts it, within two months of its release.[27]

One alternative, of course, was province-wide bargaining, a procedure in place in some other jurisdictions. But the government had never wanted any part of that particular hornet's nest.[28] Thus, for a year after the release of the Reville report, the government struggled with the problem, and finally, in the fall of 1973 – virtually coinciding with the infamous Bill 274 – introduced 'Bill 275,' which retained the principle of compulsory arbitration favoured by trustees but, as a sop to the teachers, included working conditions as a negotiable item.

In other circumstances, the proposal might have been successful. Giving teachers the right to strike was still highly controversial; many feared it would set a dangerous precedent for other public servants; until late 1973 at least, the federations were not united on the issue; and many individual teachers flatly opposed it as incompatible with their responsibilities as professionals.[29] But Bill 275 rapidly became hopelessly entangled in the uproar over Bill 274, condemned holus-bolus with it, and was abandoned in early 1974.

Solutions that might have been possible in 1973, in any case, ceased to be so after that, as teacher opinion coalesced around the right to strike, and turned into a resolute determination to extend legal bargaining to cover working conditions. By this point, moreover, both opposition parties were prepared to concede these issues to the teachers and even trustees were beginning to agree that compulsory arbitration would not, in fact, put an end to job actions ranging from work-to-rule to mass resignations. The Conservative caucus remained deeply divided over the right to strike, nonetheless, and only in March 1975 did cabinet conclude that something had to be done, and done quickly, before the government went to the polls.

The result was 'Bill 100,' which completed passage through the legislature in June 1975 and was formally known as 'The School Boards and Teachers Collective Negotiations Act.' It introduced collective bargaining on both salaries and working conditions, and gave teachers the right to strike (and trustees the right to lock them out). The bargaining unit for the teachers was to be the local branch of the affiliate federation (though the right to strike was denied those members who were principals and vice-principals). If local bargaining encountered difficulties, there was a complex system of voluntary mediation and arbitration procedures that might be pursued, and the whole process was to be supervised by a provincial 'Education Relations Commission,' which was also assigned the task of recommending government intervention when a conflict remained unresolved long enough to threaten the public interest – which meant, in effect, a significant threat to students' education.

Bill 100 did not put an end to the severity of either conflict or controversy. The months from autumn 1975 to the spring of 1976 were especially tough as teachers (along with other public servants) were brought under the terms of the federal anti-inflation legislation by the Ontario government, and agreements rolled back which teachers thought had already been settled. By the later 1970s and early 1980s the number of strikes declined, but several of those that did occur were long and headline-grabbing, including the Sudbury high school strike of 1980, which set a record, to that point, of fifty-six school days. Meanwhile, contract 'leap-frogging'* and generous settlements continued to provoke calls for province-wide bargaining as the best solution to rationalize teachers' wage demands. In its final report, the Committee on the Costs of Education came out solidly against the right to strike, which, in its view, amounted to strikes against children, and proposed compulsory arbitration as an alternative much to be preferred.[30] Its views were widely shared in the press, and in an opinion poll of 1979 a slight majority of Ontario respondents agreed.[31] By 1979, with a possible election in the wind, Stuart Smith, the Liberal leader, reversed the party's previous stand and called for the provincial government to strip teachers of the right to strike.[32]

Bill 100 had its protagonists. When Owen Shime stepped down in 1979 as the first chair of the Education Relations Commission, he pointed out that while there had been twenty-eight strikes in the three years before the legislation, there had been only eighteen since then, adding that 'compulsory arbitration could not guarantee an end to teacher strikes – experience has shown that legislation does not prevent strikes.'[33] Yet the controversy ran deep enough to provoke Bette Stephenson to establish a review of the act, though when the commissioners recommended only modest changes, the government conceded, announcing that it was not considering repeal, or even major amendments.[34]

THE PROVISIONS OF BILL 100 immeasurably strengthened the role of the federations, confirming rights in law that had gradually been established de facto in the bargaining arena during the two previous decades, and more especially in the early 1970s. While improved salaries and a voice in determining their conditions of work were achievements accomplished in increments across the decade, the School Boards and Teachers Collective Negotiations Act was rightly viewed by teachers as landmark legislation,

*One of the common phrases for a settlement with one board that would then set the minimum demands for negotiations with the next.

the decisive victory of the militant seventies, and a turning point in the history of the organized occupation.

There was a price to be paid, however. Aggressive tactics and large wage demands during the 1970s contributed to the alienation of public opinion, which hardened into a widespread view that teachers' organizations were primarily interested in their own aggrandizement, and individual teachers in their own personal welfare, rather than in the best interests of their students. That such perceptions tended towards a sentimental view of a golden age when teachers' dedication to the cause of education was unalloyed by material interests, and they were universally cherished because of it, is beside the point. The perceptions were no less potent because of that. In the late 1970s and early 1980s, teachers who went on strike certainly faced a hostile press: 'The innocent pay in teacher disputes,' 'Strike against children,' 'The student as hostage,' were typical headlines, and almost as routine as weather reports.[35] A large portion of the public agreed. Nor did teachers do themselves any favours when they insisted in public that pupils were unaffected by strikes. To the cynical it only raised the inevitable rejoinder: if that was true, just what was going on in classrooms when teachers *weren't* on strike? And even while they insisted that teachers were being unfairly maligned, federation leaders were worrying about the loss of public esteem the occupation as a whole was experiencing. Said Margaret Wilson, the president of OSSTF, at its 1979 annual meeting, and only half-jocularly, 'I often hear teachers say that they go almost in disguise to parties, afraid to reveal themselves as teachers lest they become the butt of criticism and comment.'[36]

EVEN AS THE LEVEL of outright conflict between local boards and their teachers began to decline, the conviction that teaching was an occupation under siege grew stronger. Stuart Smith's Liberals and a significant portion of the press were accused of 'teacher bashing' during the election of 1981 for suggesting that the right to strike should be abolished, but also for their criticisms of the state of Ontario's classrooms.[37] More important, a whole series of issues in the late 1970s and early 1980s where teachers' opinions appeared to be ignored or discounted, or where their financial or bargaining rights were threatened, left them at loggerheads with the government and its minister of education.[38] Above all, there was the 'College of Teachers' – a proposal to give teachers a new professional body, like those in medicine and law, that would govern their qualifications, license them to practise, and take responsibility for professional ethics and discipline. A notion originating in the late 1960s from within OTF itself, it had been firmly rejected by Thomas Wells, but was revived in 1980 by Bette Stephenson, who, with her medical background, saw it as a means of raising the status of teachers but also of increasing their sense of professional responsibility.[39]

Though favourable in principle to a measure that would give them the trappings of professional status already possessed by others, federation spokesmen were leery of anything that would infringe on bargaining rights or the existing prerogatives of the federations.[40] They were made more leery by the fact that the initiative came from the government. 'One of the things that worries us,' said a local federation leader in London, 'is that it is the minister who is pushing the issue and not the teachers. As far as we are concerned, that is reason enough for wondering exactly what she intends with the college.'[41] And the minister certainly didn't help by proposing at one critical point that 'membership in the college be mandatory and membership in the OTF be optional.'[42] Her intent was probably benign – that was essentially the kind of arrangement that then existed between the College of Physicians and Surgeons of Ontario (the governing body for medicine) and the Ontario Medical Association, the doctors' union; it was the case with other professional organizations as well. But in the snarly atmosphere of the early 1980s, it looked to many teachers like straightforward 'union-busting,' and there was talk of closing the schools in protest, until Premier Davis stepped in to announce that the government would not pursue the proposal without 'the enthusiastic support of the teachers.'[43]

The teachers won on that one, but then, during the Stephenson years, with their public image already battered and their jobs under siege because of declining enrolments, they seemed to be losing any collective influence with the government and, indeed, were confronting government initiatives they saw as inimical to their interests. One way or another, their relationship with the provincial government, and more particularly with the Conservative leadership, was badly strained.

On June 12, 1984, it suddenly got much worse.

The Completion of the Separate School System, 1960–1987

Early in the afternoon of June 12, 1984, William Davis rose in the legislature to embark on one of the most historic speeches of his political career. The government, he began, 'has undertaken a careful and fresh review of the outstanding issues surrounding public support for the Roman Catholic school system, and ... I wish to outline a new course we have decided to pursue.' In the name of both justice and 'common sense,' it was time 'to permit Roman Catholic school boards to establish a full range of elementary and secondary education and, as part of the public system, to be funded accordingly. This new program will be introduced at the rate of one year of secondary education for each school year, beginning in September 1, 1985.'[1] While the speech earned Davis a standing ovation from all three parties in the House, it was also a bolt from the blue, stunning the press, the public, and the Tory caucus alike. Not even the cabinet, including the minister of education herself, had been informed of the decision until a few scant hours before.[2]

Reaction was swift. For Catholics it was a moment to cherish, a vindication of decades of struggle to maintain and extend the scope of their schools. In sharp contrast, the president of the Ontario Public School Trustees' Association declared that she was 'horrified' by the move.[3] The president of OSSTF was 'shocked and dismayed.'[4] A leading evangelical pastor described it as an 'ugly discrimination' to fund the schools of one Christian denomination but not those of others.[5] The Loyal Orange Lodge issued its own condemnation, and a few days later a group of prominent Protestant clergymen declared it a betrayal of the ideal of a common education for all.[6] Thus the stage was set for the most divisive conflict over an educational issue in Ontario since the middle decades of the nineteenth century; indeed, over the same issue – the right of a minority to public funding for its own religious schools.

AT MID-TWENTIETH CENTURY, as I suggested in chapter 2, the separate school system suffered substantial disadvantages compared to its public counterpart. Its public funding ceased at the end of grade 10 and even for earlier grades its tax base was less adequate; it survived in large part because it could rely on the religious orders to offer much of its instruction. Increasingly in the post-war years, however, that solution no longer worked. On the one hand, immigration and the baby boom sent Catholic school enrolments soaring far above the rate of increase in the public schools. On the other, the increase in the number of teaching nuns lagged far behind, and thus separate school boards were forced, more and more, to turn to lay teachers. In 1949, for example, 46 per cent of the teaching force was drawn from the religious orders; by 1965 the proportion had fallen to 15 per cent. But lay teachers had to be paid competitive salaries, an increasing number of them had to be recruited, and schools had to be built or expanded just to keep up with the enrolment boom. The demand far outran the available resources, every year it seemed to get worse, and by the early 1960s Roman Catholic leaders, lay and clerical alike, believed they faced the possible collapse of the separate school system itself. Their response was to begin an intensive public-relations campaign, attempting to rally the entire Catholic community behind them and then to press the politicians for new legislation. Two of the most important remedial measures demanded were changes in the law to give them access to corporate property taxes, and public funds for grades 11 to 13.

The government found itself in a political dilemma. Giving Catholics access to corporate taxes would direct money out of the public school system and rouse the anger of those Protestants opposed to any concession to Roman Catholics, and of others who believed that separating children according to their religion was 'divisive.' Quailing before the political consequences of that option, in 1964 Robarts and his advisers fell upon another strategy. Assuring public school supporters that no local corporate revenues would be diverted from their schools, Robarts announced that Catholics would receive a special provincial grant to compensate for their lack of access to corporate property taxes. The effect was to rescue the separate schools from the financial imbroglio they faced without setting off a political uproar. Major inequities persisted, but the plan enabled the Catholic schools to compensate for the declining number of

nuns and teaching brothers by offering competitive salaries to lay teachers, and to match, more or less, the facilities available in the public
elementary schools despite the expansionary pressures of the sixties. In
extending this support to the separate schools, Robarts and Davis had also
firmly rejected any extension of funding to grades 11 to 13. Yet one effect
of the new arrangement was to allow the private efforts of the denomination to be redirected to the improvement and expansion of the Catholic
high schools.

Despite the rebuff over secondary education in the early 1960s, Catholic
leaders were encouraged by the success of their public campaign and
private lobbying efforts, and during the second half of the decade they
launched a vigorous new initiative to persuade all three of Ontario's
political parties to support full funding to Catholic high schools. In many
respects they had a good case. If separate schools were a legitimate part of
the public system it hardly made sense to starve the secondary schools of
the financial resources necessary to meet objectives set for the whole
system. If equality of opportunity meant anything, it surely meant that
young people should have access to the full set of options and programs
within the schools their parents chose for them. And these arguments, no
doubt supplemented by the desire to appeal to Catholic voters, carried the
day among the opposition parties: by 1969 both the Liberals and the NDP
had come out in favour of full funding. The question then became, Could
the Conservatives be persuaded? Mounting pressure was put on MPPs,
earnest private appeals were made to key cabinet ministers, and one of the
culminating events in the campaign, a giant rally in 1970 at Maple Leaf
Gardens organized by the Ontario Catholic Students' Federation, attracted 15,000 people.

In the end, however, the Conservatives failed to come through. In late
summer 1971, Davis warned of the additional costs (especially heavy at the
senior high school level), the unease about further fragmentation and
divisiveness, and the concern that if funding were extended to Catholics,
other groups would inevitably come knocking at the door. Most probably
Davis also believed that, with an election looming, there was enough
opposition in key ridings to influence the outcome of his first election as
leader of the party. The Conservatives went into the election of October
1971 opposed to full funding and won a decisive victory.

That setback left Catholic organizations in some disarray, and for the
rest of the seventies they were unable to apply the kind of pressure that
they had in the sixties. Despite the fact that both opposition parties were
on side, the Tories refused to budge, and separate-school issues did not

play a significant role in the elections of 1975, 1977, or 1981. Catholics' only success was to win increased funding in the late seventies for grades 9 and 10, but it still remained well below the amount given for the same grades to non-Catholic high schools. A more vigorous campaign began to take shape in the early 1980s; even then, Catholic leaders were more optimistic about the chances of getting equal funding for the junior than the senior grades.[7]

ALL OF WHICH BRINGS US back to 12 June 1984, and the reasons for Davis's historic turnabout. We do not know the exact causes, and may never know; but there are plausible explanations.[8] Not only had enrolments in Catholic elementary schools continued to increase, but so had those in Catholic high schools – from some 32,600 students in 1968, to over 70,000 in 1983. The sheer illogic of this situation undoubtedly played its part: here was the most expansive part of the school system underfunded in grades 9 and 10, and cut off from funding after that, forcing parents to pay hefty fees for their children to complete their education within a system that had served them since kindergarten – *and* forcing them to pay property taxes to support the senior grades of the public system as well. If there were to be Catholic schools at all, something guaranteed by the constitution, did it make any sense to limit public provision to the lower reaches of the secondary school alone? Davis also estimated the costs at a modest $40 million annually, in part because the anticipated demise of grade 13 would mean funding for only two years of high school rather than three.

There was also the apparent decline in Protestant opposition revealed in Tory-sponsored opinion polls, coupled with the growing importance of the Catholic vote. Catholics now represented something like a third of the Ontario electorate, they were particularly strong in Metropolitan Toronto, and their loyalties were solidly Liberal. Davis expected that the party was likely to go to the polls in late 1984 or 1985 and there was the hope that a Tory initiative on the school question might cut into Liberal support. Throughout the 1970s and early 1980s, moreover, Davis had established close ties with key Catholic leaders, above all Cardinal Carter of Toronto, and that undoubtedly influenced him as well. Davis would always deny that there was a 'deal' struck over the issue, but the nature of the relationship may well have increased his sympathies for Catholic claims or nagged at his conscience: he would later say of his 1971 decision, 'I believed in what I said at the time, but I was never totally comfortable with the position I had taken.'[9] The threat in early 1984 by a Catholic student organization to launch a constitutional challenge to the inequities of the existing arrangement may have played a part as well.

Finally, it was not as though the issue appeared out of nowhere. According to Bette Stephenson, the ministry had been talking about it 'very quietly' for several years, and it had been 'discussed in caucus almost annually.'[10] It had been a major topic at a 1981 policy conference attended by a select group of senior Tory ministers and political advisers.[11] It was one of the most contentious and time-consuming issues preoccupying the steering committee of the Secondary Education Review Project.[12] Davis's closest advisers and key cabinet ministers were badly split on the issue, nonetheless, and thus in the spring of 1984 planning for the announcement was shrouded in secrecy, with only a handful of Davis's personal aides in the know. Though the Catholic bishops were kept informed of possible terms for a settlement, apparently not even they were aware of the full sweep of the decision until the announcement was made.

The terms Davis proposed in his June 12th speech represented an attempt to keep both public and separate school supporters happy.[13] The former were promised that the public system would remain sheltered from undue hardships the transition might entail. Buildings would be transferred from one system to the other and there would be inevitable enrolment shifts; but public high school teachers who were declared redundant were to be guaranteed jobs in the Catholic system regardless of their denominational affiliation and without penalties in terms of rights or seniority. Davis also expressed hope that, where accommodation allowed, Catholic schools would be open to all students who chose to attend.

At the same time, he announced that three related commissions were to be established. One was to play a vital role in the transition process: a 'Planning and Implementation Commission' charged with overseeing the transition, locality by locality, as well as with proffering advice to the minister of education on the details of the legislation required. A second was the appointment of a six-member commission on educational finance. Chaired by H. Ian Macdonald, a former deputy treasurer of Ontario and professor at York University, it had a much wider mandate than full funding alone, but recommendations aimed at eliminating inequities between public and separate school access to local property taxes were integral to its work. Finally, the extension of funding to Catholic high schools raised the question of the rights of other minorities to funding for their schools, and thus a third commission was to study and report on that issue – a job that fell in the lap of Bernard Shapiro, at that time the director of OISE.

Whatever the merits of the decision itself, the timing of the announcements would exacerbate the political difficulties full funding would encounter. Already contemplating his own retirement, Davis nevertheless delayed going public until mid-June, 'too late,' as Rosemary Speirs argues, 'to allow for the preparation and passage of legislation in the fall session. Had Davis been ready even a month earlier, he could have defended and passed the new law himself – instead of bequeathing it to a successor who was uncomfortable with the change and therefore not credible defending it.'[14]

IN THE WEEKS IMMEDIATELY following the announcement, those with a direct stake in the decision began to mobilize all their resources to resist, or support, Davis's initiative. During the summer and fall of 1984, however, public reaction remained muted. Opinion polls continued to show that confidence in the Davis government remained high, the separate school question appeared to be only a minor irritant, and since all three political parties were now in accord, the politicians refused to debate the subject, treating it as a fait accompli.

In December the mood began to change. Public hearings by the implementation commission were now under way, and would, over a period of three months, include 190 presentations from groups and individuals all across Ontario.[15] There were slick and lengthy set-pieces by the various provincial organizations with a large stake in the issue. OSSTF claimed that implementation would result in the loss of 8500 jobs and 100 schools, and the further fragmentation of Ontario's public education system.[16] As well, it wanted implementation delayed at least one year to allow a full public debate on the issue beforehand.[17] The Ontario Public School Trustees' Association warned that there would be a drop in enrolments in public secondary schools of up to 15 per cent, and as much as 75 per cent in some areas. The results would be devastating: cuts in optional subjects, rising class sizes, more school closures, less money to maintain facilities, more busing, and higher per-pupil costs for transportation.[18] OPSTA also disputed Davis's claim about the cost of full funding, estimating it at double the $40 million he had predicted.[19] Catholic organizations argued that all of this was exaggeration, that good sense and co-operation could smooth difficulties, and that 'completion' of their system was as necessary as it was wise. But they also pointed out in no uncertain terms that there must be a transfer of resources and physical plant from a shrinking to an expanding system. And there was also some unease expressed about being required to treat non-Catholic teachers equally, or allowing access to their schools by a large number of non-Catholic students, both of which might threaten the spirit of Catholic education itself.[20]

This much might have been expected. But what the hearings also revealed was that things were on the boil at the local level. In small communities everywhere, there were fears that the introduction of a second high school might siphon off enough students to make the public high school unviable. Wherever there were large concentrations of Franco-Ontarians, the possibilities seemed especially horrific – the splintering of schools into French and English public, French and English separate. Such scenarios divided English and French, Catholic and Protestant, and Franco-Ontarians themselves. In the larger urban areas, frictions developed – pockets of public school supporters angered at the potential loss of what they saw as 'their' local secondary school, and, on the other side, Catholics eager to take over half-empty schools that they had helped build with their tax dollars. Reporters might retain their scepticism about the self-serving claims of the big provincial stakeholders, but they were also filling the daily press with accounts of local divisions, fears for the future of both systems, and, in some cases, passions dangerously inflamed.[21] The implementation commission did its best to insist that the hearings were about *implementation* and only that; but in presentation after presentation, and in the newspapers as well, Davis's decision was itself the central issue.

In March the Macdonald Commission on School Finance held its own public hearings. The 'Ontario government has been slowly strangling its public school system,' the Ontario Teachers' Federation brief declared, and on that point – a rare event in these years – both OSSTF and the Ontario English Catholic Teachers' Association (OECTA) agreed.[22] But OECTA also called for major changes in local school finance in order to equalize access to industrial and commercial property taxes. The federations' demand for larger government grants and a return to 60 per cent provincial funding was greeted with scepticism by the commissioners; the inference drawn by reporters was that the commission was unlikely to recommend that full funding be accompanied by more money to ease the pain.[23]

The federations' annual meetings in late March contributed to the din. For OSSTF, the central issue was full funding, with the executive threatening to close the schools in protest if jobs were not protected by legislation or regulation. The meeting also revealed that OSSTF thought it still possible to delay or even kill the measure through the combined impact of a constitutional challenge, organized protest, and an aroused public opinion.[24] For OECTA, entirely different issues were at stake. In their enthusiasm for full funding, Catholic authorities had rather overlooked the salary disparities that had long existed between public and Catholic secondary school teachers. Now, with boards promised financial parity, the teachers wanted it too. As one reporter summarized it, OECTA was 'more concerned with contract negotiations across the province than the introduction of government funds for a high school system ... Teachers at the meeting said they anticipate that almost 8,000 of the 23,000 Catholic teachers may be on strike this spring.'[25]

MEANWHILE, A NEW GUARD had taken over the Ontario government. In October 1984, William Davis resigned as premier and as leader of the Conservative party. Following the leadership race that ensued, Frank Miller, a Muskoka businessman with a political agenda considerably to the right of the Davis era, became premier and leader of the party. Eager to win his own mandate from the voters, and overconfident about the abiding strength of the Tory party without the personal popularity of William Davis, Miller called an election in late March 1985. Among other things, the election meant that legislation on full funding, long expected for the spring session, would be delayed, and at least some of Miller's advisers warned of the explosive consequences. With both opposition parties already committed, on the other hand, the Tories apparently concluded that the matter could be kept off the political agenda until after election day.

For most of the campaign, that turned out to be the case. Spluttered the editorial voice of the *Globe*, 'A burning Ontario issue is being treated by all three parties as a non-issue, a *fait accompli* with details to be worked out somehow in time to force the plan into operation, somewhere, by September. It is the antithesis of responsible management of public affairs.'[26] Others were outraged as well. OSSTF offered to provide funding for up to twenty-seven independent candidates who would run on the issue in marginal ridings; they found only six willing to do so.[27] The Metropolitan Toronto board launched a tough advertising campaign against the politicians' 'veil of silence.'[28] The leaders of the three parties were flushed out only in the last week of the campaign when Lewis Garnsworthy, archbishop of the Anglican Diocese of Toronto, made an impassioned plea for public debate, at one point comparing Davis's tactics to Hitler's in regulating education by decree.[29] A ruckus ensued, but even then the talk was of bigotry and the danger of inflaming religious passions, not about the central issue or its implications. Polls, nonetheless, revealed voters to be deeply divided on the issue, while some reporters and politicians thought it the hottest door-to-door subject of the campaign. The polls also showed, however, that it was hurting the Tories most, alienating traditional Protestant supporters in both urban and rural ridings, while drawing little support from Catholics: the Liberals and NDP, after all, had advocated the measure for years, while the Tories were 'johnnies-come-lately.'[30] On

2 May 1985, the voters delivered their verdict: the Conservatives won
52 seats, David Peterson's Liberals won 48 – their best showing since 1957 –
and Bob Rae's New Democrats raised their count to 25. The Tories
remained the Ontario government, but by the narrowest of margins, and
the combined votes of the other two parties could bring them down in a
moment.

That moment came soon enough, and full funding played a role in the
outcome. At a news conference the morning after the election, still shaken
by the result, Miller declared that the separate school issue was the main
reason for the loss of Tory seats and implied that, given the new situation,
he might well consider reversing Davis's decision. It was a major gaffe, he
was abruptly informed in public and private, and he recanted the next day.
But it raised the spectre for both opposition parties of a Tory party
defeated in the House, calling an early election, and making the separate
school question a central issue in a new election campaign. That, writes
Rosemary Speirs, 'helped drive the Liberals and New Democrats into one
another's arms.'[31] An agreement was quickly reached: in return for a
Liberal pledge to push forward with legislation on a variety of social
policies favoured by the NDP, that party would support a Liberal government for a period of two years. Included in the pact were clauses ensuring
that full funding would begin in September, that the requisite legislation
would be introduced promptly, and that there would be public hearings
before the bill became law.[32] Accordingly, the government was defeated on
18 June 1985. It was, in its way, a historic moment: few Ontarians then
under the age of fifty could remember a time when the province was
without a Conservative government at the helm.

IN PETERSON'S NEW CABINET, Sean Conway, a thirty-four-year-old, politically astute MPP from Renfrew County, was handed the job of minister of
education. But when Peterson re-convened the legislature for a short
session in early July, it was the premier himself who introduced the separate school legislation, known as Bill 30, and issued a statement of intent
on the subject. In the latter he promised three things. First, there would be
a 'full, fair and unfettered' public hearing on the terms of the bill. Second,
in order to avert the threat of a later legal challenge the government itself
would refer the bill to the courts for a ruling on its consistency with the
constitution. And third, he reaffirmed the Liberal government's commitment to proceed with full funding for grades 9 to 11 in September 1985.[33]

In its detail, Bill 30 was consonant with the principles set out by Davis a
year earlier. Separate school boards were given jurisdiction to establish

secondary schools with the full range of academic and vocational programs. To pay for them, Catholic boards would be given access to government grants and local property taxes. Pending the report of the Macdonald Commission, only the question of equal access to industrial and commercial taxes remained to be settled. The Planning and Implementation Commission was to continue to supervise and adjudicate disputes over the transfer of property, buildings, and staff. For a period of ten years following passage of the bill, secondary school staff made redundant by shifts in enrolment from one system to the other were to be identified by their board as 'designated persons'; Catholic boards were required to employ them at either classroom or supervisory level before hiring others to do the job, and to do so regardless of creed and without penalties with respect to salary, seniority, or opportunities for promotion. So long as accommodation permitted, non-Catholic students were allowed to enrol in Catholic schools.[34]

The bill received first reading on 4 July 1985, and was approved in principle the next week by a vote of 117 to one.[35] The government's intent, however, was not to proceed with third and final reading until after the public hearings and the reference to the court had been completed – which meant a delay of at least several months. The job of sounding out the public on Bill 30 was handed to the eleven-member Social Development Committee, which included senior members of all three parties.

The Peterson government probably had no choice but to pursue the course it did, and there were certainly pressing political and legal reasons for doing so. Yet it compounded the problems of Davis's delay the year before. In the weeks and months that followed, positions hardened, voices grew more shrill. Hopes were renewed that by one means or another the course of public policy might be altered. Though founded the previous May, the 'Coalition for Public Education' now became the chief voice of organized opposition. Established by the leadership of five Protestant denominations, three teachers' federations, and three trustees' groups, it claimed to represent a million people and carried on a vigorous campaign through public rallies and in the media during the summer and fall of 1985. Its central argument was that opponents of Bill 30 had been reduced to 'political orphans' and its platform was a call for a referendum on the principle of extended funding for separate schools.[36] Catholics made concerted efforts to counter the campaign, but an internal split that had first appeared shortly after the Davis decision became more open through 1985–6. Some clergy and laity denounced the compromises made over the hiring of 'designated' teachers and principals as a sure road to the dilution

of Catholic education, while others, including at one point Cardinal
Carter himself, declared such fears excessive zealotry and warned that they
might put the entire project at risk.[37]

OTHER VOICES HAD ENTERED the fray as well. During the 1960s and 1970s,
the number of private schools in Ontario had grown significantly, and by
the early 1980s enrolled some 80,000 students.[38] In many cases, private
schools existed from hand to mouth, their finances always precarious;
others were more secure but their resources, measured by per-pupil expenditure, remained far below those of the public system. Like Roman
Catholics, private-school organizations had lobbied the politicians in 1970–
1 for access to public funds.[39] And when the Conservatives failed to
respond, it became clear that a more concerted effort was necessary. In
1974, the Ontario Association of Alternative and Independent Schools
(OAAIS) was founded by participants from the Roman Catholic, evangelical Christian, and Jewish educational communities, along with representatives of some non-sectarian schools.

There were three common arguments made in support of public funding for private education.[40] The first focused on the inherent unfairness of
'double taxation': forcing parents who opted out of the public system to
pay private-school tuition fees on top of the taxes they paid to support the
public schools. Second, if Roman Catholics had the right to even partial
funding, which they did in Ontario, it was discriminatory to deny it to
other religious groups – an argument that gained substantial force in 1982
when the Canadian Charter of Rights and Freedoms, with its provisions
guaranteeing religious freedom and equality under the law, was embedded
as part of this country's constitution. Finally, there was the prior right of
parents to select an educational environment they believed best fostered
their children's intellectual and spiritual development. In the case of Roman Catholics and evangelical Christians this meant schools that reinforced
the teachings of home and church. Evangelicals in particular were often
bluntly outspoken about the baleful influence of 'secular humanism' in the
public schools, which included lax standards of behaviour, the destructive
divorce of moral instruction from its religious grounding, and curriculum
materials or content that denied or challenged church doctrines.[41]

In the late 1970s and early 1980s, private-school supporters had some
reason to be hopeful that public funding might be forthcoming. Several
other provinces already offered such aid. There was much talk across
North America about raising educational standards through increased
choice and competition: one favourite nostrum was the 'voucher system,'
in which educational grants would be given to parents rather than directly

to schools, allowing the former to purchase education at the school of their choice. And perhaps of more import, there were indications that some prominent Tory and Liberal politicians appeared sympathetic and others were at least willing to consider the matter; only the NDP remained resolutely opposed.[42]

The pact that brought down the Tory government cast the first pall – the Liberals were unlikely to push forward a project opposed by the NDP. Then, in early July 1985, Sean Conway said that while he looked forward to the Shapiro report with interest, the government 'does not contemplate at the present time funding anything other than the last few grades' of the Roman Catholic school system.[43] In September he slammed the door shut, bluntly reiterating that 'we do not contemplate extending that funding to third (or private) schools.'[44]

Thus pre-empted, Shapiro submitted his report in October 1985.[45] In clear, forceful prose he subjected the arguments on both sides to thorough scrutiny, concluding that neither parents nor the state have unqualified prior claims over the education of children, but that it was indeed discrimination to fund some religious schools and not others. There were, in any case, other convincing reasons for funding private schools from the public purse, but such funding must be accompanied by guarantees that they would meet minimum academic standards, be accessible to students regardless of religious creed or ethnic background, and be responsible to locally elected public authorities.

That conclusion was rejected outright by those who believed state funding would entail restrictions they were not willing to live with.[46] Others were more favourable, including OAAIS. By the summer of 1985 it was ready to continue the fight, joining in the government's reference case on Bill 30 even though it now found itself having to switch sides, to oppose full funding for Catholic schools on the ground that it discriminated against other religious groups. And other groups of private-school supporters were also preparing to make their voices heard during the public hearings of the Social Development Committee.

THE HEARINGS PROVED TO BE the longest ever held by a provincial legislative committee, lasting from mid-July to mid-November 1985, and attracting 879 submissions.[47] Even Bill Davis agreed to appear, offering his own version of why he had made the decision. The *Globe*'s Robert Matas provided this vivid portrait of the committee's work: '[It] sat through public hearings in the mornings, afternoons and evenings. The politicians met Saturdays. They travelled to the North, to Eastern Ontario, to Southwestern Ontario. They held hearings in French and in English. They listened with uncommon restraint to people insulting them and their political beliefs. They showed as much interest in the opinions of high school students as in the glossy presentations of well-heeled professional education groups.'[48]

All the issues received a thorough airing, not only before the committee but in newspaper columns and editorials, church journals, and on radio and television. There were, of course, the specifics: jobs, school transfers, the plight of small schools in rural and northern areas. There was no shortage of self-interested claims and counter-claims, and some bigotry to boot. But it was also a public debate about fundamental issues. Catholics did not rest their case on narrowly legal grounds alone but spoke of the essential unity of religion and education, the vital need for schools infused with moral and religious values, and the prior rights of parents in determining how their children were to be educated. Jews and evangelical Christians chimed in with similar arguments. Mainstream Protestants contended that while schools must teach moral and religious values, doctrinal differences could and should be excluded from the classroom. Others maintained that however necessary separate schools had been in an earlier era tinctured by religious prejudice, they were an anomaly in a pluralistic multicultural society where education had a large responsibility to instil common values and loyalties. To allow publicly funded institutions to discriminate on religious grounds against students and teachers, moreover, was to deny the spirit of fairness and equal rights incorporated into the Ontario Human Rights Code and the federal government's brand-new Charter of Rights and Freedoms.[49] Overall, the hearings represented an impressive public debate over the nature of the good school, the good society, and the terms of the social contract that should bind Ontarians together.

A useful seminar perhaps; but did it matter that substantive issues were thoroughly aired? The problem here was much the same as it had been a year before. As the OSSTF brief put it, the Social Development Committee, like the implementation commission before it, was 'determined to discuss only how best to implement full funding to Roman Catholic separate secondary schools, not the crucial question of whether it should be implemented at all.'[50] And that was the gist of it. The committee listened long and earnestly to concerns and criticisms about particular aspects of Bill 30, and did indeed take them seriously: it would later offer amendments that reflected this. But a 'full, fair, and unfettered' consideration of the fundamental question was not on the political agenda.

Meanwhile, in October, the Ontario Court of Appeal – the province's highest court – heard the government's reference on Bill 30.[51] The question the attorney-general, Ian Scott, put to the panel of five justices was this: 'Is Bill 30 ... inconsistent with the provisions of the Constitution of Canada including the Canadian Charter of Rights and Freedoms and, if so, in what particulars and in what respect?' In their decision, issued in February 1986, three of the five judges ruled in favour of the government. Section 93 of the Constitution Act, 1867, prohibited the province from limiting the legal rights of denominational schools held at the time of Confederation but did not prohibit it from extending such rights if it so wished. Nor had Ontario violated the Canadian Charter of Rights, because section 29 of the Charter explicitly exempted Catholic denominational schools from the more general clauses guaranteeing freedom of religion and equality before the law.

SO THAT WAS THAT? By no means. For the opponents of Bill 30, a three-to-two decision was proof of legitimate grounds for doubt, and within days of the ruling the Metropolitan Toronto Board and OSSTF announced they would launch an appeal to the Supreme Court of Canada.[52] By spring, a consortium of groups had been established under the aegis of the Coalition for Public Education to finance and organize the appeal, with the result that the question of Bill 30's constitutional status remained uncertain.

The government read the ruling differently: the question had been tested and the bill found to be consistent with the constitution; the legislation would go forward for third and final reading during the spring session of the legislature.[53] With public opinion still divided, however, and pressed by criticisms from the two opposition parties, Conway was prepared to give ground on issues that had provoked some of the loudest outcries throughout the months of hearings by the Social Development Committee. Thus three key amendments were introduced in late April.[54] First, those 'designated persons' who had conscientious objections to being transferred to the Catholic system would be offered financial assistance and retraining opportunities. Second, the original clause which had made access for non-Catholic pupils subject to conditions was abandoned, and all students were given unrestricted entry to either public or separate secondary schools. Finally, non-Catholic students would not be required to take religious instruction in the separate secondary schools.

The latter two amendments caused an uproar in the Catholic community. The transfer of 'designated' staff was something their schools could absorb: such transfers could be made only as a result of verified shifts in enrolment between the two systems; thus the numbers were expected to be limited. But now Bill 30 was starting to look like a Trojan horse, allowing an unregulated influx of non-Catholic students, exempt from the discipline of religious instruction, to dilute and perhaps undermine the very purpose of Catholic education.

Worse was to come. By May the New Democrats were facing open splits over Bill 30 and, with an annual party conference looming in June, the pressure on Bob Rae and his senior colleagues was particularly intense. The most explosive issue was the rights of non-designated teachers. To reiterate, designated staff – those who were displaced by enrolment shifts over a period of ten years – were guaranteed jobs regardless of creed. But in all other cases the Catholic system retained the right to discriminate on religious grounds in hiring and promotion policies. And that stuck in the craw of many a New Democrat, especially among party loyalists outside the caucus. The public record remains murky about what exactly ensued, but in a last-minute compromise, made only in order to get the bill passed, Conway accepted an NDP amendment which said, in effect, that ten years after the passage of Bill 30, Catholic boards would lose the right to discriminate against non-Catholic applicants for teaching or other jobs.[55] What would eventually become section 136 of the Education Act allowed separate school boards to require 'as a condition of employment' only that teachers, principals, and supervisory officers 'agree to respect the philosophy and traditions of Roman Catholic separate schools in the performance of their duties.'

With that, Bill 30 passed into law in late June 1986.[56] Leading Catholics, however, were already warning that section 136 violated their constitutional rights; the Liberal government was no less persuaded of it. In October, as the Supreme Court appeal case got under way, the government announced that it was prepared to challenge the constitutionality of its own amendment![57] Lawyers for the Ontario attorney-general's office asked the court to rule on section 136 as part of the larger issues at stake. The court, however, declined the request, declaring that the case must be restricted to the version of the bill on which the Ontario Court of Appeal had originally ruled.*

THE SUPREME COURT CASE was a replay of the Ontario court's hearings of the previous year, but on a much grander scale. Though preparations went on throughout the autumn of 1986, the appeal against Bill 30 was heard over six days of sittings that ended on 5 February 1987. The case attracted

---

*In 1995 the Ontario Separate School Trustees' Association began a constitutional challenge to section 136; the latter was struck down by the courts in 1997. For the judgment see *Daly v. Ontario (Attorney-General)* (1997), 154 DLR (4th) 464 (Ont. Gen. Div.).

a capacity crowd, with loyalties divided so sharply that public school supporters sat on one side of the courtroom, Catholics on the other; not even in the long line-ups to get in was there much banter between them. The documentation submitted in evidence extended to several thousand pages: there were 2000 pages of historical evidence alone, and that constituted only one of the issues at stake. The cream of Ontario's legal establishment was well represented on one side of the case or the other: J.J. Robinette, Aubrey Golden, Ian Scott, Paul Lamek, and John Sopinka, to name only a few. Altogether forty-four lawyers were present, sixteen of them QCs. Collectively they represented the government of Ontario, a large number of public and separate Ontario school boards, OSSTF, FWTAO, and OECTA, the Loyal Orange Lodge, the Canadian Jewish Congress, the Canadian Civil Liberties Association, two separate organizations speaking for the independent schools, the English and French Catholic Trustees' Associations, the Coalition for Public Education in Ontario, and, because there were issues that might have consequence beyond Ontario, the governments of Alberta and Quebec, along with the Quebec Association of Protestant School Boards.

The issues before the court were complex, including the relationship between the Charter of Rights and section 93 (both integral parts of the Canadian Constitution), the extent of Ontario's plenary powers over education under section 93, the legal rights of Catholic schools to offer secondary instruction before Confederation, the nature of the Confederation settlement itself, and whether or not it was discriminatory under the Charter to fund one set of religious schools and not others. The stakes were high. As Rosemary Speirs would summarize it in a perceptive column in the Toronto *Star*, the judges might find that Bill 30 was constitutional; or 'they could argue that funding for Catholics was legal as long as all other similar groups are similarly entitled ...; or, the Court might rule ... that separate schools don't have the right to full-funding.' The first would satisfy large numbers of Ontario's Catholics and the Ontario government but leave many public school supporters restless and alienated. The second might cost an estimated $75 million dollars and further sap the hold of the public school system on Ontario's people. The last was the most intimidating: the government might invoke the 'notwithstanding clause' in the constitution, overriding the judgment of the courts, something it was loath to do; but the alternative would be chaos – it had already gone ahead with funding, schools and teachers had already been transferred, and the disruption of the education of 89,000 Catholic high school students was also at risk.[58]

Not surprisingly, given the stakes and the complexity of the case, when the hearings ended the court reserved its decision. Judgment was rendered nearly four months later, in June 1987, almost three years to the week William Davis had made his historic announcement. The court ruled against the appellants, finding that section 93 gave the government the right to extend funding to Catholic schools, and that provisions in the Charter of Rights protected section 93 against the more general Charter injunctions about religious equality rights. It defined its mandate narrowly, however, confining its focus to Bill 30, and side-stepping the larger question of the rights of other religious groups to funding as well. At the end of the fifty-page majority judgment, the author of the opinion, Madam Justice Bertha Wilson, concurred with, and quoted, the majority opinion of the Ontario Court of Appeal: 'These educational rights, granted specifically to the Protestants in Quebec and the Roman Catholics in Ontario, make it impossible to treat all Canadians equally. The country was founded upon the recognition of special or unequal educational rights for specific religious groups in Ontario and Quebec. The incorporation of the *Charter* into the *Constitution Act, 1982* does not change the original Confederation bargain. A specific constitutional amendment would be required to accomplish that.' Thus, she concluded, 'even if Bill 30 is supportable only under the Province's plenary power and s. 93 (3) it is insulated from *Charter* review.'[59] With the appeal dismissed, Bill 30 was finally rendered a secure part of Ontario's Education Act.

Reaction was predictable. The Liberal government was vindicated in the risks it had taken. Catholic leaders were jubilant. In the immediate aftermath there were some bitter words from prominent Protestant churchmen and other public school supporters, but having lost the final round in the courts they were forced to come to terms with the extension of separate school funding at last. Yet, even before the Supreme Court's decision was released, the overall level of antagonism between the main contenders was already beginning to diminish as the Peterson government applied the best salve of all. A sharp upturn in the economy during the mid-eighties allowed the Liberals to increase education grants substantially, easing the insecurities of public secondary school teachers and trustees, and providing additional resources for the expanding Catholic system.[60]

IN THE FOUR OR FIVE YEARS immediately following the passage of Bill 30 there would be bitter struggles in some local communities over the transfer of schools, or the reduction of a small but thriving public secondary school when a new Catholic high school was built or Catholic students were bused to another jurisdiction; there would also be conflicts over the transfer of designated teachers. Yet the overall effects of Bill 30 were relatively modest. Between 1985 and 1990 some 1300 designated teachers were transferred from public to separate boards.[61] Though the number is unknown, some of them were Roman Catholics and presumably had little difficulty adapting to the new environment; a significant number were teachers who were part of *en bloc* transfers of Franco-Ontarian schools from the public to the separate system. Altogether, twenty-six buildings were transferred, seventeen of these *en bloc.* Between 1985 and 1987 only some nineteen thousand students transferred out of the public system, and most of the growth in separate school enrolments – from 63,000 in 1985 to 171,000 in 1990 – resulted from the separate schools' new ability to retain their own students. That undoubtedly exacerbated the decline in public secondary school enrolments, which continued to fall throughout the 1980s, levelling off only in the early 1990s. But a more pertinent contributor was the long-term consequences of the declining birth rates of the 1960s. OSSTF was right to claim that full funding made a bad situation worse, but overall, the effects were much less worse than the federation had made them out to be in 1985 or 1986. For Catholics, on the other hand, it meant not just rapidly expanding numbers but the capacity to offer the full range of programs and special services long offered in public secondary schools.

MODEST ADJUSTMENTS to the immediate circumstances of the educational enterprise, perhaps; but Bill 30 had far-reaching consequences. Ontario's public school system, divided since the middle decades of the nineteenth century, was now entirely sundered by differences in Christian doctrine. Students learn in separate environments and sometimes learn quite different things. There are potent arguments for and against this arrangement. But the sheer *fact* remains a legacy of the events set in motion by William Davis's speech of 12 June 1984.

8

Broadening the Mandate

On 26 June 1984, only two weeks after William Davis's announcement on full funding for Roman Catholic schools, the Ontario Court of Appeal handed down a judgment of no less historic proportions. The Education Act, the court declared, was inconsistent with the Canadian Charter of Rights and Freedoms because it placed limits on the right of individual Franco-Ontarians to a full and complete elementary and secondary education in their own language. 'Fundamental fairness,' it added, 'impels the conclusion that those parents whose children use minority-language educational facilities should participate in managing them.'[1]

It was an enormous victory for francophone parents and educators who had struggled for decades to secure for their youngsters the kind of education that most Ontarians had long taken for granted. The development of francophone education, and of *rights* to that education, was not the only way in which the mandate of Ontario's educational system was broadened and made more inclusive between the 1960s and the 1980s, but because of its significance it deserves pride of place in this chapter.

IN ONTARIO, FRANCO-ONTARIANS constitute a minority twice over. Representing only a small proportion of Ontario's entire population, they are also substantially outnumbered within the Roman Catholic community as well. Some 500,000 Ontarians call French their mother tongue, about 5 per cent of the total population. They are not spread evenly across the province, however; in the eastern and northeastern regions of the province they represent about 15 and 23 per cent of the population respectively, and in some communities they form a near or outright majority. There are also significant clusters in the Niagara Peninsula, Toronto, and the Windsor area.

Despite their small numbers, they were traditionally treated with a good deal of suspicion by many Ontarians because they were both Roman Catholic and French. During the late nineteenth and early twentieth centuries, the Ontario government went to some lengths to limit French-language teaching, forcing pupils to switch to English at a very early age, a policy symbolized by the infamous 'Regulation 17' of 1912. Having failed at outright suppression, by the late 1920s the government began to concede the right of French students to be taught in their own language in the elementary schools, insisting only that students be exposed to progressively greater amounts of English instruction in the senior grades. Thus, by the early 1960s, there was a well-established system of 'bilingual' separate schools giving instruction in French to grade 8, and in some cases to grade 10. To complete their secondary education, however, students had either to attend one of the private French-Catholic high schools, which for many students meant leaving home to attend school elsewhere in Ontario, or go to Quebec. With few exceptions, the only other choice was to switch to an all-English public high school. The result, even in the 1960s, was a massive dropout rate far exceeding anything exhibited by their English-speaking peers.

By the early sixties there was a growing sense that something had to be done. There had long been demands for redress from Franco-Ontarian educational and cultural organizations, but the decisive factor was undoubtedly the explosion of nationalist sentiment in Quebec. For other Canadians the message of the 'quiet revolution' was simple: either recognize the existence of two founding cultures and languages, or risk the break-up of the nation. Many changes followed, among them significant shifts in educational policy. In Ontario two problems had to be addressed. One was *legal* recognition of the right of Franco-Ontarians to instruction in their own language: despite the growth of French-language elementary schools since the 1920s, they existed de facto only, at the discretion of the minister.[2] The other was the provision of French-language secondary education.

In the second half of the 1960s, John Robarts played an admirable role in a number of issues relating to national unity, and French-language education was one of them. In a historic speech in August 1967 he announced that the government would encourage the establishment of, and provide financial support for, the development of French-language secondary schools. The next year the government adopted the report of an advisory group, the Bériault Committee, which recommended enshrining in law the rights of Franco-Ontarians to an education in their own language.[3]

There was a problem with the expansion of secondary education, however. Franco-Ontarians were mainly Catholic and sent their children to
separate schools. But the government could not very well extend funding
to Catholic francophone secondary schools and refuse it to their
anglophone counterparts. Thus Robarts' solution to the problem was to
create French-language secondary schools but to lodge them within the
public sector. There would, in other words, be francophone secondary
schools but not francophone Catholic secondary schools.

The key legislation was enacted in 1968. Where there were at least thirty
French-speaking pupils in the primary, junior, or intermediate divisions,
and at the request of ten or more French-speaking ratepayers, a French-
language class had to be established. Where numbers warranted, there
had to be a French-language elementary school. For the secondary schools
there were to be two options: certain subjects might be taught in French
within an existing secondary school, or a distinct secondary school might
be established. That decision, however, was left in the hands of local
boards. Finally, boards with francophone instructional units were to establish advisory committees, composed of three members of the school
boards and four ratepayers chosen by francophone ratepayers, to make
recommendations on all matters relating to the education of francophone
students. But the committees were advisory only; jurisdiction was still
vested with the board itself.[4]

Especially in light of the record of earlier political leaders in Ontario,
Robarts deserves great credit for establishing the principle that Franco-
Ontarians had a right to instruction in their own language from kindergarten to grade 13. And the impact of the legislation at the secondary level
was quite dramatic: a rise in the number of francophones enrolled in
Ontario's high schools from just under 10,000 in 1967–8 to nearly 25,000
in 1970–1, and over 31,000 by 1975–6.[5]

BUT THE LEGISLATION also bred a festering sore. Through the decade that
followed, there would be a series of spectacular local conflicts over the
establishment of French-language secondary schools – bitterly divisive
conflicts pitting French and English neighbours against each other in
battles that sometimes went on for years. Because other historians have
offered detailed accounts of these disputes, I will not reiterate them here;[6]
still, the names rang through the 1970s: Sturgeon Falls and Cornwall early
in the decade, Essex County and Penetanguishene in its latter half. The
major dust-ups may have been few, and some boards and their advisory
committees worked in harmony throughout the entire period; however,

French-language instruction was never far from the headlines or the nightly newscasts, and eruptions occurred not just in Sturgeon Falls or Penetanguishene but in Toronto, Burlington, London, Kirkland Lake, Elliot Lake, and other places besides.[7] In nearly every case the central issue was whether or not the board was going to follow the advice of its French-Language Advisory Committee (FLAC) and create a distinct French-language secondary school.*

Part of the problem lay with the legislation itself. The right of individual students to instruction was not embedded in law. A threshold of twenty secondary students was required before boards had to provide it; and after that the extent of provision was governed by the phrase 'where numbers warrant,' something determined by each local board. A board might agree to provide an entire building, or it might house a French unit within an existing school, or it might provide French-language classes in some subjects. It might take the advice of its French-Language Advisory Committee or it might not; certainly it didn't have to. Thus the legislation incorporated a generous vision but also assumed a fund of goodwill on the part of anglo-dominated boards and the ratepayers who elected them. It also assumed a generous capacity to pay for the expansion of French-language instruction.

Right from the beginning, many francophone parents, most FLACs, and provincial organizations claiming to speak for francophones argued that there was only one best solution – distinct French schools where not only the language of the classroom but the language of the halls and playgrounds was French. They had good grounds for this stance, and a growing body of research backed them up. Mixed schools where enrolments and ambience were overwhelmingly English were 'assimilation factories' undermining the raison d'être of French-language instruction itself. In too many mixed schools, moreover, francophones had to switch over to English-language instruction for most of their senior high school subjects, especially mathematics and sciences, a circumstance that invited failure, disproportionately increased dropouts, and restricted opportunities for post-secondary education. Given these two arguments, it is not surprising that advocates of francophone education, French and English alike, condemned any compromise that fell short of distinct secondary schools. The sustenance of two official languages and cultures in Ontario, as in other parts of Canada, demanded the sustenance of an education in a genuinely French environment.

*I will use the word 'distinct' throughout to avoid any confusion with 'separate' schools.

There were, however, some very real constraints in achieving that goal. The legislation of 1968 virtually coincided with the beginning of an era marked by declining enrolments and financial restraints imposed by both the provincial government and pressures from local ratepayers. Capital expenditure was tightly capped and people knew that by the late 1970s there would be empty classrooms in high schools across the province. In some areas this provided the opportunity to create distinct francophone schools; in others it meant consolidating space and resources by providing French-language instruction within an existing school. Declining fertility rates were even more dramatic among francophones than other Ontarians, resulting in fewer francophone children to be educated and greater conflict over the 'where numbers warrant' clause. Moreover, francophone immigration from northern and eastern parts of the province to large urban communities in southern Ontario meant that they were more dispersed among a sea of anglophones. Francophone parents were themselves divided, some favouring distinct educational environments, others believing that mixed schools would ensure their children learned the English skills they needed to prosper.[8] While there was always some bigotry, in the main trustees did not oppose French-language instruction per se; to them, the issue was distinct buildings, staff, and principals, and all the extra costs that entailed. And then there was the political pressure from anglophone parents angered about losing a neighbourhood elementary school when it was converted to a French-language unit, or about a decline in the level of service their own children might experience when a small-town high school was split in two.[9]

All of this made the issue contentious under the best of circumstances. But the larger political environment ensured that it was an explosive one. During the 1970s, as the 'Quebec question' came to dominate the national agenda, some of the most influential voices in Ontario politics were adamant that francophone rights, in education as in other things, be protected or extended. Sturgeon Falls and Penetanguishene were national stories, and especially in Quebec were used as proof of enduring anglo bigotry. Even the *Globe and Mail*, normally death on anything that increased educational spending, was at the forefront of those calling for an end to a situation that allowed local boards to refuse to build brand-new schools for francophones.[10]

AFTER MORE THAN A YEAR of parental protests, student boycotts, and sit-ins over the Nipissing Board of Education's refusal to create a distinct French school in Sturgeon Falls, in 1971 the minister of education ordered an inquiry, headed by Thomas Symons, then president of Trent University, into French-language education across the province.[11] Symons made some valuable recommendations on the subject which would be enacted into law; but he failed to address the critical issue before him: exactly how many students were necessary before a board was required to provide a distinct French-language high school. And thus the *dénouement* in Essex and Penetanguishene, where the government allowed local disputes to explode into national headlines before finally being forced to settle matters that were making it difficult to convince outsiders that Ontario had any interest in a renewed Confederation.

The solution was easy in theory: give francophones control over their own schools and the resources to sustain them. By the late 1970s two models of governance had their advocates: entirely independent francophone school boards; and some less radical arrangement allowing francophone ratepayers within each board a much greater say in the structure and administration of their schools. The first option, long preferred by francophone lobby groups,[12] was flatly opposed by the government; as Bette Stephenson would put it in 1979, 'Such an action would, in effect, initiate the establishment of a third separated school system in Ontario, a development the government does not support.'[13] Davis and Stephenson were, nonetheless, now willing to consider some more limited form of local francophone governance, especially in areas like Ottawa-Carleton where there were large numbers of francophone students, and much agitation on the subject.

WHAT REALLY BROKE the issue open, however, was the passage, in 1982, of the Charter of Rights and Freedoms as part of the country's constitution. Though negotiations had been tough, and some provinces reluctant, the federal government had finally been able to get an agreement, enshrined in section 23 of the Charter, on minority educational rights across the country. The critical phraseology was that English or French parents, regardless of where they resided, 'have the right to have their children receive primary and secondary instruction in that language.' Included was a 'where numbers warrant' clause, but that too would be subject to judicial review.

Though the implications of section 23 would remain uncertain until the courts interpreted the Charter, there was now no question that some changes had to be made, and in March 1983 Bette Stephenson embarked on two major initiatives. First, Ontario's 'where numbers warrant' clause was to be dropped entirely: every French-speaking child would be guaran-

teed the right to a French-language education, either through direct
provision, or by a school board purchasing adequate services from another board. Second, forthcoming legislation would add a minimum of
four French-language school trustees to all school boards with at least five
hundred francophone students or where francophones constitute at least
10 per cent of total enrolment; and these trustees would have jurisdiction
over both the finance and administration of French instructional units.[14]

In order to head off the possibility of a constitutional challenge, the
government also referred the matter to the Ontario Court of Appeal,
asking for a ruling on two key questions. Did the 'where numbers warrant'
clause in the Education Act violate section 23 of the Charter? And was the
Education Act inconsistent with the Charter because it did not give
francophones a role in managing their own schools? On 26 June 1984, as
we have already seen, the judges replied that the Education Act violated
the Charter on both counts.

The nearly coincident announcement of full funding for the Roman
Catholic schools had its own impact. While the vast majority of francophone
elementary schools had always been part of the Catholic system, their
secondary schools were in the public sector. Did full funding mean that
Ontario would now see the emergence of a dual system of francophone
high schools? The prospect split francophone communities, especially in
northern and eastern Ontario, and created much acrimony. But negotiations between French and English Catholics, and between public and
separate school boards, resulted in a substantial number of *en bloc* transfers
of entire schools from one system to the other. This did not occur everywhere, however, with the consequence that in some communities
francophone loyalties remain divided between public and separate high
schools, and two small secondary schools exist where one larger one might
serve young people better, and at less cost. That outcome was virtually
inevitable once two incongruent political decisions were placed in conjunction: in 1967, to encourage francophone secondary education within
the public system in order to avoid funding Roman Catholic high schools;
and, in 1984, to fund Roman Catholic as well as public high schools.

The uproar over full funding, on the other hand, had one indisputable
advantage: as Stacy Churchill remarks,

Franco-Ontarians were spared a vast, province-wide outcry over the implications of the Appeal Court decision. Public attention was directed mainly at
the joust between the great education bureaucracies and power groups
concerned with the Catholic funding issue. In December 1984, the Education Act was revised and Bill 119 received Royal Assent. With little fanfare,

Franco-Ontarians received ... the right to have an education in French even
on an individual basis, thus going beyond the constitutional guarantee of
'where numbers warrant.'[15]

The governance issue proved more difficult.[16] Here, proposed legislation was delayed first by the political turmoil of spring 1985, then by the
new Liberal government's preoccupation with the full funding issue.
Peterson and Conway were no more enthused than Davis and Stephenson
about creating distinct francophone school boards for the entire province.
But they were committed to some form of francophone governance, and
their own proposals emerged in the form of Bill 75, which became law in
July 1986. Beginning with the school board elections in 1988, there would
be French-language sections on local school boards, with francophone
trustees, elected by francophone voters, responsible for the management
of French-language schools. Because of their special circumstances, two
distinct French-language school boards were to be created as well, one for
Metropolitan Toronto and the other for Ottawa-Carleton.

BILL 75 DID NOT ELIMINATE all the problems of preceding decades, and in
the aftermath many francophones continued to chafe at the constraints of
legislation that made them participants in local decision-making rather
than independent policy-makers for their own schools. That question
would only be fully resolved in the late 1990s. Between 1967 and 1986,
nonetheless, enormous gains had been made in achieving an equitable
educational environment for francophones. It could not have been accomplished without a certain magnanimity on the part of key politicians
and a large number of English-speaking Ontarians. Yet too much should
not be made of that. The outcome might have been very different had
influential Ontarians not been so alert to the consequential rumblings
emanating from Quebec. And even then the gains had to be fought for,
and fought hard for, by Franco-Ontarian students, parents, teachers, trustees, and provincial organizations. As late as the mid-1980s, francophones
from Penetanguishene had to go to court, and *fight an appeal by their own
government*, before they won the right to funding and facilities for secondary education equivalent to that given local anglophone students. Still, by
1986, Ontario was most of a world removed from Regulation 17.

II

Throughout the post-war decades large numbers of immigrants had settled in Ontario and enrolled their children in the public or separate

schools. Their presence elicited three sorts of responses. One was the development of 'English as a second language,' designed to assist children whose mother tongue was not English to make the transition to English-language instruction. In the city of Toronto, ESL had a history reaching back to the 1950s, and in the following two decades the program spread to most communities with significant immigrant populations. A variation, increasingly common in the 1970s, was 'English as a second dialect' for those from English-speaking countries whose form of speech was not standard Canadian English.[17]

A second response was to rewrite textbooks and other course materials to remove the exclusive emphasis on the anglo-Canadian experience and, more important, to eliminate stereotyped or demeaning characterizations of other customs and cultures. More positively, this effort meant celebrating the variety of heritages that composed modern Canada, teaching tolerance and the virtues of pluralism. By the mid-1970s, when visible minorities were subjected to taunts and attacks in and out of school, anti-discrimination programs began to be incorporated by boards and the ministry as part of their more general policies on multiculturalism.[18]

Neither ESL nor the ministry's brand of classroom multiculturalism stirred up much dissent. What was much more controversial was the language-of-instruction issue.[19] While most parents might be anxious to have their children learn English, it was common for them to want to pass on their own language and culture as well; indeed they found it hard to imagine one without the other. There were also practical reasons: communication between the generations was an essential prerequisite for cohesive families. Thus it was not surprising that groups of parents or voluntary organizations established weekend or after-hours classes to keep the mother tongue alive and to maintain the fundamental link between language and culture. By the late 1960s and early 1970s, however, there were groups beginning to press for such instruction in the public schools, and in some metropolitan boards, trustees prepared to back their demands. The problem was that the Education Act was quite explicit in this matter. Except for transitional ESL programs, there were only two languages of instruction permitted in Ontario schools: English and French.

By the mid-1970s intense pressure to change the legislation was being brought to bear on the ministry by the Toronto Board of Education, and even more so by the Metropolitan Toronto Separate School Board, which had established a large and vibrant program of Italian-language instruction, taught during an extended school day, and substantially subsidized by the government of Italy. Once again, the Tories were caught in the

cross-pressures of politics, pushed in one direction by those who opposed
the divisive effects of separate classes in the culture and language of a
variety of ethnic groups, pressed in the other by a hunger for the votes of
ethnic constituents eager for some public funding and for a concrete
recognition of their place in Ontario's school system.

Facing an election later in the year, the Tories hit upon the compromise
that became the 'Heritage Language Program' of 1977. English and
French were to remain the only legal languages of instruction during the
official five-hour school day. However, boards were permitted to establish,
and a funding formula for government grants was put in place to support,
third-language instruction after school or on weekends.[20] Five years later
some 82,000 students, representing more than fifty language groups, were
enrolled in heritage language classes.[21] While there was renewed pressure
from Toronto activists in the early 1980s to incorporate the program into
the school day proper, the Tories refused to budge, in part perhaps because the compromise appeared to satisfy the majority of ethnic parents.[22]

WHILE THE EDUCATION of native children living on reserves located in
Ontario is the constitutional (and financial) responsibility of the federal
government, a substantial number attend the province's public schools.[23]
Many families of native ancestry are not legally members of a reserve
community and thus are not eligible to attend schools financed by the
federal government. Others choose to live in urban areas in both northern
and southern Ontario. Especially since the 1960s, moreover, there has also
been a growing tendency for band councils to enter into contracts with
local school boards to provide all or part of the schooling of children
living on reserves. While the total number attending provincial schools
remained relatively small in the 1970s and early 1980s, enrolments tended
to be concentrated in a relatively few boards.

The hopeless inadequacy of the education provided for native children
was well documented by the mid-sixties, and both the federal and provincial governments, prodded vigorously by native organizations themselves,
began to abandon disastrously unsuccessful policies devoted to assimilat-
ing children as quickly as possible into white society. In Ontario, one
thrust was to try to ensure that wherever there was a significant bloc of
native children bused into the public schools, there would be a native
representative to speak for their interests on the school board. In 1967 the
government introduced legislation permitting boards to appoint a native
member.[24] Most boards did so, but when the Kent County Board of
Education resisted despite the comparatively large native population in its

schools,[25] the government moved to mandatory legislation requiring boards with a hundred or more native children in attendance to appoint a representative named by the band council.[26] Other policy initiatives addressed curricula and classroom issues. On the one hand, there was an attack on stereotyping in textbooks and other learning materials – putting an end to a situation where natives were routinely portrayed as 'savages' or 'heathens,' and replacing such images with more positive portrayals. Indeed, the first vigorous efforts in Ontario against stereotyping generally were focused here.[27] During the seventies, experimental native-studies units and courses began to emerge in some localities, as well as ministry resource guides for instruction.[28] And by the early 1980s the ministry had approved Canada's first senior secondary credit course in native studies and a program of native-language instruction, incorporated (unlike heritage-language instruction) within the regular school day.[29]

III

Given the conviction that all of Ontario's children must have greater opportunity *and* equality of educational opportunity, it is perhaps not surprising that special education became another major preoccupation during the 1960s and 1970s.[30] A few boards, most notably Ottawa, Toronto, and London, had long had exemplary programs for some children with special needs. By the late sixties the majority of boards offered a modicum of services, most commonly classes for 'slow learners,' including the moderately retarded. But coverage was spotty at best, both in terms of geography and the variety of needs met; and services at the secondary level hardly existed at all.[31]

There were two main reasons for this state of affairs. First, children with marked physical, mental, or emotional exceptionalities were considered to be outside the purview of the school system. For decades, school boards had had the legal right to exclude children they deemed 'unable by reason of mental or physical handicap to profit by instruction in an elementary school.' To the extent such children were looked after at all, they became the responsibility of charitable organizations (severely retarded or crippled children, for example), of government ministries other than education, or of parents themselves. Second, the existence of a large group of children with a variety of 'learning disabilities' (dyslexia is just one example) was only beginning to be recognized. In the main, they entered regular classrooms, failed to keep up with their classmates, and were relegated to 'opportunity classes' or some other segregated setting.

As was the case for so many other things discussed in this and preceding chapters, the sixties laid the groundwork for change. The belief that all children had the right to the best education that society could provide, and the kind of education that would enable them to fulfil their aspirations, implicitly encompassed those with special needs. Influential lobby groups demanding that such commitments be made explicit were established. There were several of these, but within the province perhaps the most important was the Ontario Association for Children with Learning Disabilities (OACLD). Founded in 1963, it gradually established local chapters throughout Ontario, united parents and those who worked with exceptional children in a variety of capacities, and not only lobbied vigorously for better services but provided parents with a place to go for assistance and advice. The Hall-Dennis Report, in a passionate and compelling chapter, argued that special education must become a prime responsibility of the school system, and from at least the mid-1960s the Ministry of Education itself was committed to that proposition: grants rose steadily, a special branch of the ministry was created to promote the development of special services, and in 1969 boards were mandated to assume responsibility for all but the most severe cases of mental retardation. Above all, there was school board consolidation, intended, among other objectives, to ensure that boards had the resources to sustain a full range of services for children with exceptionalities.

Paralleling these developments was the emergence of a new pedagogical model. People began to argue that most children with exceptionalities were better served when they stayed with their peers in a regular classroom, receiving special assistance along the way, rather than being isolated in segregated classes or schools. Much influenced by American research and experience during the 1960s, this notion became known as 'mainstreaming' and was quickly adopted by advocates in Ontario as the ideal solution.[32]

Still, there were constraints. Effective response to exceptionalities required early identification and special services. That in turn demanded not only adequate facilities but personnel trained to the task – everyone from school psychologists and social workers to a new breed of special-education teachers who, with sensitivity and skill, could provide assistance to regular classroom teachers, or run their own classrooms. In many cases, the latter required pupil-teacher ratios far below those in regular classrooms. All of this was expensive; indeed it was generally recognized that meeting the demand across the province would constitute the single most costly innovation of the 1970s. And this need coincided with a decade of fiscal restraint. Government grants for special education steadily increased throughout the decade but compulsory provision was not, under these circumstances, contemplated. Though school boards generally tried to maintain their special-education programs, expanding them or creating new ones was less feasible. By 1978, some $369 million was being spent on special education in Ontario's schools, there were nearly 11,000 special-education teachers, and 120,000 students were being provided for;[33] yet it was estimated that 15,000 students were on waiting lists, and another 15,000 had yet to be diagnosed.[34]

By that point, the politics of special education had become irresistible. A minority government could not help but be on the lookout for any policy initiative that would catch the voter's eye and raise its standing in the polls. Both opposition parties were demanding that special education be made mandatory, regardless of cost.[35] Parents in dire need of help were turning to private schools, and paying hefty tuition fees, to give their children help unavailable in the public schools; and their plight was widely publicized by journalists, by the OACLD, and by leading opposition politicians.[36] American legislation of 1974, which had mandated special education in schools across the country, was being hailed by advocates as an exemplar for Ontario.[37] Nor were there the kinds of political cross-pressures that might have made the government hesitate. The expansion of francophone education had its sceptics and its detractors. So did the teaching of 'exotic' languages in the schools. Nobody stood up to denounce helping a dyslexic child to read, or to decry building ramps to accommodate the physically disabled. Whatever its reluctance to commit the province to an expensive new program, the government itself was cognizant of the need.[38] The new minister of education, Bette Stephenson, had her own strong convictions on the matter.

And thus the context for what would become known as 'Bill 82.'[39] Within six months of assuming the job, in December 1978, Stephenson announced three interrelated initiatives. The first was a directive to boards, 'requiring them to offer an Early Identification Program to ensure the learning needs of every child entering schools will be identified. It is essential that physical, mental, emotional, or learning disabilities be identified early, so that remedial programs can be provided promptly. Boards will begin to implement this program by September 1979; it should be fully operational by September 1981.' A second memorandum instructed boards 'to provide educational programs for children with learning disabilities.' And, finally, she promised legislation to spell out the details of how all this was to be accomplished.[40]

It took much longer than expected – a full year – to put the legislation in place. There was much controversy over the extent to which school boards were to be accountable to parents or the courts for the efficacy of their special-education programs, and school boards protested against the costs the bill would impose. The boards were mollified by two guarantees: that there would be a five-year phase-in period for implementation, allowing them time to plan facilities, find personnel, and anticipate their own costs; and a promise by Stephenson of some $75 million in extra government grants. 'Bill 82' became law in December 1980, and was to be fully implemented by all boards in 1985. Though complex in detail, its principles were straightforward: all exceptional pupils were to have, by right, access to appropriate education programs without additional fees. Following diagnosis, pupils were to have a program containing specific objectives, an outline of services that met their needs, and annual review of the suitability of the placement. Parents were given the right to appeal an identification or request a review on behalf of their child. Much to the displeasure of some of its most committed advocates, Bill 82 stopped a long way short of its American exemplar – it largely shielded the government and school boards from legal accountability, and it withheld from parents a substantial voice in the process.* The schools, nonetheless, had now taken on a broad new responsibility for the education of all of Ontario's children.

IV

Though not quite all children, quite yet. There were, after all, large numbers below the age of compulsory attendance, which began at six. By the late 1960s, half-day kindergarten for five-year-olds was well established throughout urban Ontario, and school consolidation made it accessible to rural children as well: by the mid-seventies, kindergarten enrolments virtually mirrored those in grade 1. During these same years, however, there was growing momentum to put four-, and even three-, year-olds in school as well.

Working mothers needed day care. The American 'War on Poverty' in the middle sixties threw up an enormous number of experiments designed to help black and other disadvantaged children succeed at school by offering 'head-start' programs aimed at three- and four-year-olds. The

---

*Parents' rights to determine placement were tested in the courts through the Eaton case in the mid-1990s and denied by the Supreme Court of Canada. For a brief introduction see William J. Smith, 'The Placement of Students with Disabilities and the "Best Interest" Standard,' *Education & Law Journal* 8 (1998): 251–4.

interest in 'compensatory education' quickly spilled over into Canada. Academic research, which grew in volume throughout the 1960s and 1970s, reaffirmed the critical importance of the pre-school years in establishing learning-readiness, not just for the disadvantaged but for all children. Middle-class parents responded with enthusiasm, sending their children to Montessori schools, organizing co-operative nursery schools, or making use of those established by other private or charitable agencies. Lobby groups, such as the Association for Early Childhood Education, began to press boards of education and the Ontario government to make greater provision for young children.

Throughout the period there was a good deal of confusion, and some acrimony, about the primary purpose of pre-school programs: day care or education, compensatory or necessary for all. There was also divided opinion about who should provide them: private or charitable agencies, or public authorities, and if the latter, the school system or some other department of government? By the late 1960s, nonetheless, the emphasis on early childhood *learning* encouraged both school boards and the Department of Education to see pre-school education as a jurisdiction for which they should take responsibility. Initially, the focus was on compensatory education,[41] and that remained the primary concern for most school boards throughout the 1970s, but the notion of universality was never far below the surface. In its inimitable fashion, the Hall-Dennis Committee thought schooling for *all* meant just that: 'priority in time should be given to developing Nursery Schools in the socio-economically deprived areas throughout the province, but the nursery school movement should be given support for all children.' It went on to recommend that the prime responsibility be shifted from the Department of Welfare (later, Community and Social Services) to the Department of Education, and nursery school viewed 'as an educational instrument, not as a child-caring, baby-sitting service.'[42]

The department, and many others, agreed. By the early 1970s government stimulation grants were covering just over 50 per cent of the costs of operating junior kindergartens, Metropolitan Toronto boards had established universal programs, and a handful of other boards were following suit.[43] The motives were not purely altruistic: the grants were tempting, and declining enrolments meant space was available. Catholic boards committed themselves whole-heartedly, and the competition for little bodies encouraged public boards to do likewise. The teachers' federations were supportive in part because JK would prevent redundancies, and in part because there were fears in the early 1970s that the government would allow those outside the federations to qualify as teachers in early childhood education.[44] But the main reason for providing the programs was enormous demand from parents. Their motives may have been mixed, ranging from the desire for day care to more purely educational considerations. It probably also mattered that school board programs were free and most others were not. But for whatever reason, the demand certainly existed. Before 1966, the numbers in JK were so small the ministry did not even bother to report them; by 1975, enrolments stood at nearly forty-four thousand – despite the fact that in these years the number of children born was at its lowest in decades.

The momentum would almost certainly have been even greater except for the financial constraints of the 1970s and early 1980s. A few boards were forced to abandon embryonic JK programs because of the expenditure ceilings, and many more drew back from universality because of the costs.[45] Following a pattern that recurs throughout this chapter, the provincial government was prepared to encourage early childhood education through stimulation grants and other forms of promotion. But during the 1970s there was no talk about requiring boards to offer JK – on the part of the government at least.[46]

Yet demand continued to swell. By 1985 the difference between grade 1 and JK enrolments in Roman Catholic elementary schools was only 10,000 students. In effect, separate school enrolments in JK were beginning to approach universality. In the public system the proportion was lower, but it still represented nearly 35 per cent of grade 1 enrolments.[47] In other words, though neither kindergarten nor JK was mandatory, by the end of the sixties Ontario had added one full year of schooling – the kindergarten year – for the vast majority of children, and, a decade later, was well on the way to adding yet another.*

V

At the beginning of the Second World War, Joan Sangster writes of Ontario, 'only one in twenty married women worked for pay ... by 1961 it was one in five. By the mid-1960s the census indicated that one-third of Ontario's workforce was female, and that more than 50 per cent of these women were married.'[48] They moved into an occupational structure, nonetheless, that was highly segmented by sex. Their aspirations were

---

*Almost all of the senior and junior kindergarten programs, however, were half-day, not full-day.

often contained within occupational ghettos such as clerical work, sales, nursing, and elementary school teaching. In most jobs, they were paid less than men and they had far fewer opportunities for advancement.

Women only had to look around to notice these inequities, and not surprisingly, their entry into the workforce was accompanied by growing discontent about the disadvantages they faced. By the mid-1960s, established women's organizations were calling for a general reassessment of women's place in Canadian society – an initiative that would result, in 1967, in the appointment by the federal government of the Royal Commission on the Status of Women in Canada (RCSW).[49] At the same time, a new generation of highly educated young women was emerging from Canada's colleges and universities, self-confident about their skills and abilities, often radicalized by the student movement of the 1960s, and eager not just to participate in the country's existing political and economic structures but to reshape gender relations within them. Together, these two groups would give birth to what has become known as 'second-wave feminism,' a movement that would have a large impact on the last thirty years of the twentieth century.

In education, the first tremors were already being felt by the late 1960s. There were only five women (out of a total of twenty-four members) on the Hall-Dennis Committee, but each had the kind of activist background typical of those who were also agitating for the creation of the RCSW – women who had played senior leadership roles in the federations or trustees' associations, who had held elected office on school boards, or were prominent in other areas of Canadian life. In part because of that, *Living and Learning* presaged the RCSW on two important points: it contained a specific recommendation on the need to open promotion opportunities to women teachers; and, as part of the more general argument about greater curriculum choice, it called for an end to the sex-role stereotyping of subjects and program options.[50]

It was the report of the RCSW, however, that provided the chief impetus. While not its only focus, education occupied a long chapter that reviewed schooling from kindergarten to PhD, adult education and training, and the special needs of immigrant and native women. At its centre was one basic proposition: '[E]qual opportunity for education is fundamental: education opens the door to almost every life goal.'[51] By 1970, few educational opportunities were formally closed to girls, but a wide variety of pressures from families, teachers, peers, and the media tended to foreclose choices and steer girls into areas of traditional female work – into program options like commercial courses, into arts and social studies rather than science and mathematics, into job training at the end of high school rather than preparation for post-secondary education.

Access, in other words, was fundamentally dependent on the elimination of sex-role stereotyping. This could not be done by the schools alone, the commission warned; families, government, and business all had to do their part. But schools reinforced such stereotypes in powerful ways, through teachers' unexamined assumptions and classroom practices, and, above all, by the way in which learning materials portrayed the typical activities of girls and boys, men and women. Mothers, textbooks told children, stay at home; fathers go to work; boys 'are typically active and adventurous but girls are not.' The sex roles described in too many textbooks 'provide few challenging models for young girls and they fail to create a sense of community between men and women as fellow human beings.'[52]

Young girls also needed 'role models,' examples to awaken aspirations and proofs that their aspirations were capable of realization. Here the key arena was the workplace, including the schools. In Ontario, for example, there were far more women elementary school teachers than men; yet in 1967, 'of a total of 3,459 elementary school principals only 925 were women.'[53] But the issue was broader than role models alone: as a matter of basic equity, women must have the same opportunities as men to participate in making the decisions that shaped economic, social, and political policy.

The RCSW was enormously influential. It provided a national forum for discussion of all the relevant issues, the report itself was a best-seller – it was reprinted three times – and the momentum it helped generate gave birth to national and provincial organizations devoted to translating its recommendations into policy and law. In education, as in so many other areas, it set most of the agenda for the two decades that followed its publication in 1970. The one element to be added was the distinctive contribution made by young academics and activists only just beginning their careers in the late 1960s and early 1970s in reorienting a wide range of academic disciplines in order to recover women's past and rethink gender relations in contemporary society.[54]

THOUGH ITS RESPONSE was sometimes halting or half-hearted, government could hardly ignore the demands for change on a range of issues.[55] Within the school system, however, second-wave feminism had this great advantage: highly educated women were already employed in large numbers, they had a pre-existing organizational base in the federations, the FWTAO

in particular had a long history of decorous feminism, and by the late
1960s it also had an experienced leadership committed to equity issues. In
some boards there was also a caucus of trustees ready to press forward
themselves, or work co-operatively with federation affiliates. By the mid-
1970s, for example, the Toronto Board of Education had a sophisticated
curriculum-development and equity unit that would provide much of the
early impetus in developing new learning materials, and in establishing
more equitable promotion policies.[56] And Toronto was soon joined by
most large boards, which by the late seventies and early eighties had part-
time or full-time consultants or committees at work on these issues;[57] from
1973 onward, so did the Ministry of Education.[58] The work involved both
consciousness-raising and policy change. Research by women teachers and
academics drew attention to the sex-role stereotyping pervasive in the
textbooks of the day, and to the entire absence of girls and women in high
school course materials ranging from history, English literature, or 'Man
in Society' to mathematics and science.[59]

But content was not the only problem; there were also the routines and
unexamined assumptions embedded in classroom practice. Summarizing
the work of a task force on women established in 1975 by OSSTF, the
authors of *At What Cost?* remarked that it had found that teachers 'discriminate between boys and girls, that male and female teachers discriminate in different ways, and that male and female teachers had different
expectations for their students depending on the sex of the student.
Secondary school teachers must become aware of the subtle ways in which
they discriminate on the basis of sex and make a conscious effort to free
themselves of sexual bias.'[60]

The message was disseminated not only in research reports and academic articles, but in federation journals, professional development semi-
nars, conferences, popular magazines, and the daily press.[61] Accompanying
mounting evidence about the forms and diversities of sex discrimination,
moreover, there was a growing volume of material that offered alternative
ways of doing things: resource guides on sex stereotyping, inclusive language, and women's studies; new materials for guidance, model teaching
units, or even entire courses devoted to women. Initially, much of this was
generated by school boards or local federation affiliates, but from the mid-
1970s the ministry was increasingly engaged in producing its own material
and promoting the use of such resources across the province.[62]

Ministry policy reflected these enthusiasms as well. *The Formative Years*
(1975) condemned all forms of sex-role stereotyping in the primary and
junior grades; *HS1 1979–81* discountenanced sex segregation in high

school courses or programs. In the mid-1970s, moreover, the ministry established criteria for vetting all new textbooks not only for sex-role stereotyping but to ensure a balanced portrayal of boys and girls, men and women in a variety of roles, and an adequate representation of women's contributions to society.[63]

By the mid-1980s, a decade or more of hard work by people within and without the ministry was rewarded when *OSIS* included a section on sex equity that incorporated all of the bases. It repeated the directives of *The Formative Years* and *HS1 1979–81*, but it also went a good deal further, demanding 'a balanced representation of the achievements of women' in all learning materials, and it concluded that 'the philosophy of sex equity ... should permeate all aspects of the school's curriculum, policies, teaching methods and materials, and assessment procedures, as well as attitudes and expectations of its staff and all their interactions with students, parents, and the community.'[64]

WHILE ONE THRUST of second-wave feminism in education focused on curriculum and classroom practice, the other zeroed in on the gross imbalance between men and women in managerial roles. In 1967 the RCSW had found 'only' 925 women principals in Ontario's elementary schools; by 1974, that number had dropped to 230. Why? a *Globe* reporter inquired. 'Officials at the FWTAO say the answer is simple. Many of the women principals were heads of small schools. When the schools were consolidated with others, the men became principals.'[65] There was no parallel decline in the high schools because women principals had always constituted a tiny minority: as OSSTF's Task Force on Women noted in 1975, women represented 37 per cent of high school teachers, 5 per cent of vice-principals, and 2 per cent of principals.[66]

There were a variety of reasons for this imbalance,[67] but the most specific barrier was the Principal's Certificate, a prerequisite for the job. Though the certificate came from the ministry, nominations for entry to the course came from board selection committees. As one senior FWTAO executive put it in 1970, 'It's a vicious circle. You have to be named as a principal before taking the course, and women don't get named to be principals.'[68] The solution was double-barrelled: raise the aspirations and ambitions of women, and break down the barriers that excluded them.

Though other federations, most notably OSSTF, were active as well, the role of FWTAO was especially important in both respects. From 1969, for example, it began to run summer leadership courses for its members,[69] as well as engaging in a variety of other initiatives to equip and encourage women to apply for promotions. It was also at the forefront in lobbying for change at both the provincial and local level. Through the 1970s and early 1980s, nonetheless, it was hard slogging. Some school boards had affirmative-action plans in place by the mid-1970s; others did nothing. Beginning in 1973 the government introduced policies to improve the representation of women at senior levels of the civil service, and one result was an increase in the number of women in leadership roles in the Ministry of Education.[70] But local boards hired their own personnel, and Thomas Wells was reluctant to do more than express his concern and issue memoranda exhorting the boards to do better.[71]

Under Bette Stephenson's leadership, there was more determination – in 1979 the ministry established 'an Equal Opportunity / Affirmative Action Unit' to promote equity at all levels of the education system.[72] Still, the Conservatives shied away from imposing it, and the lack of progress led FWTAO, at its annual meeting in 1980, to adopt affirmative action as its major goal for the following five years.[73] One immediate outcome of its lobbying effort was to persuade Stephenson, in 1981, to open the principal's course to anyone who wanted to apply. Three years later, coinciding with the release of a major federal study on equality in employment,[74] Stephenson went a good deal further, launching the Ontario government's 'Affirmative Action Incentive Fund' in December 1984, a plan in which the province would pay school boards 75 per cent of the start-up costs of hiring an affirmative-action co-ordinator. In return, boards were asked to 'adopt a formal policy of affirmative action for women employees,' appoint a senior staff member to develop and co-ordinate an affirmative-action plan 'which would identify goals and timetables for hiring, promotion, and training women employees at all levels,' and collect data on the subject to submit to the Ministry of Education.[75] It remained a voluntary program – even in the mid-1980s government was still not prepared to require school boards to act. But in less than two years some seventy-nine boards had taken the money and met its terms.[76] In December 1986, the Liberal government extended the plan – now renamed the Employment Equity Initiative Fund – for a further three-year period.

WHAT, THEN, HAD BEEN accomplished a decade and a half after the RCSW report? There was a much greater awareness of the sources and effects of sex-role stereotyping for both girls and boys. There was a wealth of new guidance materials about non-traditional career options for young women. Many boards had put an end to sexual segregation in such courses as home economics and industrial arts. There were resource guides on strategies for implementing non-sexist classroom practices, new texts and teaching units on women's studies, new curriculum guides more balanced in the attention they paid to the activities and achievements of both women and men. Women teachers were enrolling in large numbers for the courses that led to the Principals' and Supervisory Officers' Certificates – by 1986 they constituted 44 and 36 per cent of enrolments respectively.[77] Provincial policy had itself undergone a sea-change: by the mid-1980s, sex equity in Ontario's schools, both for students and teachers, was a matter of ministry doctrine.

The extent to which those policies penetrated the routines of most schools was much more uncertain. In an era of financial restraint, textbooks had long shelf lives, and even in the mid-1980s many remained in use that incorporated the most flagrant forms of sex-role stereotyping. If some teachers, principals, and trustees were committed to sex equity, others were indifferent or hostile.[78] If the number of female principals and supervisory officers was increasing, the figures in 1986 were only marginally better than they had been in 1982.[79] By the mid-1980s, the advocates of greater sex equity in Ontario education could claim a beachhead, but it remained to be seen if that gain could be converted into a victory. Within feminist circles themselves, moreover, a debate was already beginning to emerge about just what constituted 'victory' and how it should be measured.[80]

VI

Treating a list of apparently disparate policy initiatives in serial fashion, as I have done in this chapter, may well leave the impression that each is a discrete story with few broad implications for the school system as a whole. That is assuredly not the case. After 1980, no child could be defined as uneducable and thus excluded from access to a suitable education; but the growth of special education was a much broader initiative than that, encompassing by the mid-1980s nearly 10 per cent of all those enrolled in Ontario's schools and absorbing a significant share of total expenditure on public education. Along with the completion of the Catholic system, new provisions for francophone students changed the structure of Ontario's education system in fundamental ways. Junior kindergarten was initially introduced as a form of compensatory education; by the early 1980s some boards were already offering universal access to a full additional year of schooling and a ministry report was calling for mandatory legislation. The attempt to eliminate sex-role stereotyping was not just about greater opportunities for girls but also about avoiding stereotypes for both sexes. To view the initiatives addressed in this chapter as 'add-ons' to the extant school system, or simply as specific accommodations to special-interest groups, is to misapprehend their significance. Cumulatively they were changing both the structure and the mandate of the school system as a whole.

Translating the pressures for change into policies proceeded unevenly at best during the 1970s and early 1980s; but it proceeded nonetheless. Influential advocacy groups were crucial to the process, and so was the political situation during the period of minority government, from 1975 to 1981, when the Tories shopped for any and all additional support they could find. While that is the nature of democratic politics, it should not invite mere cynicism. Advocacy groups, parents, and voters demanded redress for what they viewed as legitimate grievances. Politicians responded not only to political exigencies but also to what appeared to be conclusive research and compelling argument. Obviously they did so within the context of their own assumptions about what was good for the province and what was not, how much the province could afford to pay, their own assessment of policy priorities, and the political cross-pressures they confronted. The Davis Tories did not set out to make a social revolution; but they presided over one in the making, and inevitably put their own stamp on it, in education as in many other things.

9

The Contexts for Policy-Making, 1985–2000

Unlike the long era of Tory rule that preceded it, Ontario's political history during the last fifteen years of the twentieth century was volatile.[1] I have already described, in chapter 7, the fall of the Tory dynasty in June 1985. An accord with the New Democratic Party kept David Peterson and his minority Liberal government in power for two years, until September 1987 when the Liberals went to the polls and won a large majority. Despite a mandate that could have run into 1992, Peterson called an early election in the summer of 1990, and to everyone's astonishment, including their own, Bob Rae and the NDP found themselves holding the reins of office, the first social-democratic party ever to do so in Ontario. Caught up in a vicious recession, but caught up too by their own mistakes, the NDP was booted unceremoniously out of office by the electorate in June 1995, and replaced by Mike Harris's Tories, a very different group of Progressive Conservatives from those led by John Robarts or William Davis.

My review of the era begins with the contexts for education policy-making in the decade or more following 1985. These included demographic and economic trends, government fiscal policy, the acrimonious debate over the quality of public education that reached an apogee in the early 1990s, and a variety of social changes that had implications for Ontario's schools. In the next chapter I will pursue the issues of finance and governance that set the stage for the reorganization of educational administration that took place in the late 1990s. In chapters 11 and 12, I will return to the program of studies and address the policy outcomes of the debate over excellence, accountability, and equity. I will conclude with an overview of educational policy under the Harris government.

I

During the fifteen years after 1985, demographic trends played nothing like the dominant role in Ontario's educational history that they had between the late 1940s and the early 1980s. But they were not without influence. From a high of nearly four children per woman in the late 1950s and early 1960s, the fertility rate in Ontario plunged to something more like 1.5 by the early 1970s, and it remained at that level throughout the 1990s. Because of their sheer numbers, however, the baby boomers were bound to produce a large number of babies. Thus, despite a fertility rate well below zero population growth, the number of births in Ontario began to rise in the early 1980s (see figures 2 and 3). Aptly named the 'baby-boom echo,' its peak years occurred in the late 1980s and early 1990s. After that the number of births began to subside as the last of the baby-boom women passed beyond their peak years of fertility and the much smaller cohort of baby-bust women entered theirs.

Coinciding with the baby-boom echo was a sharp rise in immigration to Canada. Changes in government policy and, more important, the return of good times from 1983 on, boosted the flow of migrants from 84,000 in 1980 to over 250,000 in 1992. Each year just about half of all these newcomers settled in Ontario. About 20 per cent of them were of school age – between four and seven years old – and many more were young adults soon to have children of their own.[2]

It was primarily these two phenomena that reversed the enrolment decline of the 1970s and returned Ontario's schools to an era of modest expansion. For elementary schools the upturn in enrolments began in the mid-1980s (see figure 4). Thereafter numbers would continue to increase through the 1990s, and are predicted to level off just after the turn of the century. Rising enrolments, first in the elementary and later in the secondary schools, were not exclusively due to the baby-boom echo and immigration; increasing attendance of four- and five-year-olds in kindergarten and junior kindergarten mattered too, as did higher retention rates among older adolescents and a large number of adults enrolling in high school courses.[3] Some parts of the province experienced only the most modest change in enrolments, or no change at all; but continued suburbanization caused tremendous stresses in others, especially in the Greater Toronto Area, and around the fringes of most larger cities. Some school boards embarked on building programs unmatched since the 1960s; more commonly, schoolyards were increasingly packed with portables. In such cases the demand for capital expenditures to expand physical plant remained insatiable throughout the entire period.

II

The recession of the early 1980s, with its runaway inflation and double-digit unemployment, was followed by a return to good times. Between 1983 and 1989, economic growth in Ontario exceeded 4 per cent a year, and was accompanied by relatively low rates of unemployment, modest inflation, and rising family incomes. In 1989, however, and again in the first half of 1990, the rate of economic growth declined sharply; by the summer, the Ontario economy had begun a descent into a deep recession – the worst since the Great Depression of the 1930s. The contraction of the economy continued through 1991, with only a marginal improvement in 1992, and that, in turn, was followed by a slow, shaky recovery through the mid-1990s. Once again, unemployment rates spiralled upwards, from 5 per cent in the late 1980s to over 10 per cent in the early 1990s. Previous gains in family incomes were wiped out, and even in the mid-1990s had yet to return to their 1988 peak. From 1991, on the other hand, inflation dropped off dramatically and remained very low through the rest of the decade, at 1 to 2 per cent. For many individuals and families, that was about the only good news during the first half of the 1990s; an aura of uncertainty and anxiety became pervasive in both private life and in public forums like the legislature and the media.[4] And it was only in the late 1990s that strong economic growth began to dispel the gloom.

Anxiety was fed not just by the reality of the recession but by more long-term fears, stretching back to the late 1970s and early 1980s,[5] about the future of the Ontario economy in a changing world. Together, the 'globalization' of economic life and the march of technology appeared to pose a massive threat to both the province's economic well-being and its social structure. By the late 1980s and early 1990s, the pressures of international competition to cut costs and raise productivity led to wholesale restructuring of entire industrial sectors, and of individual firms large and small; in the process, not only blue-collar workers but layers of white-collar and managerial workers lost their jobs. Economic change might well produce some high-tech, knowledge-based, secure, well-paid jobs, though even that seemed doubtful at the height of recession. But equally, it appeared to be producing many more low-skilled, routine jobs vulnerable to displacement, or no jobs at all. Indeed, in 1990 the Economic Council of Canada issued an influential report that documented the development of two distinct kinds of work – *Good Jobs, Bad Jobs* was its title – with little in between.

THE DEBATE ABOUT the nature and demands of the new economy would have a large impact on the rhetoric of educational reform throughout the period after 1985. The bricks and mortar of government fiscal policy, however, had a far greater influence in shaping the politics of schooling under Liberal and NDP governments alike.

As is usually the case, good times meant growing government revenues. The economic boom of the latter half of the 1980s generated enormous tax revenues and filled government coffers to overflowing. Robert Nixon, the Liberal treasurer of the province, was prudent enough to want to run Ontario's public affairs on 'pay as you go' principles, keeping government spending more or less in line with revenues: relative to gross domestic product, there was no increase in expenditure and, in fact, a slight decline. The Liberals, nonetheless, spent most of what they received from the windfall revenues produced by the boom, and raised taxes substantially as well. In real dollars – that is, controlling for inflation – program spending (which constitutes the bulk of government expenditure) rose 4.5 per cent under the Liberals, a substantially greater increase than during the last Davis government or under the NDP.[6] There were large investments in capital projects such as roads, hospitals, schools, and the like, as well as some major program innovations in health care, social assistance, pay equity, and more generous transfer grants to municipalities. What the Liberals did not do was put anything away for a rainy day.

In its first year and a half in power, the NDP pursued a similar path. Determined to fight the recession through government spending, and to cushion its core constituents against hard times, it spent more, not less, money than even its Liberal predecessor, and raised taxes with equal vigour. Beginning in the summer of 1990, however, government tax revenues plummeted relentlessly as profits shrank, and unemployment and bankruptcies rose. The result was that both the deficit and Ontario's debt spiralled upwards. By late 1991, as business and bond-rating agencies began to warn that Ontario was about to hit 'the debt wall,' Rae and his inner cabinet became increasingly convinced that fiscal probity had to become their prime concern. And thus, in January 1992, there was a sharp reversal of the policy pursued over the previous half-decade by both the Liberals and the NDP. Transfers to municipalities, universities, schools, and hospitals, which had routinely increased at anywhere from 6 to 11 per cent a year, were reduced to a 1 per cent increase in 1992–3 and 2 per cent in the two following years. Predictably this provoked great gnashing of teeth from public-sector employers and unions, despite the fact that it amounted to a 5 per cent increase over three years at a time when many private-sector employers and employees were taking a harsh beating. This and other measures, nonetheless, proved inadequate to halt the government's deteriorating financial situation, and thus it attempted a much more drastic remedy in 1993.

What the government needed, Rae and his advisers concluded, was a significant reduction in public expenditure, and it settled on a three-part strategy: more tax hikes, more spending cuts, and a reduction in the total wage bill paid to civil servants as well as to those employed in the larger public sector – two groups that, together, totalled close to a million workers. The latter goal could be achieved by large-scale layoffs or an outright reduction in salaries. For political and other reasons, both were unpalatable alternatives, especially for an NDP government. The government then settled on a three-year wage freeze accompanied by 'temporary layoffs' of so many working days each year, to be taken by all employees in the public sector. The effect was equivalent to a 5 per cent wage cut for each of those three years, or, for the government, about $2 billion in savings. The original plan was to negotiate the details with managers and unions, the government believing that the latter would agree to participate in a 'social contract' designed to further the interests of all Ontarians. When the unions refused to play ball, the 'contract' was imposed by legislation, a step that alienated large numbers of NDP supporters, fractured the government's alliance with the powerful public-sector unions, and contributed mightily to its defeat in June 1995.

In conjunction with a succession of tax hikes and cuts in program spending, the 'social contract' helped put a modest dent in the total amount spent during the last two years of the Rae government. The impact of a decade of Liberal and NDP rule, however, was to increase substantially the level of public expenditure in Ontario – from $29 billion in 1985–6 to $52 billion in 1993–4. Even when estimated in real dollars, the increase was dramatic, and more dramatic yet was the growth in the proportion spent just to service Ontario's public debt, a result mainly of the recession but of NDP policy as well.[7]

HOW DID PUBLIC EDUCATION fare in this fiscal environment? Under both the Liberals and the NDP there was a substantial increase in capital spending for school construction and renovation. Expenditure on operating grants is a rather different story. First, consider the proportion of the Ontario budget devoted to education. In the glory years of the late 1960s, education (K to PhD) constituted the largest single category of expenditure, claiming 33 per cent of every dollar spent by the provincial government. By the time the Liberals took office that figure had declined to 20 per cent and it remained at that level until 1992–3. Then it declined further until it stood at 17 per cent in 1994–5.[8] Spending on elementary and secondary schools followed a similar trajectory: 24 per cent of the budget in 1971–2; 12.5 per cent by the late 1980s; 11.5 per cent in 1994–5.[9] In financial terms at least, education simply did not occupy the pride of place on the public agenda that it had from the late 1950s to the early 1970s.

A second approach to the question leads to a similar conclusion. Between the mid-1980s and the fiscal year 1991–2, spending by the Ministry of Health increased by an average of 11 per cent a year; growth in spending on social assistance was over 10 per cent in every year from 1986–7 to 1992–3 – that is to say, not simply in hard but in good times as well.[10] Increases in operating grants for schools were much more modest: indeed, just above the rate of inflation. And if one deducts money earmarked for a variety of new programs, it is probably more accurate to say that increases were designed to account for inflation and nothing more. The exception was the NDP's 'recession fighting' 7.9 per cent in 1991–2. After that came the historically low increases of 1, 2, and 2 per cent.

The story is told most graphically in figures 7 and 8. Measured in current dollars, government grants grew modestly but steadily until 1993, increasing each year under the Liberals and NDP as they had under the Conservatives before them. But controlling for inflation, one gets something that more closely resembles a flat line: grants remained steady, but there was no significant increase in their value before 1993, and beginning in that year, a slight decline. Thus the pattern is one that transcends the policies of particular political parties in power. From roughly the mid-1970s under the Conservative, Liberal, and NDP governments alike, provincial spending on Ontario's elementary and secondary schools was held roughly in line with inflation. Wherever all the growth in provincial expenditure during these years was being directed, it was not into public education.[11]

III

At the very same time, the educational enterprise was faced with a deepening crisis of confidence over the quality of instruction offered in Ontario's elementary and high schools. 'Educators will argue that the schools are every bit as good today as they were 20 years ago,' wrote the editors of the Toronto *Star* in 1987, 'but doubts about quality persist and become stronger ... There's a chasm between public expectations of the schools and what they are accomplishing.'[12] During the late 1980s similar sentiments were expressed in dozens of newspaper columns, and by the early 1990s had become unremitting and far more shrill.[13] A 1993 *Star* editorial, accompanying its ten-part series on the state of public education, was titled 'A failing grade for our schools.' 'A tidal wave of parental anger and frustration,' the editorial began, 'is eroding the bedrock of Ontario's education system,' and it went on to speak of 'the stunning vote of non-confidence' the *Star*'s survey of public opinion had handed the school system.[14] Lambasted in the newspapers, the schools were also targeted in government reports, magazine articles, and angry books – one typical example, by Andrew Nikiforuk, subtitled 'the catastrophe in public education.'[15]

What exactly was wrong with the schools? Illiteracy was widespread because the schools failed to teach the basics. High school graduates were ill prepared for the demands of higher education or the world of work. Large numbers of adolescents dropped out of school because their programs of study were irrelevant to their future needs or present interests. Ontarians invested huge and ever-increasing sums in public education, but no one was accountable for ensuring quality or guaranteeing that big bucks bought big returns.

Newspaper editors and columnists laid such charges again and again; so did groups of angry parents. Virtually unheard-of before the late 1980s, especially outside Toronto, middle-class parent activism blossomed in the early 1990s.[16] The best-known of these groups were the Organization for Quality Education and the Quality Education Network, the latter 'an umbrella organization of 6,000 parents, teachers, and taxpayers' formed in 1991.[17] Though far more evanescent, local groups of militant parents, sometimes joined by disaffected teachers, organized from Kingston and Ottawa to Sarnia, from Toronto to the Lakehead, to lobby trustees and MPPs and harass school administrators in the name of a better education they believed their children deserved and were not receiving in Ontario's schools.

Nor was the discontent limited to a handful of jaundiced journalists or a relatively small minority of parent activists. When OISE carried out its biennial survey of public opinion on education in 1988 the poll yet again confirmed 'an almost continuous decline in satisfaction with the situation in Ontario elementary and secondary schools. In 1979, 50% of respondents ... pronounced themselves satisfied ... only 30% were dissatisfied. In 1988, opinion was almost balanced – 36% satisfied, 37% dissatisfied.'[18] Asked in the 1990s whether they believed the quality of the schools had improved or deteriorated, far more of those polled thought the latter was the case.[19] Other polls revealed worse results. In 1992 a Gallup survey found that 61 per cent of Ontarians were dissatisfied 'with the education children are receiving today.'[20] Of no less import, several Canada-wide polls indicated far greater dissatisfaction with the schools in Ontario than in other provinces.[21]

During the 1980s and early 1990s, Ontario, along with other Canadian provinces, participated in a series of international assessments of knowledge and skills in mathematics and science, conducted on students in selected elementary and high school grades.[22] Though Canadian ten-year-olds did well enough on these tests, from age thirteen or fourteen they began to fall behind youngsters from other countries, and by the end of high school the lag was quite marked. This in itself was enough to provoke predictable headlines across the country, such as 'Canadians "flunk" world science competition,'[23] as well as much hand-wringing about the superiority of Japanese, Korean, or Singaporean schools and students – a virtual industry among commentators at the time. Of considerably more import, the same tests showed that Ontario's results were sub-par compared even to other participating Canadian provinces.[24] Here, on the face of it at least, was hard evidence – the kind of evidence so rarely available in the 1970s – that Ontario's schools were, indeed, in trouble.

THE TEST RESULTS in mathematics and science might have had far less impact had they not coincided with three major reports which exercised great influence among the province's political and policy-making elites, and which received a good deal of attention from the press as well. Two of these were written by George Radwanski, a policy consultant, ex-editor of the Toronto *Star*, and confidant of key members of the Liberal party. The other was produced by the 'Premier's Council,' a blue-ribbon committee of cabinet members, prominent businessmen, academics, and labour leaders, chaired by David Peterson himself, which had been created by the Liberal government in April 1986 and given the mandate to 'steer Ontario into the forefront of economic leadership and technological innovation.'[25] The earliest of the reports was Radwanski's *Study of the Service Sector*, commissioned by the government only a few months after it came to power, and published in December 1986. The second Radwanski report, published in February 1988, was the *Ontario Study of the Relevance of Educa-*

tion, and the Issue of Dropouts. Just two months later, in April 1988, the Premier's Council issued its first report, *Competing in the New Global Economy.*[26]

All three reports were driven by one central issue: the urgent necessity to come to terms with the economic and social consequences of globalization and the new technologies. And all three concluded that if Ontario were to maintain its high-wage economy and its network of essential but expensive social services, it had to adapt to the transforming effects of these two forces. One central component – perhaps *the* critical component – necessary to success was high-quality education. As Radwanski put it in 1986, 'To compete effectively in a new knowledge-intensive global economy that relies primarily on human capital, excellence in educating our workforce is our single most important strategic weapon ... An economically advanced society's ability to compete will depend increasingly on having sufficient world-class experts to provide innovation and leadership, and a general workforce with the skills and flexibility to carry out sophisticated and rapidly changing tasks.'[27]

Neither *Service Sector* nor *Competing* was primarily concerned with education, and neither gave much space to analysing the state of the schools. But Radwanski took it as a given that the schools would have to change 'to meet the needs of a changing economy,'[28] while *Competing* offered a brief but savage indictment, concluding with this punchline:

> Increasing the commitment to educational achievement and completion is the central educational challenge facing Ontario policy makers, educators, and students. All partners in the education system must respond to the fact that student performance on basic skill tests is sliding or comparatively mediocre, that illiteracy rates among those in and out of school are alarmingly high, that almost a third of our students are dropouts, and that our students need earlier and more effective exposure to an expanded scientific and technological knowledge base.[29]

What needed to be done? The old and new basics had to be better taught and levels of proficiency guaranteed through province-wide testing; the curriculum had to be renovated to make it more relevant to the world of work; and there had to be greater accountability to parents and the public to ensure that Ontarians received value for their relatively high level of investment, by either international or Canadian standards.[30]

In contrast to either *Service Sector* or *Competing,* Radwanski's second report, published in 1988, was exclusively focused on education. In this case, his mandate was 'to identify and recommend ways of ensuring that

Ontario's system of education is, and is perceived to be, fully relevant to the needs of young people, and to the realities of the labour market they are preparing to enter, with particular emphasis on the issue of drop-outs.'[31] He began by briefly reiterating the arguments about the changing economy and the critical importance of a highly educated workforce. He then reviewed the statistics on dropouts, which suggested that about one-third of Ontario's young people left school before completing grade 12. That in itself was 'shameful, in a society that purports to understand the importance of education,' he wrote, but it was only the 'most visible manifestation, the symptom, of broader issues that require attention. If fully one-third of the client group for something as vital as education, in a society as education-conscious as ours, is sampling the product and walk-ing away from it in dissatisfaction, the right strategic question isn't "What's wrong with the clients – how can we get them to stay?" It's "What's wrong with the product – how can it be improved?"' That question led Radwanski to launch a swingeing attack on what he saw as a soft, ineffective, rudder-less school system, still mired in mindless Hall-Dennis rhetoric. There was the excessive emphasis on process rather than content that Radwanski claimed was typical of child-centred approaches to education. There was the optionalization of the curriculum that led to excessive choice and the avoidance of essential knowledge and skills. There was the pedagogical focus on affective attributes such as self-esteem, creativity, and a capacity for teamwork, all of which were valuable but not sufficient in themselves: 'education should not be confused with group therapy,' he wrote. 'We ought no longer to shrink from affirming explicitly that education is ultimately about the acquisition of knowledge and skills.'

Radwanski offered a large number of specific recommendations de-signed to improve the situation and I will return to some of these in chapter 11. But his agenda for change was organized around three overarching principles. One of these was 'excellence' – the need for high standards of achievement and a worthwhile curriculum. Ontario had neither of these, but both were prerequisites for a more relevant school system. Second, there was the principle of equity: a worthwhile curriculum must be taught to, and high standards of achievement demanded from, *all* students. That, too, Radwanski argued, we failed to do. Finally, there was the principle that 'there can be no effective pursuit of excellence ... without meaningful accountability.' The school system must be responsi-ble to parents and taxpayers – there must be proof that our goals are actually being achieved, something, he argued, that had been lacking for decades.

Taken issue by issue, there was not much that was new in Radwanski's report. What was original and important was the package itself. Radwanski took the disparate concerns expressed about the state of the schools and bundled them into a coherent platform for the restructuring of education, addressing, at one and the same time, questions about educational standards for all students, dropouts, and accountability to the public for both the quality and the costs of education. And he did this relatively briefly and in readable prose, refreshingly free of the clichés and jargon that marked (and marks) the eduspeak so pervasive in Ontario educational circles, as elsewhere. Many of his proposals were highly controversial, raising hackles and provoking strong reactions.[32] But for that reason, as well as others, *Relevance* was widely discussed in the media, in public forums, and in teachers' and trustees' professional journals. Indeed, more than anyone else it was Radwanski who focused public attention on most of the issues that would dominate the educational agenda from the late 1980s to the end of the century.

THERE WERE OTHER goads. During the 1980s some Canadian provinces were launching their own reform projects, introducing more rigorous or more uniform curricula and assessment regimes, changes that were carefully watched by Ontario commentators.[33] In Britain, Margaret Thatcher's Tory government was in the midst of its own educational revolution, engaged in what a *Globe* editorial described as a 'bare-knuckled assault on the "progressive" school of thought that had dominated British pedagogy since the 1960s.' The *Globe* went on to highlight the main emphases: a national curriculum outlining the content in major subject areas, the introduction of national examinations to monitor achievement, the publication of school-by-school results, parental choice of schools, and funding of schools that might operate independently of Britain's local educational authorities.[34]

Inevitably, however, it was the American example that drew the most sustained attention in Ontario, as in the rest of Canada. In 1983 the National Commission on Excellence in Education published *A Nation at Risk*, which bluntly warned of 'a rising tide of mediocrity that threatens our very future as a Nation and a people.' Its publication, Diane Ravitch remarks, 'was followed by a frenzy of public concern about the quality of education.'[35] An apt description. The mood is nicely captured in the opening lines of an article, 'Saving the Schools: How Business Can Help,' published in *Fortune* in 1988. 'It's like Pearl Harbor. The Japanese have invaded and the United States has been caught short. Not on guns and tanks and battleships – those are yesterday's weapons – but on mental might.

In a high-tech age where nations increasingly compete on brain power, American schools are producing an army of illiterates.'[36] Suddenly the American debate over the reform of education was full of the language of excellence, rigour, achievement indicators, standards, national goals.

Canadian politicians and policy-makers adopted the rhetoric as though it were their own. If George Bush wanted to be known as 'the education president,' then Brian Mulroney wanted to be Canada's education prime minister. If the United States needed national standards and national goals, so indeed did Canada. If 'excellence' was the reigning slogan of corporate America and of that country's educational aspirations, it is not surprising that it quickly became the slogan of choice in Ontario. If *Fortune* asked how business could help save the schools, it was just a matter of time before Canadian business magazines did the same.[37] And when, in 1993, the Toronto *Star*'s Judy Steed interviewed Ontario's deputy minister of education, she noted a book on his coffee table 'that [Premier] Rae is asking everyone in government to read, *Thinking for a Living: Education and the Wealth of Nations*, an American look at "the need for coherence between economic strategy and educational strategy."'[38] As usual, American developments did not merely run parallel to those in Ontario; they played a large role in shaping the way Ontarians identified problems, conceptualized them, and imagined solutions.

ONTARIO ALSO HAD its own, home-grown revolt over pedagogical practice. An issue that had only occasionally surfaced in the 1970s and early 1980s, teaching methods in the elementary schools were a fruitful source of conflict in the decade after 1985. One reason for this was the emergence of a new approach to the teaching of reading, known as 'whole language.' It emphasized informal rather than direct instruction, and exposure to a wide variety of print sources rather than traditional 'readers,' since learning to read was supposed to occur as naturally, and easily, as learning to speak. Children began with whole words and stories, on the theory that they would decipher meanings from the context, thus learning to read by becoming acquainted in this unselfconscious fashion with the look and rules of written language.[39] To puzzled parents, however, it often seemed as if reading was being learned by accident, and the dismissal of phonics instruction by the more rabid whole-language advocates became a particular source of unease. So intense was the controversy that the newspaper editors and reports took to describing it as 'the reading wars.' In fact, the number of articles in the popular press on a subject that in most other eras would only have provoked yawns in all but a handful of reading specialists is quite remarkable.

Whole language, however, was only one subset of a larger conflict over child-centred and activity-oriented approaches generally. More honoured in the breach than the observance even in the 1970s, when much of the primary-school teaching corps relied on pedagogical methods they had learned in the decades before the Hall-Dennis Report, 'child-centred' learning became *de rigueur* as those weaned on the enthusiasms of the late 1960s and early 1970s entered teaching or, more important, became local administrators responsible for determining the learning styles in elementary classrooms.[40] Many parents, on the other hand, were worried, and some infuriated, by teaching strategies that appeared to turn classrooms into noisy playrooms, in which youngsters seemed to learn or not learn as they saw fit, in which children seemed abysmally ignorant of the common rules of spelling or grammar.[41]

To a large extent, the 'debate' over pedagogy was a conversation of the deaf. Too many local directors, superintendents, and other spokespeople for school boards were smugly complacent when parents raised their concerns, and were dismissive even when the weight of research raised serious doubts about the classroom teaching methods they promoted. Indeed, instead of addressing the challenges, they simply discounted those who demanded direct instruction, orderly learning, and accountability as back-to-the-basics fundamentalists, intent on returning the schools to the bad old days of nothing but rote and drill – an educational scenario which virtually no thoughtful contemporary critic wished to contemplate and, more to the point, which had never existed in good classrooms in any case. Their opponents replied in kind, one typical riposte by the Quality Education Network asserting that Ontario 'has one of the worst education systems in the developed world,' and 'anything short of a complete renewal will not do the job.'[42] Particularly in the early 1990s, a middle ground was hard to find. And even before that, one acute observer described it as a 'tug of war between the 3 R's and the pedagogy of joy' which profoundly split communities of parents, educators, and academics alike.[43]

THOUGH NEVER ENTIRELY absent, it was only in the mid-1990s – beginning, indeed, about 1993 – that a literature, and a set of arguments, began to accumulate to counter the critique of public education. Throughout the 1980s and early 1990s, the conventional estimate of the number of dropouts was about 30 per cent; by 1993 better data collection made it clear that it was nowhere near as bad as that: once authorities began to count those who 'stopped out' and then returned to school months or years later, the Ontario figure dropped to something more like 14 per cent, and in some local jurisdictions as low as 5 to 10 per cent.[44] The findings on illiteracy rates for recent high school students were effectively challenged. The significance of international test results was contested on the grounds that, among other things, comparing highly selective and unselective secondary school systems was like comparing apples and oranges.* The pervasive human-capital arguments of the late 1980s also came under scrutiny, observers pointing out that while Ontario might need a cadre of highly educated workers, who might well earn high salaries and hold secure jobs for life, there was much less evidence that staying in school only until high school graduation had any pay-off; that skill levels for large numbers of jobs were dropping, not rising; and that continuing high rates of unemployment even among well-educated young people contradicted the notion that all one had to do to ensure success in the new global economy was tinker with the schools.[45] Even the opinion polls were far from unambiguous: people could, at one and the same time, express dissatisfaction with the quality of the schools, and on more specific or different questions assert a high degree of support for them. Articles and books began to appear that took the critics to task for distorting the evidence and pursuing their own political agendas – most notably a spirited defence of public education by Maude Barlow and Heather Jane Robertson, called *Class Warfare: The Assault on Canada's Schools.*[46]

Until the mid-1990s, nonetheless, the critics had it mostly their own way. While disaffection with the schools had existed since the middle 1970s, moreover, the volume of the din and the level of vituperation during the early 1990s was unprecedented. And even though alternative voices were more frequently heard during the last half of the 1990s, more international and intra-provincial comparisons seemed to confirm Ontario's mediocre educational record, the 'reading wars' persisted, and the attack on soft pedagogy and lax standards continued to be a staple subject for the disenchanted and the cynical. However one-sided, biased, partial, or just plain wrong such assessments might be – and in many cases they were just that – what matters here is their political consequences. In the media, and in the minds of many politicians, policy-makers, academics, businessmen, parents, and taxpayers, the schools stood condemned for their lack of either financial or academic accountability, dismal standards of achievement, suspect pedagogy, and irrelevance in the face of a changing economy. And it was these views which would establish the environment and shape the agenda for curriculum change in the decade or more after 1985.

*The problems were real enough. But those academics and practitioners who dismissed the international tests on that account rarely drew attention to the fact that Ontario's own provincial reviews were producing some equally unimpressive achievement results.

IV

There were other pressures on public education besides. As I have already suggested, the sheer volume of immigration in the last fifteen years of the century had its own impact. But of more importance was the long-term shift in the origins of Ontario's immigrants. Increasingly they had come from places other than Britain or northern Europe, and a growing proportion consisted of what came to be called 'visible minorities.' Throughout the late 1960s and 1970s, a wave of Black immigrants arrived from the Caribbean. They were joined in the 1980s and 1990s by growing numbers from Asia, Latin America, the Philippines, and other parts of the world. Together European and non-European migrants changed the face of urban Ontario. By 1991, Hamilton's population was 24 per cent immigrant, and the figure stood at 20 per cent for Kitchener, Windsor, London, and the St Catharines–Niagara region; for Toronto it was 38 per cent. By 1996 close to half the population of Metropolitan Toronto had been born outside Canada; one in ten had arrived in the previous five years. In the same year, more than half of all visible minorities in Canada lived in Ontario; almost all of them – 1.3 of 1.7 million – lived in the Toronto census area, where they constituted a third of the population.[47]

The newcomers' children flooded into Ontario's elementary and high schools, in sometimes staggering numbers. There are many eye-popping statistics on this point: in 1990, for example, one Scarborough high school had only 39 per cent of students whose mother tongue was English; Cantonese came a close second at 36 per cent, and the rest spoke fifty other languages.[48] But perhaps the most indicative figures came in 1997, when test results recorded the percentage of Grade 3 pupils across the province who spoke a language other than English at home. The provincial average was 21 per cent. For the Metropolitan Toronto Separate School Board, it stood at 49 per cent; in the Dufferin-Peel Catholic schools, 35 per cent; among public boards, Toronto recorded 39 per cent, Etobicoke 42 per cent, North York 51 per cent, Ottawa 36 per cent, Windsor 25 per cent.[49]

The challenge to the schools was enormous. Metro required 1112 ESL teachers in 1990–1 to cope with 96,500 immigrant children, compared to 310 teachers and 9000 students in 1985–6.[50] There were the associated costs of allied services for testing, placement, counselling, social workers, and interpreters. And beyond that there were the psychic costs as teachers and students alike struggled to adjust to the clash of cultures in the classroom, the hall, and the playground.[51] It was not the first time Ontario's urban schools had been faced with the task of educating large numbers of new Canadians, but the particular problems – and successes – of the last two decades of the twentieth century deserve an account of their own.

DURING THE SAME TWO decades, rising divorce rates, and an increasing number of single-parent families and of those where both parents worked, provoked widespread concern in educational circles. While single-parent children had more than their share of educational problems and drew a disproportionate amount of attention, the numbers of single-parent families had grown only modestly between 1971 and 1991.[52] The vast majority of children continued to live with two parents. Not all of the families with two working parents were struggling to survive, but many were, and the pressures to make ends meet, along with the stresses of daily life, appeared to leave more and more children ill-prepared for school either intellectually or emotionally. According to *Globe and Mail* columnist Michael Valpy, writing in 1994, 'split families, two-parent-earner families, stressed and overworked parents, deepening poverty and the tolls of recession and economic restructuring are exacting a price: Canadian society is dumping a lot of distraught, distracted, unhappy and insufficiently loved and nurtured children onto the school system.'[53] Teachers were forced to cope with the consequences; and many voices insisted that the schools had a moral or social obligation to do so effectively.

Though it could hardly be blamed exclusively on the family, the level of violence in the schools seemed to confirm the breakdown of traditional means of socializing the young. By the mid-1970s the organized protests and disruptions of a few years earlier had subsided. They had been replaced, however, by a worrisome increase in problems with individuals. Most children and young people, most of the time, teachers tended to agree, were responsible and well behaved. Yet there were enough challenges to the authority of principals and vice-principals, enough violations of school rules, enough confrontations between teachers and individual students, ranging from outbursts of foul language to assault, to create a substantial conviction among teachers that their authority was under attack. During the 1980s and early 1990s there was a steady increase, year by year, in the volume of reports about schoolyard bullying, racial and sexual harassment, and student assaults on peers and teachers on and off school premises. Indeed, with the exception of the quality debate, no other educational issue received such extensive press coverage, invited so many blaring headlines, or provoked the amount of concern among trustees and teacher federations as this did; conferences, task forces, research studies, and reports piled up on one another in search of its causes, and of solutions that would ensure safe schools.[54]

As with all crime statistics, the issue of rising school violence needs to be treated cautiously and hedged with qualifications. More pressures to report schoolyard incidents, less tolerance for behaviour such as bullying, more encompassing definitions of 'violence,' more complaints about various forms of harassment than in previous decades all contributed to the belief that the phenomenon was out of control.[55] My impression, nonetheless, is that there was some substantial increase in problems with both discipline and violence during the last two or three decades of the century. And given the fact that much larger numbers of older adolescents were now staying in school, it is plausible to think that more of them brought their penchant for rebellion, mischief, and mayhem into the classroom with them. More certainly, the rise in school violence was a *perception* shared by large numbers of teachers and by the public as well, and one that contributed to the unease about a school system in crisis. Said one member of the Royal Commission on Learning in 1993, 'The problem of violence in the schools has been raised at our hearings more than any other issue.'[56]

SCHOOL VIOLENCE MIGHT hog the headlines but yet another issue was far more recalcitrant and more fundamental. When it came to achievement, academic success in elementary and secondary school, persistence through the upper grades, and entry into post-secondary education, the poor fared far less well than the comfortable or prosperous majority.[57] There was, of course, nothing new about this. It was already well documented by the mid-1960s. But despite all the program changes designed to address inequalities of opportunity, the disparities persisted, and with each decade the volume of documentation grew. Even more so than before, moreover, the links between school achievement, ethnicity, and race were obvious. Afro-Canadians, the children of Portuguese immigrants, Latinos, and some Asian groups were disproportionately at risk. The least well-off, native and immigrant alike, did less well in school tests in the basics, fell behind their peers in language acquisition or failed to attain it fast enough to keep up, were more likely to be placed in special-education classes, more likely to be found in the basic or general streams of the high schools, more likely to be segregated into the vocational and technical schools of the larger cities, more likely to drop out before graduating from high school.

Explanations varied: poverty and poor nutrition; inadequate parenting;

other forms of social or emotional deprivation; language difficulties and
cultural differences; the systemic biases of a school system attuned to
'middle-class values'; a Eurocentric curriculum; the inexorable effects of
streaming and the role of the school in a capitalist system devoted to the
reproduction of social and economic inequality. Whatever the causes, the
raw reality of inequities of outcome was not at issue. People might differ
on the former; the latter was there for all but the wilfully blind to see.

   But the meaning of equality of educational opportunity was itself under-
going change. Traditionally, the chief criterion used to measure it had
focused on equal access to the services the schools had to offer. Beginning
in the 1960s, however, in both Europe and North America, there was a
substantial reassessment of that view. Access alone, academics and activists
contended, was not in itself enough. What did equal opportunity mean if it
did not break down barriers for those who had been excluded, or subjected to crippling stereotypes? What did it mean if access to education was
formally guaranteed but children who needed special help and extra
resources failed to receive them? Increasingly, access to schooling per se
was ceasing to be viewed as an adequate definition of equality of educational opportunity, and more subtle arguments were emerging that stressed
the need for affirmative action on behalf of children and young people to
ensure equality of outcome.[58] This reconceptualization had given impetus
to the measures designed to broaden the educational mandate that I have
discussed in the previous chapter. But it would be of no less import when it
came to debates about equalizing chances in the last fifteen years of the
twentieth century.

   That, however, was only one part, and perhaps the most academic part,
of changes in expectations that had been under way since at least the
1960s. When earlier generations of immigrants had failed to adapt to
Ontario's schools nobody had much worried about it, or, at least, identified it as a failure on the part of the school. Many families had always lived
under stress; many children had always been ill prepared for school by
virtue of their intellectual, emotional, or physical disadvantages and thus
fell behind or dropped out. In the late twentieth century, however, there
was far less tolerance for such outcomes, far more criticism of institutions
that failed to address them, far more voices demanding changes designed
to promote both equity of access and greater equality in outcomes. Whether
or not politics and policy-making could respond effectively to these challenges remained to be seen.

The Crisis in Finance and Governance, 1985–1995

In the decade after 1985, I suggested in the previous chapter, government grants to Ontario's schools were held roughly in line with inflation. Yet overall expenditures increased at a quite remarkable rate (see figures 7 and 8). Even when we adjust for inflation, spending on Ontario's public schools rose from just over $6 billion in 1985 to $9 billion in 1993 – in current dollars, from $6 billion to $12 billion! Where did all the additional money to finance the schools come from? The answer is straightforward: it was raised by local boards of education through the levy on property taxes. Or to put it another way, while total spending increased rapidly, the proportion paid by the province dropped precipitously: from 60 per cent in 1975, to 45 per cent a decade later; under the Liberals and NDP, it declined further, to something like 40 per cent in 1991.[1]

Why did local costs rise in this fashion? In the main, the reasons were not much different than they had been a decade or so earlier. There were a lot of costs that local boards could not control. Rising enrolments in the late 1980s and early 1990s meant hiring more teachers, providing more space, adding more buses. So did initiatives mandated by the province, such as special education or the reduction of the pupil–teacher ratio in grades 1 and 2. While young teachers began to be hired again in the latter half of the 1980s, the workforce continued to age, and a steadily increasing percentage of elementary school teachers had undergraduate degrees,[2] pushing more teachers to the top end of the salary grid (see figure 9).

In principle, trustees had some control over annual salary increases and improvements in working conditions. But it was never easy for them to turn thumbs down on teacher demands. Few trustees wanted to provoke the wrath of parents by allowing the schools to be closed by a strike or a lockout. Many trustees, moreover, were sympathetic to arguments, com-

monly put forward by teacher representatives, that improved working
conditions such as a lower pupil–teacher ratio translated into direct gains
in student learning. Thus the outcome of collective bargaining contributed substantially to increasing expenditure. Pupil–teacher ratios continued to fall, from a provincial average of 18:1 in 1981 to 15:1 in 1993.[3] Caps
on class size, and provision for preparation time in the elementary schools[4]
– parts of the school day when teachers did not have to teach – became
conventional provisions in collective agreements in Ontario, and both
raised the number of teachers boards had to employ.

There is some disagreement about how much teachers gained in salaries
and benefits during the 1980s and early 1990s. One specialist in educational finance has claimed 'dramatic real gains' were made; other research
points to more modest increments.[5] But even the latter suggests that
teachers did better than just keep up with inflation. And since salaries
account for the lion's share of school-board budgets, that too was an
important factor in explaining increasing expenditures.

Boards of education, their administrators, and teachers were also on the
front line in coping with the social pressures of the era. The federal
government controlled the flow of immigration but offered no funds to
provide for the education of immigrant children. The province provided
no funds for Canadian-born children whose first language was other than
English or French. Yet such children had to be educated by local schools.
In 1988 alone, as one reporter described it, the Metropolitan Toronto
public board expected to hire two hundred new teachers at a cost of $10
million, in addition to 'the millions already spent on students in ESL.'[6] A
few years later, the same board estimated that it cost $273 extra per pupil
to provide ESL, which helped to boost Metro's average per-pupil spending
well above the provincial average; and when some boards tried to cut back
on ESL programs in the tough years of the 1990s, they incurred the wrath
of immigrant groups and equity activists.[7] Pressed to 'do something' about
school violence, boards responded with research and policy initiatives,
special programs to deal with disruptive and violent students, adult hall
monitors, surveillance cameras in high school corridors, and other measures to enhance security. Anti-racist programs and gender-equity policies,
which might involve additional personnel, were introduced in some boards
well before such measures became mandatory. To boost achievement in
inner-city schools, there were enrichment and nutrition programs, extra
teachers and assistant teachers, social workers and counsellors. Urban
boards expanded their co-op and French immersion programs, moved
towards universal JK, introduced day-school programs for adults, reduced

distance limits for students walking to school, invested in computers and other trendy technology. Some of all this was necessary, indeed essential, to provide all children with a good education and fair chances in life; some of it was, perhaps, not. But the pressures on boards – urban boards especially – were intense, and the additional costs high.

Finally, the ranks of non-classroom personnel blossomed. Between 1980 and 1990, when the student population increased by only 6 per cent, the number of consultants and supervisory officers grew by 22 per cent; by 1993–4, the latter figure had increased to 27 per cent.[8] And board employees of other sorts increased as well. This was not merely the result of featherbedding: more new programs (many of them mandated by the province) demanded more supervision, co-ordination, and central office assistance; the devolution of curriculum control in the late 1960s and 1970s left local boards with the responsibility of designing and implementing their own programs of study; special-education classes needed teacher assistants and psychologists. All in all, by the late 1980s and early 1990s there were a lot of board employees, many of whom were not routinely working in classrooms, and all of them cost money.

BUT WHY SHOULD local property owners have to pick up such a disproportionate share of the bill for the explosive growth in spending on education? To many trustees, and to many others as well, the overriding cause was patently obvious – the failure of the province to honour its commitment, made in the late 1960s, to pay 60 per cent of total costs of education. The Liberals (as well as the NDP) had spent years in opposition hammering the Davis government for funding policies that allowed more and more of the financial burden to fall upon property taxes. And during the 1985 election campaign, Sean Conway was only one prominent Liberal to condemn 'the niggardly, miserable funding' of education by the Tories, promising to restore the provincial share of operating costs to 60 per cent over a five-year period.[9]

Once in power, however, the Liberals dragged their feet. Nothing was done in the first two years to redeem the pledge, and during the run-up to the 1987 election, the Liberals would only promise 60 per cent within a larger effort to reorganize the entire structure of education finance.[10] In 1988, and again in 1990, all-party committees of the legislature urged the government to increase its share of education costs, but without success.[11] In the election campaign of 1990, the NDP launched a biting attack on the Liberals for their failure to provide adequate funding, and reiterated earlier promises that if elected to office they would move to restore 60 per

cent funding over a period of five years, relieving property owners of some
$1.5 billion by transferring it to the provincial income tax.[12] Within six
months of the election, however, Marion Boyd, the NDP's first minister of
education, told the House that there 'won't be much of an improvement'
in the near future, in part because of the recession, but also because the
whole question of financing Ontario's schools needed review.[13] And that
was just about the last anyone heard of the 60 per cent target – something
that had run like a leitmotif through Ontario educational politics since the
late 1960s.

There was actually a perfectly good reason why, once in power, prominent politicians changed their minds about fulfilling election promises.
Taken to task during the 1987 election campaign for not increasing the
province's share of education funding, David Peterson was wont to respond by asking, 'Sixty per cent of what? You can't commit yourself to
60 per cent of the blue sky ... What you have to do is enter into a
relationship with a school board, to make sure there's an agreement on
the approved expenditures.'[14] And in part at least, it was the same question
that had led William Davis to establish the Macdonald Commission on
educational finance at the same time as he announced full funding for
Roman Catholic secondary schools.*

During the first half of the 1970s, Davis had been certain of the answer
to '60 per cent of what?' Because the expenditure ceilings set limits on
what any school board could spend, the government could predict what
the 60 per cent target amounted to. Once the ceilings came off, however,
that safeguard was gone. The government might establish grant ceilings,
thereby setting a maximum limit to its own contribution to local education
costs; but boards could raise, from the taxpayers, any amount they wished,
and by the 1980s, the vast majority of boards raised more than required by
the grant ceilings – in some cases far more.[15]

Trustees' and teachers' organizations claimed that this was necessary
because the grants were inadequate to ensure a quality education for all of
Ontario's children. That might well be the case: there were good arguments to suggest that levels of 'approved expenditure' – the standard
which determined the size of the government grant – ran well below the
real costs of education. The solution to that, as the Macdonald Commis-

---

*The commission, chaired by H. Ian Macdonald, an ex–deputy treasurer of Ontario, was
given a wide-ranging mandate to review and make recommendations about 'the equitable
distribution of financial resources in future years.' While issues relating to Catholic funding were important to its work, the full-funding announcement was the occasion rather
than the cause of the review.

sion pointed out, was for the government to establish a realistic level of approved expenditure and then raise its funding to 60 per cent, or some other appropriate portion, of that figure. But the commission also argued that no government could live with '60 per cent of the blue sky.'[16] In the first place, much larger annual expenditures, requiring a substantial tax hike, would be necessary. As *Star* columnist Rosemary Speirs would later explain, 'In 1986 Ontario paid 45.5 per cent of total school board funding of $7.3 billion. Picking up 60 per cent of the tab would cost the treasury $1.1 billion more. To raise that $1.1 billion, Ontario would have to increase the sales tax to 8.5 per cent from 7 per cent, or increase the provincial share of income tax from 51 to 57 per cent. These are treasury calculations.'[17] Even more to the point, the government had no guarantee that boards would not spend greater sums the next year, and more again the year after that, each increment requiring a proportionate increase in the amount raised by Queen's Park. The government, in other words, would have lost control over its own budget.

If, on the other hand, government wished to exercise control over the costs of education, it could assume all of the expense itself, or return to imposing expenditure ceilings on boards. The latter option had already proved a more difficult (and more politically unpalatable) exercise than expected; equally, both these alternatives would encroach upon – or destroy outright – an effective local voice in education. To remove the right of boards to raise money for education, or to dictate how much could be raised, violated the long-established principle that locally elected representatives were best able to reflect the needs and preferences of their community, and should, therefore, determine appropriate levels of local expenditure.

Thus one conundrum of educational finance in the last third of the twentieth century was, Who should pay for public education, and how should the money be raised? If education was a social good, of benefit to the entire community, then perhaps it should be funded by the province out of provincial revenues. But that would render local autonomy a dead letter. Local autonomy, on the other hand, rested on the power to raise levies on property, long recognized as a regressive form of taxation because it takes from owner and renter alike without regard to income or condition in life.

The Macdonald Commission was not the first to struggle with these issues: they had been a staple of government committees and reports since the 1960s.[18] While the commission found 'provincialization' an attractive option because it was fairer in many respects, it concluded that it was not 'a

viable option for Ontario in the immediate future, given the administrative and political realities in the province today.'[19] Nor was the commission
content to see local autonomy and local responsibility set at naught. It was
essential, however, to lessen the burden on residential and farm properties. To that end the commission recommended three interrelated measures. First, the province needed to establish a realistic level of approved
costs, which would allow government to move to a 60 per cent share and
still maintain control over its own budget. Second, property taxes should
remain an important component of local school finance, but those who
paid residential and farm rates would be eligible for an equivalent credit
on their income tax – a credit to be financed by a designated education tax
levied on personal income. Finally, school boards would only be allowed to
raise amounts in excess of approved expenditure from residential and
farm assessment alone – that is, from local property owners who were also
local voters and who would thus select only trustees prepared to exercise
fiscal self-discipline. By these means, a significant local voice would be
maintained, the provincial government would bear a greater share of
costs, more of the total expenditure would be transferred to the income
tax, and some controls would be put in place to restrain spending.[20]

There was, however, a second critical issue that also had to be addressed
by the Macdonald Commission, or, indeed, by anyone else concerned with
the adequacy and equity of education finance in Ontario. Individual
Catholics had long had the right to direct their residential property tax to
the school system of their choice. But the separate schools had also been
denied equal access to commercial and industrial taxes, which in the mid-
1980s equalled 22 per cent of total school board spending.[21] This was a
source of grievance among separate school advocates, not only because it
denied equity to Catholic school boards, but for the very practical reason
that it left them much poorer than their public counterparts. Full funding
meant that Catholic schools had to be given one of two things: either their
fair share of commercial and industrial assessment or some equivalent
amount from provincial coffers; that much was on the table from the
moment the funding decision was made.

The more important issue, however, concerned the inequities inherent
in commercial and industrial property assessment, which was distributed
very unequally across the province. Indeed that is a bit of understatement:
the lion's share was concentrated in a handful of localities, above all in
Metropolitan Toronto and Ottawa-Carleton. As a result, these assessment-
rich boards found it relatively easy to raise large amounts of money
through modest increases in the property tax rate. To raise the same per-

pupil amount, assessment-poor boards would have had to tax their property owners extremely heavily. Provincial equalization grants were designed to offset that disadvantage by giving larger grants to poor boards, and smaller grants to rich boards. But provincial grants were only paid up to a set per-pupil ceiling. While most boards taxed beyond the ceilings, rich boards could and did raise enormous amounts beyond them. By doing so they were able to raise money for all kinds of educational programs that poor boards could only dream of offering their students.[22]

'From the outset,' the Macdonald Commission concluded, 'we have stressed the importance of equality of educational opportunity in Ontario's education system, and hence, the equalization of financial resources. Having looked at the distribution of wealth among school boards, in terms of taxation revenues from commercial and industrial assessment, we have become acutely aware of wide disparities ... Fairness is the key consideration'; and that meant the ability 'to provide a fair share of the available resources to each pupil, irrespective of location of residence.'[23] The commission's recommendations were explicit: in the name of equity, commercial and industrial assessment should be pooled and then distributed across the province, by the provincial government, in such a fashion as to ensure that every student, regardless of geographic location or choice of school system, had access to equal resources for his or her education.[24]

SUBMITTED TO THE GOVERNMENT in December 1985, the Macdonald Report was released to the public in early 1986, and boards or other interested parties were invited to respond by October. A ministry committee was established to examine its recommendations and prepare plans to change Ontario's methods of financing the schools. By spring 1987 it was clear that pooling was among the reforms the committee was considering; indeed, Sean Conway, the minister of education, was on record as saying that any move to increase operating grants was tied to pooling.[25] But opposition, which had been gaining momentum ever since the Macdonald Report had been released, was now intense. In the midst of the bitter struggle over full funding for Catholic secondary schools, public school boards interpreted pooling as a raid on their own tax base to pay for the expansion of the separate school system. In Metropolitan Toronto, the *Star* had already dubbed it 'the Robin-Hood scheme' and urban trustees across the province endlessly warned of the loss of programs and rising residential taxes that would result if pooling were introduced.[26] During the 1987 election campaign the Liberals ducked the issue: the party was 'committed

to paying 60 per cent of *approved* school board costs,' but decisions about
the means to achieve this would not be announced until the ministry
committee had laid its recommendations before the government (conven-
iently, not till after the election).[27] And though they emerged from the
election with a huge majority, the Liberals remained acutely aware of the
level of opposition to pooling.

Committed to Catholic full funding in any case, and knowing the only
alternative to pooling was a large infusion of provincial revenues to meet
its capital and operating costs, the Liberals finally announced their decision in the spring 1989 budget. 'Coterminous' boards – that is, public and
Roman Catholic boards with overlapping jurisdictions – would share the
revenues of commercial and industrial assessment. The scheme would
begin in 1990 but be phased in gradually, over a period of six years, during
which (but not beyond) public boards would be compensated through
larger grants for any losses they experienced.[28]

For the Liberal government, it marked the last significant step in implementing full funding for Catholic schools. And certainly it went some way
towards closing the gap between the financial resources of public and
separate school boards.[29] At the end of five years of government, nonetheless, this was the only financial issue the Liberals had addressed; meanwhile, the disproportion in the share of education costs borne by the
property tax had gotten worse, not better, and the inequities amongst rich
and poor boards, urban and rural boards, had widened, not narrowed.

THE NDP HAD LONG been critical of Ontario's (and Canada's) system of
taxation. Once in office, Floyd Laughren, the new government's minister
of finance, launched the Fair Tax Commission to review and overhaul the
entire system, including the way in which education was financed.[30] Its
report, issued in 1993, was scathing. Referring back to the findings of a
1967 tax commission, it concluded 'the assessment system was in chaos
then; it is in chaos now. The extent to which property tax was relied upon
for financing education was of concern then, as it is now. Efforts at reform
have failed.' The commission added that 'the issue of funding education
from property taxes dominated discussion of local government finance in
our public consultation program. Virtually every aspect of the education
funding system was questioned.'[31] The report went on to document the
inequities, to *both* taxpayers and students, of reliance on local property tax,
and then made three recommendations which, in intent, were similar to
those of the Macdonald Commission. The provincial government should
set a basic standard for education expenditures and assume responsibility

for funding up to that standard. Commercial and industrial property taxes would be set by the government and distributed across the province in an equitable manner. And third, a local levy on residential property 'should be restricted to a fixed percentage – not greater than 10 per cent – of the total amount of provincial funding provided to that board.' Leaving this limited power in the hands of school boards would allow a degree of flexibility in local provision for special circumstances. But it also had to be 'tightly restricted ... to ensure that pressure is kept on provincial governments to maintain a realistic level of formula funding for education.' Otherwise, the commission emphasized, there would be 'an almost irresistible temptation for provincial governments to abandon tax fairness principles and to tap the local property tax base indirectly by restricting formula funding below realistic levels.' Indeed.

There might well be a rough consensus, among the experts at least, about the central problems in education finance and what needed to be done about them.* As it stood, the system promoted inequities, provided inadequate support to sustain the program the government itself mandated, and allowed costs to increase almost without restraint. The answer was greater central control over total amounts designated for education, the pooling of local corporate resources among school boards, and greater use of provincial sources of revenue to pay for education. After two major reports, the government knew what should be done, as indeed the Liberals had before it.

But whatever the experts said, when it came to reading the political ledger, things looked different. By the mid-1990s there had been no diminution of opposition by wealthy boards or municipalities to the 'Robin-Hood scheme' of pooling. The polls revealed that Ontarians were split right down the middle about transferring the costs of education to the provincial income tax.[32] There was a ticking time-bomb at the core of the finance reform agenda that only the Macdonald Commission had had the temerity to address: if the province determined all or most of a board's budget, would the province have to assume responsibility for collective bargaining, or modify bargaining rights granted under Bill 100? – something an NDP government was especially loathe to contemplate.[33] Not even an NDP government, moreover, was about to raise provincial taxes or

---

*The Royal Commission on Learning, which had also been established by the NDP government, devoted a short chapter to educational finance, and heartily endorsed both the critique and the recommendations in the *Fair Taxation* report: see Royal Commission on Learning, *For the Love of Learning* (1994), 4: chap. 18, 127–34.

introduce large additions to government appropriations for education in
a political environment rife with criticism of excessive government spending. And, to give politicians and civil-service mandarins their due, the devil
was in the details: changing the system of education finance was a complex, intricate, messy task. In 1994, Laughren announced a significant
modification to the way in which the pooled funds of coterminous public
and Catholic boards would be distributed – a move that increased the
degree of equity between such boards.[34] But by the end of its mandate, the
NDP government had done nothing further except appoint yet another
committee – a Ministry of Education 'Working Group on Education Finance Reform.'

II

The political price of doing nothing fell upon Ontario's boards of education. From the mid-eighties to the mid-nineties, I have said, spending on
the schools rose from $6 to $12 billion; by 1990, 60 per cent of the annual
costs were borne by local taxpayers, and the dollar amounts that had to be
raised from property taxes increased inexorably every year. In the boom
years, taxpayers swallowed their medicine with little more than annual
grumbling at budget time. But as the province slid into a savage recession,
trouble began to brew. By 1991 and 1992 discontent had become so
intense that a well-organized tax revolt was taking shape across the province, not directed solely at the school boards but certainly not excluding
them.[35] In January 1992, moreover, the government announced its cuts in
transfer payments – a 1 per cent increase in 1992–3 and 2 per cent in the
two following years. Accustomed to complaining about 'inadequate' grant
increases that had run at 6, 7, or 8 per cent, Ontario's school trustees were
appalled. Many were stuck with previous contract settlements that promised wage increases in the 5 per cent range[36] – well above the 1 per cent
grant increase. Fixed costs to deliver existing programs didn't come unfixed
just because the government decided to reduce its spending. The outlook
had appeared bleak at other times – and had certainly been declared bleak
by those who cried wolf many times earlier; but 1992 was a harbinger of
tough times to come.

WHILE THERE HAD BEEN some notable conflicts in the mid- to late 1980s
between teachers and local boards, good times had kept labour relations
tolerably cordial and strikes few. After that, however, the situation deteriorated. The year spanning September 1991 to August 1992 was described by

the head of the Education Relations Commission as 'the most turbulent year since Bill 100 was passed,' with eight strikes, the largest number in any year since 1976, and negotiations generally 'more prolonged and more difficult than in any year since 1983,' the year after provincial public-sector wage controls had been lifted.[37] The federal government imposed wage settlements of 0 and 3 per cent over two years on its employees, and Ontario's civil servants settled for 1 per cent in 1992 and 2 per cent in the two following years. The school boards took these as models and substantially reduced their offers compared to the two previous years; teachers, on the other hand, behaved as though it was business as usual. Toronto's 9200 secondary school teachers demanded 6 per cent; they finally settled for a 3 per cent increase in each year of a two-year contract, but only after an eight-day work-to-rule campaign that cut out all extracurricular activities.[38] In Ottawa-Carleton, two boards were struck, one of the unions demanding 9 per cent over two years, and both strikes ended only when the government threatened to legislate the teachers back to work.[39] Other settlements came more easily, but those that exceeded 1 per cent, which included nearly all of them, meant program cuts or rising taxes.

Generally, it meant both. Peel cancelled its JK program; Ottawa cut 873 jobs and trimmed 'everything from field trips to furniture to bus passes.' Dufferin-Peel Separate School Board abandoned its family-studies program for two years and sent one hundred consultants and specialist teachers back to regular classrooms. East York cut back on English as a second language, Oxford laid off eleven psychologists and speech therapists. OSSTF claimed that 2000 jobs had been cut in fifteen school boards.[40] Even then it was a struggle to keep tax increases single-digit. Meanwhile anger over education spending mounted. 'The pain isn't going to stop,' Anne Vanstone, a long-time Toronto and Metro board trustee, told Jennifer Lewington. 'It's different from any time I have been involved ... The people that pay the bills are saying, "We're not paying more money; we largely don't like you and don't like the way you spend it, and get your hand out of our pocket."'[41]

Grounded in a decade or more of increasing taxes, and escalating with the impact of the recession, discontent with Ontario's school boards had other sources as well. 'Cut school bureaucracy not services' became a rallying cry in the budget warfare of 1992 and 1993. '"Hundreds of supervisors, co-ordinators, and consultants who hold high paying jobs have been protected for too long,"' said one parent, speaking for many others at a meeting of the Toronto Board of Education. '"We have glossy education centres all over the city, full of these people, while students sit in

portables," she fumed.'[42] And it certainly didn't help that in at least a few
Ontario boards, trustees were busily shooting themselves in both feet. By
the end of the 1980s the Toronto Board of Education had already established a reputation as a busy-body in political, social, and economic issues
wholly beyond its jurisdiction.[43] In 1990 the York Region board vetoed
a plan to introduce junior kindergarten because of the costs, but left
$13 million in its budget earmarked for a new administrative building; not
surprisingly, many parents with young children were irate about the board's
sense of priorities.[44] After a whopping 14.7 per cent increase in education
taxes in 1990, the London board proposed early in 1991 to renovate its
administrative centre to the tune of $700,000. And that, a *London Free Press*
editorial pointed out, was shortly after administrators 'found themselves in
hot water for spending $45,000 in two-day training seminars at Niagara-
on-the-Lake.'[45]

But the issues that made critics foam at the mouth were trustees' salaries
and perks. Traditionally, the job of school trustee had been viewed as a
part-time avocation and a call to public service. For some years before
1982, they had been accorded a modest honorarium based on the number
of students enrolled in the board. In that year, however, the law was
changed to allow an outgoing board to establish salary levels for an
incoming board, and in 1989 trustees were given the right to set their own
salary levels.[46] Since most trustees in most boards were re-elected, they
were in effect voting on their own salaries from 1982 onwards. In a few
boards, trustees appointed themselves full-time employees of the people
and paid themselves generously. By the 1990s the Toronto Board of
Education topped the list with salaries of over $49,000 and generous
expense accounts besides.

A good deal of the criticism trustees and their employees were subjected
to during these years was trivial or over-drawn. Trustees had responsibilities they couldn't duck, and the political pressures to maintain spending
on people and programs was intense. Well paid or not, serving as a trustee
on a large school board was a demanding, time-consuming job. But the
discontent and frustrations bred during the recession made them easy
targets, and highly visible ones once the press and other critics zeroed in
on them. The issue of trustees' salaries is one good example. Set in
provincial perspective, it was a relatively minor one: as the Royal Commission on Learning would emphatically point out in 1995, in only seventeen
boards did trustees earn more than $15,000 and in only seven was the
amount more than $22,000.[47] But all of these boards were in the Greater
Toronto Area, where annual school-tax increases were among the highest,

where the school accommodation crush was at its worst, where citizen activism was most common, and where the local media provided coverage and commentary that had a province-wide audience.

Beginning in the run-up to the school-board elections in autumn 1991, and multiplying during 1992, questions began to be asked about the possible savings that would accrue to public education if local administration were reorganized. Sometimes the talk amounted to no more than reducing the number of trustees. Sometimes it was about board amalgamation. Occasionally someone would suggest outright abolition.[48] Tony Silipo, the NDP government's second minister of education, was ordering boards 'to explore ways to end duplicated services.'[49] The *Star* was running front-page stories on the extent of 'duplication' and 'waste' within Metro, pointing, with rhetorical outrage, to its nine administrative centres employing 14,300 non-teaching employees, its nine directors of education, ten assistant directors, 123 superintendents, 48 assistant superintendents, all for 360,000 students.[50] And it was calling for an end to 'Bloated Bureaucracy.' 'The NDP government ought to act quickly,' one November 1992 editorial maintained, 'on a recent cabinet suggestion to review the structure and operation of Ontario's school board system. In Metro alone, there are 112 trustees in nine different boards ... We need our scarce resources in the classroom, for the children, not for the trustees and burgeoning bureaucracies. The province's over-managed and over-priced school board system badly needs a shake-up.'[51]

The public might increasingly despair of the boards; the politicians had their own, more hard-edged reasons to want their wings clipped. By early 1992 there was substantial opposition to some of the government's policy initiatives, especially those which cost large amounts of money. Mandatory junior kindergarten was a particular flashpoint with several wealthy boards. Because of the equalization formula they received minimal grants from the government – or no grants at all. Yet they were expected to implement government policies like any other board, even if it meant paying the entire cost through local taxes. Not surprisingly in the hard economic circumstances of the 1990s, some boards balked. After a public slanging match at a meeting in Mississauga between the minister of education and York Region's director of education, the latter warned that the price of mandatory junior kindergarten might be reductions in spending on math and science. 'I find it absolutely intolerable,' he said, that transfer payments had been reduced to 1 per cent while 'at the same time, we're being forced to pay for other items we don't even want.'[52] In April 1992, Peel flatly refused to implement mandatory JK.[53] At the same time, several other large southern Ontario boards were threatening to ignore the government's injunction to destream grade 9 the following September.[54] By 1992 and early 1993, in other words, school boards were bluntly challenging the government's right to determine their educational priorities, and, in a few cases, were openly defying the NDP's political agenda for the schools – something that powerful politicians could hardly have welcomed.

Scarborough provided the last straw. In June 1992 the board's trustees voted themselves a salary increase of 64 per cent over three years. A city hard-hit by the recession exploded in anger. When confronted by a mass protest in January 1993, the board compromised but refused to back down gracefully, 'voting 8 to 6 to keep the 36 per cent raise they gave themselves last year but freeze their salaries this year and next.'[55] According to the *Star*'s account, 'the incensed taxpayers have vowed that if the province doesn't step in – soon – they'll force it to. [Bob] Rae found the pay raise so bizarre he laughed. Then, reflecting more seriously, he said it may be time to do away with such bureaucratic duplication and put more money into classrooms.' Now a belated convert, Tony Silipo, who, as chair of the Toronto Board of Education in the late 1980s, had not only voted for a large salary increase but defended it in an unusually brazen manner, was heard to say that 'the "very serious" issue of the pay raise just hammers home the need for comprehensive reform.'[56]

AFTER THAT, IT WAS no longer if, but when and how. The thrust of the proposals to reform educational funding was to remove nearly all taxing power from the local boards. That, in turn, raised an obvious corollary: if the provincial government set the agenda *and* provided all the money, did Ontario really need school boards, and if so, for what? A 1993 poll found that nearly half of Ontarians favoured increasing the powers of the province at the expense of the school boards; those who believed trustees did 'a poor job' of representing them outnumbered those who believed the opposite; no less telling, people's faith in trustees was much lower in Ontario than elsewhere in Canada.[57] Though few people wanted to abolish boards altogether, two different 1994 polls indicated that public opinion was strongly in favour of reducing their number.[58] Ontarians were also well aware of experiments in other provinces and in Britain and New Zealand, where school boards were being either amalgamated or abandoned altogether.[59]

Moreover, one alternative had been gaining an enthusiastic following for a decade: the school or community council, sometimes envisioned as a substitute for school boards, or intended more commonly to bridge the gap between a board and each of its schools. A school council, its proponents argued, would put management back in the hands of those who had the greatest stake in the school: parents, teachers, and other members of the local community. It would ensure that both policy and practice were more responsive to local needs. At the same time, it would give parents the opportunity for greater involvement in their children's learning, and greater contact with staff, which would play a large part in improving discipline and academic achievement.[60] There was no talk of actually replacing the boards with school councils, but the discussion about a new unit of local policy-making was yet another indication that the government was serious about restructuring.

The most telling sign, however, was the attitude of Dave Cooke, who became minister of education in early 1993 (and, one might probably add, the attitude of his new deputy minister, Charles Pascal).[61] A social worker and ex–school trustee from the Windsor area, an experienced MPP, a Rae loyalist, and a member of the inner cabinet, Cooke had a bee in his bonnet about the school boards. Believing that it would save money by eliminating duplication, as well as redirect funding from administration to classrooms, amalgamation was high on his agenda from the beginning. Not only did he issue dire warnings that if boards didn't do it, the government would,[62] but he immediately appointed consultants to make recommendations about amalgamation in Windsor-Essex and Ottawa-Carleton, and pressed ahead with a similar plan for London-Middlesex. The latter, he believed, had far too few students to merit its own school board;[63] Ottawa-Carleton, he pointed out, had five school boards with eighty-eight trustees serving 128,000 students; Windsor-Essex had four boards and fifty-six trustees serving 69,000 students. As one *Star* reporter wrote, 'Cooke says the $1 billion a year growth in education costs of the past five years poses the question, "Has all of the increased cost done much for the outcome in education? How much of those dollars ended up in the classroom?"'[64]

All perhaps true. But his two consultants disagreed, arguing that outright amalgamation would cost more than it saved, and in Ottawa-Carleton was unworkable in any case; a better alternative, they suggested, was to insist on sharing costs of common services like busing, purchasing, and printing.[65] And the Royal Commission on Learning, which enthusiastically supported the establishment of school councils, was forthright in its opposition to any large-scale amalgamation: certainly there were advantages to greater co-operation among boards. But 'local representation and control' must be preserved. There was, however, 'no formula, nor do there

seem to be any objective criteria, that would allow us to conclude that
there are too many school boards in Ontario ... Here, as everywhere in this
report, we encourage communities to use local strategies and solutions to
fit local situations. Any more general consideration of amalgamation of
school boards must take into account their incredibly varied nature and
size, and must also consider mechanisms for sharing services, as well as for
dealing with political representation.'[66]

Cooke remained adamant, nonetheless. Determined to make education
a major part of their platform in the forthcoming election, and no less
eager to exploit a public mood that had been hardening since the late
1980s, Cooke announced in February 1995 that the number of school
boards would be cut in half, and trustees' salaries capped at $20,000. 'This
will have a dramatic effect on the way school boards are organized in
Ontario,' he said, and promised that 'it will result in significant savings
being put back into the classrooms of the province.'[67] To that end, he
established a four-person task force, headed by John Sweeney, an experienced educator and former Liberal cabinet minister, to work out the
details: to draw up new boundaries, consult with the public, report by
31 December 1995, and then monitor amalgamation.

That spring, the government also announced that all schools would be
required to establish school councils, consisting of parents, community
representatives, the principal, a teacher, and for secondary schools a
student, to 'advise the principal and, where appropriate, the school board'
on such issues as curriculum and program priorities, reporting, budget
priorities, selection of principals, and other related matters. The councils
were to be 'fully operational' by June 1996.[68]

Thus was the stage set for a major change in the way education in
Ontario had traditionally been financed and organized. All of the arguments were in place to justify sharp restrictions in the right of locally
elected school boards to determine how much money was to be raised for
local schools. And a major overhaul of the number of school boards was
now official policy. All that remained to be determined was the date when
the axe would fall, and who would wield it.

The 'Pedagogy of Joy' Meets 'Mental Might'

Addressing the chorus of complaints about the quality of Ontario's education system had been a long-standing commitment of Liberal leaders, dating back to Robert Nixon in the early 1970s. When the Liberals took office in 1985, restructuring Ontario's economy to meet the high-tech competition in world markets was defined as the central long-term priority for the provincial government; and Peterson made it clear that changing the school curriculum was a key part of accomplishing that goal.[1]

Looking for fresh ideas to renew a bureaucracy that had grown stale and inbred, Sean Conway, the new minister of education, recruited Bernard Shapiro as his deputy minister of education. A specialist in educational psychology and measurement with a PhD from Harvard, Shapiro was unusually well versed on a broad range of educational issues and had also acquired substantial administrative experience at the university level, most recently as director of OISE. By the mid-1980s, he was hardly an outsider to either the field of education or its politics in Ontario. William Davis had commissioned him to report on the funding of private schools. And like the Liberal government itself, Shapiro inherited a working agenda from the Tories, including the reform of the high school program and the commitment to more systematic assessment and evaluation. Shapiro, indeed, had played a part in generating the ideas that underpinned some of these initiatives and, as deputy minister, was not about to abandon them. He was, however, an outsider in the sense that he was the first senior ministry appointment who had not risen through the ranks of the education bureaucracy, and thus had not been socialized into its values and shibboleths.

The Liberals had decided at least as early as September 1986 that education would be an important part of their election platform when the accord with the NDP expired in 1987, and Shapiro was given the task of providing the specifics.[2] Raising standards and increasing accountability had to be part of that agenda: Liberal politicians were too well aware of the public outcry to ignore it. But along with greater public accountability there was the promise of curriculum renewal for the general and basic levels of high school, including new approaches to the dropout problem, an emphasis on learning skills in elementary education, and an extended role for schools in providing day care, something that was a particularly hot topic at a moment when large numbers of working, baby-boom women were now also mothers, and when women's groups were pressing for new initiatives. These were the core objectives Shapiro set for the ministry and offered to the Liberal party in early 1987.[3]

PERHAPS BECAUSE IT WAS the area where political consensus was greatest, and where, because of his previous experience, Shapiro felt on solid ground, he moved fastest on assessment and accountability.[4] It was also a field of good intentions gone awry. Nearly a decade earlier, Thomas Wells had promised better testing and evaluation of students, and the Davis government made a firm commitment in 1984 to a province-wide testing initiative. For a variety of reasons that remain obscure, nothing actually happened.[5] Assessment, in any case, was a political minefield for any government. Whatever the exact format, ordinary citizens tended to equate assessment with traditional paper-and-pencil tests, and to treat them as a fair gauge of educational achievement. At least some influential experts, however, dismissed such commonsensical views as simple-minded: assessment was a broad and continuous process that relied on 'holistic' approaches including observation, evaluation of projects and portfolios of work, oral presentations, co-operative and individual research, role-playing, and journal-writing. Paper-and-pencil tests might have a modest place in this array of assessment tools but they were of only limited value.[6] Externally set examinations were even more of a red flag, as was the phrase 'standardized testing.' Such tests, it was said, did little more than measure recall of factual trivia, were insensitive to cultural, racial, or class differences, rewarded product not process, encouraged rote learning rather than creative or critical skills, forced teachers to 'teach to the test,' might expose individual schools and teachers to unjust criticism, and undermined the autonomy of practising professionals.

Those academics and curriculum specialists who dismissed or belittled external or standard assessment had enormous support among senior school administrators and federation leaders.[7] Virtually every proposal to introduce such devices, above all those that would report on, or rank, individual teachers, schools, or boards, was adamantly opposed. To the critics of the schools, on the other hand, this all looked like smug complacency and the reticence of bureaucrats, union leaders, and rank-and-file teachers to expose their practices to public scrutiny. 'There can be no effective pursuit of excellence ... without meaningful accountability,' George Radwanski had written; but, he added, 'there can be no meaningful accountability without measurable standards of accomplishment.'[8] On this point, he had a lot of support. Influential newspaper editors and columnists, business organizations, the Premier's Council, and large majorities in the public-opinion polls wanted both more accountability and more transparent assessment procedures.[9]

Thus did the Peterson government enter the minefield on tiptoe, but tiptoe in it did. And here, Shapiro's contribution was critical: he understood the assessment literature, knew how to navigate around the strengths and weaknesses on both sides of the argument, and, as a former chair of the ministry's advisory committee on assessment, was already familiar with the problems, the politics, and the extant provincial initiatives. He also believed that accountability, assessment, and quality went hand in hand. Asked, for example, by the Select Committee on Education in 1988 about the efficacy of child-centred pedagogy, he would say, 'Although people say such things as the child-centred approach certainly yields wonderful results ... the public policy question is whether, in general, ... [it] yields the kind of results one hopes it will. I think quite likely it does actually; that is where my intuition takes me. But ... we cannot rely simply on intuition.'[10]

Within weeks of his appointment, Shapiro had launched a test project, focusing on grade 9 or 10 geography in 1986–7, that would become the model for a revivified system of 'provincial program reviews' designed to evaluate the level of success achieved in the teaching and learning of particular subjects at various grade levels.[11] Following the April 1987 Throne Speech, Conway promised similar reviews, over the next five years, in a series of elementary and high school subjects.[12] The aim of the provincial reviews, however, was not to introduce external subject tests for every pupil in the province or report to parents on the progress of individual students, not even, indeed, to report publicly on the relative standing of individual boards and schools.[13] Rather the reviews were intended to assess curriculum implementation, pedagogical practices, *and*, using a variety of tools, student achievement through sample testing in a relatively small number of schools.

Under Shapiro's leadership, the ministry also initiated other assessment projects. One involved participation in a series of large-scale international assessments of student achievement in mathematics and science. The results, as we have already seen, presented Ontarians with a comparison report card and precipitated an outcry over the apparently poor showing of their students. A second project originated in response to pressures from the universities to impose greater consistency in the evaluation tools and award of marks for the examinations mandated by the Ontario Academic Course guidelines.[14] Pioneered for OAC English by a group of ministry-led senior high school teachers, it provided guidance on the type of examination, and how to maintain common standards. Evaluation would remain in teachers' hands; but consistency was to be monitored: all schools that offered OACs would be required to submit samples of examinations and marked student responses for review and appraisal. In 1988 the Liberals also committed the province to participation in a national project sponsored by the Council of Ministers of Education of Canada. Achievement tests, administered to a nation-wide sample of students, would allow provinces to assess the performance of their own schools against Canada-wide standards and issue system-level accountability reports to their voters, taxpayers, and parents.[15]

PERHAPS THE LIBERALS' most significant accountability and assessment initiative, however, was a program first broached in the April 1987 Throne Speech and then fleshed out in ensuing months during the election campaign and the legislative session that followed it. The province, Ontarians were promised, would establish 'new provincial benchmarks for literacy and numeracy in grades 3 and 6,' and would 'develop more effective ways of measuring student achievement against those benchmarks.'[16]

Because of its impact in the years that followed, the context for this new departure deserves some comment. The Provincial Benchmarks Program – renamed the Provincial Standards Program in the early 1990s – was the product of a larger trend towards 'outcomes-based' education that swept across North America during the 1980s, and exercised a large influence in other parts of the world as well.[17] It was driven by several diverse pressures: by the demand for more effective schools generally; by the conviction that underachieving students and disadvantaged groups in particular were being ill served by existing approaches to curricular goals and pedagogy; and by the cry for greater accountability to taxpayers and parents for both the costs of education and its results. The movement was also rooted in the search for greater quality and efficiency in public institutions through the application of techniques pioneered in the process of corporate restructuring so characteristic of the 1980s. But whatever its origins, outcomes-based education was the most potent movement to hit the schools in a decade.

The aim was not simply to state intentions or objectives, which had always been done, but to ensure results, and to ensure not simply success for some but success for all. This was to be accomplished, in the first place, by defining objectives that all children could and should achieve. These objectives were to be specified in behavioural terms – that is, as 'outcomes' that could be demonstrated by students and observed by others. Benchmark testing was designed to measure achievement in these standards and to identify, for remedial help, those who had yet to attain the standard. Exemplary benchmark testing tended to adopt 'holistic' evaluation techniques, or at least some measures beyond paper-and-pencil tests so that evaluation included both product and process, cognitive and affective characteristics. To its proponents, the particular virtue of benchmark assessment was its ability to wed the imperative of accountability to 'sophisticated' assessment techniques and teacher autonomy. It provided, in theory at least, publicly expressed standards against which the success of teaching and learning could be measured, leaving teachers to decide the means of achieving those goals without telling them, in any prescriptive way, what to teach. It gave teachers diagnostic tools to use in assessing student progress and reporting to the parents of individual students. It enabled school boards or the ministry to monitor and report on system-wide achievement, and to identify trouble spots in pedagogy or curriculum. And such monitoring could take the form of either universal testing or less intrusive sampling procedures.

In the atmosphere of the 1980s and early 1990s, this happy combination of pressures and preferences made outcomes and benchmark testing a wildly popular idea. The first step in achieving excellence and accountability in education, Radwanski argued in his report, was to shift the province's educational goals from vague objectives, such as giving children *opportunities* to learn – the language of the extant curricular guidelines – to outcomes that would specify what children were expected to learn, and when.[18] Nor was Radwanski alone. Pressed hard by reform-minded trustees and their constituents to improve reporting and ensure that children were learning what they should, administrators at the Toronto Board of Education embarked in 1987 on an ambitious, and very expensive, experiment in producing sophisticated libraries of video, print, and other materials indicating what students could actually do at certain ages and the range of variation in the accomplishments they might be expected to exhibit.[19]

Though generally adopting more conventional approaches and assessment tools, other big urban boards, including Ottawa and North York, launched large-scale benchmarks programs and smaller boards began more modest ventures.[20] Not to be left behind, the Ministry of Education had announced in 1988 that it would have its language and mathematics benchmarks for grades 3 and 6 in place as early as the end of 1989,[21] though it actually took far longer than that, for reasons we shall see.

Early in the following year, the government took a more dramatic step, the minister declaring that the benchmarks would be accompanied by the development of province-wide 'diagnostic tests' in reading, writing, and mathematics, to be administered at the end of grades 3 and 6 – something which went much further than anything hitherto proposed, and which provoked sharp condemnation from the teachers' unions.[22] Be that as it may, what was common in all these initiatives of the late eighties was a new attention to accountability, in terms both of assessing and reporting the progress of individual students according to some declared performance standard, and of assessing and reporting the success of the system at board or provincial levels.

FROM THE TIME he became deputy minister, Shapiro emphasized the critical importance of the early school years; his agenda reflected that emphasis,[23] and so, in consequence, did the direction Liberal educational policy took before, during, and immediately after the election of 1987. In Shapiro's view – though he was hardly alone in this at the time – most later learning problems originated in the early years. 'I am really convinced,' he told one reporter in 1987, 'that most of the problems we see later can be, I wouldn't say resolved, but dramatically decreased, by enriching the environment of the elementary schools.' That included a substantial reduction in the pupil-teacher ratio in the primary grades.[24]

It was these convictions that gave shape to key parts of the Liberal election platform in the summer of 1987. If re-elected, Peterson promised, his government would, forthwith, hire 4000 more elementary school teachers, at a cost of $170 million, in order to reduce the pupil-teacher ratio in grades 1 and 2 by fully one-third, from 30:1 to 20:1. The government would also buy '40,000 more classroom computers in a bid to teach young students "the new basics,"' and additional money would be allocated for the purchase of educational software, new textbooks, and other learning materials for the elementary schools. The benchmarks program was announced at the same time, and there were to be new, provincially mandated report cards to parents at grades 3, 6, and 8.[25]

When the government decided, late in the fall, that it couldn't afford the entire $170 million all at once, a ruckus ensued, senior cabinet ministers expressing surprise that they would be taken at their word over election promises. Things were made worse by the discovery that the policy advice had been a piece of sloppy homework: the pupil-teacher ratio was actually less than 30:1, 4000 teachers weren't needed to do the job, 4000 new primary specialists didn't exist, and there weren't enough classrooms to house them all in any case.[26] But the class-size reduction was formally introduced in May 1988, to be phased in over a three-year period beginning that September.[27] By 1988 the government had also committed itself to rewriting *The Formative Years*, a virtual inevitability once it had decided to introduce the benchmarks program. The new document, the minister told the legislature's Select Committee on Education, would be 'more explicit in its learning expectations with regard to skills, concepts, and attitudes right across the curriculum for the primary and junior divisions. In fact, this government has made the renewal of the primary and junior divisions a major priority.'[28]

Despite the intrinsic importance of these initiatives, the one that really captured headlines came in 1989. In a ministry-sponsored review of early childhood education, begun under the Tories but submitted to the Liberals in 1985, Frances Poleschuk had urged that junior kindergarten be mandated throughout the province and that full-day senior kindergarten be encouraged.[29] In his most radical recommendation, Radwanski had gone even further, proposing the extension of schooling downward, to begin at age three. His justification was straightforward. Early childhood education was the most crucial stage for learning. Deficits that showed up at age five or six were already very hard to make up. An early start, especially with those at most risk, would enable large numbers of children to cope with the demands of a challenging curriculum once they started school.[30]

Though Radwanski's recommendations on early childhood education met with some criticism and considerable scepticism, there was plenty of enthusiasm as well. And while putting three-year-olds in school was generally deemed a bit much, making more provision for four- and five-year-olds garnered wide support. Thus the government was not about to pass on an opportunity that seemed to promise large gains in both educational and political capital. The April 1989 Throne Speech looked forward, as a 'long-term vision,' to the day when the government could make 'full-day senior and junior kindergarten' available to all four- and five-year-olds. But as a 'first step' it announced that it would require all school boards to expand their existing senior and junior kindergarten programs. Attendance would remain voluntary but the government would ensure that boards 'offer half-day junior kindergarten for four-year-olds as well as half-day senior kindergarten for five-year-olds.' Both initiatives were to be implemented over the following five years. As well, the province would 'provide funding for school boards to offer full day senior kindergarten programs, where classroom space permits.'[31]

FROM THE LATE 1970s onwards, 'the dropout problem' had been of growing concern to politicians and policy-makers alike, and the Liberals were no exception. Early in 1987 the government had hired Radwanski to report on the question, while Shapiro identified it as one of the key priorities for the Ministry of Education. It became, as well, one focal point of the April Throne Speech. As part of its 'excellence in education' campaign, the government promised to 'take steps to reduce the drop-out rate in Ontario by one-third within the next 5 years. Further substantial reductions will be achieved in subsequent years.'[32] Though the rhetoric drew headlines, few concrete commitments were made. More money was to be put into co-operative education programs; studies and pilot projects were to be funded; but beyond that, all the government really promised in its April 1987 Throne Speech was to try to figure out just *how* the dropout rate could be reduced by a third in only five years.

Between 1986 and 1989, the studies piled up. Appointed Ontario's Youth Commissioner by the previous government, Ken Dryden had submitted a report to the Liberals in which he speculated at some length about the causes of early school-leaving and described the province's high dropout rate as 'my biggest shock' as commissioner.[33] In February 1988, the Radwanski report was published. Just a month earlier, the ministry had released an analysis of the effects of *OSIS* – the new high school program of studies introduced in 1984 – carried out by a group of OISE researchers led by Ken Leithwood.[34] The ministry also set up the Student Retention and Transition Project, designed to support additional research on, and to promote and evaluate a variety of innovative approaches to, the problem. One outcome of the project was several more volumes of research.[35] In November 1987, the Liberals had established an all-party committee of the legislature, the Select Committee on Education, to review the entire system, including the high school curriculum. It released its own report on the latter issue in late 1988. Meanwhile OSSTF and some school boards were conducting their own research or experiments that paralleled those of the provincial government.[36] Altogether, 1988 was a banner year for the dropout problem; indeed by 1989 it was in serious danger of being studied to death.

WHY, THEN, DID teenagers drop out of high school? The new Ontario studies confirmed what was one of the most widely recognized reasons in the international literature: students failed one or another subject in the early high school years, and as they did so, began to fall further and further behind their peers in accumulating the credits necessary to graduate.[37] The introduction of *OSIS* appeared to have made the situation worse. In order to graduate under the new regime, three additional credits were required, and the number of compulsory academic courses had been increased substantially. It was still too early to be sure of the full impact of these changes because the first cadre of students to enter high school under *OSIS* did not reach grade 12 until 1987–8. But researchers believed there was already enough evidence to indicate that the dropout rate was actually rising.[38] As Ken Leithwood pointed out, moreover, dissatisfaction with the general-stream courses had been one major stimulus for the entire SERP/*OSIS* project; yet when it came to implementation, most of the energy had been poured into the revision of the advanced program, especially into the creation of the new OAC courses. Little had been done, on the other hand, to rethink the curriculum of the two lower streams. Thus, on a number of fronts, Leithwood argued, general and basic students were paying the price for reforms that had promised higher standards and a more rigorous curriculum.[39]

Be that as it may, there was also the charge that the curricular fare offered to general-level students, little more than a 'watered-down' version of the academic courses designed for the advanced program, had little relevance to either students' present lives or the world of work they were soon to enter. Dryden, Leithwood, Radwanski, and several other commentators would press this argument hard. But students also did badly, or so the argument went, because of the very nature of the school environment. As an OSSTF curriculum committee put it, 'Individual timetables, eight different teachers, as many as 200 peer contacts frustrate students' attempts to establish a sense of identity and focus their attention on school work. The relative isolation of subject disciplines hinders the school's attempt to remedy skill deficiencies and integrate learning.'[40] The result too often was alienation, low morale, and a loss of motivation.

The interface between elementary and secondary school was also a source of concern. The legislature's Select Committee on Education had consulted parents, teachers, and community groups across the province and remarked in its first report that 'perhaps one of the most troubling problems we heard of was the difficult transition from elementary to secondary school.'[41] It marked a significant change at a trying time in students' lives and meant a shift from close contact with a single teacher to a very different environment, a different pedagogy, and, at the end of grade 8 – at thirteen or fourteen years of age – the imperative of choosing a program of studies that would substantially determine career choice.

There was, however, one other influential explanation for the dropout problem, and one that encompassed all the rest: the negative effects of streaming itself. An interpretation widely shared by researchers in Britain and North America during the 1980s, it resonated through most of the Ontario studies completed in the latter half of the decade. Radwanski put the case most eloquently. The relationship between streaming and dropouts, he began, was obvious and direct. Only 12 per cent of those enrolled in the advanced program dropped out. The figures for the general and basic streams were 62 and 79 per cent respectively![42]

Why this pattern? In answering that question, Radwanski did not reduce the schools to scapegoats; parental attitudes mattered, he insisted, as did the influence of part-time jobs, youth subcultures, as well as other individual attributes and social factors. Yet the phenomenon was also caused by the alienation engendered by the two lower streams with their dead-end courses, low standards of achievement, and seeming irrelevance to students' lives. To offer such a stunted and useless program of studies to any student was just plain bad educational practice. But it was more than that. Most of those enrolled in the general and basic streams, Radwanski went on to argue, were children of parents in the two lowest socio-economic categories. Thus dropouts were drawn disproportionately from the children of parents who were among the least well-off and least educated, or were recent immigrants. As a result, streaming was more than just a case of bad educational practice; it was unjust. It denied equal opportunity to poor children by channelling them into dead-end courses and then into dead-end jobs (or no jobs at all). 'If all young people need the same foundation of knowledge and skills to be able to participate fully in the workplace and in society at large,' he wrote, 'then a streaming policy designed from the outset to impart different levels of knowledge and skills to different groups of students cannot be rescued by improvements. And if the current advanced program represents even an approximation of the content and quality we believe are required for a first-class education, then placing young people in any other program necessarily consigns them to a second-class education.'[43]

NO SHORTAGE OF ADVICE there might well be. But it was much more difficult to achieve consensus about what should be done. Not only did commentators disagree among themselves on some issues, or assign priority to different sorts of solutions, but policy-makers had to consider the views of trustees, school administrators, teachers' unions, parents, and public opinion generally. In some areas there was near-universal accord. Promoting more co-operative education was one example, along with the need to rethink both the nature and role of technological studies.[44] Similarly, there was a good deal of consensus about the need to anchor teaching and learning around specified outcomes.[45] If all students were expected to meet the outcomes and the efforts of teachers focused on that goal, then many of the sources of alienation, low self-esteem, and lack of motivation might be removed. As the select committee discovered, moreover, there was also broad consensus about the negative effects of the discontinuities between elementary and high school, and a concomitant belief that changes needed to be made in the curriculum and organization of the junior grades of the high school rather than the senior elementary school. Indeed, a greater focus on 'caring and concern' was a common diagnosis. More monitoring and supervision of students through everything from home-form teachers to school-attendance officers, more mentoring of individual students by teachers, more stability within peer groups, more links between home and school, and a more supportive and positive school atmosphere generally were only some of the proposals to reduce the degree of alienation high school students were said to experience.[46]

When it came to the more fundamental question of what students should actually be taught, however, rifts were everywhere. Radwanski mounted a powerful case against the principle of curricular choice embedded in the credit system, arguing, among other things, that it penalized students from less-educated families because they lacked the information and advice to choose wisely, and that the individual timetables it required 'make school a more alienating place as students move from class to class and teacher to teacher without being part of any cohesive social unit.' The extensive choice of courses, moreover, implied that it didn't matter what students chose to study, and that in turn implied that it didn't much matter whether or not they stayed in school.[47]

Radwanski's alternative was a common curriculum consisting of English, mathematics, science and technology, Canadian and world history and geography, French, the arts, and physical education. There would be two cross-curricular emphases, 'clear thinking and effective learning,' and citizenship. Old-fashioned trades training would be replaced by 'Work in Society,' a broad-based approach to technological education. This unstreamed or common curriculum would be taught to *all* students, from grades 1 to 12. A limited menu of options would be available only in the last two years of high school to enable students to meet university or college entrance requirements or pursue other special interests.[48]

The reaction of many practitioners was stark incredulity. Not only did Radwanski's curriculum look like a return to the discredited past, a futile hankering after an irretrievable golden age when a handful of academic subjects, sustained by the grade 13 departmentals, reigned supreme, but it contradicted their intuitive sense that choice and flexibility were essential if individual interests and needs were to be met.[49] Some of the research on school atmosphere appeared to support their views.[50] Nor did everyone agree that the general courses were merely watered-down versions of the real thing; indeed, as one thoughtful critic argued, offering subjects like mathematics with a practical bias had its own academic integrity, while the attempt to teach advanced subjects to every student would result either in high failure rates *or* the dilution of the advanced program itself.[51] Even those who agreed with Radwanski's assessment of the credit system took issue with his views about what constituted a suitable curriculum.[52] Others described it as giving students more of what they already hated.[53]

The educational community was equally divided over the abolition of streaming. Radwanski had some important allies on this issue, including much of the media, the Ontario Federation of Labour, and many academics. Though initially opposed to abolition, OECTA reversed its stand in the light of a thorough literature review by Robert Dixon, a senior Catholic educator and historian.[54] An OSSTF curriculum committee, in a widely circulated report to members, recommended abolition, and a group of OISE academics did the same before the Select Committee on Education.[55] OSSTF members, on the other hand, rejected the recommendations of their curriculum committee and opposed abolition, as did FWTAO, the latter arguing that ability grouping had a place among a teacher's pedagogical tools.[56] Opinion polls demonstrated that Ontarians were sharply split over outright abolition or, indeed, the age level at which some form of streaming should begin.[57] In their own research report, Alan King and his colleagues expressed scepticism, suggesting that abolition was impractical given the sorting function the Ontario high schools were required to carry out as part of their mandate to prepare students for post-secondary education – a view shared by Bernard Shapiro.[58] King also pointed out that the most influential American critique of streaming offered no comparisons of the relative effectiveness of streamed and non-streamed schools, did not 'identify non-streamed secondary schools that are working effectively, nor ... offer anything that might be considered a concrete proposal.' King went on to add that 'the credit system with its individualized student timetables actually goes a long way towards reducing some of the negative effects' that Radwanski, relying on this American research, had described.[59] What he meant by that was demonstrated in one 1990 study of London's high schools: some 60 per cent of grade 11 students were taking 80 per cent or more of their courses at either the advanced or general level (about 30 per cent in each); the other 40 per cent took a mix of both, and the figures were similar in the other grades. *OSIS* and the credit system, in other words, provided students and their parents with opportunities to choose courses at either level according to their interests and abilities, and there was a high level of fluidity in the choices students made.[60] In such circumstances many teachers and administrators found it difficult to subscribe to a view that portrayed their schools as rigorously streamed, or as imposing dead-end programs on large numbers of their students.

The first report of the Select Committee on Education reflected the complexities of the issue nicely. During its hearings many people had expressed unease about the effects of streaming, and 'research reviewed by the committee underscored their concern ... Data from other countries clearly showed that streaming reinforces educational inequality ... The limited amount of Ontario research seemed to indicate similar patterns. On the other hand, many witnesses argued that streaming is not itself the cause of unequal educational outcomes and other problems. A major body of opinion believes that grouping can address the differing specific capacities and needs of students.'[61]

Befuddled by the contradictions and divided among themselves, committee members gingerly reached a compromise that tied the abolition of streaming not to the larger issues of social justice or the provision of a second-rate education in the lower streams, but to the difficulties associated exclusively with the transition from elementary to high school. Declaring that students were too young to make irrevocable decisions about their future at age thirteen or fourteen, it recommended the abolition of streaming in grade 9, thus delaying it by one school year. Even then the committee warned that no precipitate action should be taken without pilot projects, professional development for teachers, and careful planning before implementation, all underwritten by adequate funding.[62]

In the Throne Speech of April 1989, the government fell upon this modest proposal as its only substantive response to the long and large-scale public discussion over the dropout rate and the related problem of what and how to teach the majority of Ontario's high school students who would not be going on to post-secondary education. In order to ease the transition from elementary to high school, grades 7 to 9 would be reorganized. A core curriculum would be introduced, for all three years, that 'emphasizes the development of basic skills and progressive problem-solving.' Such a core would improve the academic skills required to handle the secondary curriculum and delay, by a year, the choice of academic future. To that end, streaming in grade 9 would be abolished. Grades 7 to 9 were retitled 'the transition years' and grades 10 to 12 designated 'the specialization years.' But the only specific proposal for the latter was the redesign of technical courses into an approach that would become known as 'broad-based technology.'[63]

THE APRIL 1989 THRONE SPEECH was the high-water mark for Liberal policy-making in education. And though they would rapidly become known as the 'restructuring' initiatives – one of the buzzwords of the era – the Liberal agenda was fairly modest in scope. Enrolments in junior and senior kindergarten were already very high; mandating the provision of school places for four- and five-year-olds was a relatively small step forward, though moving from half- to full-day kindergarten was not without significance. While controversial enough, the government's actual destreaming initiative encompassed only a single high school grade. Despite all the talk about a more relevant high school curriculum, Bernard Shapiro had told one reporter that the high school curriculum 'is more likely to be fine-tuned than fundamentally changed.'[64] Perhaps the most radical departure was the various assessment initiatives. Though only just under way they seemed to portend an about-face within the ministry. It was 'amazing' just how much had been accomplished in testing in only two years, remarked Dennis Raphael, at the time the ministry's provincial review manager. 'It's really changing. There is a [new] sense throughout the ministry that it has to be more active in setting standards, in measuring and evaluating.'[65]

GIVEN ALL THE RHETORIC about the renewal of education so pervasive amongst Liberal politicians and their advisers in the previous four years, and given the sheer magnitude of the Liberal election victory in 1987, which gave the government a free hand and a convincing mandate for change, one is entitled to ask why it took so long even to formulate the 1989 initiatives.

There were, I suggest, four reasons. First, the Liberal government and the Ministry of Education already had their hands full dealing with other issues. The introduction of full funding for Roman Catholic secondary schools ate up prodigious amounts of time and energy from the moment the Liberals came to power until at least 1989. During the same years the government and the ministry were grappling with the politically explosive and administratively complex problems associated with the provision and governance of francophone schools. The government was also trying to come to terms with the problems of educational finance, including the vexed issue of pooling local property taxes. And, in the late 1980s, proposed legislation to change the governance and financing of the teachers' pension plan caused a horrendous dust-up between the government and the teachers' unions.[66] As Thomas Courchene and Colin Telmer have suggested, moreover, pressed by the terms of the Liberal-NDP Accord, and after 1987 by other matters, the Liberals' initial enthusiasm for an economic agenda focused on making Ontario more competitive 'in the new global and informatics order' took second place to 'an incredibly ambitious social agenda.'[67] While education tended to be on the margins of this shift, it could hardly escape the impact.

After some prodding by the NDP, and much adverse publicity in the press over the refusal of the Scarborough Board of Education to introduce Heritage Languages Programs in its schools, the Liberals reviewed the entire issue and made such programs mandatory for all boards in Ontario upon the request of the parents of twenty-five or more children.[68] The ministry was also engaged in developing a model 'anti-racist and ethnocultural policy' that could be used by boards to tackle the concerns about racism and other discriminatory practices, promote respect for cultural diversity, and reduce the number of students assigned to lower streams because of cultural differences or difficulties with the English language.[69] Beyond that, the government invested a good deal of time in issues relating to gender equity. As it became clear that many boards were failing to respond to earlier incentives to increase the number of women in Positions of Added Responsibility, the Liberals amended the Education Act in 1989 to give the minister authority to require boards to establish affirmative-action policies and, a year later, set a goal of 50 per cent or more women in PARs in both the elementary and secondary panels, to be achieved by the year 2000.[70] Thus, aside from anything else, the Liberal government and the ministry had a wide-ranging series of issues to deal with from the beginning, and the agenda broadened as time went on. Amidst all this, the restructuring of the learning program did not exactly get lost, but it certainly had to compete with things that had a higher priority or were enormously time-consuming for the politicians and senior bureaucrats alike.

Second, after the election victory of 1987, the Peterson government temporarily lost some of its sense of direction, and with that, a good deal of its momentum. There is a first-rate account of these difficulties elsewhere and I will not reiterate them here.[71] But it was not until the Throne Speech of April 1989 that the government managed to get back on track. Education as well as other initiatives languished in the interim.

Third, in their concern to construct policy that was based on a broad public consensus, Peterson, his inner cabinet, and their advisers became obsessive about 'consultation.' Said one top bureaucrat in 1988, 'If I had one word to describe this government it would be "consultation." We are so busy consulting that no one is noticing that nothing is happening.'[72] That was as true in education as in other policy areas. Not content with the advice they were getting from Radwanski and the Premier's Council, for example, the Liberals had established an all-party Legislative Committee on Education that toured the province, consulting the public as well as a panoply of experts, and issued four reports between 1988 and 1990. For his part, Shapiro commissioned a plethora of research reports, which, whatever their value as foundations for policy, also delayed decision-making.

Finally, the extent to which research studies and consultative processes were pursued between 1987 and 1989 suggests a government and a ministry determined to 'get it right' before proceeding, confident they would be able to implement their initiatives during a second (or even a third or fourth or fifth) Liberal term. Certainly the political history of the province was conducive to such a view, as were the Liberal ratings in all of the opinion polls right up to the moment David Peterson called the election of 1990.

HAD THERE NOW, at least, been enough deliberation, enough consultation? Not at all. The Throne Speech initiatives, to be introduced over the succeeding three to five years, had to be turned into concrete policies which could be implemented in the schools; that in turn had to be done in ways concordant with the consent and support of the educational community. Thus the ministry embarked on a massive consultation project that included the creation of a new mini-bureaucracy at the centre, yet more commissioned research, and a blizzard of paper designed to test policy options and solicit opinion.[73] Special emphasis and yet more research money was put into planning for the 'Transition Years,' because that was where the most dramatic and controversial changes were expected to take place, including the destreaming of grade 9. Altogether, the consultation papers constituted hundreds of pages of print, which by 1992 had elicited some three thousand written suggestions that, collated into 'response summaries,' were intended to guide policy decisions.[74]

Having set this behemoth in motion, Shapiro left the ministry, in January 1990, to become deputy minister of cabinet, where he was engaged in a large-scale project to streamline and downsize the civil service. At the very time the Ministry of Education was taking on an enormous restructuring project, it entered a period of prolonged decline in the number of its employees, including those at the senior levels where the quality of decisions and the competence of management were mostly determined.

The NDP and a Royal Commission, 1990–1995

Meanwhile, amidst all the consultation and strategic planning, David Peterson called his surprise election for 6 September 1990. And lost, badly, in part because of an energetic, well-financed campaign by the teachers' unions attacking the Liberals for spending too little on education.[1] In the immediate aftermath the question arose, Would the new NDP government proceed with the Liberal education initiatives, or start over with a different agenda that was distinctly its own? While the Ontario NDP had some sharp internal divisions on educational policy, it came to power with a record of substantive debate over education issues, and a backlog of thoughtful position papers, the product of an energetic organizational effort by its most recent education critic, Richard Johnston.[2] There was, on the other hand, a good deal of common ground between the NDP and the departing Liberals. Though hardly satisfactory to the party's left wing, the 1989 Throne Speech initiatives went some way towards meeting the objectives of many mainstream New Democrats. Radwanski's assault on the class biases of the streaming system went down well among large numbers of the party faithful, and the party's economic policy advisers were favourably disposed towards much of the argument of the Premier's Council's reports, including the emphasis on the importance of education and training to Ontario's economic future.[3] There was, in other words, no automatic disjunction between Liberal and NDP education policy to push the new government towards a different course.

Contingency pressed towards continuity as well. In September 1990, the most likely candidate for the education portfolio was Tony Silipo, a thirty-five-year-old lawyer, long-time school trustee, and most recently chair of the Toronto Board of Education.[4] Silipo knew the ground, the hot education issues, and brought to them a perspective to the left of the party's mainstream. He might well have set educational policy on a new course right at the beginning of the party's accession to power. But he was temporarily knocked out of contention when he appeared to have run afoul of the Law Society's ethics rules, and the appointment went, *faute de mieux*, to Marion Boyd.

An experienced social activist, Boyd brought to the job strong opinions on equity issues and pressed forward with these on a number of fronts, including one major policy initiative not on the Liberal list – making the integration of exceptional pupils the norm in Ontario's classrooms. But beyond that she supported the general thrust of Liberal policy and was enthusiastic about the broad canvass of all stakeholders the consultation process entailed.[5] As a consequence the Liberal agenda remained in place throughout Boyd's year as minister of education, and she functioned, in effect, as a political caretaker for a bureaucracy already fully engaged in its own restructuring initiatives.

The one exception occurred over the assessment of student achievement. Boyd created a brouhaha when she reversed a Liberal commitment to provincial participation in the student achievement tests that were part of the national indicators of the Council of Ministers of Education, thus offering the more paranoid critics of the schools one more proof that the educational establishment did have something to hide and was indeed hiding it.[6] But that was probably less significant than the downgrading of the benchmarks program. Though never formally abandoned, the predilections of the party, pressure from the teachers' unions, and probably the predisposition of senior ministry officials combined to consign it to a policy backwater, and to jettison the development of the diagnostic tests which had been intended to give the benchmarks program its teeth.[7]

IN THE AUTUMN OF 1991 a ministerial resignation forced Rae to make some cabinet readjustments, and he took the opportunity to move Boyd to Community and Social Services. Already rehabilitated and a member of cabinet, Tony Silipo took her place as minister of education. Eager to leave his mark on the province's school system and sure he could do it swiftly, Silipo brought in his own small team of political advisers, and prepared to get on with the job. High on their agenda were the long-standing objectives of the left-wing education caucus within the NDP: destreaming the schools and delabelling students, the virtual abolition of the special-education empire, vigorous employment-equity and anti-racism initiatives, curricular reform that would lessen invidious distinctions between academic and practical subjects, a pedagogy that promoted co-operative and

shared, rather than competitive, learning styles, and changes in governance that would short-circuit local bureaucracies and give greater voice to
parents and other lay members of school communities.[8]

Like Boyd before him, Silipo inherited the Liberal restructuring initiatives and the ministry's consultation and implementation strategies. Silipo
did nothing to redirect this activity except to ensure that it reflected the
party's emphases and priorities. But he also initiated a more fundamental
project intended to lay out a vision of what a genuinely 'democratic
socialist' school system might look like, and articulate the larger policy
framework that would inform specific ministry initiatives.[9] This task, the
preserve of Silipo's political team, was begun early on. By March 1992
Silipo was promising that 'a comprehensive policy statement for Education in Ontario, designed to provide a framework from junior kindergarten to graduation, is planned for the fall of 1992.' This would 'provide a
context for the development of learning outcomes for each initiative.'[10] As
he himself described it, the document would fulfil his 'commitment to
redesign the whole elementary and secondary school system in Ontario';[11]
on another occasion he spoke of providing 'a coherent statement of
direction for the school system.'[12] Thus from autumn 1991 through to
autumn 1992 there were two overlapping policy thrusts at work: the
ministry initiatives, on the one hand, and, on the other, an ambitious
attempt to reorient the premises of the system along politically 'progressive' lines and to indicate the policy changes this might entail.

Silipo became minister just about the time the furore over standards
and accountability was reaching its crescendo, and however unenthusias-
tic they were, neither he nor his advisers could sidestep assessment and
testing issues. Indeed, one of Silipo's first initiatives was to reverse Boyd's
decision to withdraw from the national indicator achievement tests.[13] In
December 1991, he also gave the flagging benchmarks program new life,
directing that the production of provincial standards for mathematics in
grades 3, 6, and 9 be given priority.[14] The issue became far more urgent in
February 1992 with the release of another set of international test results
which showed that Ontario's nine- and thirteen-year-olds were doing worse
in math and science than their counterparts in several other countries and
some Canadian provinces. Silipo took the opportunity to release all the
bad news at once, simultaneously revealing the results of a provincial
review of grade 8, 10, and 12 mathematics achievement that was equally
unsatisfactory. Amidst predictable cries of outrage from all the usual
suspects, Silipo admitted that the results were 'disturbing' and declared
that the new provincial standards would be in place by June.[15] The minis-

ter, his advisers, and ministry officials, nonetheless, bent over backwards to insist that the standards would not be accompanied by province-wide testing, that teachers alone would use them to assess individual students, that only teachers would control which assessment tools they used to measure achievement of the standards, and that the province would use them only to monitor the success of the system as a whole.[16]

When it came to destreaming, on the other hand, Silipo was prepared to push hard. In an unexpected announcement in January 1992 he confirmed that there would be no delay in the schedule for grade 9 – it would be destreamed in September 1993. That in itself put teachers' teeth on edge; he then went on to add that discussions would also begin about extending the policy to grade 10, something that had hardly been whispered in policy circles since 1988.[17]

By the spring, moreover, the ministry had worked out the principles that would guide curriculum reform.[18] Rather than treat the formative and transition years separately, there would be a seamless curriculum for grades 1 through 9, and one that was the same for (or common to) all students, an inevitable concomitant of the decision to abolish homogeneous ability grouping. It would be based on learning outcomes that all students were expected to achieve. Organizing the curriculum around subjects, a practice specifically sanctioned by *OSIS* for grades 7 onwards, was to be abandoned; instead, content was to be integrated within four core areas: language; the arts; self and society; and mathematics, science, and technology.* Each area would have its own set of learning outcomes and these, in turn, would be tied to the provincial standards – criteria for ascertaining whether or not a pupil had, at given points, achieved the outcome. Not all students were expected to reach the same level, but all would meet the outcome at one level or another – or, alternatively, would be identified as candidates for remediation. Thus the attempt to give substance to the rhetoric of excellence, equity, and accountability: a common curriculum for all, with worthwhile, relevant, and challenging outcomes, and with explicit criteria (or standards) for assessing and reporting achievement to parents and public. That, at least, was the theory of how the new program of studies, grades 1 to 9, would work, and why it was supposed to represent an improved model for teaching and learning in Ontario.

The destreaming and curriculum decisions were translated into a minis-

---

*In staffroom parlance, integration was quickly tagged 'decoursing' and joined 'destreaming' and 'decrediting' as part of the ministry's trinity of policy changes.

terial directive in June 1992, and two others were added as well.[19] Integration of exceptional pupils into regular classrooms would become the norm beginning in September 1993. School boards would also be required to provide senior kindergarten for all children whose parents sought it by the same date, and a year later, in September 1994, mandatory provision of junior kindergarten would begin.

All this, in itself, was a mouthful for trustees, administrators, and teachers to swallow. By the autumn it got worse. The draft benchmarks (or 'standards') for mathematics were released, and an initial overview of the new curriculum, entitled *Everybody's Schools: The Common Curriculum*, was circulated to all and sundry despite being stamped, in large letters, 'Confidential.' Beyond that, there was the comprehensive policy document. We do not know the ideological framework it proposed or its contents, for it was never released.[20] But we do know that it was submitted to cabinet late in the fall and that the following specific changes were under consideration at the same time: the elimination of grade 13, the end of streaming in grade 10, the integration of heritage language instruction within the regular school day, and mandatory parent advisory councils for every school.[21] Taken altogether, the agenda that emerged between June and November 1992 promised quite dramatic and comprehensive change.

The result was growing uproar. Opposed from the beginning to destreaming – opposed at least without all kinds of qualifications about implementation – the OSSTF was caught off guard by Silipo's January 1992 decision to proceed and came out swinging. Union leaders contended the initiative was ill planned and ill financed. There were no suitable curricular materials, they pointed out, teachers were unprepared, and the results of the ministry's much-vaunted pilot projects were not yet available.[22] In April the union won the backing of OTF, representing the other teacher unions, for a motion condemning the initiative, and, following its own spring conference, OSSTF launched an all-out campaign of opposition, including a failed attempt to defeat the initiative at the NDP party convention that June.[23] While opinion among the rank and file may have been divided about destreaming grade 9, large numbers of teachers were either opposed in principle or profoundly anxious about their ability to cope with unstreamed classes. 'I received more letters on the destreaming issue,' OSSTF president Liz Barkley would later remark, 'than I did on any other, including the Social Contract.'[24]

But it was not just destreaming and not just OSSTF. The integration of exceptional pupils caused general unease among teachers. There was confusion about just how the benchmarks program was supposed to work, and anxiety about how the government might use it to control curriculum or to evaluate individual teachers and schools. By autumn 1992 there was even more confusion about what teachers were expected to teach: in less than a year they were supposed to offer a new curriculum, yet there were no guidelines beyond the 'confidential' draft version of *The Common Curriculum*, which gave virtually no direction at all. Capping it all was the leaked cabinet document (and the accompanying front-page headline in the *Toronto Star*) about the abolition of grade 13. Given the potential job losses that change might entail, it came as no surprise when OSSTF condemned it outright; by late November, an emergency meeting of OSSTF delegates voted unanimously for a motion demanding Silipo's resignation and a moratorium on classroom reform.[25]

Nor was it only teachers who were upset by ministry initiatives. Under intense taxpayer pressure to contain their own costs, school trustees were outraged when told to introduce junior kindergarten or pay for the expenses attendant upon everything from destreaming to the integration of exceptional pupils. At a time when 73 per cent of Ontarians said they wanted province-wide testing in the schools, they were being offered instead a benchmarks program that (whatever its actual merits) looked like voodoo assessment. Destreaming provoked controversy, both in the press and among trustees and parent groups. *Everybody's Schools* was slammed as gibberish, gobbledy-gook, holistic hogwash, mumbo-jumbo, or edubabble gone mad, judgments that were only somewhat understated. 'Ask anyone outside government to explain Ontario's education policy,' wrote Jennifer Lewington in September 1992, 'and the common response is a burst of laughter. The province claims to be on the verge of reforming its education system. But after a decade of stop-and-go change ... the current exercise is being greeted with confusion and cynicism.' A November *Star* headline read, 'Discord, confusion dog school reforms.'[26]

By that point, it was clear that Silipo could no more persuade his cabinet colleagues to support him than he could the teachers and large parts of the public. Silipo's 'comprehensive policy document' was rejected in cabinet and then suppressed by Rae.[27] The common curriculum was thrown back for rewriting. By the end of 1992, the premier had lost confidence in Silipo's ability to manage the education portfolio, and, perhaps, in the competence of senior ministry personnel to manage their own affairs.

By late 1992 and early 1993, indeed, the problem of public confidence was paramount. Anger and confusion over program reforms peaked at the same time as the outcry over education costs, school trustees' extravagance, and school administrators' smug complacency about standards. And education issues were contributing to growing disaffection with the Rae government itself.

But what was to be done? Beginning at some point in the late fall, the idea of an independent review of educational policy began to crystallize in the minds of politicians and senior civil servants. 'Another study!' the sceptical reader might well remark: What about Radwanski, the two Premier's Council reports, four separate reports from the Select Committee on Education, the volumes of research commissioned by Shapiro, and, most recently, the massive consultation exercise conducted by the ministry itself? Did Ontario really need yet one more canvass of public opinion, one more survey of the issues confronting education? Obviously a commission had the great political advantage of buying time, taking the heat off government and its education policies; that was no doubt one vital argument in its favour. But there was more to it than that: given the ferment that existed by late 1992, it was not hard to conclude that a large number of issues needed a thoughtful second look and, most important, some ground for consensus about both means and ends in education.

Though its mandate and membership had yet to be determined, the decision to establish a commission on education was made by mid-January 1993.[28] At best, however, that was a long-term solution. A more immediate form of damage control emerged from a February 3 cabinet shuffle: Silipo was moved to another ministry and Dave Cooke, who had proved his mettle during a difficult stretch at Municipal Affairs, took on the job at Education.*

COOKE HAD FAR MORE experience in provincial politics and was now a seasoned cabinet minister. He didn't share the ideological zeal of the party's left wing and would make no attempt to refashion the entire school system in a 'democratic socialist' image. Nor was he about to add fuel to the fire by destreaming grade 10 or promoting changes in the senior high school program. Issues such as these could safely be left to the royal commission. But there was no wholesale change in the direction of established educational policy. Though willing to make some modest compromises over implementation dates, within a month of assuming office Cooke had reaffirmed the government's commitment to a destreamed

---

*Cooke actually took over the new 'Ministry of Education and Training,' a product of the civil-service streamlining initiated by the Liberals, which absorbed the three existing education-related ministries, those of education, skills training, and colleges and universities.

grade 9, the benchmarks program, the integration of exceptional pupils, and the introduction of mandatory junior kindergarten. Despite the fact that it was controversial, and in some parts of the province deemed unnecessary, he pushed ahead with plans already under way to mandate the introduction of anti-racism and ethnocultural equity policies in all of Ontario's school boards.[29] In February 1993 he released a rewritten *Common Curriculum*. It was, in his own view (as well as in the opinion of others, including Premier Rae), still jargon-ridden[30] and its approach to curriculum remained controversial. To deal with both problems Cooke labelled it a 'working document,' promised that the ministry would listen seriously to suggestions for change, and established a review committee to canvass public opinion and prepare a final revision.[31] He also hired a private consulting firm, at a cost of $10,000, to translate the document into English for parents and the general public; he had to go to an outside firm, he reputedly told a reporter, 'because everyone in his 3000-person ministry speaks bafflegab.'[32] But the essential principles of *The Common Curriculum* remained in place: an integrated curriculum that was outcomes-based, and with as heavy an emphasis on equity and social goals as on academic learning more narrowly conceived. The revisions completed, a final version was published early in 1995.[33]

ONE NEW DEPARTURE came over the uses of assessment. As Cooke would put it the day after he became minister, 'I am not afraid of issues like testing, because if we don't get more public confidence in the education system I think that's a greater threat to the ... system than anything else right now.'[34] In the months that followed Cooke would speculate repeatedly about introducing province-wide achievement tests at several grade levels[35] – something unheard of since the Liberals' brief flirtation with the idea in 1989. But he put off a final decision on that one, pending the report of the royal commission. He believed, however, that some interim measure was imperative. Thus, in April 1993, Cooke ordered that a planned provincial review of grade 9 reading and writing skills, based upon a sample of pupils, be rejigged to include a system-wide assessment of every grade 9 student in the province.[36]

While both the process and the results are interesting,[37] what mattered more was the significance of the experiment. The test constituted something of a minor revolution in Ontario education: the first province-wide, universal assessment of achievement in decades. There was a second consequence of greater importance. The grade 9 test results were provided to school boards and to individual students, their teachers, and parents. Cooke, however, had not intended to release school-by-school results or require boards to do so.[38] But a previous decision by Ontario's privacy commissioner made it all but inevitable, and a few hardy souls used freedom-of-information legislation or some other method to extract school-level results from recalcitrant boards or administrators.[39] Even before that, some boards had been converted to the advantages, and legitimacy, of openness, and had begun to release all their own school-level results.[40] In a few cases, most notably in North York, where its director, Veronica Lacey, was setting precedents in establishing results-based education, much more detailed, multi-grade rankings were being released.[41] The release of the provincial grade 9 test results reinforced this trend. In doing so, it contributed to changing the environment of the assessment enterprise and thus served a more useful purpose than simply as a source of aggregate or individual test results.

The other 'public confidence' issue Cooke tried to address was violence in the schools. He was hardly alone in this: most of the pioneering work on the problems had been carried out by the teacher federations or individual boards, and while the province had been slow to formulate its own response, work had been on-going under the Liberals, Boyd, and Silipo. Cooke, however, made it a priority, working with the school boards and through a recently established Ministry Violence Prevention Secretariat; by June 1994 a provincial Violence-Free Schools Policy was in place, requiring all boards to develop violence-prevention policies and implementation plans.[42] Undoubtedly mainly of symbolic value, the policy at least indicated that the government recognized and was prepared to respond to a major source of public unease about the schools.

STILL, ALL OF THESE developments were sideshows compared to the decision, back in January 1993, to establish Ontario's first full-fledged royal commission on education since Hope, and the first comprehensive review since Hall-Dennis. Two full-time co-chairs were selected, Monique Bégin and Gerald Caplan. A formidable pair of political veterans, Bégin and Caplan knew how to read public opinion, and how to get things done in the public arena. Bégin had been a teacher, worked as executive secretary to the Royal Commission on the Status of Women, entered federal politics in 1972, served as minister of national health and welfare in the Trudeau government from 1977 to 1984, and by the mid-1990s was a senior administrator at the University of Ottawa. Though a lifelong Liberal, her political and social commitments put her in the left wing of the party. Caplan, a long-time NDP activist and past national director of the party, had also served as co-chair of a federal royal commission on broadcasting, had been a key strategist on the Ontario NDP election planning and transition team in 1990, and was working as a newspaper and television commentator. The part-time members of the commission included two well-established and highly experienced members of Ontario's education community and a senior-high-school student from Cornwall.[43] The mandate of the commissioners was a broad one: to review and make recommendations about the program of studies, accountability, and the governance of the school system. Only finance was left out, and even then the commissioners included a short chapter on the subject because it was so integral to their reform proposals.

During the year that followed their appointment, the commissioners spent a significant amount of time inside schools and classrooms, solicited expert opinion on a wide variety of subjects, carried out an intensive program of public consultations with teachers, parents, students, citizens' groups, and community organizations, and 'spoke hundreds of times to newspaper, radio, and television reporters.'[44] The views they heard were diverse and contradictory, and touched on many different aspects of schooling. But 'underlying the concerns of all those who made submissions,' the commissioners remarked, 'is a distinct sense of unease and uncertainty about the educational system. People spoke about unclear purposes and overload; they questioned whether the material students were learning was necessary and important, whether they were learning it at an appropriate level, whether the system was equitable, and whether it was cost-effective.'[45] Or, as the commissioners summarized it elsewhere, 'The major issues around which the debate about education and educational reform centres ... include quality, focus, fairness, openness, and efficiency.'[46]

And how did the commissioners respond to what they heard? Rejecting the list of vague and indiscriminate 'goals' set for the schools since the 1970s, their first step was to try to reassert some clarity of purpose for the educational enterprise.[47] How are schools different from other social institutions, they asked? The school has many responsibilities, some shared with families and other community organizations, and some uniquely its own. But its primary responsibility was 'children's learning and the development of competence.' The commission listed five key goals for the schools: 'intellectual development, learning to learn, citizenship, preparation for work/career development, [and] instilling values.' But 'we see the first priority ... to be the intellectual nurturing of students.' The commissioners went on to cut through, in incisive fashion, the debate over the

links between education and the economy. It didn't matter whether or not
the economy required high or low levels of skills from most workers: 'We
would argue that the central or primary purpose is intellectual development ... and that preparing young people to participate in a modern
democratic society requires quality programs for all.'

What did intellectual development entail? The school must ensure that
students acquire 'high-level literacies, beginning with basic reading and
writing skills, leading to increasing knowledge, intellectual understanding, problem-solving skills, and critical thinking in a wide range of subjects.'[48] These characteristics were to be acquired in the first instance by
induction into a group of generic or foundation skills – the 'grounding for
further learning,' as the commissioners termed it; 'they include the traditional basics – literacy and numeracy – as well as the "new basics" – group
learning and interpersonal skills and values, scientific literacy, and computer literacy.'[49] These generic skills were to be taught and learned from the
beginning of elementary education through to high school graduation,
sometimes as subjects in their own right, and sometimes as outcomes of
the process of learning other subjects.

While the schools were not doing nearly so badly as most critics claimed,
the commissioners continued, there was still a substantial gap between
what needed to be done and what the schools were actually doing. 'We
believe, in no uncertain terms, that almost all students have the capacity to
complete secondary school with a great deal more academic excellence,
more rigorous analytic capacity, more genuine intellectual understanding,
more power of thinking, reasoning, problem-solving, than is now generally the case.'[50] How, then, was the gap to be closed? There were, the
commissioners believed, four crucial 'engines' of change – 'four driving
forces ... essential to major transformation of the system, to support
key partners in playing new roles ... and to drive the other reforms we
recommend.'[51]

The first was early childhood education, which was vital to the intellectual development of all children and which promised greater equality of
opportunity for the disadvantaged. Next were teachers, who were at the
heart of the enterprise; all other reforms depended, at base, on enhanced
professionalism and improved teacher education. Third was Information
Technology, a subject that provoked the commissioners' uncritical enthusiasm. Information Technology was to become a transformative influence
on the way students learned and teachers taught, changing relationships
among students, and between students and teachers. Finally, there was
'community education.' This involved a greater say for community repre-

sentatives in how schools were organized and run, including the establish-ment of parent councils. But the commissioners were adamant that it cut both ways. The schools were badly overburdened, and it was essential that 'social agencies, community and religious organizations, local businesses and trade unions, and community colleges and universities share the load, particularly the non-academic load, that has been thrust on our schools. Such alliances would allow teachers to focus on their central tasks, namely teaching and learning, and to address the issues of curriculum overload and system over-extension.'[52]

Having set out this framework for change, the commission then turned to its review of specific parts of the system. Despite the importance of early childhood education as one of the commission's four 'engines,' the report dealt with it relatively briefly, presumably because the commissioners believed its merit was obvious and overwhelming. Covering much the same ground as Radwanski, they reviewed the research and concluded, as indeed Radwanski had, that Ontario's schools should be required to provide education 'to all children from 3 to 5 years of age whose parents/guardians choose to enrol them.' As space became available 'early child-hood education would gradually replace existing junior and senior kin-dergarten programs, and become part of the public education system.'[53]

Whereas that recommendation proposed an ambitious new departure, the commissioners' review of the learning program for six- to fifteen-year-olds (grades 1 to 9) did little more than rubber-stamp government policy and the nostrums of its advisers.[54] All in all, outcomes-based education was a good thing; indeed it should be extended throughout the high school years. Despite bitter controversy, the decision to destream grade 9 was a wise one. Although there was no research to suggest that subject integra-tion improved student achievement or that it contributed to teaching 'the essential skills of each subject logically and cumulatively,' integration was 'intuitively appealing.' Thus the commission pronounced its blessing on the main outlines of *The Common Curriculum* even as it quibbled with some of the details: there should be a sharper focus in the primary and junior years on the foundation skills, above all literacy and numeracy; the out-comes listed in *The Common Curriculum* were too numerous and too vague – revisions were needed to produce a shorter and more focused set. One substantial change in direction was put on the table, however. The out-comes needed to be accompanied by detailed curriculum guidelines to help teachers understand 'what they are expected to teach and what students are expected to learn.' These should be drafted by the ministry, and teachers required to devote 90 per cent of class time to meeting them.

Though the reorganization of the senior high school had been on the agenda since 1989, the ministry's consultation project had not even begun until late 1991, was only completed in 1993, and policy decisions were put on hold when the royal commission was appointed. Thus, unlike the situation with grades 1 to 9, the commissioners had a clear field.[55] They began by canvassing, yet once more, the dropout problem and the various analyses of the previous decade. They also added their voice to the long succession of observers who had called for the abolition of the fifth high school year (still conventionally called grade 13), reiterating the familiar arguments about this unique and purportedly unnecessary Ontario institution. The idea of destreaming grade 10 had its virtues, but for practical reasons should not be pursued: teachers had found the decision to destream grade 9 'traumatic, and they told us they feel beleaguered by the pace of educational change ... in the last decade.' With some regret, the commissioners also rejected Radwanski's proposal for a common curriculum through to the end of grade 12; given the variety of aptitudes and interests among students, it was necessary to offer some choices and encourage some degree of specialization.

They recognized, however, that there was a pressing need for 'more successful alternatives [to *OSIS*] that will help lower the number of students who leave school without a diploma, and will increase the percentage who attend college.' With that goal in mind they fashioned a modest but 'do-able' scheme that would also reduce, if not eliminate, the invidious distinctions between the advanced program and the general and basic streams. They recommended that there be only two sets of differentiated courses, one geared to meeting university requirements and the other, of equally high quality, designed to emphasize applications and connections outside the classroom. Beyond that, as many subjects as feasible would be offered at a single, or common, level. Students would be encouraged to take a mix: those, for example, intending to enter a university engineering program might take specialized university preparation courses in mathematics and science but could also take the more applied history and English courses and common-level subjects such as physical education and music. The commissioners proposed to raise the total number of required subjects to fourteen of twenty-one credits in grades 10 to 12 so that individual programs of study would become more structured; all students, moreover, would organize their selections around packages of courses based on career plans or an interdisciplinary theme. The commissioners did not expect any of these changes to revolutionize the high school or create dramatic changes in student enrolment patterns. But they did hope that they might increase the degree of focus, relevance, and inclusiveness, better equip students to enter the world of work, or qualify them to enter the community colleges.

As important as these programmatic recommendations were, the commission was also alert to the emphasis, pervasive in the research literature, on 'caring and concern' – the need to reduce alienation among high school students, and, indeed, ensure that individual pupils, elementary and high school alike, received closer supervision and more emotional and intellectual support. Thus the commissioners endorsed proposals to organize house systems or 'schools within schools,' more effective guidance and mentoring systems at all grade levels, and a variety of other innovations to encourage a supportive environment.

While the commission made a number of recommendations designed to improve the quality of teaching, the most contentious was the proposal to establish a 'College of Teachers,' a step intended to recognize and regularize the status of teaching as a profession, much like other professions. 'The college would be responsible for determining standards of teaching practice, regulating initial and on-going teacher certification, and accrediting teacher education programs.'[56]

Given the sheer volume of debate about evaluation and accountability, it was not surprising that the commissioners devoted a good deal of attention to the topic.[57] They circled it warily, however, attempting, without much success, to keep accountability and the evaluation of individual student achievement in air-tight compartments. In the main, their response to the latter was little more than a gloss on the reigning consensus among the educational establishment. The commissioners reiterated the conventional horror stories about the effects of large-scale assessment. Yet, in the end, for both educational and political reasons, they gave it a reluctant endorsement. 'While we want to be very clear about our lack of enthusiasm for extensive, expensive, universal testing, as opposed to sample-based assessment, we recognize the public's need for some measure of basic student achievement that is applied in the same way to every student at a few points in time. That is why we are recommending two province-wide assessments.' These were to be used, not, 'most emphatically ... to place or sort students for any reason,' but strictly for identification and remediation, and for system monitoring. One test, based on specific learning outcomes in literacy and numeracy, should be held at the end of grade 3, and the other, a literacy test, should be administered in grade 11 – that is, before students received their graduation diplomas. In order to ensure public confidence in the results, test construction, administration, and reporting should be put in the hands of an agency independent of the Ministry of Education and Training.

The commissioners were, however, unequivocal in their support for system-level monitoring, which could be done by sampling, and which they saw as crucial to ensuring accountability to the public. 'Those who are responsible for the overall quality of the system – the provincial government and local boards – must not only ensure that individual students are progressing, but that the curriculum is being delivered effectively, and that, on the whole, students in each grade and subject are learning what they are expected to learn.'

Quite critical of the ministry for its failure to provide leadership and direction, the commissioners were convinced that its role, which had become so attenuated over the previous three decades, had to be reasserted.

> We believe that in a province with the scale and diversity of Ontario, and especially in such uncertain times, there must be a clear and consistent direction for education ... The Ministry must ... generate a sense of common purpose in the educational community. This will reduce the fragmentation of many local school boards and schools 'doing their own thing,' and ensure that there is some shared understanding throughout the province ... The Ministry must set the priorities for Ontario education, clarify goals, and define the desired outcomes.[58]

The commissioners went on to argue that providing firm and clear leadership did not mean the ministry had to exercise direct control or 'over-regulate' the system. But the signal was clear: the province had substantially abdicated its responsibility for public education; it was time for a change in direction and the restoration of provincial leadership and provincial responsibility for the effectiveness and efficacy of Ontario's *provincial* school system.

THOUGH MOST OF THE key recommendations were leaked to the press in late December 1994 in order to test public reaction and prepare the ground for quick policy decisions, the report was released a month later, in late January 1995.[59] Titled *For the Love of Learning*, it was given its own distinctive packaging. Hall-Dennis had been a book for the coffee table; Bégin-Caplan came in a box with the techie look of a software manual and actually included a CD-ROM. Far longer than Hall-Dennis (though not quite as long as Hope), it was published in four separate volumes, presumably to make it appear less intimidating. Lest that fail to entice, a fifth summary volume was enclosed, comprising a sprightly once-over-lightly of the main themes of the report. More eloquent than the good grey prose of Hope, it was less jargon-ridden and, generally, far better written than Hall-Dennis. Indeed, like the Shapiro and Radwanski reports, it is one of the more readable official analyses of Ontario education written during the last half of the twentieth century.

For the Love of Learning did not, however, garner the near-universal praise initially accorded to Hall-Dennis, though that may have merely reflected the cranky mood of the mid-1990s compared to the panglossian temper of the age of Aquarius. Some of the criticism was predictable. The leadership of OSSTF expressed unease about the College of Teachers infringing on its turf, and even before the report was released the union was reportedly 'fighting mad' about the proposal to abolish grade 13.[60] Centralizing program control at Queen's Park, said representatives of several large urban boards, would do nothing to improve learning.[61] The *Globe* declared the report 'on the whole, rather timid' largely because it did not go far enough in advocating large-scale testing and unrestricted reporting of school-level results.[62]

The editors of the Toronto *Star* thought it a hard-hitting report that pointed in the right direction, expressing their enthusiasm in remarkably similar fashion, though in less florid prose, as the co-chairman of the Coalition on Educational Reform: 'The soft and mushy and warm and fuzzy education system that we have had for the last 25 years has been officially brought to an end.'[63] Mike Harris, leader of the Progressive Conservatives, was supportive of most of the report, the Liberals were clearly on side, and Dave Cooke not only said nice things but promised a swift response.[64] The one area that provoked substantial controversy was the commission's recommendations on early childhood education. Here, opinion was sharply divided. Influential voices in academe and the media expressed fervent enthusiasm; Harris, on the other hand, declared the proposal to extend public education down to age three, 'the stupidest recommendation I've ever heard.'[65] Liberal leader Lyn McLeod worried about busing three-year-olds in rural areas, and opinion polls indicated that parents and taxpayers were badly split on the issue.[66]

BEGINNING IN EARLY February, only days after the report's release, Ontarians were confronted by a month-long blizzard of related government announcements. By March, these had been bundled into a single policy document entitled *New Foundations for Ontario Education*. Though written in the form of a response to the royal commission, *New Foundations* was also a broader summary of recent government policy decisions, including several that either ignored or ran counter to recommendations in the commissioners' report. The new departures were grouped into eight distinct topics. Two focused on governance: the introduction of school councils and the amalgamation of school boards, issues I've addressed in chapter 10. The rest dealt with teachers, program, and accountability.

Following the lead of the commission, *New Foundations* promised to create a College of Teachers, to massively expand the use of computers in the schools, and to put much greater emphasis on access to, and use of, a wide range of information technology. The high school program of studies was to be rewritten to eliminate grade 13, expand work experience, improve support for educational and career planning, and ensure a relevant provincial curriculum that would build upon *The Common Curriculum* and enable students in grades 10 to 12 'to acquire a common core of knowledge, skills, and values in the areas of language, mathematics, science, technology, critical thinking, and interpersonal skills.'[67] Because it was expensive and controversial, extending formal education to three-year-olds was rejected in cabinet.[68] But the government proposed a comprehensive program, mandatory on all school boards, which, by the year 2000, would provide a combination of day care and early childhood education, available to four- and five-year-olds, from seven in the morning to six in the evening. If that marked something of a retreat from the commission's recommendations, Bob Rae and Dave Cooke were prepared to go much further when it came to assessment and accountability. There would be annual, mandatory testing in reading, writing, and mathematics for all students in grades 3, 6, 9, and 11 – a degree of universal testing wildly beyond anything the commissioners were willing to countenance. The government, on the other hand, found the argument for an independent testing agency compelling, creating the Education Quality and Accountability Office, and assigning it the responsibility for test construction, administration, and reporting. The government was similarly sympathetic to the commission's case for greater centralization of control of the curriculum: organized around 'outcomes' from junior kindergarten to grade 12, a province-wide curriculum would be introduced, accompanied by sets of standards for all the core subjects, and school-ready curricular materials. A standard report card would clearly indicate each student's level of achievement according to the public criteria established by the outcomes and subject standards.

Dismissed by some as little more than pre-election grandstanding by a government desperate to revive its dismal standing in the polls, *New Foundations* was a good deal more than merely that. It reflected many reform initiatives going back to the early 1980s, and reflected as well Dave Cooke's convictions about the need to restore public confidence and his assessment of the measures necessary to achieve that end. Moreover, Cooke didn't wait till after the election to set the wheels in motion. The establishment of school councils was mandated by ministry directive in the spring of 1995, as was the establishment of a committee to redesign the high school program of study.[69] The membership of the Education Quality and Accountability Office was settled in February and it began work immediately. The same was true for the Sweeney committee on school-board amalgamation and the committee to design the structure of the Ontario College of Teachers.[70]

But the education initiatives encapsulated in *New Foundations* were indubitably intended to serve electoral purposes as well.[71] Sitting third in the opinion polls, far behind Lyn McLeod's Liberals and even Mike Harris's Tories, the NDP needed a popular issue that would revivify its fortunes. The promise of educational reform seemed a likely candidate. It might also bring the teachers' unions back on board after the hostilities over the social contract. That didn't pan out, however. On top of the social contract, there were the NDP proposals to eliminate grade 13 and create a College of Teachers: the one threatened members' jobs and the other the power of the unions. There was, besides, patent disaffection among the rank and file over destreaming grade 9: two years of experience implementing it had increased rather than diminished discontent and frustration.[72] This time around, the teachers sat on their hands. Nor could the NDP turn educational reform into an effective election issue among the public. While there were some important differences of emphasis, all three parties endorsed most of the royal commission report and the general thrust of *New Foundations*. The only significant exception was Mike Harris's resolute condemnation of its early childhood education proposal.

All in all, then, educational issues played almost no role in the election campaign that began on 19 April and ended, on 8 June, with a smashing victory for Mike Harris and the Progressive Conservatives. With 45 per cent of the popular vote, a relatively high figure for a winning party in Ontario, and 82 of 130 seats in the legislature, it now fell to the Tories to deal with the educational agenda that had been taking shape since the early 1980s.

13

The 'Common Sense' Revolution, 1995–1998

Between June 1995 and the spring of 1998, the 'Mike Harris government' imposed changes on Ontario schools that were remarkable in scope, in the sheer speed of execution, and in the turmoil they engendered.[1] In order to impose some clarity on a complex and, at times, chaotic story, I propose in this chapter to deal only with the lineaments of Tory policy itself. I will then turn, in the next chapter, to the conflicts that surrounded policy-making and to the immediate aftermath of the '"common sense" revolution' in education.

The phrase came from a twenty-one-page campaign pamphlet that warrants more attention than such documents ordinarily merit. As John Ibbitson remarks, *The Common Sense Revolution* (*CSR*) was 'both an election strategy and a statement of neo-conservative political philosophy.'[2] Carefully 'road-tested' long before the election was called, it was designed to woo all those voters disenchanted by rising taxes, spiralling deficits and debt, and the intrusion of big government in their lives; but at the same time it was intended to articulate a set of convictions and a course of action that would keep a Tory government on course throughout its years in office.

The focus of the *CSR* was on job creation, economic recovery, and renewed growth by reducing the tax and regulatory burden as well as the excessive layers of bureaucracy that had developed over the previous ten years under the spendthrift and interventionist policies of the Liberals and New Democrats. After '65 tax increases' since 1985, including '11 hikes in personal income taxes,' the Tories would cut provincial income taxes by 30 per cent over three years, and balance the budget by the end of their first term. These two key measures would stimulate consumer spending and investment, and boost international confidence in the Ontario economy. To pay for the lost revenue entailed, *and* to put the government's house in order, spending on 'non-priority items would be cut by 20% over three years.' The intent, however, was not simply to slash spending, but to make the public enterprise more effective and efficient. In a slogan that will recur throughout this chapter, the Tories promised that they would 'provide the people of Ontario with *better* for *less.*' That applied, moreover, to both levels of government in the province. There is, said the *CSR* in big bold letters, 'ONLY ONE TAXPAYER.' Traditionally, municipalities responded 'to provincial funding limits by simply increasing local property taxes ... We will work closely with municipalities to ensure that any actions we take will not result in increases to local property taxes.' That meant that local government also had to do better for less. 'It is rare that politicians and bureaucrats voluntarily surrender power. But it must happen. *It's time to stop government growth once and for all.*'

Along with health care and law enforcement, 'classroom funding' was identified as a priority area to be protected from government spending reductions. But that did not mean there would be no cuts in education. The *CSR* trotted out the now-familiar international and interprovincial achievement comparisons, concluding that 'Ontario spends $14 billion a year on education – more per pupil than any other province – and still gets a failing grade.' The system, moreover, was overburdened with education personnel who '*don't teach,*' and with massive duplication of programs and services among boards and between boards and the ministry. Cuts in these areas would 'save Ontario taxpayers at least $400 million.' Though the *CSR* didn't promise board amalgamation, it pointed to the financial savings that might be realized through rationalization and condemned those trustees who were 'full-time politicians with full-time salaries.' The high school program would be reduced to four years and, until a review demonstrated its worth, junior kindergarten would be left optional. 'With a core curriculum set province-wide, and standard testing at all levels, we know we can spend more efficiently while improving the quality of education.'[3]

DESPITE BEING DISMISSED by his enemies as merely a 'golf pro,' Mike Harris was not only a successful North Bay businessman, but an ex-teacher, former school trustee, and by the late 1970s chair of the Nipissing Board of Education. Other members of the cabinet had similar backgrounds, including Elizabeth Witmer and Dianne Cunningham, both experienced teachers, trustees, and then chairs respectively of the Waterloo and London school boards. These leading Tories may have shared a common commitment to make changes unpalatable to many, but they were not neophytes when it came to things educational, especially governance and finance. Much of the impetus for change arose from powerful politicians who understood how the education labyrinth actually worked.

Determined, nonetheless, not to allow 'insiders' to be co-opted by their bureaucracies, and wanting a tough-minded manager as minister of education, Harris appointed a total outsider. A high school dropout, as frequently remarked, John Snobelen had made himself rich in the haulage business and in management consulting before he was elected MPP for Mississauga North in 1995. Afflicted by a penchant for the latest buzzwords in the human-relations industry, he almost immediately got into trouble by speculating on the need to 'invent a crisis' as a means of promoting rapid change, by describing teachers, to their face, as 'front-line service providers' who should be more accountable to their 'clients' and 'customers,' and by pronouncing on any and every occasion possible, however inappropriate or inflammatory his comments, that the system was 'broken.'[4] In public, at least, he was undoubtedly the most aggressive, tactless, and outspoken minister of education in Ontario's long history. He could also be smooth and congenial, and proved able to move large parts of his agenda forward. But he was too inclined to preface every policy proposal by lobbing a grenade. He was, on the other hand, only an outrider for a leadership that was generally confrontational, and that description applied to the premier as much as to Snobelen himself.

Snobelen's problems may have been exacerbated by the lack of strong support from senior levels within the ministry.[5] Early on, the government had fired the deputy minister installed by Dave Cooke in 1993 and had given his successor two ministries to handle – education and intergovernmental affairs – which meant he could not devote all his attention to education.[6] It was not until autumn 1996 that education acquired its own deputy minister in Veronica Lacey, the ex-director of the North York public board, and an individual who brought to the ministry, for the first time since Bernard Shapiro, the requisites both of managerial skill *and* an intimate familiarity with educational issues ranging from program to governance and finance.

LOVE IT OR HATE IT, academic observers and journalists alike have remarked on the Harris government's level of commitment to its election platform and its determination to move rapidly and forcefully on a wide variety of fronts – move, indeed, beyond the signal goals of the *CSR*, ambitious enough in themselves, to an equally ambitious second phase focused on the restructuring of local and provincial government services.[7] Education was no exception. Within weeks of assuming office, Snobelen cancelled the junior kindergarten pilot project begun by the NDP, and then abandoned mandatory junior kindergarten.[8] The government was equally quick to jettison a decade's worth of equity initiatives, repealing, among other things, the provisions of the Education Act designed to improve the representation of women in positions of administrative responsibility.[9]

Snobelen did, however, proceed with other initiatives already launched by the NDP. The minister encouraged the Sweeney committee to pursue its work on school-board amalgamation, while the Working Group on Education Finance Reform continued to struggle with the vexed issue of a new funding formula and the sources of revenue to underpin it. Despite intense teacher opposition, he also pushed ahead with the creation of the Ontario College of Teachers, shepherding the legislation through the House until it became law in June 1996.[10] The Education Quality and Accountability Office (EQAO), set up in spring 1995, submitted its first report in October recommending a much scaled-down version of Dave Cooke's testing regime. Instead of universal testing in grades 3, 6, 9, and 11, it was to be restricted to grades 3 and 11; only sample testing, in the tradition of the provincial reviews, was to be carried out in grades 6 and 9. Part of the reason for this was educational: four universal tests were considered excessive. But money was also a factor. Universal testing was expensive and the EQAO's budget had been cut from the $25 million promised by Cooke to $15 million under Snobelen.[11] The minister, nonetheless, concurred with the EQAO recommendations and proceeded in December with the legislation to establish the EQAO as a semi-independent Crown agency.[12] Test design was contracted out to a consortium of school boards with proven expertise in the business, field tests were carried out in the fall of 1996, and the first grade 3 and 6 assessments were carried out in spring 1997. Like the grade 9 reading tests introduced by the NDP, the new assessments were multifaceted, avoiding the pitfalls of multiple choice or narrowly conceived paper-and-pencil tests. The ministry also got on with the job of field-testing a standard report card, which was in place across the province by September 1998.

THE TORIES HAD COME to power with a pledge to improve achievement for all, and to introduce a more 'rigorous and relevant' curriculum. Snobelen was quick off the mark, announcing in early November 1995 that a new, four-year secondary school program would be in place for those entering grade 9 in September 1997.[13] That, however, entailed not simply excising a year from the existing program, but reorganizing the program of studies itself – rewriting course content and replacing *Ontario Schools: Intermediate and Senior* (*OSIS*) with a new set of program rules. The latter had to come first because the nature of the courses depended on the kind of overall program to be offered. Would, for example, grade 9 be left as part of *The Common Curriculum*, unstreamed and organized around areas of study rather than subjects? Would the organizational and thematic principles of *The Common Curriculum* be extended upwards or would a different pattern prevail?

The ministry's first stab at a draft provoked howls of outrage.[14] Leaked to teachers' groups and the press in the spring of 1996, it appeared to be a muddle of competing models. The outcomes of *The Common Curriculum* would remain in place for grade 9, and no credits would be earned for completion; but the list of required content was shifted to a mix of subjects and areas, and local boards were to determine whether or not grade 9 students would be streamed. In grades 10 to 12 the credit system was to be modified to increase flexibility: the value of a credit was set at thirty hours in order to allow courses to be offered through single or multiple units. More time was to be devoted to mathematics and science, but English requirements were substantially reduced. The emphasis in all subjects seemed to fall upon practical, career-preparation activities. All students, moreover, would be required to complete a minimum co-operative/work experience credit, and for those not planning to go on to post-secondary education, work experience could count for up to 40 per cent of their senior high school credits.

Condemned by OSSTF and by the Secondary School Principals' Council as academically unsound and a timetabling nightmare, the draft document also invited an obvious question about the co-operative/work experience proposals: how were the schools to supervise such large-scale field experiences, or ensure that they had enough educational value to warrant academic credit?[15] By July, Snobelen and his advisers had conceded. The abolition of the fifth year would be delayed until 1998 and a new round of consultations about the future of the high school would be carried out during the autumn of 1996.[16]

What followed in September was a much more tempered set of proposals[17] that left a number of controversial topics open to debate: How should grade 9 fit into the new program and should it remain destreamed? What proportion of the program, and which subjects, should be made compulsory? How should work experience be integrated? Should the amount of testing be increased and how should the results be used? The public consultations that followed elicited more than 20,000 written replies and a good deal of public debate, all of which revealed that divisions about what constituted a sound high school program of studies remained deep.[18] Perhaps the most notable exception was the large majority of respondents who favoured the reintroduction of streaming in grade 9.[19]

The government's response was set out in two policy statements, one in June 1997 and the other in January 1998.[20] In order to allow adequate time for planning and implementation, the introduction of the new four-year high school program would be delayed yet one more year, to September 1999. Grade 9 would revert to a streamed, credit-based year. The basic credit value would remain 110 hours and graduation would require the accumulation of 30 credits. Though courses in grade 9 would be differentiated in their emphasis on academic or applied, a common core of content would ensure that no student would be locked into a particular stream at age 13 or 14. In grades 10 to 12, distinct streams (or series of courses) would continue, as they had in the past, to prepare young people for entry to post-secondary education or the world of work, though there would also be a 'series' of transfer courses enabling students to change their minds and switch streams. All students would be required to complete forty hours of non-credit 'community involvement' before graduation. Though no details accompanied the announcement, improved and expanded co-operative and school-to-work programs were to be developed. The high school literacy test would be moved downward, 'prior to the end of Grade 10,' to allow sufficient time for remediation, and the test result would be recorded on the student's transcript. The number of compulsory mathematics and science credits would increase modestly and those for English would drop by one credit, from five to four; otherwise, there was not much change from the old *OSIS* requirements. With the exception of grade 9, it was all rather like the cautious approach taken by the Royal Commission on Learning to the reform of the high school program.

What now remained was a much more ambitious and, in the end, much more important task – rewriting the high school curriculum, course by course, a process that began in early 1998, and which the minister of education promised would be completed within eight months. Lurking on the horizon there was also the formidable problem of the 'double cohort,' as the last group to complete the five-year program and the first group to finish the four-year program doubled the number of competitors for entry to post-secondary education in the year 2003.

While the Harris government may have intended to rewrite the elemen-

tary school curriculum all along, the immediate stimulus seems to have
been the uproar over the draft high school document in the spring of
1996. If improved achievement was the government's aim, its critics per-
suasively argued, one could not take a full year out of the high school
program without demanding a more rigorous elementary school program.[21] That at least appears to have been the key consideration which
convinced Snobelen and his senior bureaucrats to proceed with both
projects in tandem and to delay the introduction of the four-year high
school program until the requisite changes had been made at the elementary level.[22] By the fall of 1996, in any case, the latter was under way and in
June 1997 new curriculum documents were released for language and
mathematics, grades 1 to 8. A combined Science and Technology guideline was published in March 1998, and others appeared in the months that
followed.[23] The documents replaced all of the pertinent sections of *The
Common Curriculum*, moved some content to earlier grades, stated the
intended 'expectations,' a word that now replaced 'outcomes,' with greater
clarity and less verbosity, and specified them grade by grade, rather than at
grades 3, 6, and 9 only. Since many school boards had already moved in
this direction, these changes hardly warranted the hype surrounding the
new ministry guidelines. But they did offer something brand-new – the
promise of province-wide consistency about what was to be taught when,
written in language that parents and the general public could understand.

While the specifics might appear to be modest innovations at both the
high and elementary school level, taken together they also indicated some
significant changes in direction. The movement to destream the high
school had been gaining momentum for a decade. For many of its advocates – and it is well to remember they were not all members of the political
left – the aim had been not simply destreaming but a common core
curriculum that promoted both equity and fraternity. The restreaming of
grade 9 by the Harris government (with, it must be added, the support of
large numbers of teachers and parents) and the concomitant introduction
of 'flexible' streaming in the later grades, with differentiated course content, constituted a substantial reassertion of more traditional views. So,
indeed, did the new elementary guidelines, stripped as they were of the
values, equity, and anti-racism rhetoric that pervaded *The Common Curriculum*. The school grade was also back in fashion: the new elementary
guidelines were unequivocally organized by grade, from 1 to 8, and the
successor to *OSIS* indicated that the same would be true for the high
school. More than five decades after it began to gain currency, in other
words, the very notion of an 'intermediate division' (or any other 'divi-

sion') had disappeared, including its last incarnation, 'the transition years,' which had absorbed so much research money, generated so much organizational turmoil in the schools,[24] and produced so much half-baked edubabble in the early 1990s. Ontario's schools were now to be organized conceptually (as indeed they always had been in reality) around the elementary school, grades 1 to 8, and the secondary school, grades 9 to 12. Finally, with *The Common Curriculum* dead as a doornail, there was a perceptible shift from a curriculum organized around interdisciplinary areas of study to a more traditional focus on discrete subject content. And though the comparison should not be overdrawn, if the new elementary school guidelines resembled any particular ministry document of the last fifty years, it was the 'little grey book' from days of yore.

ALL OF THESE INITIATIVES, from the establishment of the EQAO and the College of Teachers to the reform of the curriculum, had their own importance. Still, they were hardly more than preliminaries to the main event. For government and public alike, that was the expenditure reductions. On the cards from the beginning, the only question was how big and how permanent they would be. The answer came swiftly enough. But the attempt to implement the cuts triggered a train of events which ended in a radical restructuring of the way Ontario's schools were to be governed and financed.

The overriding priority for the new government was to put their two key promises on track – eliminating the deficit and introducing the 30 per cent cut in provincial income tax. In the *CSR* the Tories had estimated that would involve $6 billion in cuts, including at least $400 million from education. On taking power, however, they found a deficit ballooning far more rapidly than they had predicted, and, during the autumn of 1995, revenues failing to increase at the expected rate. Thus the stage was set for much deeper cuts – more like $8 billion overall. Education's share of that reduction was estimated to be in the neighbourhood of $1 billion. Over the years that followed, leading Tories would repeatedly justify that figure as a legitimate reduction intended to bring Ontario's spending on its schools down towards the national average. But it first emerged as a policy target in the autumn of 1995, as the Tories grappled with program cuts larger than they had originally thought necessary.[25]

Though a modest cut in transfer payments to the schools had been introduced in July 1995 as part of the government's initial response to the deficit figures, the major announcement came from the minister of finance, Ernie Eves, in his economic statement in late November. Operating grants for September to December 1996 were to be slashed by $400 million, about 9 per cent of the government grant.[26] Hardly a modest reduction in itself, on an annualized basis it amounted to $1 billion dollars – or a staggering 22.7 per cent reduction in the annual provincial operating grant to schools.[27] Reiterating the commitment made in the *CSR*, moreover, Eves emphasized in the legislature (and to reporters afterwards) that the government 'fully expects' school boards to absorb the reductions without increasing the tax burden on local ratepayers. 'The object of this exercise isn't to push a tax burden from one level of government to another,' but to 'rethink and restructure' the provision of all public services. 'Classroom funding,' however, was to be spared, Eves declaring that boards must 'take every reasonable step to cut costs outside the classroom,' which 'now account for at least 30 cents of every education dollar.'[28]

How was that to be done? As in other sectors where large cuts were to be introduced, the government had been consulting its 'stakeholders' during the autumn. In education that meant, among others, the Ontario Public School Boards' Association, which offered up a series of recommendations including new powers for boards to abrogate collective agreements relating to employees' benefits and working conditions.[29] The Ministry of Education then cobbled together proposals specifying how, exactly, $1 billion was to be extracted from the system.[30] Its aim was a set of targeted reductions, imposed on boards through legislation and regulation, that would lessen the costs of central and in-school administration along with various support services, require more sharing of services among boards, limit retirement gratuities, and reduce the amount of preparation time available to teachers. That last item, it was estimated, cost taxpayers close to $1 billion and amounted to 8 per cent of school-board operating expenditures. Bringing preparation time down to something more like the national average would, in a single stroke, save $400 million in salary and benefits – close to half, that is, of the $1 billion in savings the government was looking for – by reducing the total number of teachers necessary to staff the schools. The Sweeney Report, submitted in early 1996, added its two cents' worth. Classrooms must be protected, it insisted, but items like administration, preparation time, and retirement gratuities offered savings that could better be focused on the core tasks of the schools.[31]

With this advice in hand, Snobelen promised a package of legislation designed to give boards the flexibility to meet the reduced provincial grant. His January 1996 'tool kit,' as he called it, included, among many other things, measures to allow boards to modify existing collective agreements. Key politicians, among them the premier himself, took exception. That stemmed in part from the conviction that it was up to the boards to decide how cuts were to be made. Unwilling to shoulder the blame for tampering with collective agreements, cabinet was also reluctant to take on the teachers on the eve of a looming confrontation with its civil servants.[32] As a result, the 'tool kit' emerged from cabinet, as one columnist put it nicely, 'a few hammers short of a bag.'[33] Not just a few, indeed: the legislation was shorn of nearly all the powers the boards believed they needed to meet the reductions they faced.[34]

Whether from panic, malice towards spending cuts that many trustees (including some prominent Tory supporters) believed unconscionable, or the sheer weight of habit formed over many years, the school boards responded by cutting program services and issuing September lay-off notices to an enormous number of mostly young teachers.[35] The outcry was strident and the Harris government took most of the flak. Of more import, the boards met the provincial reduction by raising property taxes: of 129 major boards, 100 increased their rates, and 45 of them by amounts of 2 to 5 per cent.[36] Unless the boards had been prepared to take on the teachers' unions, it is hard to see what alternative they had. But that in itself was partly the issue for the Harris government. So long as the boards oversaw large portions of total expenditure it was their job to manage their own affairs within the context of overall government policy; for the Tories, the course pursued by the boards was merely one final example of a long history of irresponsible spending increases. On top of that, in late spring the Working Group on Education Finance Reform made its own contribution to Tory disenchantment. Though it made useful recommendations about the more technical aspects of a revised funding model for the schools, it bogged down hopelessly on the larger issues of how money was to be raised and shared. Overloaded with 'stakeholder' groups ranging from the teachers' unions to representatives from public, separate, and francophone boards, it could agree on little of substance and when it did, rubber-stamped the status quo.[37] Still a leading member of the NDP caucus, Dave Cooke was as contemptuous of its self-serving nostrums as was John Snobelen himself.[38]

While there had been talk of 'disentanglement' and restructuring in the *CSR*, just what that might entail remained as uncertain during the first nine months of Tory rule as it had been undefined in the *CSR*. In February 1996, the Sweeney committee submitted its final report, recommending, as directed, a massive reduction in the number of school boards, but warning as well that finance reform must accompany amalgamation. Even at that point, however, Snobelen was preoccupied with solutions that lay in the realm of adjustments to the status quo rather than root-and-branch reform. As for the kind of large-scale amalgamations recommended by Sweeney, Queen's Park reporters were still speculating that the Tories were unprepared to waste political capital on a massive administrative reorganization that offered modest savings and that they had never shown much commitment to in any case.[39] But the failure of the 'tool kit' and the events that followed in its train marked the end of tinkering with the existing system. By late spring 1996 the government was set on an entirely new course, historic in its radical restructuring of both finance and governance.[40] Local administration was to be substantially reorganized and, what was far more revolutionary, the province itself would assume responsibility for determining how money was to be raised, how much money was to be raised, and how these funds were to be distributed to schools across the province.

OVER THE MONTHS THAT followed, the enemies of restructuring contended that it was nothing more than another means of cutting expenditure – merely a different 'tool kit' designed to bleed the system of its existing resources. But there was a good deal more to it than that. Undoubtedly the Tories believed the school system not only could but *should* be bled. They would reiterate, time and time again, their conviction that the system was over-governed and, through the connivance of boards and unions, promoted featherbedding that taxpayers could not afford – while, at the same time, producing results in student achievement that were mediocre at best. In defence of such views they offered everything from statistic-laden reports and what they at least believed were reasoned arguments, to unalloyed invective: as one *Star* reporter recounted, 'In discussing what he calls "a lot of fat, a lot of waste," in Ontario schools, Harris rattled off this litany: "Too many boards, too many trustees, too many bureaucrats, *too many certificated teachers.*"'[41]

In education, above all, the Tories were determined 'to do better for less.' *Better* meant refocusing resources on the classroom, improving student achievement, and clarifying lines of accountability for educational and fiscal results between the ministry and localities. It also meant reducing 'the variations in spending among boards, [now] ranging from $4,723 to $9,148 per student. The excessive reliance on local tax wealth has led to unacceptable differences in programs and services across the province.' *Less* meant bringing down expenditure to something closer to the average of other provinces and easing the burden of education tax rates on both residential and business property. 'Between 1985 and 1995,' Tories liked to point out, 'school enrolment increased by only 16%, but school board spending increased by 82%, and education property taxes by 120%. Taxpayers can no longer afford such property tax increases.'[42]

But the Tories also knew that meat-cleaver cuts were no answer. The November expenditure reductions had been applied to all boards according to the existing grant and equalization formulas. As a result, some boards suffered cuts of up to 4 or 5 per cent while others experienced only a marginal change, or no change at all.[43] And in many cases the boards that were assessment-poor were hit the hardest, while assessment-rich boards escaped unscathed. The November cuts, in other words, actually increased the inequities in an already inequitable situation. That, as John Snobelen, other key Tories, and their senior bureaucrats recognized, was patently unfair.[44] What was needed was fiscal restructuring, not simply more reductions in transfer payments.

Transferring the entire cost of education to the provincial treasury had long had influential advocates, and the arguments had merit. But the price would be enormous – by 1996 about $8 billion. Transferring residential property taxes would alone amount to $5 billion. And those sums could only be raised by a massive increase in provincial income taxes or other revenues available to the provincial treasury.[45] No government in recent history had been prepared to follow the reasoning of academics and policy analysts on this point. Though it might remain a long-term goal for the Tories,[46] in the short term it was hardly a conceivable option for a government committed to a 30 per cent income tax cut, and, simultaneously, a balanced budget. The alternative the Tories adopted was to assert control over local property taxes.

That decision, in turn, set the stage for the 'disentanglement' exercise that would drag on, in private and in public, from late spring 1996 until June 1997. The story has been told by John Ibbitson and I will not reiterate it here;[47] but it was a fiasco of the government's own making. After months of wrangling in cabinet, rampant rumours, and panicky opposition outside it, the government issued its first final decision in mid-January 1997. Among a 'megaweek' of announcements about the more general restructuring of provincial-municipal relations, John Snobelen promised to remove education taxes from the residential property rates and transfer the cost to the provincial treasury. Equivalent sums, other ministers explained, would be 'downloaded' to the municipalities, including responsibility for welfare and related social services, so that neither local nor provincial governments would incur higher taxes. In the ensuing months the municipalities and many others, including powerful business spokesmen and prominent Tory supporters, said it could not be done (which was almost certainly true), and in June 1997 a compromise was hammered out. The government would download fewer services, and reduce residential education rates by only half. It would, however, take control of establishing the education portion of the taxation rate for residential, commercial, and industrial property alike, and it would determine how and where that money would be spent.

SCHOOL BOARD AMALGAMATION was a subsidiary question to fiscal restructuring, and the one was not necessarily dependent on the other. Throughout his term as minister, Snobelen huffed and puffed about excessive board spending, producing this study and that which purported to prove it. Even if true, the problem could have been solved through the assertion of government control over the spending of the existing boards. Merely rearranging board boundaries offered few advantages in that respect. True, there were savings to be realized through administrative consolidation. Fewer trustees, administrators, and their support staff, co-operative arrangements for transportation and purchasing, greater efficiencies in custodial services and the like might well reduce local expenditure. But the savings would be relatively modest. By the late 1990s, nonetheless, the extant boards had shot their bolt. If they still had friends, they had at least as many enemies.[48] And while the Tories might not have entered power committed to amalgamation, the boards' response to the November 1995 expenditure cuts sealed their fate.

For contingent reasons, the subsidiary question took precedence over the more fundamental question of fiscal reform. If changes were to be made, they had to be in place before municipalities began the lengthy process of preparing for the November 1997 school board elections. By the autumn of 1996, the rumours were flying out of Queen's Park: all boards would be abolished and their powers divided between the province and much-strengthened school councils; no more than a handful of regional boards would be established; much-reduced local responsibilities for schools were to be handed over to the municipalities.[49] By late autumn, however, cabinet had concluded that some intermediary body between the province and the schools had to be left in place. Leading off on megaweek Monday, Snobelen introduced Bill 104, a piece of legislation that remodelled the existing structure of local governance for education.[50]

Bill 104 introduced four substantive changes.[51] It reduced the number of Ontario's major school boards from 129 to 72, and renamed them 'district school boards.'[52] This included the abolition of the federal structure in Metropolitan Toronto, creating a single public 'megaboard,' one of the largest school districts in North America. Second, it entrenched in legislation francophone public and separate boards covering the entire province. Third, it reduced trustee representation from about 1900 to 700 and put a cap of $5000 on their remuneration. Finally, it established an 'Education Improvement Commission' to oversee the transition from old to new boards, with far-reaching power to monitor and approve such things as budgets, administrative appointments, and the initial operation of the new boards. A few months later Snobelen was able to announce a small political coup: Dave Cooke, the NDP minister of education, and Ann Vanstone, a highly experienced Metro Toronto school trustee and a vigorous critic of the government's education policies a few months earlier, would serve as the commission's co-chairs.

BILL 104 WAS, HOWEVER, only a modest first step in restructuring education in Ontario. The centralization of financial control announced at the beginning of megaweek still required legislation to put it into effect. A new funding formula had been promised, but not even its principles were settled. And Bill 104 said nothing at all about the powers the new boards would exercise or those the government might arrogate to itself. It was these three issues that constituted the substance of Bill 160, the landmark legislation introduced by John Snobelen on 22 September, and passed after some amendment on 1 December 1997.[53]

Bill 160 made two fundamental changes in the traditional structure of Ontario education.* First, it put exclusive control of revenue in the hands of the provincial government. This would continue to be raised, as it always had, from a combination of property taxes and provincial funds; but the government would now determine both the level of provincial funding and the amount to be levied on local property. In effect, local school boards lost the right to determine how much money they would raise to support local education; all of the key decisions would be made at the centre.

---

*There was, however, nothing simple about the bulk of the bill. Because it revised, repealed, or added new provisions to huge portions of the existing Education Act, as well as other provincial statutes, it was very long (232 pages), very intricate, and highly technical. Indeed it was the most complex piece of educational law since the integration and revision of disparate pieces of legislation produced Ontario's consolidated Education Act of 1974.

Second, the overriding principle governing the new funding formula was written into law: funds were to be distributed in a 'fair and non-discriminatory manner' between English-language public and Catholic boards, and French-language public and Catholic boards. The act did not provide any additional detail about the funding formula itself. But the intent was clear: to put an end to the geographical and other disparities that had long made a mockery of claims of fiscal equity between different localities and between public and Catholic school boards. By these two measures the Harris government proposed to cut the Gordian knot of education funding, resolving issues of control, accountability, and equity that had exercised policy-makers and analysts for decades.

In sorting out the relative powers of the province and local boards, Bill 160 left most of the long list of traditional board responsibilities in place. They would continue to hire teachers, provide accommodation, prepare and administer budgets, manage schools in their jurisdiction, and deliver the program of studies, all within the context of provincial policy guidelines. They would also retain responsibility for collective bargaining. Bill 160 repealed the School Boards and Teachers Collective Negotiations Act (Bill 100), and placed bargaining under the aegis of the Ontario Labour Relations Act. But bargaining remained in the hands of local boards and the affiliates of the Ontario Teachers' Federation. Though still allowed to perform the duties of a teacher and required to hold teaching certificates, principals and vice-principals (along with supervisory officers) were removed from the bargaining unit – a major change in their traditional affiliations and loyalties.

The bill also transferred a handful of specific responsibilities from the boards to the provincial government. A maximum average class size per board of twenty-five pupils for elementary schools and twenty-two for secondary schools was written into the legislation, as was a formula designed to set limits on the amount of preparation or release time for administrative duties. Reducing the number of professional-development and examination days effectively extended the academic year by a few instructional days for both the elementary and high schools.

The inclusion of these latter changes in the legislation remains a bit of a puzzle. Long before Bill 160, the legal powers of the Ontario government were near-all-encompassing. By statute or regulation, there were few limits on the power of the minister to control the interna or externa of Ontario's public education system. Indeed, one critical section of the extant Education Act (11.1) opened with this blanket phraseology: the minister 'may make regulations in respect of schools or classes ... for the establishment, organization, administration and government thereof.' And regulations already existed to govern, for example, the length of the school day, the school year, the licensing of teachers, and myriad other details of students' and teachers' lives. To suggest that the government was arrogating large new powers to itself – powers it had never had before – is misleading to say the least. But why, then, were these particular provisions incorporated into Bill 160? The Tories' motives may have been purely political: adding them would focus attention on its quality agenda, garnering the support of parents and taxpayers who thought teachers should be doing more with less. Alternatively, there may have been doubts about the broad regulatory powers conferred upon the minister by the existing act, or worries that even a favourable outcome of a court challenge would cost millions or delay the introduction of the legislation itself. But what several of these provisions did, in any case, was to remove powers – preparation time above all – that had long been the subject of negotiations between local boards and teachers' unions.

BILL 104 REORGANIZED local governance, reducing the number of school boards by half; Bill 160 centralized control over the amount of money to be raised for education and how that money was to be spent; the third part of the Tories' restructuring initiative was the new funding model: the formulas which would spell out how much money each local board would receive and what that money was to be spent on. The problems of the existing funding model had been recognized for years. Consisting of some thirty-five different kinds of grants, it was generally considered excessively complex and, as new funding for a variety of different purposes was added to it, increasingly incomprehensible. The provincial government had limited control over how its grant money was actually spent by the boards. And despite equalization features designed to ensure that youngsters in assessment-poor boards had the same opportunities as those elsewhere, local per-pupil spending still varied enormously. By the mid-1990s, the NDP and then the Tories not only wanted a formula with more clarity, accountability, and equity across the province, but one that would focus a larger amount of expenditure directly on the classroom.

Building on the efforts of both the Sweeney committee and the Working Group on Education Finance, the Ministry of Education outlined a new model in September 1996, and invited reaction from the education community.[54] In May 1997 it released a detailed proposal, and while more public discussion followed, the May document, with only modest revisions, became the funding model which would be used to calculate the grants to

Ontario's school boards.[55] There was not much that was new in principle; indeed it maintained the traditional tools of educational finance: a 'foundation grant' designed to provide basic per-pupil funding for the common needs of every classroom, and a series of 'special-purpose' grants to cover variable costs ranging from special education to transportation. But the latter were reduced to seven (later nine) categories – on the face of it, at least, a major simplification.[56] As well, there were now to be three areas where spending had to be targeted: in response to long-standing complaints, special education was moved out of the foundation grant and the allocations could only be spent for that purpose; the school board and governance grant (mainly for central office costs) represented the maximum a board could spend in that area; and funding designated for school renewal and new pupil places had to be allocated to that alone.

Having taken steps to ensure that these three special-purpose grants were spent for their intended purposes only, the government went on to add that every board would be required to issue an annual 'Financial Report Card' detailing how its total budget had been allocated and spent. Between May 1997 and March 1998, moreover, the categorization of 'classroom spending' was defined.[57] It included the cost of classroom teachers, supply teachers and teacher assistants, learning materials and classroom supplies, library and guidance services, classroom computers, professional and para-professional services such as school psychologists, and staff development. Everything else was categorized as 'non-classroom spending,' including teacher prep time, in-school administration (principals, vice-principals, and department heads), teacher consultants, and custodial services. A board's 'report card' could be organized by grant category, in other words, but also, or additionally, by the relative costs of those items designated as classroom and non-classroom spending. And just to make sure the public got the message, the province itself would issue an annual report that provided board-by-board spending comparisons.

But a formula is only a formula. The real challenge was to write in the dollar amounts. How much money was to be spent overall? And how much of that was to be put in the various 'envelopes' the formula encompassed? Following the release of the May document, four ministry-appointed teams went to work on some of the more technical problems, such as the cost of school accommodation and maintenance, or the per-pupil cost of special education; the Education Improvement Commission was also asked to proffer advice on instructional costs such as preparation time.[58] Based on this expert advice, or so at least the government and its senior officials claimed, the dollar amounts were finally released in late March 1998.

Funding, the minister of education announced, would remain stable 'at over $13 billion for each of the next three years.'[59] And that did not include an additional $385 million for a restructuring and transition fund. 'In its first three years, the new funding model will increase the share of resources directed to the classroom from 61% to 65%.' That would be accompanied by a decline in non-classroom spending and 'waste.' The 'new emphasis' on accountability – targeted allocations monitored by the province, the annual board 'Financial Report Card,' and the provincial 'Report to Taxpayers' – would 'let parents and taxpayers see where their education dollars are being spent.' A new 'Class Size Protection Fund' would provide $1.2 billion over three years to hire new teachers to accommodate enrolment growth within the legislated class sizes. All boards choosing to offer half-day JK for four-year-olds would receive funding through the foundation grant. But JK would not be mandatory; boards that did not opt to introduce it would have access to equivalent amounts from an Early Learning Grant 'to design alternative early learning programs that best meet the needs in their communities.' Half-day senior kindergarten would, of course, continue to be funded, but full-day programs, which enrolled about 10 per cent of all kindergarten students, would only be funded for 1998–9. 'In future years, boards could choose to continue these programs, using resources from efficiencies achieved in other areas of their budgets.' A new Learning Opportunities Grant would underwrite special programs for children at risk. Overall, the new funding model was not only simplified, but of more consequence, it would ensure that students, regardless of geography or the kind of public school attended, would receive equal funding. 'Each and every student in Ontario deserves the best education our province can give him or her – this idea provides the spirit and the basis of today's announcement of Ontario's new, student-focused approach to funding.'

THUS THE GENERAL THRUST of restructuring carried out by the Tories between January 1997 and spring 1998: the reorganization of local governance, the centralization of control over educational spending, and the introduction of the new funding model. What remains is to explain key aspects of the 'architecture' of restructuring. Why were the boards amalgamated but not abolished in favour of some more radical form of local governance? And how was it possible to impose central control over finance when a significant portion of the public school system – all of the Catholic boards in Ontario – appeared to be guaranteed the right, *by the Canadian constitution*, to levy taxes on their own school supporters?

The answers to these two questions overlap; but for clarity's sake I will tackle the first question first. There may have been several reasons why the boards survived, but the main one was legal. Section 93 of the Constitution Act guaranteed Catholic trustees the right to manage and control their own schools. While prepared to tolerate a reduction in the number of their boards, they would not countenance their abolition; any attempt to do so would provoke a court challenge and almost certainly result in a defeat for the government.[60] No one had ever imagined a scenario where the legal rights of Catholic boards would be preserved while public boards were stripped of theirs. So Bills 104 and 160 kept the existing structure intact, albeit in modified form.

But there was another, no less imperative constitutional restraint on the Tories. Ever since the legislation had been passed under the Liberals, many leading Franco-Ontarians had expressed dissatisfaction with Bill 75, which had extended their rights to school governance but still left key aspects in the hands of anglophone-dominated boards. And between 1984 and 1993 a series of important court cases, in Ontario and elsewhere in Canada, had made it clear that francophone educational rights, under section 23 of the Charter of Rights, included substantial measures of self-governance. The courts did not try to tell the provinces exactly how these rights were to be enshrined in legislation, but the thrust of the decisions tended to favour entities independent of anglophone majorities. The Ontario Liberals had struggled with this issue in the aftermath of Bill 75 and towards the end of their mandate the NDP decided the solution was to establish francophone boards of education across the province. This was probably not the only plausible response to Supreme Court directives, nor, necessarily, the optimum one for the entire province, but the Harris government apparently never reconsidered it, simply incorporating it into Bill 104. As a result, for the first time in its history Ontario had four different categories of school boards, each province-wide: English and French public, and English and French separate school boards.[61]

The establishment of francophone boards, however, created its own fiscal dilemma. Small numbers of ratepayers meant a weak assessment base; and, in addition, francophone separate boards would suffer the same inequities as Catholic boards generally.[62] Yet the courts had made it clear that adequate financing must underpin the guarantee of equitable provision for francophone children. The government could not permit continuing inequities in this respect – it would almost certainly lose any subsequent court challenge – nor was it willing to provide enormous compensatory grants from the public treasury. That was one of the reasons why it was important to lay hands on the money raised from local property taxes: once accomplished, grant regulations could ensure that such funds could be redistributed to help sustain per-pupil equity for Franco-Ontarian pupils just as it would for those in other assessment-poor boards.

But the centralization of financial control *also* raised a different constitutional question, and one that was even more fundamental: the right of English and French Catholic boards to manage their own schools included the right to levy local property taxes. How, then, could the government get away with removing that right, as it did in Bill 160? The answer was a political deal struck between Catholic trustees and the government – perhaps not a deal formally speaking, which both sides denied,[63] but a deal nonetheless. For some years, reaching back at least to the early 1990s, a few Catholic leaders had suggested that they were willing, in return for equitable financing, to suspend or put in abeyance their constitutional right to levy property taxes for schools.[64] That, in turn, might mean that the government could centralize control of finance in the name of equity and the pertinent legislation would survive a constitutional challenge by dissident Catholic parents or others who took exception to such a compromise by their trustees. Though the details remain murky and the extent of collaboration unclear, meetings between representatives of the Catholic trustees' association and Ministry of Education officials took place in late December 1996 and early January 1997 to consult on the shape of legislation, and the association's lawyer, retained by the government itself, offered 'policy advice' on the drafting of Bill 160 and 'reviewed' the draft legislation.[65] The outcome, in any case, is not in doubt. Bill 160 promised that funding would be distributed in a 'fair and non-discriminatory manner' to all boards in Ontario. The extent to which funding was indeed 'fair and non-discriminatory' would be subject to review by a committee of the legislature in 2003, and its report made public. Catholic boards would suspend for five years the right to levy local property rates. The Catholic trustees' association was virtually the only organized educational lobby group to defend the bill during passage, at one point issuing a report designed, in the words of its president, to correct 'a great deal of misinformation that was limiting the opportunity for rational discussion' and in the process offering the government its only succour.[66] In March 1998 the new funding model established equal per-pupil funding for all boards, public and separate alike. What price equity? The courts would begin to answer that question a few months later.

14

Disarray

Teachers had not been indifferent to the unfolding drama during the first two years of Tory rule. Already unsettled by the policies of the previous regime which had seen salaries frozen under the Social Contract, declining operating grants never fully matched by rising property taxes,[1] a substantial reduction in support services, a modest overall decline in the number of teachers employed despite increasing enrolments and class sizes,[2] substantive and in some cases unpalatable curriculum change, and the threat to the role and powers of their federation implicit in the proposed creation of the College of Teachers, they could hardly expect better from a government committed to the dogma of the *CSR*.

They had good reason to worry. The cost of teachers' salaries, benefits, and working conditions constituted the lion's share of total expenditure. Substantial spending reductions meant that by one means or another these costs had to be contained. There were few ways to do that except by limiting the power of the teachers' unions to determine education budgets through the collective-bargaining process. It appeared increasingly likely that the Tory government was prepared to do just that. Key politicians from Harris downwards missed few opportunities to remind the public that a $14 billion enterprise produced mediocre results, that it was necessary to do better for less, that spendthrift trustees and powerful unions combined to fleece taxpayers of their hard-earned dollars. A ministry report released by John Snobelen in August 1996 purported to prove that, by national standards, Ontario's teachers were overpaid and underworked.[3] The Sweeney committee had already recommended that bargaining rights be restricted;[4] in autumn 1996 yet another ministry-sponsored report called for major changes in collective bargaining that would substantially reduce the unions' influence over working conditions, and advocated as well that their right to strike be abolished.[5] Snobelen's megaweek announcement that the government would take control of educational finance heightened anxieties, as did the talk of forthcoming cuts even larger than those of November 1995.

An open confrontation might have come sooner had cabinet allowed Snobelen's 'tool kit' to proceed unaltered. But with its teeth removed and the long interval during 1996 as the government struggled with its restructuring initiatives, there was nothing beyond the November cuts except omens. First the activists and then a growing number of rank-and-file teachers joined labour-sponsored protests and demonstrations against the Harris government, or organized their own.[6] The unions reached out to secure new alliances with community groups and the labour movement,[7] while also attempting to counter government propaganda about 'a broken system' or excessive salaries through studies and publicity drives of their own.[8] Beginning in late 1996, they also began to arm themselves with a more concerted strategy to defend their interests, including, by May 1997, an overwhelming vote by OSSTF members to take job action if the government attacked their bargaining rights.[9] Yet the operative word remained 'if.' For nearly two years the tough talk on both sides had steadily escalated. But until the late summer of 1997 there was no certain target to justify a call for job action or to mobilize the rank and file in support of it.

The crisis began in June 1997 with the introduction of Bill 136, designed to ensure smooth labour relations during the restructuring of school, municipal, and health authorities. The bill virtually eliminated the right to strike throughout the transition; if conflict did occur between unions or between employers and employees, the differences would be resolved by a government-appointed arbitration board. Though only a temporary measure, Bill 136 almost guaranteed that the terms of first contracts would be dictated by employers or the government, and those terms would become the initial benchmark for negotiations after the legislation expired. The key clauses did not cover teachers, but Snobelen promised they would be subject to parallel legislation.[10] Anathema to the unions, the bill rapidly became a *cause célèbre* for the labour movement, uniting in angry opposition parties that had been badly divided over the two previous years.

Equivalent legislation for teachers was delayed all summer, and at some point the decision was made to include it in an omnibus bill (eventually to become Bill 160) covering all the issues left unsettled in Bill 104. On 27 August 1997, senior ministry officials met with their union counterparts, presenting them with both the general thrust of government policy and an outline of their legislative proposals. Union leaders were appalled at the agenda placed before them. As OECTA's president, Marshall Jarvis, would later remark, 'The scope of the legislation we saw made Bill 136 pale in comparison.'[11] And he was surely right.

There would, teacher representatives were informed, be further reductions in spending.[12] Total expenditure would be determined by the provincial government alone. Following a forthcoming report of the Education Improvement Commission, there would be revisions made by the government in the length of the school day, the length of the school year, the number of examination and professional-development days. 'Differentiated' or 'flexible' staffing, ministry code words for uncertified instructors, would be introduced in some areas. Bill 100, the teachers' collective-bargaining legislation, would be repealed and bargaining rules would be transferred to the Labour Relations Act. The Teaching Profession Act would be repealed, ending statutory membership in the federation affiliates and allowing teachers to organize under other unions or to do without any union at all. Principals and vice-principals were declared to be part of management and excluded from belonging to teachers' bargaining units. Staffing, the assignment of preparation time, class size, and pupil–teacher ratios would all become 'management rights' – that is, the terms would be established not by negotiation but by boards or the government alone. Where contracts had already ended, further negotiations would be suspended and the first contract with the new boards would be subject to provisions similar to those in Bill 136. Teacher advice on where and how to make spending reductions would be welcomed; salary and vacation time would remain negotiable; the matter of the right to strike remained unresolved. Even that looked ominous: asked only a few weeks earlier whether teachers should continue to have the right to strike, John Snobelen had replied, bluntly, 'No.'[13]

Two weeks later the news got worse. Asked by Snobelen to make recommendations about how the proposed new funding formula might, at one and the same time, improve the quality of instruction and reduce costs, the Education Improvement Commission issued its report on *Learning Time, Class Size and Staffing*.[14] The aim, it argued, was to refocus scarce resources on the classroom. To improve learning, contact hours with students should be increased by lengthening the school year. To ensure that the new boards did not use class size as a trade-off in bargaining with employees, the average size should be capped at existing levels. Savings could be found in a variety of ways, but one key means was to reduce high school teachers' preparation time and the amount of administrative release time for department heads. The amount of 'prep time' provided to elementary teachers was about right, the commissioners thought, but a cut at the high school level of about 25 per cent would bring the figure down somewhat towards the national average. In order to increase scheduling flexibility and take account of differing needs and responsibilities, allocation of preparation and release time should cease to be a matter of collective bargaining and become the prerogative of school principals. Given the tough financial circumstances the new boards would face, all savings from such changes, the commissioners insisted, should be reinvested in the enterprise.

Snobelen liked the report, as did much of the media and many parents. His one reservation, however, was crucial: he would not guarantee that any or all savings would be reinvested in the schools.[15] Union leaders, and large numbers of teachers, hated its recommendations, on preparation time above all. Prep time, in their view, was an essential component of the job, allowing them not just to prepare for in-class contact hours but to perform a multitude of tasks ranging from interviewing parents to providing individual assistance and counselling to students. But there was more at stake than that. As Marshall Jarvis would explain to a legislative committee, 'Take 7 teachers, each handling 6 classes a day plus some prep time. If you take away prep time from each of the first 6 and replace it with an additional class, you no longer need the seventh teacher – the first 6 have effectively taken over all his or her duties.'[16]

Negotiations with the teachers' unions in early September 1997 over Snobelen's proposed legislation went nowhere; but the threat of a walkout over Bill 136 by Ontario's public-service unions, including the teachers, and a secret government opinion poll showing large numbers of Ontarians siding with the unions convinced the government to retreat on its labour legislation.[17] The bill was gutted, and immediately thereafter Snobelen announced that his education legislation would retain statutory membership in the OTF affiliates, that teachers would retain the right to strike to negotiate for salary and benefits, and that principals and vice-principals would remain members of their existing bargaining units.[18]

Four days later, on 22 September, Snobelen unveiled Bill 160. Misleadingly entitled the 'Education Quality Improvement Act,' it was essentially about finance and governance: its intent was to lay the legal groundwork the government conceived necessary to improve quality, but it did not address quality issues directly. Though most of Bill 160 remained unchanged through passage, the initial version was different on several points. Control over class size, instructional hours, the use of non-certified instructors, and the amount of prep time were all to be set by regulation –

that is, by cabinet decree, not requiring approval by the legislature. That in
turn meant that such regulations could escape public scrutiny or be
changed as ministry officials saw fit. Two days later, Snobelen announced
that once Bill 160 was enacted, the government, following the recommendations of the Education Improvement Commission, would extend the
number of teaching days in the school year. Prep time for high school
teachers, however, would be cut by something closer to 50 per cent –
nearly double that recommended by the EIC. The government insisted
that this would save $200 million and eliminate 4400 jobs – most of which
would be in the form of retirements; the unions set the figures at $450
million and 10,000 jobs.[19]

The stage was now set for confrontation. The structure of the teachers'
unions had survived intact, and, on paper at least, most of their bargaining
power. But the government's agenda included more cuts to education
spending; job losses would be significant. And, teachers asked themselves,
what was there left to bargain about: they would negotiate their contracts
with the new amalgamated school boards but the available money would
be established by the province alone, and control over working conditions
would now be in the hands of government as well. Divisions over strategy
and tactics had badly split the unions over the preceding two years.[20] Time
and again, OSSTF, under its president Earl Manners, had taken a militant
stand well beyond that of the other affiliates, though increasingly OECTA
was not far behind. Even in early September, when the other unions were
prepared at least to meet with government representatives, OSSTF had
adamantly refused to participate.[21] Now, with the leadership mantle fully
on its president Eileen Lennon, OTF and its affiliates were united. 'If John
Snobelen does not move off of his legislative agenda,' said Lennon on 25
September, 'every school in this province will be shut down.'[22]

WHAT FOLLOWED FIRST was a barrage of newspaper, radio, and television
ads, newsclips, and stories designed to persuade the public that one side or
the other was the repository of all virtue. Both the government and the
teachers' unions stood foursquare for a quality education and the true
interests of future generations. 'We won't back down' became the rallying
cry for teachers; the real aim of the Harris government and Bill 160, they
insisted, was to bankrupt public education and destroy the teaching profession.[23] The teachers' rhetoric now began to out-snobelen Snobelen,
covering the gamut from the near-scurrilous to the maudlin. In TV ads the
minister was portrayed blowing up schoolhouses, and a malevolent Tory
vehicle nearly mowed down a line of children crossing a street in a school

safety zone.[24] Snobelen, union leaders declared, was nothing but 'a slick huckster,' a 'snake-oil salesman' who wanted only to chop $1 billion out of the school system.[25] 'The bottom line is the dismantling of the system puts children at risk,' one elementary school vice-principal wailed. 'It's our responsibility to speak on behalf of the children.'[26] Bill 160, replied the government, was essentially about improving quality, rescuing Ontario from scholastic mediocrity, and ending the featherbedding that local boards and unbridled union power had saddled on the province for decades. As for more big spending cuts, the $1 billion figure only referred to spending above that by other provinces, Harris told reporters in early October. 'It's not a savings target ... We'll spend every penny required to have the best system we can possibly have. But measuring it by the way they threw money at it in the past, we don't think of it as a good way.'[27]

On the eve of new talks with Snobelen, a union rally in Toronto brought an overflow crowd to Maple Leaf Gardens, and impressive numbers demonstrated in several other Ontario cities.[28] The talks went nowhere. The poisoned atmosphere between the minister and the unions now convinced Harris that it was time to try to lower the temperature. On 9 October, Snobelen was shipped off to Natural Resources and replaced by Dave Johnson. The government's point man on a series of tough issues, Johnson brought to the job a high level of credibility, a judicious tongue, and a low-keyed personal style.[29] But he was also seasoned to crises, had no intention of backing down, and was in no hurry to resume talks with the teachers. It was not until Monday, 20 October, that the two sides would again sit down at the same table. When they did so, Johnson was presented with a lengthy OTF statement setting out a series of non-negotiable demands. School boards must retain the right to raise revenues through local taxation; teachers must retain the right to bargain all terms and conditions of employment directly with their employers, the school boards, including prep time and class size. Beyond existing ministry regulations, the length of the school year and day, or the number of examination and professional-development days, was best left to the local community to determine. Every classroom must be staffed by a certified teacher.[30]

To accede to such demands – and there were others besides in the OTF document – was to gut Bill 160 of nearly all its important provisions. Johnson dismissed it as an unacceptable 'ultimatum.'[31] The next day, Tuesday, 21 October, he offered an olive branch of sorts. Besides reiterating the government line that there were no savings targets, he promised modest amendments: non-teachers would be used only as supplementary aides in classrooms;[32] class-size caps and the formula for prep and release

time would be written into the statute itself – a shift that meant any
changes would necessarily have to be debated in the legislature and
beyond.[33] A few days later he also added that high school prep time
needed to be reduced by something like a third (rather than 50 per cent)
to bring it in line with national figures.[34] But that was all the teachers ever
got out of Dave Johnson on Bill 160.

On Tuesday night and through a long Wednesday the teachers wrangled
among themselves about what to do next, finally deciding to leave the door
open for further talks but to call a walkout on the following Monday if the
government still refused to back down.[35] Their best news, however, broke
late Tuesday just after the initial round of talks had collapsed. Howard
Hampton, the new leader of the NDP, released a leaked copy of Veronica
Lacey's 'performance contract' as deputy minister of education, in which
she was directed to slash $667 million from the schools' budget during
1998–9. By Thursday both Johnson and Harris had confirmed the additional cuts, effectively undermining their earlier claims that there were no
budget-reduction targets. Talks dragged on through the weekend. Neither
side budged. The teachers closed down Ontario's schools on Monday, 27
October.

It was not an illegal strike, their leaders insisted, but a 'political protest.'
Technically they were right. But everyone else called it 'the strike.' It lasted
ten school days, from 27 October to Friday, 7 November.* It caused a good
deal of chaos and dislocation for parents, and a good deal of pain among a
workforce that was ageing, mainly small-c conservative in outlook, largely
committed to jobs they deemed important, and, outside the larger urban
areas especially, often deeply rooted in their own communities, where they
were taking on not the abstracted face of a hostile government, but
friends, neighbours, and their students' parents. Solidarity was near-unani-
mous nonetheless. All but a handful of teachers walked out and stayed out.
A substantial number of their principals and vice-principals joined them.
The school boards sat on their hands: not a single board actively sided with
the government by taking legal action against the teachers over breach of
contract.

In order to kick-start talks the teachers dropped the demand that boards
retain independent powers of taxation and offered to negotiate a mutually
satisfactory settlement on some other issues. Johnson reiterated his prom-

---

*The phrase 'school days' is apt. Having only recently been through a nasty confrontation
of her own with the Harris government, one blue-collar OPSEU member noted wryly at
the time that teachers don't picket on weekends or, on school days, after 3:30 p.m.

ised amendments but now added a new one. Principals and vice-principals were management, had no legal right to abandon their schools for the picket line, and would be excluded from belonging to the teachers' unions. Teachers were outraged, labelling the move 'vindictive and punitive.' Negotiations stalled once more. On the opening day of the strike the government sought an injunction to end it, claiming, among other things, that the strike would cause 'irreparable harm' to students; on Monday, 2 November, the beginning of the strike's second week, the government's case was thrown out of court, Eileen Lennon declaring the judgment a moral victory for the teachers.

By mid-week, however, unity among the affiliates was cracking. The government showed no signs of further retreat. There was the double danger that some of the rank and file who favoured only a short, sharp protest would begin to drift back to work, and that prolonging the strike would shift public opinion solidly against the teachers. At least one lawyer, acting on behalf of a disgruntled citizen, was preparing to ask the Ontario Labour Relations Board to declare the strike illegal and, with the threat of heavy fines for non-compliance, order the teachers back to work, a scenario that had its own plausibility. Not even OSSTF's Earl Manners believed the strike could continue indefinitely in the face of government recalcitrance: 'As long as the government continues on this path, the political protest will continue far into the future, although the form it will take will obviously have to change.' On Thursday, solidarity crumbled. Three of the teachers' unions – OPSTF, FWTAO, and the French-language affiliate – called for their members to return to work the following Monday. Bitter militants across the province cried betrayal and staged their own protest rallies against the decision. OECTA and OSSTF leaders held out until the weekend, but confronted with their colleagues' fait accompli had few choices. The schools were back in business on Monday, 10 November.

Since the legislature had adjourned for its fall break during the conflict, Bill 160 hung on like a black cloud for nearly another month, provoking more protests and demonstrations inside and outside Queen's Park. Amidst much turmoil, it completed passage through the House during the last two weeks of November and received final reading on 1 December 1997. The only amendments to the initial version of the bill were those Dave Johnson had offered the teachers in the last two weeks of October.

WHO HAD WON the battle over Bill 160? The government, obviously, in the sense that its legislative agenda for education was now complete. As Mike

Harris was wont to say, education policy for Ontario was going to be made by the elected government of the province, and not by the unions or the multitude of 'special interests' who lobbied in the public arena on their own behalf.[36] It was a principle of no small importance and long overdue for reassertion in an environment where successive governments had ducked tough issues for fear of the political repercussions. Some of those tough issues involved the power of the teachers' unions. 'How did we get into this mess?' asked Ian Urquhart, the *Star*'s Queen's Park columnist, the week before the strike. In a column primarily devoted to an attack on Tory educational policy, he also had this to say. 'It was probably inevitable that there would be, sooner or later, a major confrontation between the teachers' unions and the provincial government. Past regimes have recognized that our schools need fixing and that union contracts are part of the problem, but they have always opted, less than courageously, to push it on to the next government. The Harris Tories have said, in effect, that the buck stops here.' Although both opposition parties were openly siding with the teachers, Urquhart added, 'some Liberals and New Democrats are privately cheering on the Tories ... Ex-ministers from both parties speak in bitter tones about the obtuseness of the teachers' unions.'[37]

Winning the war for public support, however, was a different kettle of fish. It is not easy to assess the play of public opinion during the first two years of the Harris regime. The volume of commentary and reports about educational policy was very large, the chattering classes were polarized from the beginning, and it is extremely difficult to sort out assessments of educational policy per se amidst the hubbub about Harrisite policies in general. Certainly, there was an overall tendency for columnists, editorial writers, and organized pressure groups to split along right/left lines, praising or condemning Tory educational policy according to their own political sympathies and agendas. Local groups of 'taxfighters' and education reform coalitions founded in the early 1990s continued to hammer the boards and the bureaucracies, offering their voices in support of the Harris government. New players emerged in Toronto and elsewhere in the form of activist parents' organizations dedicated to fighting the education cuts and the loss of local control, allying themselves with the teachers and, more generally, with the anti-Harris forces in the province.

Real unease rippled far out beyond the hard core of opposition. The impact of the November 1995 cuts hit programs and services ranging from ESL and special education to rural busing. Board amalgamation did indeed mean the loss of local control: backed by their constituents, the Oxford County Board of Education voted to oppose amalgamation with

London, fearing their rural and small-town interests – and thrift – would be lost in a merger with a big city board.[38] Following the Sweeney Report in January 1996, moreover, controversy over the 'pooling' of commercial and industrial assessment regained a degree of prominence it had not had since the late 1980s. Fears that pooling would be one certain Tory solution to the problem of educational finance provoked a major outcry in Metropolitan Toronto and other assessment-rich areas that continued throughout the rest of the year. Newspaper editorials and columnists, and public school board trustees, warned interminably of the injustice, and the dire consequences, of the potential outflow of local funds to rural and Catholic boards. The hubbub was quelled in January 1997 when both Harris and Snobelen promised that commercial and industrial property taxes would not be pooled, remaining in the communities where they were raised.[39] But that only prompted a variant question: if the government was about to take control of all education spending, how would assessment-rich areas like Metro or Ottawa fare under that new regime? Continuing Tory talk about deeper cuts further unsettled the uncommitted, while the disentanglement exercise and other Tory initiatives contributed to growing anxiety, disenchantment, and the conviction, even among confirmed supporters, that the government was moving too fast on too many fronts.

Teachers and boards had their detractors as well, and there was much talk about high salaries, Cadillac pensions, retirement gratuities, and a working year most others could only envy.[40] Few wept copious tears when the government promised to reduce prep time, lengthen the school year, or lighten the burden of education property taxes. The government also had on its side the long-standing public scepticism about educational quality, and the willingness of even its enemies to acknowledge that some of its proposed reforms were not only necessary but long overdue.[41] Teachers, on the other hand, were not without their own resources. While the unions had the financial wherewithal to match the government when it came to high-priced media advertising, they also had an organization that could outdo the government in reaching down into local communities across the province. The unions might be distrusted by the proverbial man in the street, but individual teachers were known qualities, respected if not always loved by parents, their opinions counted, and their hard work was usually admired. They could mobilize local opinion, while effective leadership at the centre ensured that they did so before and during the strike.

On the eve of the strike, nonetheless, it does appear that the government had the edge: the polls showed a sharp increase in hostility towards the idea of a teachers' walkout and political analysts were persuaded the government was waging the more successful publicity campaign.[42] But in the days that followed, that changed dramatically. While the shift in public opinion was due to a complex of factors, three stand out. First, after an uncertain start, the union leadership became increasingly effective in portraying the conflict as a dispute over educational quality and not a sordid squabble over labour issues: it was about the future of children and not about bargaining rights or cuts to prep time. That helped reinforce a second factor. As one experienced pollster put it nicely, 'If it's unions versus the government, government wins. But if it's the government versus the teachers, teachers win. Teachers are real people – and governments and unions are institutions. Voters will always sympathize with real people over institutions.'[43] The hinge, however, was the exposure of the cuts written into the Lacey contract. All of the government's protestations about its focus on quality, all of its talk about no fiscal 'targets,' was contradicted. The Tories stood unarmed against the teachers' charge that Bill 160 was about cuts in spending and nothing else. By the end of the strike, the polls revealed the teachers had the support of a substantial majority of Ontarians, and a variety of political observers were crediting them with a victory as well.[44]

THE WAR WAS HARDLY OVER in any case. Though they would eventually lose in the courts, the teachers almost immediately launched a constitutional challenge against the exclusion from the unions of principals and vice-principals.[45] Yet another challenge was initiated on the more fundamental issue of school boards' right to powers of property taxation. By early 1998 union leaders were laying plans to pit their organizational and financial clout against the Tories in the next election campaign. Challenging them 'to work to restore democracy in Ontario,' Earl Manners told his troops at the OSSTF annual meeting in March, 'We will never forget. We will never forgive.'[46] No less determined, OECTA's leaders had already issued an impressive little booklet outlining an anti-Harris educational platform designed to mobilize its own members for political action.[47] During the winter and early spring of 1997–8, moreover, the government found itself engaged in a ferocious brouhaha, mainly centred in the Toronto region, over continuing inequities in the business property taxes for education, inequities the Tories had half-promised to iron out and then found it politically impossible to do so.[48]

MEANWHILE, THE TRANSITION from old to new boards was taking place all across Ontario, creating its own tensions and difficulties. Some of these were inevitable in any large-scale reorganization. But they were exacerbated by long delays in releasing the government's new funding model. Initially, the ministry had hoped to make it available in October 1997. After the October cabinet shuffle, Johnson promised it for November, and then retreated to December; then to February, which also came and went without result.[49] There may well have been good reasons for this delay. The global amount had to be determined in light of other spending priorities and the continuing possibility of cuts to education. Even in January 1998 the Tories were, apparently, still debating that possibility.[50] No less important, the figures put in the various 'envelopes' had to be run board by board to see what the local consequences were. That was complex, time-consuming work; and getting it right was important not only for educational but also for political reasons. As one Johnson aide would later tell a reporter, 'We ran so many dozens of models and some of them would have been less than fun to announce. We would have had to go out there wearing flak jackets.'[51] But whatever the plausible reasons for the delay, the Tories, already hurting from the fallout over Bill 160, hardly made things easy for themselves. Well into the new year, trustees still did not know how much they would have to finance their programs for the academic year beginning in September 1998. And that, far beyond anything else, kept the political temperature far higher than might otherwise have been the case.

In the first place, the delay posed serious problems for the boards and their employees. New labour contracts had to be negotiated across the province, but that could not begin until the boards and unions knew what resources would be available. Major decisions about equalizing programs within amalgamated boards could not be made. Early in the new year, parents began to press to register their children for JK; but would JK be offered at all if adequate financing was not forthcoming? Would small district high schools remain open if the accommodation grants contained incentives to concentrate physical plant? Ontario labour law required boards intending to lay off substantial numbers of employees to give notice on or before 1 April. Boards that had reason to believe their funding might be reduced took precautions. On 23 February, Ottawa-Carleton gave September pink slips to nearly 1900 employees – according to OSSTF, one-quarter of their total workforce – including 700 classroom teachers.[52] Exacerbating all this were the persistent rumours that the Tories were about to make good on their earlier talk about further cuts to education. High-spending public boards, Toronto and Ottawa-Carleton above all, feared that they would be hardest hit, but no board in Ontario could rest assured their circumstances wouldn't get a little worse. Parents of exceptional children fretted about their children's programs; principals and vice-principals, facing a future outside the protective cover of union seniority rights, fretted about their jobs; warnings about the very survival of ESL or adult-education programs rang through the Toronto press.[53] The sheer uncertainty about funding magnified anxieties in an environment already uncertain enough.

In February and early March, bits and pieces of news escaped from the Queen's Park maw. School boards would be required to tell parents the average size of classes in each school.[54] A 'School Board Restructuring Fund' (separate from the funding model) would help ease the costs of amalgamation.[55] Boards that already had JK programs would continue to receive funding for that purpose, promised the premier.[56] The funding formula would be announced the week of 9 March.[57] No, it would be delayed yet again. For sure, 25 March, said Johnson.[58]

Well, actually, 23 March, when 'a friend of public education' kindly provided the Liberal leader, Dalton McGuinty, with all the draft press releases, backgrounders, and fact sheets relating to the new funding model.[59] McGuinty, the NDP, and the teachers' unions had a field day, giving it the worst spin possible. Two days later, with the damage already done, Johnson motored out to a Pickering high school to try to undo it. This was 'a good news story,' he retorted.[60] Stable funding for the next three years combined with the new funding formula would ensure excellence, equity, and accountability for the school system as it entered the new millennium.

A 'GOOD NEWS' STORY? With a booming economy buoying up provincial revenues and an election beginning to preoccupy Tory strategists, gone were the threats of further reductions in government expenditures on education. That alone bred a collective sigh of relief. Tory fence-mending was also obvious in some of the specifics: suddenly there was more money for JK and a recognition that 'children benefit from an early start to learning.'[61] But stable funding meant the total amount was set, for three years, at the 1997–8 level, after years of funding cuts had already been absorbed. And 'stable' meant for the province as a whole. Once board-by-board figures were released, a few days after Johnson's 25 March announcement, it looked different. True, there were winners – most Catholic boards, a few low-spending public boards, and the new French-language boards. These would receive increases, in some cases large increases, in their per-pupil resources. But most English public boards would experience losses, with no recourse to their own tax base to compensate. According to the ministry's own figures, Ottawa-Carleton would see a reduction of close to 10 per cent over three years; the new Toronto board, 5.7 per cent; Peel, 3 per cent.[62] The ministry made no bones about its justification for such reductions. As Johnson and his senior advisers would argue over and over, these high-spending boards spent more on nearly all grant categories outside the classroom, such as custodial and maintenance costs and board administration; yes, they would suffer greater overall percentage decreases than other boards, but the new funding model would ensure they actually had more dollars to spend in classrooms. Among the several problems with this argument was the distinction drawn by the government between classroom and non-classroom expenditure itself. If fewer principals, consultants, support staff, or custodial services were available, if teacher 'prep time' was reduced, did this not affect what went on in classrooms? The government, of course, said no; others disputed that mightily.

Implementation began with confusion and muddle as boards attempted to apply the complex new rules laid out in the government's 'technical paper' released 31 March. To board administrators this document was far more important than the original March announcement because it provided the 'arithmetic' of funding, item by item, that would determine what each board had to spend beginning 1 September 1998. As the implications began to emerge, near-panic ensued amongst trustees in some large urban boards, especially in Toronto where cost-cutting was made all the more complex by the amalgamation of seven pre-existing boards. Lay-off notices were issued to large numbers of teachers and administrators, the closure of many small schools and special programs predicted, and extracurricular activities, including expensive sports programs, threatened with extinction; Toronto's well-funded adult-education day schools were particularly hard hit when the board was finally forced to adjust to cuts in grants that most other boards had learned to live with two years earlier; in some cases, once the figures were actually worked out, boards found that their revenues would be substantially lower than the original government estimates had indicated.[63] Nor did it help that the government, pressed by school boards across the province, had to admit that it had some of the details wrong: by May an 'update' to the technical paper had been issued, and further revisions were forthcoming in June.[64]

The outcry against the new funding model was countered by more 'good news' announcements from the government. The April Throne

Speech brought commitments to invest in educational technology and to commission an expert review on early childhood education. In early May the budget announcement featured a pledge to increase spending on new textbooks and learning materials. In June, Johnson announced that, to meet board complaints, there would be more money for special education, additional funds to help reduce class size, and several related changes in the rules.[65] Of perhaps more import, an agreement was hammered out in mid-April between the government and the teachers' unions over the Teachers' Pension Plan, establishing a four-year window during which teachers could take early retirement and still receive full pension.[66] In its wake the number of retirements more than doubled over the previous year, as some ten thousand teachers took advantage of either the existing plan or the new opportunity, and it was predicted that retirements would total 18,000 over the life of the agreement. That meant the promise of substantial savings for boards in salaries paid to senior teachers, the cancellation of many of the lay-off notices which had made headlines earlier in the spring, and the hiring by some boards of a significant number of new teachers.

DURING THE LAST WEEKS of June 1998 yet another confrontation took place between the government and its opponents, this time in the courts. In sharp contrast to the remarkable volume of media coverage devoted to educational issues over the previous three years, this one received almost no attention whatever. That was unfortunate, for it offered the first systematic, rigorous critique of the new funding model and of the decision-making process that had shaped it. When teachers hit the pavement, it was news; when the premises underpinning the expenditure of $13 billion of taxpayers' money and a revolution in educational finance were exposed, it elicited hardly more than a comment in the province's leading newspapers.[67]

The applicants in the case included OECTA, the Ontario Public School Boards' Association, the new Toronto District School Board, OSSTF, and the two other English-language teachers' unions. Jointly, they asked that Bill 160 be declared unconstitutional on a number of grounds; but the centrepiece was the right of school boards to manage and control their own schools, including the right to tax ratepayers for their support. On the other side, the main parties were the government and the Ontario Catholic School Trustees' Association. The nature of the funding model itself was not the chief issue at stake; but its fairness and its adequacy in meeting the needs of students played an important part in the applicants' argument.

Marshalling an impressive range of evidence, and drawing on a thorough-going cross-examination of the ministry's director of education funding, the applicants' lawyers offered the court, in minute detail, a revealing and critical insight into the making of the funding formula and its implications. The data used by the government to arrive at funding levels for a wide range of grant components were, they asserted, unreliable or too dated to represent present needs. Using recent board expenditures as a proxy for 'needs' was problematic for a variety of reasons, including the fact that they reflected years of belt-tightening. Many components were set at the median for all boards in Ontario, whereas average board spending was much higher. Government claims that the model was based on years of systematic analysis were misleading or false: in many cases the funding levels were crude estimates or ministry guesswork about what per-pupil costs might be. In other cases, expert advice provided by outside consultants or ministry officials was ignored by cabinet, and lower funding levels set arbitrarily, without any plausible rationale beyond the exigencies of politics. Altogether, the model was not an attempt to gear funding to measurable or objective student needs, either within individual boards or across the province; rather, it was driven, in the first instance, by the dictates of stable funding, and then by the determination to produce a script that would play well in the public arena.[68]

Not even the much-vaunted simplicity and clarity of the new funding model could be taken at face value. When OPSBA's lawyer counted up all the subdivisions within the model, he tallied 22, or 29, or maybe even 34. 'So really,' he asked the ministry's director of education funding,

> you might as easily have said the new funding model replaces 34 different types of grants under the old funding model with 34 different components or some other number, approximately 34, could you not?
> A. I could describe it that way.
> Q. It is an exercise in nominalism, in other words?
> A. Or semantics.
> Q. Or semantics. I agree. It was a semantical exercise, was it?
> A. Mm-hmm.
> Q. You have to say yes or no.
> A. Oh, yes. Sorry.[69]

The government had its own answers to much of this, and some of them were good ones. Expert input had been put to full use, but 'in this funding decision, as in all funding decisions, the government determined funding levels based on what was necessary both to meet needs *and* to manage its fiscal resources.'[70] No funding model could 'perfectly' account for 'every variation of circumstance affecting student need in the province,' but the new model 'better accounts for these differences than the old model.' The shortcomings of the new funding model could be remedied through experience, but whatever its faults, it guaranteed, as nothing had before, real per-pupil equity for all of Ontario's children. As the applicants' own highly experienced financial expert was forced to admit, most decisions about what to fund and at what level had no 'one right answer' and would be subject to disagreements between experts, teachers, parents, ratepayers without children, and trustees. He agreed that 'one's opinion on the question of adequacy would depend upon one's pedagogical and political philosophy.'

Government lawyers, moreover, reiterated one potent argument familiar to provincial politicians and policy-makers for decades: 'You can't commit yourself to 60 per cent of the blue sky,' as David Peterson had summarized it pithily. Under the old funding model, equity could only be achieved if government raised its grants to all boards enough to match the expenditures of the highest-spending board. That was the principal solution offered by the applicants. But it would cost an estimated $2.8 billion per year, an amount that would require 'a dramatic change of priority in provincial expenditures.' More important, 'If assessment richer boards increased their spending the following year, the province would be required to increase its grant funding to keep pace in order to maintain equalization. The province would effectively have no control over the level of education spending in the province if it wished to establish/maintain equity amongst boards under the old funding model.'[71]

Faced with these two conflicting sets of arguments, Justice Peter Cumming agreed with the government that the fairness and adequacy of the new funding model was not pertinent to the constitutional issues at stake and was 'properly left to the political arena.'[72] During the hearing, nonetheless, he occasionally danced circles around government counsel over interpreting the technical details of the model or elucidating its implications, and could not resist a lengthy preliminary comment in his decision. 'The record before the Court,' he wrote,

> suggests that the funding model has been implemented with haste and without sufficient analysis as to what the funding arrangements will mean for the quality of education in the province ... The reliability of the data has been questioned by the advisory Expert Panels appointed by the Government ... There is, in effect, a substantial redistribution of monies. There is an assumption that every assessment-rich board can afford to lose some of its previous

funding and still meet the needs of its students. At the same time, there is an assumption that the amount transferred to each and every assessment poor board will be sufficient to rectify pre-existing shortfalls. It is questionable whether allowance has been made for the possibility that all relevant needs will not be met by this mechanical re-allocation of resources.

As a specific example of the applicants' concerns, Cumming referred to the nature of the teacher-salary component of the funding model, something which would, in their view, have disastrous implications for many boards. The grant for teachers' salaries constituted the major part of the government's basic per-pupil funding; yet it was based on a figure of $50,000 per teacher – and more than half the boards across the province paid their teachers, on average, more than that. In some cases this adjustment might lead to considerable underfunding. The Toronto District School Board, for example, calculated the shortfall between what it paid its teachers and what it would receive for salaries under the new model to be nearly $7 million a year.

The alternatives for boards in this situation, Cumming continued, were equally unpalatable. They could *not* make do with fewer teachers, since the funding model set maximum average class sizes that precluded such action. Thus they had the choice of reducing teacher salaries – provided they could negotiate an agreement with the unions – or perhaps even imposing a lockout, in order to keep total salaries within the amount specified by the formula; or, to pay their teachers, they would have to 'cannibalize other budget lines,' thereby reducing the resources available for students.

Cumming went on to cite other, similar examples which suggested that 'the data utilized for the inputs to determine the Foundation Grant in respect of such fundamental matters as classroom supplies, computer technology and textbooks are inadequate.' He took note as well of the applicants' contention that there appeared to be no adequate provision for enrolment growth and none for inflation. Altogether, he wrote, 'the applicants raise serious and meaningful concerns in respect of the financial limitations and impacts of the model.' He added that prohibiting school boards from raising 'any revenues at all by local property taxes runs counter to the countless studies done in respect of financing the Ontario education system' and then referred to nine of these, dating from 1950 to 1996. And he concluded his preface with this pointed paragraph:

Briefly put, the background to the present applications may be stated as follows. The present Government has introduced wide-ranging changes to

the financing structure of the educational system. There is far greater centralization of control than has ever been seen in Ontario to date. In particular, the amendments remove almost any ability on the part of local boards to
raise revenues beyond those deemed necessary to them by the provincial
government. Effectively, the government has introduced a monolithic structure into education governance, based in significant part on centralized
command and control. These changes have provoked furious and searing
criticism from a broadly based spectrum of interests. These criticisms appear
on the record before the Court to have a certain degree of validity.

Cumming's assessment of the new funding model, then, was judiciously
devastating, the more so because he really didn't have to deal with it at all.
Together, indeed, the applicants' extensive submissions and their support-
ing evidence, along with the judge's summary comments, constitute the
best critical analysis available, and may well remain so until the full impact
of the changes have worked themselves through the system, several years
into the new century. Only then will Ontarians really know for certain who
got it right, or wrong.

For the case at hand, however, the funding model was largely beside the
point. Constitutional issues decided it, and not the efficacy of the new
model. There were six interrelated questions put before Cumming and
each had its own importance.[73] But for my purposes, the crux was the right
to tax. OECTA had begun the case because it contended that Bill 160
violated Catholics' section 93 rights: the ability of a Catholic board to tax
separate school supporters was integral to its constitutional right to control and manage its own schools. The other applicants offered additional
reasons why Bill 160 was unconstitutional, including the argument that if
Catholics had section 93 rights, so indeed did public school supporters.
Lawyers for the government and the Catholic trustees' association maintained that the right to tax was not necessary to control and management,
that nothing in Bill 160 prejudicially affected Catholics' section 93 rights,
and that public school boards and supporters had no protected rights
under section 93.

On 22 July Cumming issued a decision in favour of the government on
five of the six questions put before him. But on the crucial question of
Catholics' right to tax, he rejected the arguments of government and
Catholic trustees alike. A series of judgments stretching back over decades,
and his own reading of the pertinent legislation, persuaded him that the
right to tax was guaranteed under the Confederation settlement of 1867
and protected in section 93 of Canada's Constitution Act. However willing

to co-operate with the government, Catholic trustees could not abandon their rights or put them in abeyance. 'Constitutional rights are constitutional rights for a reason; they are guaranteed and protected notwithstanding that at a given point in time it may not appear that a given right is necessary or effective. While the Government's intentions may be benevolent in regard to the Roman Catholic education community, that cannot change the fact that the taxation power is constitutionally guaranteed, and it would ill-behoove this Court to countenance its removal.'[74] And thus Cumming declared the relevant sections of Bill 160 'of no force or effect.'

That decision punched a gaping hole in the government's education-reform program. In six weeks, the schools would open and the new funding model would come into effect. For a third of Ontario's pupils it was now inoperative. Collective agreements expired on 31 August. OECTA could now contend that salary and working conditions could be negotiated in the light of their boards' right to levy taxes beyond the level of government grants. Public school supporters could point to the potentially inequitable outcomes for their own schools. And the government was saddled with a wholly asymmetrical system of funding, two different 'models' at odds with each other in providing boards with the resources to fund their schools.

In an attempt to head off disaster, the government moved quickly, announcing that it would appeal the ruling and asking Cumming to suspend his decision until then.[75] In mid-August, Cumming agreed, giving the government until the year 2000 to restore Roman Catholic rights.[76] Temporarily, the new funding model was rescued and the government given some breathing room. But OPSBA and the public school unions promptly declared that they too would appeal Cumming's rejection of their arguments, if necessary all the way to the Supreme Court. And that might leave the entire matter uncertain for years.

IN THE POLITICAL ARENA, breathing space was harder to find. The new funding model came into effect at the beginning of the school year. At the same time, new labour contracts had to be negotiated across the province. It was a recipe for renewed conflict. With no control over their own resources, school boards claimed there was little to bargain about: their costs had to be cut to meet the restrictions imposed by the funding model. The teachers' unions adamantly opposed substantive changes in working conditions. Though not the only issue at stake, prep time in the high schools proved especially contentious. In most boards, compromises were hammered out through 'interim agreements' that allowed the schools to open on schedule in September. But that left the hard issues to be settled in the months ahead, and many of the compromises challenged the government's intent to increase teachers' contact time with students. In many parts of the province, moreover, these negotiations were accompanied by rotating strikes or the cancellation of extracurricular activities and other voluntary services normally provided by teachers. In a handful of cases, bargaining broke down altogether. Lockouts or strikes ensued, and anywhere from 150,000 to 200,000 pupils lost a week or more of school during September.[77]

The disruptions fuelled parents' discontent and kept educational issues in the media limelight. But so did other implications of the new funding model. Though it had been under fire for months from the teachers' unions, from trustees and their administrators, and from parents and others with a stake in particular programs that appeared to be threatened, the funding model had been insulated from wider public scrutiny by its sheer complexities, and by a certain scepticism about the self-interested braying of both its proponents and their enemies.[78] That changed dramatically in September and October as it became clear that the formula governing school accommodation meant swift closure for large numbers of elementary and high schools across the province. When both rural and urban boards began to release lists of specific schools to be axed – schools which children actually attended and which were rooted in real communities – protests mounted in villages, towns, and cities alike. And nowhere more so than in Toronto, where the chair of the board, with only faintly disguised crocodile tears, announced that within the year, government funding reductions would force the closure of some 138 of the city's public schools.[79]

Throughout all this, the government showed an increasingly unsure hand. Tough new rules governing teacher contact time would be imposed, said Dave Johnson one week; those rules, he conceded the next, would be tempered to fit the compromises being reached by teachers and boards in many jurisdictions.[80] Would the government move to end the September strikes and lockouts in eight large boards? Solutions lay solely with boards and the unions, Mike Harris insisted in mid-September; by the end of the month the Tories had legislated an end to the conflicts and imposed the terms of local settlements.[81] Nor could the government deflect the clamour over school closures. Try as it might (and it tried mightily) to blame big-spending boards and fat-cat bureaucrats, it found its credibility and competence challenged by protests across the province. By early November, the government had virtually capitulated, promising an infusion of cash to compensate for an accommodation grant that failed to address adequately the circumstances of many boards, rural and urban alike.[82]

DISARRAY? That may be too strong a word, and the portents too ambiguous to sustain it. Key elements of Bill 160 had, nonetheless, been successfully challenged in the lower courts. Though the government recouped that loss in the spring of 1999, winning its appeal against the Cumming decision in Ontario's highest court, the legal basis for the centralization of financial control continues to be in doubt until the Supreme Court of Canada disposes of the issue sometime in the new century. There were other portents besides. A government that had hoped to remain above the fray of collective bargaining – a government that had ducked the implications of centralized funding for the future of collective bargaining – had been forced to legislate teachers back to work. The first obvious inadequacies of the funding model had been exposed for all to see by the crisis over school closures. Perhaps inevitably, but not without consequence in either the classroom or the political arena, the Tories had earned the implacable enmity of Ontario's teachers' unions and, in the main, of its teachers. Despite millions of dollars spent on advertising, the government had still not been able to persuade large portions of the public that its policies were wise or efficacious. Like the future of the Harris government itself, in the shadow of an approaching provincial election, the fate of the 'common sense' revolution in education remained uncertain.

15

Retrospect

This is not a book about the Harris government alone, but about the reshaping of Ontario's schools over the entire last half of the twentieth century. Still, at the outset of this retrospect, one can hardly help but ask how the Harris government's reforms fit into that larger history. The scope of the changes introduced in three short years was breathtaking; other than the long decade of the sixties, one is hard-pressed to think of twentieth-century parallels. But how radical beyond that?

Consider some examples. First, given the level of decentralization that held sway from the late 1960s onward, greater central control over the curriculum and more uniformity in what was taught across the province might seem like a new departure. But it was hardly more than a return to traditional ways of doing things in Ontario, at least between the late nineteenth century and the mid-1960s. Indeed, it is well within the memory and experience of those who administered and taught in the schools during the two decades after mid-century. From that perspective at least it appears more like a shift of emphasis, a rebalancing of the long-established shared responsibilities of central and local authorities in governing the province's school system.

Much of the same might be said of school-board amalgamation. That process had been going on, by fits and starts, since the beginning of the century. By far the most dramatic reorganization took place during the 1960s. Recent changes may, yet again, have increased the distance between parents and trustees, between local communities and board administration; but this is hardly more than a continuation of a well-established trend. Radicalism would have dictated the abolition of the boards altogether and the creation, perhaps, of some surrogate for the old rural school with its board of three elected trustees; strengthened school councils were one plausible alternative. That, however, is what did not happen. (At least, not yet.)

In other respects, we have seen a return to a past almost entirely forgotten. Provincial testing is one good example. Though the 'grade 13 departmentals' are usually cited as a precedent, the analogy is misleading: special-purpose tests that touched only the minority of high school students preparing for post-secondary education, they influenced teaching in the lower grades but hardly provided quality control or proofs of individual achievement for the vast majority of students who left school before that. A more apt parallel would be the testing regime of the late nineteenth and early twentieth centuries, when province-wide testing was carried out at several points – during elementary school; through the high school entrance exam, written at the end of grade 8; the 'lower-school' exams (the end of grade 10); and the junior matriculation exam at the end of grade 12. The new EQAO tests are of a different kind and conducted in a different sort of atmosphere, and there is, of course, less emphasis on the sorting function of the tests; but other than that, the purposes are similar to those which underpinned, many decades ago, the large-scale provincial testing of all pupils at several points in their school careers.

The centralization of financial control, on the other hand, was something entirely new. For at least a century and a half, since the creation of Ontario's school system in the 1840s, local autonomy had rested on the ability of school boards to raise their own revenues. Urban boards in particular had used that power to create 'lighthouse' local school systems, pioneering programs and innovative services that set the standard against which progress was judged in the rest of the province. That power is now substantially impaired, and so is the ability of all school trustees to respond in distinctive ways to distinctive local needs. Whether or not provincial authorities can respond adequately to their new responsibilities remains to be seen, but certainly this change was 'a leap in the dark,' a sharp break with the way things had been done in Ontario's past.

THE RADICALISM OF THE Harris government, in any case, has to be read in the light of a history reaching back fifteen years or more. The Tories were, after all, inheritors of, and participants in, an ongoing debate about the state of education in Ontario and its future. Most of their criticisms were common coinage among those disenchanted with current practices, and most of their proposed reforms were shared, though not universally, across the political spectrum. There was nothing new, or distinctively Tory, about the notion that to be competitive in a global economy, education needed to be more rigorous, relevant, or better at preparing young people for the job market. The 1995 election platforms of all three parties promised provincial standards, a core curriculum, and more testing – in the case of the NDP, far more testing than the Tories actually introduced; and both the Liberals and the NDP proposed to reduce the number of trustees and cap their salaries. Dave Cooke's 'New Foundations' program offered far-reaching changes on a variety of fronts; the Tories simply put a chunk of them in place.

The Tories, moreover, did not have to invent a restructuring initiative in governance and finance – it was already under way, initiated by the NDP. The Sweeney committee had been given the task of making recommendations about how to reduce the number of school boards 'by 40 to 50%,' reduce the number of trustees, and address a series of related issues including financial disparity among the boards. The Working Group on Education Finance Reform, established in March 1995, was expected to make recommendations on both raising and distributing funds for education, *assuming* that 'the level of total spending on education is adequate, but needs to be spent differently'; that 'the provincial contribution to education will not increase'; that 'expenditure on administration will be subject to a limit, in order to focus resources on the classroom'; and that these resources must be equitably distributed to ensure 'equal educational opportunity for students, wherever they live in Ontario, independent of the wealth of the local school board.'[1] The phraseology could have been Mike Harris's; but it was in fact the mandate given the working group by an NDP government. John Snobelen might have offered the following opinion, but it actually came from Charles Pascal, the deputy minister of education brought in by Dave Cooke and fired by the Tories: 'School boards as they exist right now ought to go the way of the history books, given the fact that they spend so much money and add so very little value.'[2]

Successive governments had been edging towards greater central control over the curriculum since the early 1980s, and the case for greater uniformity and more ministry direction had been made emphatically by the Royal Commission on Learning. Giving more structure and coherence to the high school program had begun, under Bette Stephenson, with the SERP-*OSIS* process, and had been one key focus of Liberal policy-making. Rewriting *The Formative Years* had begun under the Liberals and was pushed forward under the NDP. Streaming in the schools had been an issue since at least the mid-1980s, as had arguments about the best way to organize and deliver subject content in the curriculum. Finding the right balance between compulsory core and optional subjects in the high school had been a battleground since the mid-1960s.

The most radical of Tory initiatives was undoubtedly the decision to strip school boards of their powers to levy their own taxes. Yet that was different only in degree from the ill-fated expenditure ceilings introduced by the Davis government in the early 1970s – a measure that had given the province the power to set maximum limits on the amount local boards could raise from property taxes. By the mid-1990s, moreover, the equity issue could no longer be ducked. Pressed, often enough, by constitutional decisions or the threat of court challenges, provincial and state governments across North America were moving to eliminate the inequitable effects of dependence on the local tax base.[3] In Ontario, a whole battery of committees and commissions, stretching back over several decades, had made the case that education funding was a mess and in need of reform in the name of both equity and accountability. And the thrust of this advice was always towards greater central control over finance: in the name of equity, for taxpayers and students alike, provincial school systems should be paid for mainly by provincial funds; the only question was, how much should be left to the discretion of local boards? Generally, the answer had been, only a little. Despite widespread impressions to the contrary, that advice did not originate primarily because analysts were adverse to spendthrift local boards. It arose from a different source. Per-pupil equity depended on access to equal resources, and only the provincial government could ensure that such equity existed. As the Fair Tax Commission pointed out, moreover, leaving large amounts of discretion in local hands 'would provide an almost irresistible temptation for provincial governments to abandon tax fairness principles and to tap the local property tax base indirectly by restricting formula funding below realistic levels.'[4]

And that, more or less, was exactly what had been happening over the last quarter of the century. Provincial grants to schools had been held at levels nearly everyone who studied the matter agreed were less than 'realistic,' despite a plethora of new programs mandated by the province and intense local political pressures on school trustees to introduce or extend services over which they themselves had some control. As a consequence, local spending ballooned. One doesn't have to endorse the Tory solution to recognize that two or three previous governments shrank from the political consequences of fiscal reform and merely fiddled while property taxpayers burned and inequities deepened.

Be that as it may, was the new Tory funding formula adequate to meet the needs of the province's students? Large numbers of people didn't think so. But then, large numbers of people, trustees and teachers in particular, had condemned the Davis government for its expenditure ceilings, and a succession of governments for not spending more on

Ontario's schools. The essential issues that divided people in the late 1990s were not much different than they had been since the first 'cutbacks' in 1971. How much should the community pay for a 'quality education'? What constituted 'quality,' or even 'essential services' as opposed to 'frills'? How much restraint was enough, or too much?

By 1998, the worst nightmares of the government's opponents had failed to materialize. Though the spectre had been bruited in one Tory pre-election policy document,[5] and there had been undercurrents of talk within caucus and among some rabid neo-conservatives, school 'choice' in the form of the voucher system or the introduction of charter schools remained outside the scope of government policy. In late 1997 the Education Improvement Commission issued a resolute condemnation of any such innovation,[6] and as I write there is no evidence that the government intends to pursue the idea. That, however, does not mean the issue is dead. Nor should it be. There is no platonic archetype for the organization and delivery of public education; there are other ways to accomplish its goals, plausible alternatives that deserve, at the very least, serious debate.[7]

The Harris Tories were certainly confrontational, and confrontations they provoked. Though I know of no precise turmoil measuring stick, these may have been unprecedented. Yet October 1997 was not the first time teachers overflowed Maple Leaf Gardens and marched, in their thousands, on Queen's Park. Nor was it the first time teachers had effectively closed the schools over a labour issue. Nor was it the first bitter contest with government: there was the warfare over the NDP's Social Contract, with the Liberals over changes in the pension plan and again during the election campaign of 1990, and against the Davis 'cutbacks' of 1971–5. Though he was rather smugly reflecting in 1991 on the virtues of tough union tactics in dealing with previous governments, Jim Head, an ex-president of OSSTF, might equally well have been offering a prescient judgment on the effectiveness of the Harris government itself: 'Real educational change in this province comes through rough politics.'[8]

Rough politics, on the other hand, has its costs. At the end of the century, the unease among many parents about the welfare of their children was palpable, and the sheer divisiveness of the Harris years made consensus about educational policy a faint hope. Teachers in particular paid a price in morale: by 1998 the level of anger, frustration, or passive disenchantment with the classroom was worrisome. And so were the potential consequences of separating principals and vice-principals from other staff by defining them more sharply as 'managers' and removing them from their unions. In-school leadership had long had a substantial

managerial element; but it also had collegial qualities which made good
principals into educational leaders as well. To the extent that changes, it
will be a loss, and not a trivial one. High morale and a collegial environment are of crucial importance: after all the rhetoric about new departures, all the promises of excellence and accountability, all the new
curriculum guidelines and testing initiatives, what actually happens in
classrooms happens because teachers make it happen. No one can afford
to ignore that simple truth.

Even here, however, there is little point in savaging the Harris government alone. Salaries had begun to stagnate and working conditions worsen
well before 1995. Serious behavioural problems with students had been
multiplying for years. The sheer level of demands placed on teachers and
principals and the stresses entailed had been thoroughly aired during the
hearings of the royal commission. Governments, of whatever stripe, can
hardly be blamed for the large and sometimes inimical changes that have
taken place in the social fabric over the last third of the twentieth century,
and that have had an indubitable impact on the schools. Politicians and
senior bureaucrats have, however, been complicit in giving unwarranted
legitimacy to the half-baked faddism endemic in so much educational
discourse emanating from academics and practitioners alike, and in promoting sharp changes in policy direction that have had their own unset-
tling effects on teacher morale. In the high schools, for example, no
sooner was *OSIS* fully in place than governments proposed to change it.
The destreaming and decoursing experiment in grade 9 brought upheaval. Talk of the abolition of grade 13 and the reorganization of the
'specialization years' caused deep unease. Teachers, indeed, had been
complaining about the imposition of ill-considered policies, without adequate consultation, forethought, or testing, for at least three decades.[9]
Things only got worse in the 1990s, and not only under the Tories.

I hold no brief for the Harris government.[10] But writing amidst the fray
is no time to offer a considered judgment on its policies. Whether or not
the 'common sense' revolution in education is a mere blip or a genuine
new departure, the salvation of the system, its destruction, or of no
enduring impact at all, is something that can only be kenned when this
particular present is past. All that I am proposing is that it be seen in the
perspective of the recent history of Ontario education, where, in most
things, the continuities are more striking than the discontinuities.

WHAT IS NOT AT ISSUE is the sheer scope of the changes that have taken
place over the last fifty years, within the compass, indeed, of one genera-

tion. There are still people living in the province who received all of their education in a one-room elementary school, and others who went on to continuation school or boarded in a distant town to complete their matriculation requirements. There are still larger numbers of people who, in kindergarten, sat quietly in tidy rows and learned (or didn't learn) coordination by sewing thick wool through the pinholes in cardboard squares to complete a happy face; who memorized the prescribed hundred lines of poetry every year, and spouted back the three causes of the corn laws and the three causes of their repeal; who, in grade 13, long after most of their peers had left school, wrote, on a sultry day in June, a three-hour examination beginning at 9:00 a.m. on Latin Authors, in the afternoon a second three-hour paper on Latin Composition, and who returned the next morning to draw freehand and label neatly the parts of a frog. All this belongs, in Peter Laslett's evocative phrase, to 'a world we have lost.' The majority of young people now complete grade 12. Schools are bigger, better equipped, offer more choices. Elementary school teachers are better educated. The consolidation of local governance has proceeded step by step since 1964 through to 1997. Catholic children can now complete their education in Catholic schools. Francophones have not only acquired a right to an education in their own language but the right to govern their own institutions. However well or badly accomplished, schools have a mandate to provide for exceptional children, promote gender equity, and discountenance prejudice. And all this is no more than a partial list of the changes recounted in this book.

The schools also have a mandate to ensure academic achievement, from the three Rs to a more sophisticated array of skills and knowledge. How successful are they in this? That question has usually been put in a different way: Have standards fallen? If one uses the benchmarks of the past, the answer is, Of course they have. To see this, all one has to do is dig out the high school entrance examination of, say, 1898. To be allowed into high school a century ago, grade 8 students sat a province-wide examination, set by the Department of Education, which few even of the distinguished professors at Ontario's universities who carp about the work of the schools could pass with distinction, or, perhaps, pass at all. Those thirteen- or fourteen-year-olds who did pass could 'find the least common multiple of 355 and 497'; give antonyms for artless and earthly; give the date, origins, and main provisions of the Ashburton Treaty; 'sketch a map of the counties that touch Lake Ontario and write in neatly the name of each county and its county town'; read 'intelligently as well as intelligibly' a 'scene from King John'; and parse a paragraph from Macaulay or Milton. These are not achievements to be despised, or dismissed in the way they routinely are by trendy educational experts intent on denigrating the goals or the pedagogy of the past. But they did not represent, even remotely, the achievement of most elementary school pupils in 1898. Only a minority of children ever got to grade 8. Of these, only 41 per cent chose (or were allowed) to write the high school entrance exam. About 30 per cent of them failed. Its task, in other words, was a ruthless winnowing of even the relative handful of pupils who attempted it, in order to identify the even smaller handful judged equipped to benefit from the highly selective academic high school which was then, rather like the undergraduate program today, the gatekeeper of the social order.[11]

Over the course of the twentieth century, Ontario's schools have tried to ensure that all children completed elementary school, then grade 10, and, from the 1960s on, a full high school education. The challenge has been to find the means of offering a worthwhile education to not just a handful, but all young people. Whether we have been successful remains at issue. At century's end it is still unclear that much of what goes under the name of 'child-centred education' is the best means of teaching our children, or at least large numbers of them, the skills they will need in the future; indeed, there is now a considerable amount of research that indicates it is not.[12] While academic marks in senior high school remain the best predictor of success in first-year university,[13] as has been the case for decades, there are still grounds for worry that the skills required for academic work are not adequate among at least a portion of post-secondary students. A succession of 'reforms' have not abolished the effects of social class, or at least the effects of income, on student achievement or life chances.[14] Despite a plethora of studies, a significant minority of adolescents still drop out before high school graduation. Concerns about behavioural problems and lack of motivation, endemic in the schools for two decades, have begun to seep upwards into post-secondary circles.

One of the animating ideals of the last half-century, secondary education for all – or at least a *worthwhile* secondary education for all – may yet prove a chimera. The amount of theorizing on the subject has been voluminous, especially over the last fifteen years, but the general thrust has been that if we are to succeed, the schools themselves must change. Many proposals for change have been sensible and reasonable; others are little more than solemn nonsense about the academic 'bias' of the traditional high school and the 'balkanizing' effects of organizing the curriculum around traditional disciplines. But fundamental questions about the goal itself have rarely been raised. One exception was Alan King, puzzling in

1988 over the issue of student retention. 'There may be social and economic advantages to the province in keeping young people in school,' he
wrote,

> [but] there may be disadvantages to counter them. For example, ... an
> increase in alienation ... and a depressing effect on the quality of learning for
> all students. The issue, then, is what is the optimum proportion of graduates,
> so that both the young people and the society are best served. There comes a
> point when the effort to retain students is counter-productive to the quality
> of learning in schools. It is necessary to look merely at the situation of
> students in the province who take mainly General-level courses to illustrate
> this point. Over time, homework expectations have been reduced, exams are
> fewer, increased weight is being given to attitudinal indicators of achieve-
> ment, and motivation is still depressed as evidenced by mark distributions
> and the growth of General-level workshops for teachers.[15]

There is much truth in the retort that complaints about standards and
discipline are as old as Plato, and are the stock-in-trade of school critics
past and present. There have always been those who say, without rhyme or
reason, that each new generation, or its schools, is going to hell in a
handbasket. But that is hardly grounds for complacency. To those who
decry, for example, the relevance of international (and one might add,
interprovincial) comparisons of student achievement in Ontario, one
might juxtapose the response of two American scholars: 'Some dismiss the
international comparisons because our curriculum is different, and our
children cannot be expected to learn what they have not been taught. But
that begs the question as to why we would tolerate such a curriculum. It is
patently absurd to say that international comparisons of mathematics
achievement, for example, are irrelevant because few of our children have
a curriculum that includes calculus, physics, or probability when all or
most of these subjects are required for technological literacy in the modern world.'[16]

This may be a valid point in its own right; yet it also raises a different
question: Just how much technological literacy do we need? The worrisome rise in unemployment among young people, for both dropouts *and*
high school graduates, has created its own educational dilemma. Borrow-
ing some of their phraseology from several previous studies, two Ontario
analysts recently summarized the matter this way: 'The traditional prescription that better skills and more education are appropriate government policy responses seems inadequate, as evidence mounts that "young

workers" entering the labour market face a "demand deficit" rather than a "skills deficit." Education and training cannot address the full dimensions of the problem; in isolation, they simply produce "better educated unemployed people."'[17]

A nice turn of phrase; still, one might ask what would be so bad about that? Training for vocations has long been one essential task of the schools and it would be foolish to deny its importance. But the priority, as the Royal Commission on Learning emphasized, must surely fall on educating citizens, not on job-training. Nobody has much disagreed with the former goal, but means, and priorities, have been the subject of deep divisions. An underlying motif of curriculum 'reform' over the last thirty years has been what Bob Davis has termed the 'skills mania' – the emphasis on generic skills to the detriment of content, the emphasis on the 'how' of learning rather than the 'what.'[18] Critical inquiry and creative thinking have been the watchwords; learning to learn is to be valued over what is learned. No one in his or her right mind would deny the importance of thinking skills or the ability to retrieve and use information effectively. But that hardly helps us distinguish between what is worth knowing and what is not, or determine what constitutes the requisites of an educated citizen. Nor does the parallel trend to dichotomize the role of the school by pointing to its increasing burden in the socialization of the young. 'What's more important, that we graduate a kid who can read or a kid who can be a good citizen?' one high school English teacher reputedly asked at the time the royal commission was holding its consultations across the province. In their critique of the state of Ontario education in the 1990s, Peter Emberley and Waller Newell replied this way:

> We argue ... that there can be no essential conflict between good education and good citizenship. One cannot exist without the other. Neither good citizenship nor personal fulfilment is possible without a good education. Students who are unable to clarify their problems and to articulate their instinctual responses in the light of reason, history, and the known record of human experience will become neither informed, thoughtful citizens nor innovative, productive workers. For these reasons, liberal education ... is not a luxury or a matter of nostalgia. It is the indispensable condition for a young person's growth to responsible maturity and a chance to excel in life.[19]

Contrary to much progressive cant, there *is* an aristocracy of knowledge. The challenge in a democratic society is to ensure that all young people, or least the vast majority of them, inherit it as their own. That indeed is the

strongest case for a common curriculum, and it remains persuasive even
after the depredations of *The Common Curriculum.*

In a prescient formulary, an early-nineteenth-century report on an
American university described the purpose of education as 'the discipline
and furniture of the mind.'[20] The schools have other, subsidiary purposes,
of course. They must share in the task of socialization. They have vocational goals, and many others besides. But the discipline of the mind,
learning to learn *well*, and its furniture, with that core of knowledge which
ornaments both intellect and character and provides the fundament for
reflective and critical thought, remain its pre-eminent task. Indeed, it is
this which gives education its moral purpose, its social *raison d'être*, and not
something else.

THE EXPERIMENT WITH universal education, including secondary education for all, has been one of the most ambitious and compelling projects of
the nineteenth and twentieth centuries. The sheer level and volume of
controversy over means and ends in Ontario during the last thirty or forty
years, the size of the investment Ontarians have been prepared to make in
public education, the effort poured into studies, reports, and initiatives
for change all attest to the commitment of Ontario's people to do it better
and get it right. That end has proved elusive even at the close of the
twentieth century. To pursue it further may turn out to be a millenarian
delusion; our choice of means may be misguided and our goals irrelevant
in a purportedly postmodern age. Still, it strikes me as a worthy task. To
abandon it, at any rate, would be to abandon that faith which has animated
Ontario's educational history for 150 years.

Appendix

FIGURE 1 The Ontario school system: Mid-century attrition

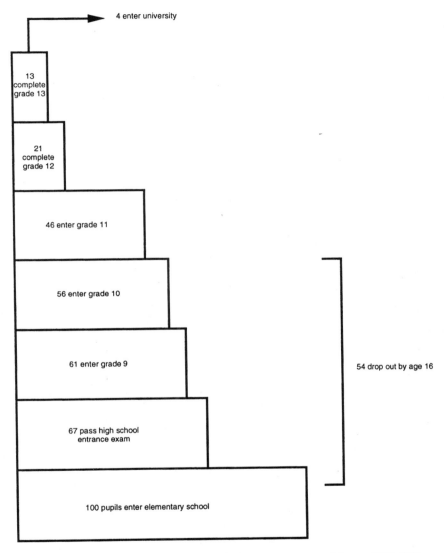

Source: Adapted from Ontario Department of Education, *Annual Report,* 1948, 107.
© Queen's Printer for Ontario, 1948. Reproduced with permission.

FIGURE 2 Ontario fertility rate, 1921–93

Note: Fertility rate is the average number of children born per woman of childbearing age.

Sources: David K. Foot, *Canada's Population Outlook: Demographic Futures and Economic Challenges* (Toronto: James Lorimer & Co., 1982), 47; Statistics Canada, *Report on the Demographic Situation in Canada, 1994: The Sandwich Generation, Myths and Reality,* November 1994, 105; Carl F. Grindstaff, 'Canadian Fertility, 1951 to 1993,' *Canadian Social Trends* 39 (Winter 1995): 15.

FIGURE 3 Births in Ontario

'000s

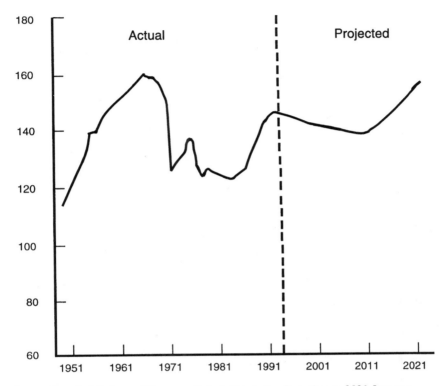

Source: Ontario Ministry of Finance, *Ontario Population Projections to 2021*, January 1994, 10. © Queen's Printer for Ontario, 1994. Reproduced with permission.

FIGURE 4 Elementary and secondary enrolment, 1955–96

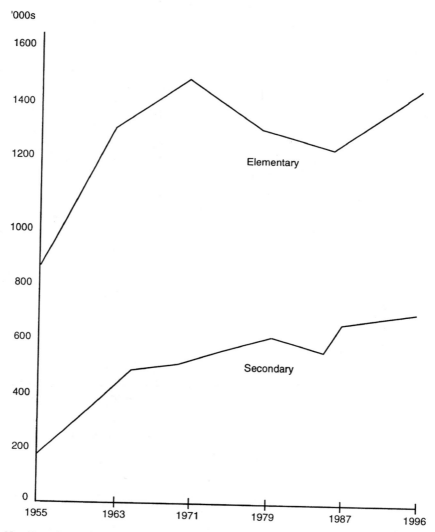

Note: Data from 1985 on are not comparable with those of previous years because of the extension of public funding to Roman Catholic schools.

Sources: Ontario Ministry of Education and Training, *Education Statistics, Ontario; Key Statistics;* and *QuickFacts.* Where figures differ, the later publications were used.

FIGURE 5 Legislative grants to school boards, 1942–72

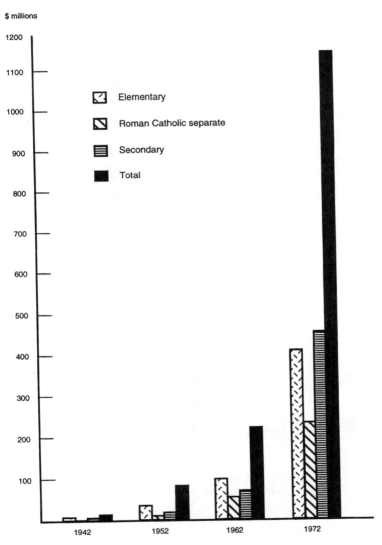

Source: Ontario, Committee on the Costs of Education, *Interim Report No. 7,* 'Financing Education in Elementary and Secondary Schools,' June 1975, 85. © Queen's Printer for Ontario, 1975. Reproduced with permission.

FIGURE 6 School board expenditures, including legislative grants, 1942–72

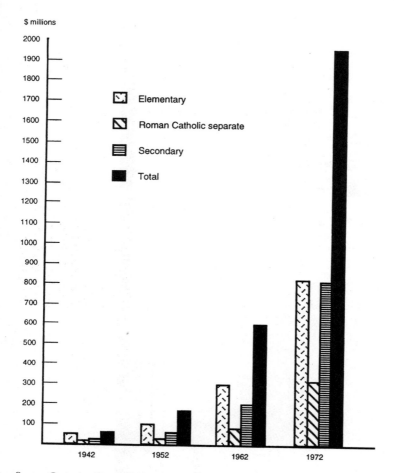

Source: Ontario, Committee on the Costs of Education, *Interim Report No. 7,* 'Financing Education in Elementary and Secondary Schools,' June 1975, 70. © Queen's Printer for Ontario, 1975. Reproduced with permission.

FIGURE 7 Provincial-local sharing of educational expenditures, 1969–97

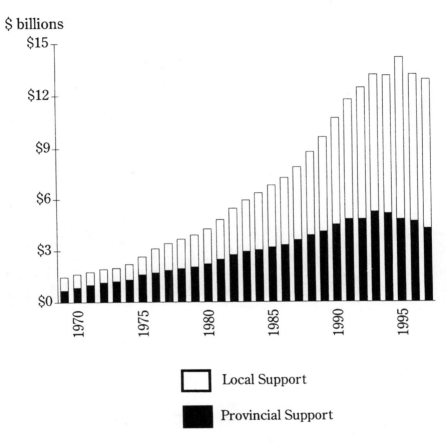

$ billions

Local Support

Provincial Support

Note: Figures exclude teacher pension-fund contributions.

Source: © Jerry Paquette. Based on data supplied by Ontario Ministry of Education and Training.

FIGURE 8 Provincial-local sharing of educational expenditure, 1969–97: 1986 dollars

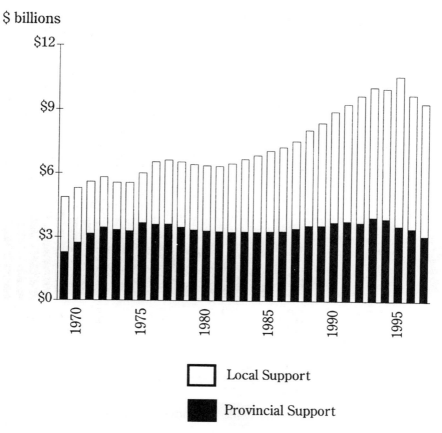

Note: Figures exclude teacher pension-fund contributions. Real dollar value adjusted with composite CPI.

Source: © Jerry Paquette. Based on data supplied by Ontario Ministry of Education and Training.

FIGURE 9 Age distribution of full-time teachers, 1978 and 1992

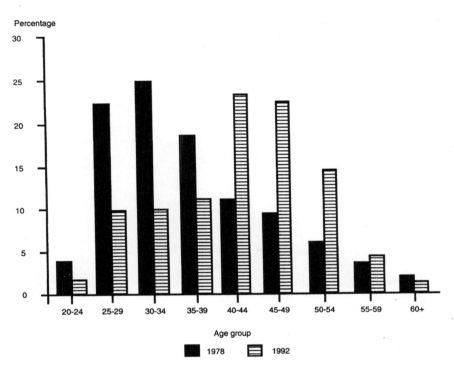

Source: Ontario Ministry of Education and Training, *1992–93 Key Statistics: Elementary and Secondary Education in Ontario,* 15. © Queen's Printer for Ontario, 1994. Reproduced with permission.

Bibliographic Note

A Note on References

In an attempt to prevent the number of notes from running riot, I have adopted the following rule of thumb: where I am charting new terrain I have provided extensive documentation, but where other easily accessible sources provide their own detailed or summary accounts, I have avoided point-by-point references. While that has been my approach throughout the book, it is particularly the case when I am dealing with the period from mid-century to the early 1970s. For that reason, I want to review some key sources for those decades.

First, there is the eight-volume work by W.G. Fleming published in 1971–2. A massive undertaking intended as a monument to the Robarts-Davis era, Fleming's work is an indispensable source for not just the sixties but much of the period before that. The volumes are not well organized or indexed and thus not always easy to use; but they remain a gold mine of information on just about any aspect of twentieth-century Ontario education.

A second 'gold mine' was produced by the Commission on Declining Enrolments in Ontario. The commissioner, R.W.B. Jackson, mobilized a large number of economists, demographers, and policy analysts to examine all the associated problems and the result was a vast compendium of historical information: aside from the three volumes of the report itself, at least forty-two related studies were printed on subjects ranging from demographic, economic, and curricular trends to teachers' salaries and teacher education.

A third key source is the annual reports of the Department of Education, which contain descriptive passages on new policies or past accomplishments, but more important, detailed annual statistics on all aspects of the school system.

The Hope Report was enormously helpful in sketching my baseline portrait. While his account of post-war developments is relatively brief, R.M. Stamp's *The Schools of Ontario* offers the standard overview of developments from 1876 to the mid-1970s. David Cameron's *Schools for Ontario* is essential on administration and finance in the 1960s (and despite the subtitle, has much to say on the 1950s as well). Stefan Dupré et al. describe the origins and implementation of TVTAA. Two indispensable doctoral theses, by Eric Ricker and John Stapleton, explore the intricate educational politics of the era, exploiting both archival sources and interviews with participants. Though it reaches only to the late 1960s, there are valuable chapters in Wilson, Stamp, and Audet, eds, *Canadian Education: A History*. No one writing about the origins and development of the separate schools can do without Franklin Walker's first two volumes on the subject; but he also offers a fine account of the post-war period in volume 3. An overview of the system of government grants to schools from the nineteenth century to the Macdonald Commission can be found in Jerry Paquette's article 'Vertical Equity.' John Porter's magisterial *The Vertical Mosaic* is critical to understanding how schooling in the immediate postwar decades interacted with class structure and social mobility. Douglas Owram's *Born at the Right Time* is pertinent for anyone interested in schooling, child-rearing practices, or youth culture during the 1950s and 1960s. And so is Mona Gleason's *Normalizing the Ideal.*

The development of the teachers' federations is tolerably well served in books by French, Hopkins, and Robinson, but all three end in the 1960s. A more recent account of FWTAO, by Staton and Light, is highly readable but lacks detail and depth. The only new study, that by Robert Dixon of OECTA, is good on both the recent and the distant past.

There are two model studies of curriculum developments in particular high school subjects, by Bob Davis on history, and Don Gutteridge on English. Both cover the post-war years as well as later decades. There is a crying need for similar surveys of other subjects at both the elementary and secondary level, including changing practices in teaching the 3 Rs in the primary grades. George Tomkins' pan-Canadian review of curriculum developments is also valuable.

K.J. Rea has written a comprehensive history of the Ontario economy from 1945 to the mid-1970s; Thomas Courchene covers some of the same ground but extends the analysis to the end of the century. S.D. Clark's *The Suburban Society* is a superb introduction to the physical and social impact of suburbanization in Ontario in the post-war decades. Two scholarly biographies of provincial premiers provide detailed portraits of the main issues in Ontario politics between the 1940s and the early 1970s, including the politics of education: Roger Graham's *Leslie Frost*, and A.K. McDougall's *John P. Robarts*. An eminently readable and often perceptive journalistic overview of the same period is Jonathan Manthorpe's *The Power and the Tories*. We have no full-dress study of the political career of William Davis, though there is a helpful overview by Claire Hoy.

Though it reaches far beyond the immediate post-war decades and only occasionally touches on education, one valuable source for the political, economic, and social context of this book is *The Government and Politics of Ontario*, now edited by Graham White (but edited in the first instance by Donald C. MacDonald). This fine collection of essays has now undergone five revisions, and readers should be aware that in each successive volume some valuable essays have been added or dropped, so that all five versions are useful.

Works Cited Above

Cameron, David M. *Schools for Ontario: Policy-making, Administration, and Finance in the 1960s.* Toronto: University of Toronto Press, 1972.

Clark, S.D. *The Suburban Society.* Toronto: University of Toronto Press, 1966.

Commission on Declining Enrolments in Ontario [Jackson Commission]. *Interim Report*, February 1978. *Interim Report No. 2*, July 1978. *Final Report*, October 1978.

Courchene, Thomas J., with Colin R. Telmer. *From Heartland to North American Region State: The Social, Fiscal and Federal Evolution of Ontario.* Toronto: Centre for Public Management, Faculty of Management, University of Toronto, 1998.

Davis, Bob. *Whatever Happened to High School History? Burying the Political Memory of Youth. Ontario, 1945–1995.* Toronto: Lorimer, 1995.

Dixon, Robert T. *Be a Teacher: A History of the Ontario English Catholic Teachers' Association.* Toronto: Ontario English Catholic Teachers' Association, 1994.

Dupré, J. Stefan, et al. *Federalism and Policy Development: The Case of Adult Occupational Training in Ontario.* Toronto: University of Toronto Press, 1973.

Fleming, W.G. *Education: Ontario's Preoccupation.* Toronto: University of Toronto Press, 1972.

– *Ontario's Educative Society.* 7 volumes. Toronto: University of Toronto Press, 1971–2.

French, Doris. *High Button Bootstraps: The Federation of Women Teachers' Associations of Ontario, 1918–1968.* Toronto: Ryerson Press, 1968.

Gleason, Mona. *Normalizing the Ideal: Psychology, Schooling, and the Family in Post-war Canada.* Toronto: University of Toronto Press, 1999.

Graham, Roger. *Old Man Ontario: Leslie M. Frost.* Toronto: Ontario Historical Studies Series and University of Toronto Press, 1990.

Gutteridge, Don. *Stubborn Pilgrimage: Resistance and Transformation in Ontario English Teaching, 1960–1993.* With a teaching unit by Ian Underhill. Toronto: Our Schools/Our Selves, 1994.

Hopkins, R.A. *The Long March: A History of the Ontario Public School Men Teachers' Federation.* Toronto: Barton, 1969.

Hoy, Claire. *Bill Davis, a Biography.* Toronto: Methuen, 1985.

McDougall, A.K. *John P. Robarts: His Life and Government.* Toronto: University of Toronto Press, 1986.

Manthorpe, Jonathan. *The Power and the Tories: Ontario Politics, 1943 to the Present.* Toronto: Macmillan of Canada, 1974.

Owram, Doug. *Born at the Right Time: A History of the Baby-Boom Generation.* Toronto: University of Toronto Press, 1996.

Paquette, Jerald. 'Vertical Equity in Ontario Education Finance.' *Journal of Education Finance* 13 (Fall 1987): 135–57.

Porter, John. *The Vertical Mosaic: An Analysis of Social Class and Power in Canada.* Toronto: University of Toronto Press, 1965.

Rea, K.J. *The Prosperous Years: The Economic History of Ontario, 1939–75.* Toronto: Ontario Historical Studies Series and University of Toronto Press, 1985.

Report of the Royal Commission on Education in Ontario, 1950 [Hope Report]. Toronto: King's Printer, 1950.

Ricker, Eric W. 'Teachers, Trustees and Policy: The Politics of Education in Ontario, 1945–1975.' PhD diss., University of Toronto, 1981.

Robinson, S.G.B. *Do Not Erase: The Story of the First 50 Years of the Ontario Secondary School Teachers' Federation.* Toronto: OSSTF, 1971.

Stamp, Robert M. *The Schools of Ontario, 1876–1976.* Toronto: Ontario Historical Studies Series and University of Toronto Press, 1982.

Stapleton, John J. 'The Politics of Educational Innovations: A Case Study of the Credit System in Ontario.' PhD diss., University of Toronto, 1975.

Staton, Pat, and Beth Light. *Speak with Their Own Voices: A Documentary History of the Federation of Women Teachers' Associations of Ontario ...* Toronto: FWTAO, 1987.

Tomkins, George S. *A Common Countenance: Stability and Change in the Canadian Curriculum.* Scarborough, Ont.: Prentice-Hall Canada, 1986.

Walker, Franklin A. *Catholic Education and Politics in Upper Canada.* Volume 1. Toronto: English Catholic Education Association of Ontario, 1955.

– *Catholic Education and Politics in Ontario.* Volume 2. Toronto: Federation of Catholic Education Associations of Ontario, 1964.

– *Catholic Education and Politics in Ontario.* Volume 3. *From the Hope Commission to the Promise of Completion (1945–1985).* Toronto: Catholic Education Foundation of Ontario, 1986.

White, Graham, ed. *The Government and Politics of Ontario.* 5th ed. Toronto: University of Toronto Press, 1997.

Wilson, J. Donald, Robert M. Stamp, and Louis-Philippe Audet, eds. *Canadian Education: A History.* Scarborough, Ont.: Prentice-Hall of Canada, 1970.

Notes

All references to government reports, commissions, etc., refer to those of the Ontario government unless noted otherwise. Other abbreviations are as follows:

EIC	Education Improvement Commission
FWTAO	Federation of Women Teachers' Associations of Ontario
Globe	*Globe and Mail*
LFP	*London Free Press*
MOE	Ministry of Education
MOET	Ministry of Education and Training
OECTA	Ontario English Catholic Teachers' Association
OPSBA	Ontario Public School Boards' Association
OPSTF	Ontario Public School Teachers' Federation
OSSTF	Ontario Secondary School Teachers' Federation
OTF	Ontario Teachers' Federation
Star	*Toronto Star*

Web References

In several chapters, but especially those on the late 1990s, I have used the Internet as a source for key documents. Many of these may also be available in 'hard copy' (i.e. paper) in various libraries and archives. Others may not. I have identified all Internet references by their full web-site addresses as of December 1998. Readers are warned, however, that web sites change over time and there-

fore there is no guarantee that the addresses will remain accurate in the future.
Where these addresses stretch over two lines they should be used exactly as
printed; no punctuation has been added.

Chapter 1 Introduction

1 For an account of religion in the schools that spans the same period as this
  book, see R.D. Gidney and W.P.J. Millar, 'The Christian Recessional in Ontario's Public Schools,' in Marguerite Van Die and David Lyon, eds, *Religion
  and Public Life in Canada: Historical and Comparative Perspectives* (Toronto:
  University of Toronto Press, forthcoming). See also Lois Sweet, *God in the
  Classroom: The Controversial Issue of Religion in Canada's Schools* (Toronto:
  McClelland and Stewart, 1997). For a serviceable short history of private
  schools, see Robert Stamp's survey in appendix G of *The Report of the Commission on Private Schools in Ontario* [Shapiro Commission], 1985.
2 The Education Act, which came into effect 1 January 1975, was a consolidation, with some new provisions, of five separate pieces of legislation, some of
  them decades old. In its most easily accessible form it is available, along with
  nearly all the pertinent regulations and other legislation affecting the
  schools, in *Consolidated Ontario Education Statutes and Regulations 1998* (Toronto: Carswell, 1998) [new edition annually].

Chapter 2 The Education System at Mid-Century

1 For illuminating graphics on this point see Department of Education, *Annual
  Report for 1949*, 115, 121.
2 This is a slightly oversimplified description of the legal requirements, which
  varied modestly from grade to grade. For the details see, for example, MOE,
  Requirements for Certificates and Diplomas, Grades IX to XIII, Circular H.S.1,
  1955–6.
3 In special circumstances a Protestant minority in Ontario could establish a
  Protestant separate school. These were always very few.
4 See the graphics in Department of Education, *Annual Report for 1949*, 115,
  121.
5 Department of Education, *Programme of Studies for Grades 1 to 6 of the Public
  and Separate Schools*, Curriculum P:1 and J:1. Various printing dates, 1937–60.
  See also Department of Education, *Intermediate Division: Outlines of Courses for
  Experimental Use*, 1951, Curriculum 1.1 revised, 15.
6 Until the late sixties there were far more women principals than popular or
  scholarly opinion recognizes. See Carol A. Small, 'An Analysis of Principals in

Southwestern Ontario, 1920–1969,' unpublished MEd. Directed Research Project, Faculty of Education, University of Western Ontario, 1996.

7 As of June 1982 the name of the men's federation was changed to the 'Ontario Public School Teachers' Federation,' deleting the word 'Men.' See [OPSTF] *News*, 15 Oct. 1982. In 1998 OPSTF and FWTAO amalgamated to form the Elementary Teachers' Federation of Ontario.

8 See E.E. Stewart, 'The 1955 Status of Recommendations in *Report of the Royal Commission on Education in Ontario, 1950*' (MA thesis, University of Michigan, 1956); Eric W. Ricker, 'Teachers, Trustees and Policy: The Politics of Education in Ontario, 1945–1975' (PhD diss., University of Toronto, 1981), esp. his summary statement, 297.

9 See George Radwanski, *Ontario Study of the Service Sector*, 1986, Appendix, Background notes, 2; *Fair Taxation in a Changing World: Report of the Ontario Fair Tax Commission*, 1993, 83.

10 It is not easy to generalize about teachers' salaries across the period, since not only average but median salaries must be considered, as well as age, level of certification, and gender. For a sophisticated analysis that also points to the complexities of the problem and the qualifications that must be made, see David Stager, *Elementary and Secondary School Teachers' Salaries in Ontario, 1900 to 1975* (Toronto: Commission on Declining Enrolments in Ontario, Working paper no. 5, 1978).

11 See R.D. Gidney and W.P.J. Millar, *Inventing Secondary Education: The Rise of the High School in Nineteenth-Century Ontario* (Montreal and Kingston: McGill-Queen's University Press, 1990), esp. chap. 15.

12 See Department of Education, Curriculum 1, *Memorandum re. Revision of Curriculum*, 10 Dec. 1949.

13 A few boards had built 'junior high schools,' usually covering grades 7–9, which captured the ideas underpinning the 'intermediate curriculum.'

14 For introductions to the nature of this tradition in nineteenth-century Ontario, and for references to the larger international literature on the subject, see Gidney and Millar, *Inventing Secondary Education*, chap. 11, and A.B. McKillop, *Matters of Mind: The University in Ontario, 1791–1951* (Toronto: Ontario Historical Studies Series and University of Toronto Press, 1994), esp. chaps. 4 and 5.

15 Hilda Neatby, *So Little for the Mind: An Indictment of Canadian Education* (Toronto: Clarke, Irwin, 1953), 15–17.

16 However, the ambience of progressivism was not entirely absent in at least some schools. See for example the study of Forest Hill Collegiate, in suburban Toronto, by John R. Seeley et al., *Crestwood Heights: A Study of Suburban Life* (Toronto: University of Toronto Press, 1956), esp. chaps. 7–9. For a

jaundiced but wonderful account of the introduction of new-fangled American innovations, as well as an instructive portrait of the Ontario high school just before mid-century, see Selwyn Dewdney's novel *Wind Without Rain* (1946; repr. Toronto: McClelland and Stewart, New Canadian Library Series no. 103, 1974).

17 Northrop Frye, ed., *Design for Learning* (Toronto: University of Toronto Press, 1962), 7.

Chapter 3 Restructuring and Refinancing Education in the Sixties

1 K.J. Rea, *The Prosperous Years: The Economic History of Ontario, 1939–75* (Toronto: Ontario Historical Studies Series and University of Toronto Press, 1985), 102–3.

2 For a summary see R.W.B. Jackson, *The Atkinson Study of Utilization of Student Resources in Ontario*, Report submitted to the National Conference of Canadian Universities, 5 June 1958 (Toronto: Department of Educational Research, Ontario College of Education, University of Toronto, 1958).

3 Desmond Morton, '*Sic Permanet*: Ontario People and Their Politics,' in Graham White, ed., *The Government and Politics of Ontario*, 5th ed. (Toronto: University of Toronto Press, 1997), 7.

4 Diane Ravitch, *The Troubled Crusade: American Education, 1945–1980* (New York: Basic Books, 1983), 237.

5 During his first year as premier, Robarts himself remained minister of education.

6 See Vernon Lang, *The Service State Emerges in Ontario, 1945–1973* (N.p.: Ontario Economic Council, 1974).

7 David M. Cameron, *Schools for Ontario: Policy-making, Administration, and Finance in the 1960s* (Toronto: University of Toronto Press, 1972), 199.

8 Maps of the 'new' county structure for both public and separate school boards, along with comparison maps following the board amalgamations of 1997, can be found at the EIC web site (eic.edu.gov.on.ca/html/dsbmaps.html).

9 While there was always a single Metropolitan Separate School Board, the administrative structure of the public system was two-tiered from 1953 to 1997. For a detailed discussion of this unique organization and its early history, see W.G. Fleming, *Ontario's Educative Society* (Toronto: University of Toronto Press, 1971), 2: chap. 7.

10 The best-documented example, and an indicative case study of the process, was the long battle by local residents to prevent the Niagara South Board of Education from closing Pelham High School, something the board finally

accomplished in 1974. See David C. Walker, 'Education in a Rural Setting: The Closing of Pelham Secondary School,' in J.H.A. Wallin, ed., *The Politics of Canadian Education*, CSSE 4th Yearbook (Edmonton: Canadian Society for the Study of Education, 1977), 69–78. Loren Lind, the *Globe and Mail's* education reporter, wrote an incisive series of articles on the consequences: see *Globe*, 7, 8, 12, 14 May 1970.

11 *Ottawa Citizen*, 5 Dec. 1970.

12 See e.g. *Globe*, 19 Nov. 1983; *Star*, 29 Aug. 1987. Nor was this mere nostalgia: the 'good school' literature of the 1990s demonstrated that much.

13 For the background and details, see Loren Lind's account in the *Globe*, 29 May 1970, and the related *Globe* editorial, 1 June 1970.

14 See e.g. *LFP*, 7 Nov. 1972, reporting the request of the chairs of '17 major boards of education' for a meeting with the minister to discuss their concerns about the matter.

15 Derek J. Allison and Allen Wells, 'School Supervision in Ontario,' in John W. Boich et al., eds, *The Canadian School Superintendent* (Toronto: OISE Press, Symposium Series 19, 1989), 94. I have changed the tense to the past.

16 Peter Hennessy, *Schools in Jeopardy: Collective Bargaining in Education* (Toronto: McClelland and Stewart, 1979), 51–3.

17 Department of Education, *Report of the Minister's Committee on the Training of Elementary School Teachers, 1966* [MacLeod Report], 53.

18 Then or now, however, the BEd. does not constitute a licence to teach in Ontario, which has always required a certificate, traditionally awarded by the minister and now by the Ontario College of Teachers.

19 The following summary of educational finance between the late 1940s and the early 1970s is based on a variety of sources, but the most important include Fleming, *Ontario's Educative Society*, 1: chap. 7; the *Interim Report* of the Commission on Declining Enrolments in Ontario [Jackson Commission] (Toronto, February 1978), chap. 1; and the various interim reports of the Ontario Committee on the Costs of Education, but above all, *Interim Report Number Seven*, published in June 1975.

20 R.W.B. Jackson, in *Interim Report*, Commission on Declining Enrolments, 7.

21 However, there were reasons for the tax increases other than the costs of consolidation per se. For an analysis see Committee on the Costs of Education, *Interim Report Number Seven*, 96–101, 204.

22 *LFP*, 16 Sept. 1969.

23 Its first chair resigned shortly after being appointed and in the early months it underwent other changes in personnel as well.

24 Quoted in Loren Jay Lind, *The Learning Machine: A Hard Look at Toronto Schools* (Toronto: House of Anansi Press, 1974), 134.

25 Quoted in Paul Axelrod, *Scholars and Dollars: Politics, Economics, and the Universities of Ontario, 1945–1980* (Toronto: University of Toronto Press, 1982), 2.

Chapter 4 The Reorientation of Curriculum and Pedagogy

1 On McCarthy's own background, and for those he recruited, see John J. Stapleton, 'The Politics of Educational Innovations: A Case Study of the Credit System in Ontario,' PhD diss., University of Toronto, 1975, 98ff.

2 Quoted in V.K. Gilbert, *Let Each Become: An Account of the Implementation of the Credit Diploma in the Secondary Schools of Ontario* (Toronto: Governing Council of the University of Toronto, 1972), 12.

3 Quoted in ibid., 45. In chap. 4, Gilbert describes the history of experimentation at each of the schools.

4 *Report of the Grade 13 Study Committee, 1964*, submitted to the Hon. William G. Davis, 12, 29.

5 Alan J.C. King and Marjorie J. Peart, *The Numbers Game: A Study of Evaluation and Achievement in Ontario Schools* (Toronto: OSSTF, 1994), 205.

6 The subject pamphlets were English, Mathematics, and Art (1966); Music, Physical and Health Education, and Science (1967); and Social Studies (1970). In their most accessible form they were reprinted, without further revision, as Department of Education, *Curriculum Guidelines, Primary and Junior Divisions*, 1971.

7 *Introduction and Guide*, 7.

8 Reprinted in *Programme of Studies for Grades 1 to 6 of the Public and Separate Schools, 1960*, 29.

9 *Interim Revision English, 1966*, 4.

10 *Interim Revision Mathematics, 1966*, 3.

11 For a much more detailed account of these developments, see Eric W. Ricker, 'Teachers, Trustees and Policy: The Politics of Education in Ontario, 1945–1975,' PhD diss., University of Toronto, 1981, esp. 302–5.

12 There was a difference in the form of the two inquiries, however. The Hope Commission was a royal commission; this was a minister's committee.

13 See Dennis Gruending, *Emmett Hall: Establishment Radical* (Toronto: Macmillan, 1985), esp. chap. 8.

14 The quotations in this and the following paragraphs are all to be found between pp. 54 and 92 of the report of the Provincial Committee on Aims and Objectives of Education in the Schools of Ontario, *Living and Learning* [Hall-Dennis Report] (Toronto: Newton Publishing Co., 1968).

15 See many of the essays in Brian Crittenden, ed., *Means and Ends in Education: Comments on Living and Learning*, Occasional Papers 2 (Toronto: OISE, 1969);

but above all, one scintillating and scathing jeremiad is not to be missed: James Daly, *Education or Molasses? A Critical Look at the Hall-Dennis Report* (Ancaster, Ont.: Cromlech Press, 1969). For a thoughtful critical review written in the aftermath, see Robin Barrow, *The Canadian Curriculum: A Personal View* (London, Ont.: Faculty of Education, University of Western Ontario, 1979).

16 Quoted in Robert M. Stamp, *The Schools of Ontario, 1876–1976* (Toronto: Ontario Historical Studies Series and University of Toronto Press, 1982), 219.

17 Ricker, 'Teachers, Trustees and Policy,' 612–13.

18 *Living and Learning*, 209.

19 Gilbert, *Let Each Become*, 11 [italics added].

20 Quoted in *LFP*, 25 Oct. 1969.

21 The quotations are from Minister of Education, *Annual Report for 1965*, 1–3.

22 The following paragraphs are no more than a brief gloss on the research presented by Stapleton in 'The Politics of Educational Innovations.' All quotations are from 140–1 and 214–15.

23 Ibid., 193.

24 The story of this shift in policy is detailed in ibid., 197ff.

25 For the details the reader can consult the various versions of the formal Circular, HS1, published between 1969 and 1973. For those who want the full flavour of departmental thinking in the period, the key source, and one that is highly revealing because the department was attempting to explain its rationale to parents, is an eight-page brochure that went out in 1972 to all parents with children in grade 8 or the secondary schools to introduce them to the credit system. Among other things, it explains the 'philosophy' of the new approach and presents a model grouping of subjects. See MOE, *Response to Change: The Facts and Philosophy of Ontario's New Credit System in Secondary Schools. An Information Guide to Parents*, October 1972. A copy is contained in MOE, *New Dimensions* 7, 2 (Oct. 1972).

26 Though the words were almost certainly the work of senior ministry officials, the quotation is from the *Address by the Hon. Robert Welch, Minister of Education, to the Chief Education Officers and Senior Program Officials of Ontario School Boards … January 17, 1972*, mimeograph, 19.

27 *Globe*, 19 March 1974.

28 Page 3.

29 The document specified a variety of educational objectives in such areas as English and mathematics, and in this respect was initially presented as a response to growing charges of illiteracy and innumeracy in the elementary schools. In fact, the same sorts of targets had been set out in the Interim Revisions. Moreover, any comparison or assessment must be based not just

on *The Formative Years* but on *Education in the Primary and Junior Divisions*, which provides a much better guide to the pedagogical drift of the era.

30 K. Leithwood et al., *The Development of Ontario Schools: Intermediate and Senior Divisions – 1984 (OSIS) and the Initial Phase of Its Implementation* (Ontario MOE, 1987), Appendices, 386: transcript of interview with G. Podrebarac.

31 *New Dimensions*, September 1972. The quotations that follow are taken from this document.

32 See Brian Burnham, *The Elementary School in Ontario, 1966–1969. Practices and Trends in Program Development, Organization and Resources* (Toronto: OISE [1969?]); Minister of Education, *Annual Report for 1972*, 39; ibid., *1975*, 126.

33 *LFP*, 11 Feb. 1970.

34 *Address by the Hon. Robert Welch*, 11–12 [italics added].

35 Ibid., 18–20.

36 For examples of the latter see two local speeches by J.K. Crossley, then the ministry's superintendent of curriculum, in *LFP*, 6 Feb. 1970 and 21 Feb. 1972.

37 For a good 'reader' containing a collection of contemporary documents and reports covering both Canadian universities and high schools, see Tim Reid and Julyan Reid, eds, *Student Power and the Canadian Campus* (Toronto: Peter Martin Associates, 1969). However, for an overview of radical opinion the indispensable source is *This Magazine Is About Schools*.

38 Stamp, *The Schools of Ontario*, 228.

39 Personal communication, Ian McKay, 1 June 1995.

40 *LFP*, 14 Jan. 1970.

41 Ibid., 25 Sept. 1969.

42 Christabelle Sethna, 'High School Confidential: RCMP Surveillance of Secondary School Activists,' in Gary Kinsman, Dieter Buse, and Mercedes Steedman, eds, *Whose National Security?* (Toronto: Between the Lines, 1999).

43 *LFP*, 3 June 1972.

44 *Globe*, 7 Apr. 1970.

Chapter 5 A New 'Philosophy' or 'Snivelling Drivel'?

1 *LFP*, 13 Dec. 1974.

2 Ibid., 23 March 1975.

3 *Globe*, 17 Feb. 1973.

4 [OSSTF] *The Bulletin*, October 1973, 223–6.

5 Page 33.

6 Ontario Economic Council, *Issues and Alternatives, 1976: Education* (Toronto, 1976), 12–14.

7 Oswald Hall and Richard Carlton, *Basic Skills at School and Work: The Study of Albertown* (Toronto: Ontario Economic Council, 1977), 85.

8 Ibid., 70.

9 Ibid., 100.

10 Ibid., 247.

11 *Globe*, 1 Sept. 1979. See Wendy K. Warren and Alan J.C. King, *School-to-Work Study* (Toronto: OSSTF, 1979). For a related study that also includes references to earlier research on the problem, see Alan J.C. King and Beverley J. Coles, *Holding Power 1: A Study of Factors Related to Student Retention in Ontario Secondary Schools* (OSSTF, Oct. 1980).

12 For this paragraph, see e.g. *Globe*, 21 Feb. 1977, 21 March, 9 June 1978, 31 Jan. 1979, 2 May 1981; J.A. Fraser, 'Education in Peel Secondary Schools' (Peel Board of Education, 1979, typescript), esp. 82ff. For some MOE responses see *Education Ontario*, Spring 1980 and Summer 1981. There is an excellent overview of the issue, the pertinent literature, and policy initiatives by both the federal and provincial governments, in OTF, *The School-to-Work Transition: Submission to [Ontario] Cabinet, 1983.*

13 MOE, *Secondary/Post-Secondary Interface Study: Summary Report*, 1977.

14 *Globe*, 27 Nov. 1979.

15 *LFP*, 2 March 1978. Similarly see *Globe*, 10 March 1978.

16 *Globe*, 3 Jan. 1979.

17 Ibid., 30 Jan. 1982.

18 *Today Magazine*, 5 Sept. 1981 [italics in original].

19 Though shorn of most of the political context I am concerned with in this chapter, the best detailed review of programmatic change in the 1970s and the impact on the organization of the high schools is to be found in John E. Davis and Doris W. Ryan, *Constraints on Secondary School Programs: The Impact of Declining Enrolments, Collective Agreements, and Regulations* (Toronto: Ontario MOE, 1980), esp. chaps. 2 and 4.

20 *Welland Tribune*, 24 Sept. 1975.

21 *LFP*, 1 May 1975.

22 See MOE, *Report of the Junior Kindergarten, Kindergarten and Grade One Task Force*, 1983.

23 *New Dimensions*, November 1971.

24 *Globe*, 28 Apr. 1972.

25 *LFP*, 17 Jan. 1983.

26 *Globe*, 4 Dec. 1973.

27 Ibid., 2 Dec. 1976.

28 *LFP*, 16 Nov. 1973.

29 *Globe*, 7 Oct. 1976. The fact that it was a political decision made by the minis-

ter and his aide against the wishes of senior bureaucrats in the ministry was confirmed in a revealing story written, a year later, by Loren Lind; see ibid., 23 July 1977.

30 Ibid., 13 Nov. 1976.

31 Ibid., 27 Nov. 1976. For an introduction see MOE, *The Ontario Assessment Instrument Pool*, Review and Evaluation Bulletins, vol. 1, no. 1, 1979. A report on the progress made to 1984 can be found in MOE, *Update '84: Results of Initiatives Identified in 'Issues and Directions'* (Toronto, 1984), 21–4. For a brief overview of OAIP origins and subsequent history see Dennis Raphael, 'Accountability and Educational Philosophy: Paradigms and Conflict in Ontario Education,' *Canadian Journal of Education* 18, 1 (1993): 35–7.

32 For English, see Don Gutteridge, *Stubborn Pilgrimage: Resistance and Transformation in Ontario English Teaching, 1960–1993*, with a teaching unit by Ian Underhill (Toronto: Our Schools / Our Selves, 1994), chaps. 3–5.

33 For more detail see Davis and Ryan, *Constraints*, 23–6; OTF, *The School-to-Work Transition*, esp. 25ff.

34 Quoted in *Globe*, 12 Apr. 1978.

35 Ibid., 3 Nov. 1977.

36 Ibid., 9 Nov. 1977.

37 The most accessible source for these developments is K. Leithwood et al., *The Development of Ontario Schools: Intermediate and Senior Divisions – 1984 (OSIS) and the Initial Phase of Its Implementation* (Toronto: MOE, 1987), 13–22. But for a much fuller account see Peter W. Baker, 'Curriculum Policy-making in Ontario: A Case Study of the Policy Formation Process Leading to the Establishment of the Secondary Education Review Project,' DEd. diss., University of Toronto, 1985.

38 See Leithwood et al., *The Development of ... OSIS*, 100–1.

39 MOE, *Report of the Secondary Education Review Project* (Toronto, 1981), 3 [italics added].

40 See William J. Lambie, 'The Renewal of Secondary Education as a Result of the Secondary Education Review Project (SERP): A Case Study of Policy Development,' DEd. diss., University of Toronto, 1985.

41 *ROSE* (MOE, 1982), 22.

42 MOE, *Update '84*, 24. The premier certainly believed 'province-wide testing' was to be introduced 'soon.' He said so in the legislature: *Ontario Hansard*, 12 June 1984, 2415. See also *ROSE*, 33.

43 See Leithwood et al., *The Development of ... OSIS*, 59.

44 *Globe*, 5 May 1981.

45 Leithwood et al., *The Development of ... OSIS*, 103.

46 See *Globe*, 9 Apr., 24 Oct. 1983.

47 Ibid., 24 Oct. 1983.

48 See Leithwood et al., *The Development of ... OSIS*, 75–9.

49 Ibid., 73.

50 *Star*, 5 Dec. 1982.

51 Alan Murray, 'The Literacy Debate: Sharing the Facts,' *Interchange* 7, 4 (1976–7): 19.

52 See David W. Livingstone, 'Educational Issues in Ontario: A 1978 Survey,' *Orbit* 9, 5 (Dec. 1978): 4.

53 See e.g. MOE, *Secondary/Post-Secondary Interface Study: Summary Report* (1977), 110.

54 A list of these research studies is to be found in Ronald J. Duhamel, 'The "Good Old Days" and Today's Academic Standards,' *Orbit* 10, 5 (Dec. 1979): 20.

55 MOE, *Interface Study: Summary Report*, 130.

56 Ibid., 111.

57 Kenneth Lee, 'Ontario – A Place to Learn,' *Orbit* 6, 1 (Feb. 1975): 26.

58 *Globe*, 13 July 1977. For the extended argument Lind was writing about here, see the sequence of articles in *Interchange* 7, 4 (1976–7).

59 See Duhamel, 'Good Old Days,' 18; H.G. Hedges, *Achievement in Basic Skills* (Toronto: MOE, 1977).

60 See e.g. Ross E. Traub et al., 'Interface Project II and Ontario's Review of Educational Policy,' *Interchange* 7, 4 (1976–7): 25–6.

61 For an example see MOE, *Interface Study: Summary Report*, 130. Note the footnote qualification to the generalization in the text.

62 See ibid.; Duhamel, 'Good Old Days,' 18.

63 Livingstone, 'Educational Issues in Ontario,' 4–6.

64 Beyond the 'new math' there were also the mysteries of 'going metric,' a shift that was to be completed in the elementary schools in 1976 and in the high schools the following year. See *Ontario Education Dimensions*, February 1976, 4.

65 *Globe*, 16 Aug. 1976.

66 MOE, *Interface Study: Summary Report*, 75.

67 See e.g. John Stevens, 'Is There a Literate in the House?' [OSSTF] *Forum* 3, 5 (Dec. 1977): 237–8.

68 MOE, *Interface Study: Summary Report*, 83.

69 Quoted in Davis and Ryan, *Constraints*, 159.

70 See the graph in King and Coles, *Holding Power*, 7.

71 Hall and Carlton, *Basic Skills*. Though the arguments are scattered through much of the book, see esp. the concluding chapter.

72 See Claire Hoy, *Bill Davis, a Biography* (Toronto: Methuen, 1985), 92 and 140. It was raised to 19 in early 1976.

Chapter 6 Demography, Economics, and the Revolting Teachers

1 *Globe,* 22 Sept. 1978.
2 Calculations based on Minister of Education, *Annual Report for 1985.*
3 *Welland Tribune,* 25 June 1980.
4 *LFP,* 23 Oct. 1984, 23 May 1983.
5 The problems declining enrolments created and the reactions, local and central, official and unofficial, deserve more attention than I have given them here. The indispensable source is the reports (and associated studies) of the *Commission on Declining Enrolments in Ontario* [Jackson Commission]: *Interim Reports,* 1978, and *Final Report,* 1979. See also John E. Davis and Doris W. Ryan, *Constraints on Secondary School Programs: The Impact of Declining Enrolments, Collective Agreements, and Regulations* (Toronto: MOE, 1980); MOE, *Issues and Directions,* 1980.
6 See Thomas J. Courchene with Colin R. Telmer, *From Heartland to North American Region State: The Social, Fiscal and Federal Evolution of Ontario* (Toronto: Centre for Public Management, Faculty of Management, University of Toronto, 1998), esp. 49–50; David Stager, 'Demographic and Economic Trends, with Consequences for Public Sector Education in Ontario,' in Ontario, *Background Papers: The Commission on the Financing of Elementary and Secondary Education in Ontario,* 1985.
7 See Claire Hoy, *Bill Davis, a Biography* (Toronto: Methuen, 1985), 210–12.
8 See Stephen B. Lawton, 'Ontario's Approach: Paying School Boards to Save,' in Barry D. Anderson et al., eds, *The Cost of Controlling the Costs of Education in Canada* (Toronto: OISE Press, 1983), 46.
9 *Ottawa Journal,* 24 March 1972.
10 See e.g. *Globe,* 8 Oct. 1971, 4 March 1972; *LFP,* 4 Apr. 1973.
11 By this point there was also a new grant system in place. For a brief, intelligible introduction to the changing methods of calculating and distributing the government grant to school boards between 1969 and 1983, see Lawton, 'Ontario's Approach,' 41–4.
12 *Globe,* 3 March 1975. A few months later, London teachers were seeking raises ranging from 29 to 50 per cent: see *LFP,* 24 Oct. 1975.
13 *Globe,* 23 Aug. 1975.
14 See e.g. *LFP,* 19 Oct. 1976.
15 MOE, *New Dimensions,* November 1974.
16 In London, for example, tax rates fell from 1968 to 1973. See *LFP,* 29 March 1973.
17 Lawton, 'Ontario's Approach,' 41.
18 *Globe,* 21 Nov. 1975.

19 Committee on the Costs of Education, *Final Report*, July 1978, 62.

20 Peter Hennessy, *Schools in Jeopardy: Collective Bargaining in Education* (Toronto: McClelland and Stewart, 1979), 54; David Stager, *Elementary and Secondary School Teachers' Salaries in Ontario, 1900 to 1975* (Toronto: Commission on Declining Enrolments in Ontario [CODE], Working paper no. 5, 1978).

21 Hennessy, *Schools in Jeopardy*, 55.

22 The detail here is taken from the report of the day's events in the *Globe*, 19 Dec. 1973.

23 Ibid., 15 Dec. 1973.

24 See Hennessy, *Schools in Jeopardy*; Bryan Downie, *Collective Bargaining and Conflict Resolution in Education: The Evolution of Public Policy in Ontario* (Kingston: Industrial Relations Centre, Queen's University, 1978); Eric W. Ricker, 'Teachers, Trustees and Policy: The Politics of Education in Ontario, 1945–1975,' PhD diss., University of Toronto, 1981, 240ff., 400ff.; Robert T. Dixon, *Be a Teacher: A History of the Ontario English Catholic Teachers' Association* (Toronto: Ontario English Catholic Teachers' Association, 1994), esp. chap. 7.

25 *Professional Consultation and Determination of Compensation for Ontario Teachers. The Report of the Committee of Inquiry, June 1972* [Reville Report], 27, 33.

26 Ricker, 'Teachers, Trustees, and Policy,' 409.

27 Downie, *Collective Bargaining*, 32.

28 See e.g. Davis's comments, *Globe*, 16 Sept. 1969, and those of the deputy minister of education in [OSSTF] *Intercom* 6 (Dec. 1971).

29 For a good example of the arguments on both sides see the articles by Anthony Ketchum and Margaret Wilson in [OSSTF] *Forum* 2, 2 (March 1976): 45–52.

30 Committee on the Costs of Education, *Final Report*, 198.

31 *Globe*, 10 Dec. 1979.

32 Ibid., 11 Oct. 1979.

33 Ibid.

34 Ibid., 31 Oct. 1980; *The Report of a Commission to Review the Collective Negotiation Process between Teachers and School Boards* [Matthews Commission], June 1980, 22–5.

35 *LFP*, 29 Apr. 1978; *Globe*, 7 Feb. and 10 March 1978.

36 *Globe*, 19 March 1979.

37 See e.g. [OSSTF] *Forum* 7, 1 (Feb. 1981): 29.

38 For more detail see *Globe*, 13 and 15 Jan. 1979; [OSSTF] *Forum* 5, 2 (March 1979): 71–3; ibid., 6, 4 (Oct. 1980): 183; *LFP*, 23 Nov. 1982 and 12 Feb. 1983.

39 *Globe*, 27 June 1980; *LFP*, 31 May 1983. For the details of the proposal see MOE, *Education Ontario*, June 1983, 1 and 4.

40 For the background see *OTF/FEO Interaction* 7, 1 (Oct. 1980): 1.

41 *LFP*, 1 June 1983. More generally, see [OSSTF] *Forum* 9, 1 (Feb. 1983): 29.
42 *Globe*, 28 Nov. 1983. The words are those of the reporter rather than Stephenson herself.
43 Quoted in ibid.

Chapter 7 The Completion of the Separate School System

1 Ontario, Legislative Assembly, *Hansard*, 4th Session, 32nd Parliament, 12 June 1984, 2414–17.
2 Rosemary Speirs, *Out of the Blue: The Fall of the Tory Dynasty in Ontario* (Toronto: Macmillan, 1986), 26.
3 *Star*, 13 June 1984.
4 *Globe*, 13 June 1984.
5 Ibid.
6 Ibid., 14 and 23 June 1984.
7 See Franklin A. Walker, *Catholic Education and Politics in Ontario* (Toronto: Catholic Education Foundation of Ontario, 1986), 3: 366–75. On the change in funding see MOE, *Report of the Secondary Education Review Project* (Toronto, 1981), 76.
8 In my view, the most judicious reading is offered by Speirs, *Out of the Blue*, 22–5, but there is also useful material in Claire Hoy, *Bill Davis, a Biography* (Toronto: Methuen, 1985), chap. 19, and Walker, *Catholic Education*, 3: chap. 13.
9 Quoted in Speirs, *Out of the Blue*, 23.
10 Quoted in Hoy, *Davis*, 275.
11 *Star*, 25 Aug. 1981.
12 See K. Leithwood et al., *The Development of Ontario Schools: Intermediate and Senior Divisions – 1984 (OSIS) and the Initial Phase of Its Implementation* (Toronto: Ontario MOE, 1987), Appendices, 405: interview with Duncan Green.
13 For this and the succeeding paragraph see Ontario, Legislative Assembly, *Hansard*, 4th Session, 32nd Parliament, 12 June 1984, 2414–17.
14 Speirs, *Out of the Blue*, 26.
15 *Globe*, 1 March 1985.
16 *LFP*, 4 Oct. 1985.
17 *Globe*, 23 Nov. 1984.
18 Ibid., 6 Dec. 1984.
19 *LFP*, 18 Feb. 1985.
20 *Globe*, 4 Oct. and 1 Dec. 1984, 25 Feb. 1985.
21 The best summary references are by Robert Matas, *Globe*, 22 and 23 March 1985. But see also ibid., 31 Jan. 1985.

22 Ibid., 25 March 1985; OECTA, *Submission to the Commission on the Financing of Elementary and Secondary Education in Ontario*, Jan. 1985.

23 *Globe*, 26 March 1985; *LFP*, 8 Apr. 1985.

24 *Globe*, 11 March 1985.

25 Ibid.; more generally see Matas's review of the issue in *Globe*, 17 Apr. 1986.

26 Ibid., 8 Apr. 1985. For similar views by columnists see ibid., 29 March, 2 and 4 Apr. 1985; *LFP*, 1 Apr. 1985.

27 *LFP*, 3 Apr. 1985; *Globe*, 22 Apr. 1985.

28 *LFP*, 11 Apr. 1985.

29 *Globe*, 24 and 26 Apr. 1985.

30 Ibid., 24 Apr. 1985.

31 Speirs, *Out of the Blue*, 139.

32 *Globe*, 29 May 1985.

33 Ibid., 4 July 1985.

34 'Bill 30. An Act to Amend the Education Act. 1st Session, 33rd Legislature, Ontario. 34 Eliz. II, 1985.' 4 July 1985.

35 *LFP*, 12 July 1985.

36 *Globe*, 23 and 24 July 1985; *LFP*, 4 Nov. 1985.

37 See three summary pieces by Robert Matas, *Globe*, 21 Feb., 22 March 1985, and 17 Apr. 1986; ibid., 23 July 1985.

38 For the background see Robert Stamp, 'A History of Private Schools in Ontario,' in Ontario, *The Report of the Commission on Private Schools in Ontario* [Shapiro Commission], October 1985, appendix G, 201–3.

39 See *Globe*, 17 March 1970; *LFP*, 18 Jan. and 23 June 1971.

40 For the best short introduction to the issues, see Bernard J. Shapiro, 'The Public Funding of Private Schools in Ontario: The Setting, Some Arguments, and Some Matters of Belief,' *Canadian Journal of Education* 11, 3 (1986): 264–77.

41 For one good example see Ontario Alliance of Christian Schools, *The Christian Day School Alternative: Report to the Commission on Private Schools in Ontario* (Hamilton: OACSS, Dec. 1984), 43–6.

42 See e.g. *Star*, 25 Aug. 1981; *Globe*, 12 Jan. 1982, 12 Feb. and 16 Apr. 1985.

43 *Globe*, 8 July 1985.

44 *LFP*, 20 Sept. 1985. Faced with this defeat in the political arena, private-school interests turned to the courts, but lost there too in the Adler case. See Maurice A. Green, 'No Constitutional Right to Public Funding for Ontario Private Schools,' *Education & Law Journal* 8 (1998): 227–38.

45 *The Report of the Commission on Private Schools in Ontario*, Bernard J. Shapiro, Commissioner, October 1985.

46 See e.g. *LFP*, 31 Jan. 1985; *Globe*, 9 Nov. 1985.

47 *Globe*, 21 Nov. 1985.

48 Ibid., 22 Nov. 1985.

49 For some of the highlights recorded in the *Globe*, see the following issues: 17 and 25 July; 30 Aug.; 18, 21 (Davis's appearance), 26 Sept. 1985. However, the written briefs by the main participants are an indispensable source.

50 OSSTF, *Bill 30: Public Secondary Education in the Balance. Submission of the OSSTF to the Social Development Committee of the Ontario Legislature ... July 1985*, 3.

51 The best introduction to the issues, the decision, and thus the question that had to be addressed by the Supreme Court of Canada the following year is Greg Dickinson, 'Denominational Educational Rights in Ontario: Section 93 of *The Constitution Act, 1867* Meets the Charter of Rights in the Supreme Court of Canada,' Canadian History of Education Association *Bulletin* 4, 2 (May 1987): 9–49.

52 *LFP*, 20 Feb. 1986.

53 Ibid., 20 and 21 Feb. 1986.

54 Ibid., 24 Apr. 1986.

55 See Speirs, *Out of the Blue*, 225–6; *Globe*, 5 and 6 June 1986. On divisions within the NDP see also George Ehring and Wayne Roberts, *Giving Away a Miracle: Lost Dreams, Broken Promises and the Ontario NDP* (Oakville: Mosaic Press, 1993), 176ff.

56 *LFP*, 24 June 1986.

57 Ibid., 3 Oct. 1986.

58 *Star*, 11 March 1987.

59 Reference Re Bill 30, An Act to amend the Education Act (Ontario), [1987] 1, SCR, 1198–9. For the legal context, analysis, and key parts of the decision itself, see Gregory M. Dickinson and A. Wayne Mackay, *Rights, Freedoms, and the Education System in Canada: Cases and Materials* (Toronto: Emond Montgomery, 1989), chap. 2.

60 See e.g. *Star*, 4 March and 16 May 1987.

61 For the major points in this paragraph I am much indebted to four fine research papers completed as part of the BEd. or MEd. program at the Faculty of Education, University of Western Ontario, by Sally Burkhart and Lois Tebbut (on Essex and Huron Counties respectively); by Laurie Langstaff (on designated teachers); and a careful analysis by Carol Mulally of the annual reports of the Planning and Implementation Commission between 1985 and 1991. For a retrospect on the Essex County crisis, see Lois Sweet, *God in the Classroom: The Controversial Issue of Religion in Canada's Schools* (Toronto: McClelland and Stewart, 1997), 38–49.

Chapter 8 Broadening the Mandate

1 Quoted in Harold E. Jakes and Hanne B. Mawhinney, *A Historical Overview of Franco-Ontarian Educational Governance* (Ottawa: Vision Education, Monographs of the Faculty of Education, University of Ottawa, 1990), 120.

2 Regulation 17 itself had never actually been repealed, but it had automatically expired at the end of 1944 when it was not renewed under the Regulations Act of that year.

3 *Report of the Committee on French-Language Schools in Ontario* [Bériault Committee], 1968.

4 The original version of the legislation, along with a detailed explanation of its intent, can be found in ibid.

5 The figures are from MOE, *Education Statistics, Ontario 1985*, 87; Commission on Post-Secondary Education in Ontario [Wright Commission], *The Learning Society* (Toronto: Ministry of Government Services, 1972), 85.

6 The most complete history in English – and one that is indispensable for the recent past – is Jakes and Mawhinney, *Franco-Ontarian Educational Governance*. This book-length typescript deserves more attention and accessibility than it now has. It includes a full bibliography of earlier works on the subject and a very detailed narrative account of developments in the 1970s and 1980s. No one, however, can afford to neglect Stacy Churchill on the subject. For the period this chapter covers see esp. Churchill, 'Franco-Ontarian Education: From Persecuted Minority to Tolerated Nuisance,' in Hugh Oliver, Mark Holmes, and Ian Winchester, eds, *The House That Ryerson Built: Essays in Education to Mark Ontario's Bicentennial* (Toronto: OISE Press, 1984); Churchill, '"So Why Aren't the French Ever Satisfied?" – Educational Rights for Franco Ontarians,' *Interchange* 9, 4 (1978–9): 59–66; and Churchill, Saeed Quazi, and Normand Frenette, *Éducation et besoins des Franco-Ontariens: Le diagnostic d'un système d'éducation* (Toronto: Le Conseil de l'éducation franco-ontarienne, 1985), 2 vols. The full version of this last report is available in French only, but there is a lengthy English summary by Churchill entitled 'Report Highlights: Education and Franco-Ontarian Needs: The Diagnosis of an Educational System.' See also Office of the Commissioner of Official Languages, *Official Language Minority Education Rights in Canada: From Instruction to Management*, 1991.

7 Jakes and Mawhinney (*Franco-Ontarian Educational Governance*) describe most of these but see also *Globe*, 10 Nov. 1972 (Elliot Lake); 16 Jan. 1974 and 15 Oct. 1975 (Burlington); 7 March 1980 (Kirkland Lake); 13 May 1980 (East York).

8 The advocates of Franco-Ontarian educational rights, including Churchill, tend to ignore this division or be rather dismissive about it. But see the story on Metropolitan Toronto francophones in the *Globe*, 8 Dec. 1977, and above all D.W. Livingstone and D.J. Hart, *Public Attitudes toward Education in Ontario, 1980* (Toronto: OISE Press, 1980), 20–1. Fifty-six per cent of *French* respondents favoured mixed or bilingual schools, another 14 per cent favoured either no special arrangements or did not offer an opinion, and only 30 per cent favoured separate French schools.

9 For Sturgeon Falls anglophones the latter was a key issue in the dispute. See *Globe*, 11 Sept. 1971. For examples of the former issue, see ibid., 16 Jan. 1974 (Burlington); 13 May 1980 (East York).

10 See e.g. the *Globe*'s editorials of 25 Feb. 1977 and 1 Nov. 1979 on Essex County; 1 Sept. 1979 and 8 Feb. 1980 on Penetanguishene.

11 Ontario, *Report of the Ministerial Commission on French Language Secondary Education* [Symons Report] (Toronto: Queen's Printer, 1972).

12 See e.g. *Globe*, 22 Jan. 1970.

13 Quoted in Jakes and Mawhinney, *Franco-Ontarian Educational Governance*, 107.

14 *Globe*, 24 March 1983.

15 Stacy Churchill, 'The Impact of the Davis Decision on Franco-Ontarian Education: A Personal Commentary,' *Orbit* 17, 2 (Apr. 1986): 15.

16 For the details, see Jakes and Mawhinney, *Franco-Ontarian Educational Governance*, 122–5.

17 For a brief introduction to the background and range of programs see Mary Hainsworth, *Report on Second and Third Languages*, Working paper no. 37 (Commission on Declining Enrolments, Sept. 1978), 8–25; MOE, *Special Populations in Education*, Review and Evaluation Bulletins 1, 3 (1979): 26–8.

18 For more detail and a guide to the literature here, see MOE, *Special Populations*, 23–5; Marie McAndrew, 'Ethnicity, Multiculturalism, and Multicultural Education in Canada,' in Ratna Ghosh and Douglas Ray, eds, *Social Change and Education*, 3rd ed. (Toronto: Harcourt Brace, 1995), 164–72; Keren S. Brathwaite and Carl E. James, eds, *Educating African Canadians* (Toronto: Lorimer, 1996), esp. chap. 1. For ministry policy by 1984 see MOE, *Ontario Schools, Intermediate and Senior Divisions* [*OSIS*], Program and Diploma Requirements, 1984, 8.

19 The best source for the brief historical review that follows is Jack Berryman, 'Implementation of Ontario's Heritage Languages Program: A Case Study of the Extended School Day Model,' DEd. diss., University of Toronto, 1986; see esp. chaps. 2 and 3. See also Jim Cummins, 'Heritage Language Education: Fact and Friction,' *Orbit* 15, 1 (Feb. 1984): 3–6; Suzanne Majhanovich, 'Official and Heritage Languages in Canada: How Policies Translate into

Practices,' in Ghosh and Ray, eds, *Social Change and Education in Canada*, 84–101; Claire Hoy, *Bill Davis, a Biography* (Toronto: Methuen, 1985), chap. 18; Jim Cummins and Marcel Danesi, *Heritage Languages: The Development and Denial of Canada's Linguistic Resources* (Toronto: Our Schools / Our Selves and Garamond Press, 1990).

20 For the details, see MOE, *Special Populations*, 8–9, 25, 29.

21 Jim Cummins, *Heritage Language Education: A Literature Review* (Toronto: Ontario MOE, 1983), 5.

22 On this point see ibid., 47.

23 Because the history of native education has been so integrally a matter of federal policy, there is no monograph on, or even adequate article-length introduction to, developments in Ontario. There are, however, good places to begin: Marie Battiste and Jean Barman, eds, *First Nations Education in Canada: The Circle Unfolds* (Vancouver: UBC Press, 1995); J.R. Miller, *Shingwauk's Vision: A History of Native Residential Schools* (Toronto: University of Toronto Press, 1996). For Ontario, see W.G. Fleming, *Ontario's Educative Society* (Toronto: University of Toronto Press, 1971), 3: 354–61; *Report of the Task Force on the Educational Needs of Native Peoples of Ontario* (Toronto, 1976); Provincial Committee on Aims and Objectives of Education in the Schools of Ontario, *Living and Learning* [Hall-Dennis Report] (Toronto: Newton Publishing Co., 1968), 111–13.

24 Fleming, *Ontario's Educative Society*, 3: 360.

25 For summary articles on this conflict, see *Globe*, 20, 21, 22 Apr. 1970.

26 Ontario, Education Act 1974, s. 162 (4).

27 MOE, *A Review of All Textbooks Listed in Circular 14 for the Purpose of Identifying Bias or Prejudice towards Ethnic Groups with Particular Reference to Indians*, by G.W.C. Nelson (June 1970). See also G. McDiarmid and D. Pratt, *Teaching Prejudice: A Content Analysis of Social Studies Textbooks Authorized for Use in Ontario* (Toronto: OISE Press, 1971).

28 For a summary of ministry policies and programs to 1979 see MOE, *Special Populations*, 10–12. See also *Ontario Education Dimensions*, December 1973, 6; April 1974, 6; October 1974, 1; March 1975, 1; December 1977, 1; Autumn 1978, 4–6.

29 *Education Ontario*, January 1982, 1; October 1984, 1.

30 For the background to 1970 see the text and references in Fleming, *Ontario's Educative Society*, 3: chap. 10; Provincial Committee, *Living and Learning*, 101ff.; Ontario, *Education for New Times. Statements by the Hon. William Davis ... to the Legislative Assembly of Ontario*, July 1967; Edward H. Humphreys, *Urban-Rural Disparity in Ontario Elementary Education*, Occasional papers no. 18 (Toronto: Educational Planning, OISE, May 1970). For government policy

throughout the period, *Ontario Education Dimensions* is indispensable. The best overview of developments to 1980 is John Vincent Mombourquette, 'Policy Implementation and Special Education: The Case of Bill 82,' MA thesis, University of Western Ontario, 1985. See also C.J. Hodder, 'The Education Act (Ontario) 1980: A Review,' *Interchange* 15, 3 (1984): 44–53; Vera C. Pletsch, *Not Wanted in the Classroom: Parent Associations and the Education of Trainable Retarded Children in Ontario, 1947–1969* (London, Ont.: Althouse Press, 1997).

31 See Provincial Committee, *Living and Learning*, 102.

32 See e.g. the MOE's 'Position Paper: A Consideration of Special Education,' *New Dimensions*, December 1971, 3–6.

33 MOE, *Special Populations*, 37. For an explanation of grant formulas, provisions, and policies just before the introduction of Bill 82, see ibid., 35–46.

34 *Globe*, 20 March 1978.

35 Mombourquette, 'Special Education,' 74.

36 By 1979, one reporter would describe the OACLD as 'one of the strongest parent lobbies in the province.' *Globe*, 27 March 1979. For the press coverage generally see e.g. ibid., 26 May and 12 July 1976, 28 and 30 Apr. 1977, 17 Jan., 13 and 23 March, 11 May 1978.

37 For an introduction see Mombourquette, 'Special Education,' 50–7; Anne Keaton, 'Special Education: By Mandate or by Choice,' *Orbit 44* 9, 4 (Oct. 1978): 6–10.

38 See *Globe*, 12 Dec. 1977.

39 Once passed, it became part of Ontario's Education Act.

40 *Ontario Education Dimensions*, Winter 1979, 4.

41 See Davis's 1967 reference in Ontario, *Education for New Times*, 14–15.

42 Provincial Committee, *Living and Learning*, 114, and Recommendations, 110–16.

43 See *Globe*, 8 March 1973; *LFP*, 4 Apr. 1973.

44 *Globe*, 8 March 1973.

45 See e.g. ibid., 1 July 1972. See also *LFP*, 21 and 26 Sept. 1979, 30 Jan. 1980, 14 Oct. 1981, 17 Dec. 1984.

46 But that does not mean there was no public discussion of mandatory JK. See Laurier LaPierre's report commissioned for the Ontario Public School Men Teachers' Federation, *To Herald a Child*, Report of the Commission of Inquiry into the Education of the Young Child (Toronto, 1980).

47 The data for 1966 to 1986 are in MOE, *Education Statistics Ontario, 1986*.

48 Joan Sangster, 'Doing Two Jobs: The Wage-Earning Mother, 1945–70,' in Joy Parr, ed., *A Diversity of Women: Ontario, 1945–1980*, (Toronto: University of Toronto Press, 1995), 98–134. An indispensable source for the larger context

this section deals with is Alison Prentice et al., *Canadian Women: A History*, 2nd ed. (Toronto: Harcourt Brace Canada, 1996).

49 For parallel concerns emerging in Ontario, see Joan Sangster, 'Women Workers, Employment Policy and the State: The Establishment of the Ontario Women's Bureau, 1963–1970,' *Labour / Le Travail* 36 (Fall 1995): 119–45.

50 See Provincial Committee, *Living and Learning*, 55, 134, 192. For the committee's membership see p. 7.

51 Canada, *Report of the Royal Commission on the Status of Women in Canada* (Ottawa: Information Canada, 1970), 161.

52 Ibid., 174–5.

53 Ibid., 92.

54 The best introduction is Ruth Roach Pierson and Marjorie Griffin Cohen, *Canadian Women's Issues*, vol. 2: *Bold Visions* (Toronto: Lorimer, 1995), chap. 3.

55 For an overview see Hoy, *Davis*, chap. 17.

56 See *Ontario Education Dimensions*, October 1975, 4–5.

57 See *Globe*, 19 March 1981. Written by Dorothy Lipovenko, the article offers a good overview of the kind of activities Ontario school boards were engaged in by that point.

58 See *Ontario Education Dimensions*, May–June 1976, 3.

59 For some influential examples of this literature see Ad Hoc Committee Respecting the Status of Women in the North York System, 'The Rape of Children's Minds,' unpublished report, 1975; E. Batcher et al., ... *And Then There Were None* (Toronto: FWTAO, 1975); Linda Fisher and J.A. Cheyne, *Sex Roles: Biological and Cultural Interactions as Found in Social Science Research and Ontario Educational Media* (Toronto: MOE, 1977); Priscilla Galloway, *What's Wrong with High School English? It's Sexist, Un-Canadian, Outdated* (Toronto: OISE Press, 1981). See also *LFP*, 10 Nov. 1977.

60 OSSTF, *At What Cost? A Study of the Role of the Secondary School in Ontario* (Toronto: OSSTF, 1976).

61 For typical reports and articles see [OECTA] *C.T. Reporter*, December 1985, 10–11; *Ontario Education Dimensions*, September 1975, 6; January–February 1977, 3; Valerie Miner Johnson, 'Fighting (Nervously) the Sexual Stereotypes,' *Saturday Night*, January 1974, 23–6; *Globe*, 2 June 1975, 21 Dec. 1977; *LFP*, 11 Apr. 1978.

62 For two examples from the MOE, see *Changing Roles in a Changing World*, 1976, and *Sex Role Stereotyping and Women's Studies* [1978?]. For the publications and activities of the Toronto Board of Education see *Ontario Education Dimensions*, October 1975, 4–5. See also Becky Kane and Margot Smith, 'The Women's Kit,' *Orbit* 5, 4 (Oct. 1974): 10–11.

63 The criteria, along with the justifications, can best be traced through the introductions to successive versions of *Circular 14*, the ministry's publication listing all textbooks approved for use in Ontario schools.

64 *OSIS*, 10.

65 *Globe*, 10 Jan. 1974.

66 OSSTF, *At What Cost*, 94.

67 See ibid.; see also FWTAO views reported in *Globe*, 10 Jan. 1974.

68 *Globe*, 27 March 1970.

69 Pat Staton and Beth Light, *Speak with Their Own Voices: A Documentary History of the Federation of Women Teachers' Associations of Ontario* (Toronto: FWTAO, 1987), 168. For more detail on the various FWTAO initiatives during the period this section covers, see chaps. 5 and 6.

70 Though *Ontario Education Dimensions / Education Ontario* generally provides the details, there is a handy checklist of government and ministry initiatives from 1973 onwards in MOE, *The Status of Women and Employment Equity in Ontario School Boards. Report to the Legislature by the Minister of Education*, 1992, 9–12.

71 See *Ontario Education Dimensions*, September 1975, 6, and April 1976, 3.

72 *Education Ontario*, Spring 1980, 2.

73 Staton and Light, *Speak with Their Own Voices*, 171.

74 Canada, *Report of the Commission on Equality in Employment*, October 1984.

75 *Education Ontario*, January 1985, 2.

76 Ibid., June 1986, 4.

77 Ibid. See also Pierson and Cohen, *Canadian Women's Issues*, 2: 203–6.

78 For examples of the debate in London see *LFP*, 4 and 19 May, 9 June 1983, 19 Nov. 1984, 5 June 1985, 24 May 1986.

79 *Education Ontario*, June 1986, 4.

80 For a retrospective view and an introduction to the critique of earlier sex-equity concepts and strategies, see Rebecca Coulter, 'Gender Equity and Schooling: Linking Research and Policy,' *Canadian Journal of Education* 21, 4 (Fall 1996): 433–52. See also Linda Briskin and Rebecca Coulter, 'Feminist Pedagogy: Challenging the Normative,' ibid., 17, 3 (1992): 247–63.

Chapter 9 The Contexts for Policy-Making

1 There are several good accounts of the politics, and economic and social policies, of the Peterson and Rae governments. For the early years of Liberal rule see Rosemary Speirs, *Out of the Blue: The Fall of the Tory Dynasty in Ontario* (Toronto: Macmillan, 1986). Georgette Gagnon and Dan Rath pick up the story in *Not Without Cause: David Peterson's Fall from Grace* (Toronto:

HarperCollins, 1991). For the NDP years see Thomas Walkom, *Rae Days: The Rise and Follies of the NDP* (Toronto: Key Porter Books, 1994); and Patrick Monahan, *Storming the Pink Palace: The NDP in Power: A Cautionary Tale* (Toronto: Lester Publishing, 1995). Generally, see Thomas J. Courchene with Colin R. Telmer, *From Heartland to North American Region State: The Social, Fiscal and Federal Evolution of Ontario* (Toronto: Centre for Public Management, Faculty of Management, University of Toronto, 1998). For the latest overview, carrying the story to summer 1998, see Randall White, *Ontario Since 1985* (Toronto: Eastendbooks, 1998).

2 For the numbers see MOE, *Key Statistics, 1988–89* and *1992–93*.

3 On this point see François Gendron, 'Does Canada Invest Enough in Education?' *Education Quarterly Review*, 1994, 21. For enrolment figures in the 1980s and 1990s, and projections into the twenty-first century, see MOET web site (www.edu.gov.on.ca/eng/document/brochure/quickfac/facts98/facts98e.html).

4 Most of the detailed figures in this paragraph are drawn from the 'statements' or related papers in the Treasurer of Ontario's annual budget statement. On family incomes, see Bruce Little's review and the accompanying graph (1978–94) in the *Globe*, 6 Apr. 1996.

5 For a helpful summary of the early debate well before the Liberals came to office, and of the related literature, see OTF, *The School-to-Work Transition: Submission to [Ontario] Cabinet, 1983.*

6 *1994 Ontario Budget*, 16. Note that the figures are in real dollars. In current dollars the pattern looks dramatically different.

7 See Courchene and Telmer, *Heartland*, 40–3.

8 Almost every Ontario budget document contains a table, usually including comparisons with other years, showing government expenditure by major categories.

9 Figures supplied by Jerry Paquette.

10 *1994 Ontario Budget*, 76–7.

11 Yet one more measure suggests a similar conclusion. The percentage of GDP spent on elementary and secondary education in Ontario actually declined from a high point in 1977 to its lowest point in 1989. Though it turned sharply upward in the two following years, by 1991 it was still only at its 1977 level. See Jerry Paquette, *Publicly Supported Education in Post-Modern Canada: An Imploding Universe?* Background to Education: Issues and Analysis, vol. 2 (Toronto: Our Schools / Our Selves, 1994), 125.

12 *Star*, 8 Sept. 1987. Similarly see the *Globe* editorial, 21 Nov. 1988.

13 For some examples see *Star*, 5 Nov. 1991 (Carol Goar); *Globe*, 29 Nov. 1991 (Jeffrey Simpson), 4 May 1992 (editorial), 22 Sept. 1992. See also *Report Card*

on *Our Schools: A Reprint of a 6–part Series, Star,* 1987; the 10–part series in the *Star* beginning 29 May 1993; *Globe,* late Dec.–early Jan. 1992–3; Southam Press series 'Report on Illiteracy in Canada,' published in September 1987 in the *Star, LFP,* and other Ontario newspapers.

14 *Star,* 12 June 1993.
15 Andrew Nikiforuk, *School's Out: The Catastrophe in Public Education and What We Can Do about It* (Toronto: Macfarlane, Walter and Ross, 1993). Nikiforuk had already established a reputation for incisive, controversial, and critical commentary as the author of a weekly education column for the *Globe and Mail* in the early 1990s. See also Joe Freedman, *Failing Grades: Canadian Schooling in a Global Economy* (n.p.: Society for Advancing Educational Research, 1993); Jennifer Lewington and Graham Orpwood, *Overdue Assignment: Taking Responsibility for Canada's Schools* (Toronto: John Wiley and Sons, 1993).
16 For an analysis and an exploration of the changing forms of parent activism, mainly in the former city of Toronto, see Kari Dehli with Ilda Januario, 'Parent Activism and School Reform in Toronto,' Dept. of Sociology in Education, OISE, October 1994.
17 *Globe,* 29 Dec. 1992. For an accessible introduction to the views of such reform groups, see *Could Do Better: What's Wrong with Public Education in Ontario and How to Fix It ... By the Coalition for Education Reform* (Toronto, 1994).
18 D.W. Livingstone et al., 'Public Attitudes towards Education in Ontario – 1988,' *Orbit,* February 1989, 5.
19 D.W. Livingstone et al., *The Tenth OISE Survey, 1994: Public Attitudes towards Education in Ontario* (Toronto: OISE Press, 1995), 22.
20 *Star,* 7 Sept. 1992. See also ibid., 29 May 1993.
21 See ibid., 26 Sept. 1990, 7 Sept. 1992, 5 Feb. 1993.
22 For a brief, clear introduction to the nature of the tests and to some of their strengths and weaknesses, see Alan J.C. King and Marjorie J. Peart, *The Numbers Game: A Study of Evaluation and Achievement in Ontario Schools* (Toronto: OSSTF, 1994), 284–6.
23 *Star,* 24 March 1988.
24 See Dennis Raphael, 'Accountability and Educational Philosophy: Paradigms and Conflict in Ontario Education,' *Canadian Journal of Education* 18, 1 (1993): 38. Similarly, see Economic Council of Canada, *A Lot to Learn: Education and Training in Canada* (1992), 47–8.
25 Ontario Premier's Council, *Competing in the New Global Economy,* 1988, Preface.
26 A second report by the Premier's Council, *People and Skills in the New Global Economy,* published in 1990, addressed the province's educational needs in much greater detail.

27 George Radwanski, *Ontario Study of the Service Sector* (Government of Ontario, 1986), 18.

28 Ibid., 21.

29 Premier's Council, *Competing*, 223.

30 Ibid., 223–4; Radwanski, *Service Sector*, 24–5.

31 George Radwanski, *Ontario Study of the Relevance of Education, and the Issue of Dropouts* (MOE, 1988), letter of transmittal. In some library catalogues, and consequently in some references to the report, the date of publication is 1987. While technically correct, that is the date it was submitted to cabinet. It was released to the public in February 1988: see *Star*, 16 Feb. 1988. For this and the following paragraph, including quotations, see ibid., 6–7, 51–2, 56, and generally 25–40.

32 To sample the reactions immediately upon its release, see *Star*, *Globe*, and *LFP*, 16–18 Feb. 1988. For the way the teachers' unions disposed of the report, see *Star*, 16 March, 1 and 6 July 1988. For a thoughtful academic assessment that is generally sympathetic but also critical, see the essays in Derek J. Allison and Jerry Paquette, eds, *Reform and Relevance in Schooling: Dropouts, Destreaming, and the Common Curriculum* (Toronto: OISE Press, 1991).

33 For an overview see Paquette, *Publicly Supported Education*, chaps. 1 and 2.

34 *Globe*, 3 May 1993. For a brief, highly accessible introduction to the spectrum of school-reform issues in Britain, America, and other Western countries in the late 1980s and early 1990s, see *The Economist*, 21 Nov. 1992, 'A Survey of Education.'

35 Diane Ravitch, 'The Search for Order and the Rejection of Conformity: Standards in American Education,' in Diane Ravitch and Maris A. Vinovskis, eds, *Learning from the Past: What History Teaches Us about School Reform* (Baltimore: Johns Hopkins Press, 1995), 180.

36 Nancy J. Perry, 'Saving the Schools,' *Fortune*, 7 Nov. 1988, 42.

37 See e.g. Rona Maynard, 'Look Jane, Dick Can't Read,' *Report on Business Magazine*, May 1989, 91–6. The subtitle reads in part, 'Can business rise to the challenge?'

38 *Star*, 16 July 1993 [Ray Marshall and Marc Tucker, *Thinking for a Living: Education and the Wealth of Nations* (New York: Basic Books, 1992)].

39 For the novice, one good place to begin is an introductory spread on the background and key figures by James Collins, 'How Johnny Should Read,' *Time* (Canadian edition), 27 Oct. 1997, 56–9. Also useful are two special issues on the subject in *Orbit* 21 (Dec. 1990) and 22 (Dec. 1991). For a thorough and relatively dispassionate analysis see Andrew Biemiller and David Booth, 'Towards Higher Levels of Literacy in Ontario,' in Royal Commission on Learning, *For the Love of Learning: Background Papers for the Royal Commission on Learning*, 1: 153–84.

40 See Mark Holmes, 'The Values and Beliefs of Ontario's Chief Education Officers,' in K. Leithwood and D. Musella, eds, *Understanding School System Administration: Studies of the Contemporary Chief Education Officer* (New York: Falmer Press, 1991), 154–74.

41 See e.g. *Star*, 4 Dec. 1989; *LFP*, 21 May 1994. But for the best 'horror story' of administrator/parent non-communication, see Nikiforuk, *School's Out*, 19–21, and a related *Star* editorial, 22 July 1992.

42 Quoted by Nikiforuk in *Globe*, 26 June 1992. For an example of the competing views, see the exchange between Curran and Nikiforuk in ibid., 2 and 3 Dec. 1993.

43 Bernard Shapiro, quoted in *Star*, 25 Apr. 1987.

44 See Sid Gilbert and Bruce Orok, 'School Leavers,' *Canadian Social Trends* 30 (Autumn 1993): 2–7; Warren Clark, 'School Leavers Revisited,' *Canadian Social Trends* 44 (Spring 1997): 10–12; *Globe*, 5 Apr. 1993.

45 For an overview of the literature and the arguments, see Jerry Paquette, 'Universal Education: Meanings, Challenges, and Options into the Third Millennium,' *Curriculum Inquiry* 25, 1 (1995): 23–73.

46 Toronto: Key Porter Books, 1994. For typical articles see Diane E. Meaghan, 'Fixing What Isn't Broken,' *Orbit* 26, 4 (1995): 34–8; David S. Ireland, 'Dispelling Myths of Student Underachievement,' *Orbit* 26, 4 (1995): 2–4; Diane E. Meaghan and François R. Casas, 'On the Testing of Standards and Standardized Achievement Testing: Panacea, Placebo, or Pandora's Box?' *Interchange* 26, 1 (1995), and subsequent discussion and replies; William A. Hynes, 'Lies, Damned Lies, and Statistics,' *Our Schools / Our Selves*, February 1994, 93–104. For the counterattack in the daily press, see Meaghan and Casas, *Globe*, 1 Feb. 1994. A book that cuts through the rhetoric on both sides and offers an evocative insight into the classrooms of the mid-1990s is Ken Dryden, *In School: Our Kids, Our Teachers, Our Classrooms* (Toronto: McClelland and Stewart, 1995).

47 See e.g. Jane Badets, 'Canada's Immigrants – Recent Trends,' *Canadian Social Trends* 29 (Summer 1993): 8–11; Viviane Renaud and Jane Badets, 'Ethnic Diversity in the 1990s,' *Canadian Social Trends* 30 (Autumn 1993): 17–22; *Star*, 4 Jan. 1998; *Globe*, 3 Dec. 1997; Frances Henry, *The Caribbean Diaspora in Toronto: Learning to Live with Racism* (Toronto: University of Toronto Press, 1994), 27–9, 121; Karen Kelly, 'Visible Minorities: A Diverse Group,' *Canadian Social Trends* 37 (Summer 1995): 2–8; *Globe*, 18 Feb. 1998.

48 *Globe*, 3 May 1993.

49 EQAO, Provincial Report on Achievement ... 1996–7, Board by Board Results, Appendix D (www.eqao.com/eqao/vendor_information/html_docs/public/highlights.html [archives]).

50 *Star,* 17 March 1991.

51 One of the best examples is reported in Michael Valpy's column on Somali children in the *Globe,* 23 Feb. 1996.

52 See Pina La Novara, *A Portrait of Families in Canada* (Ottawa: Statscan, 1993), 16, table 1.5; ibid., 'Changes in Family Living,' *Canadian Social Trends* 29 (Summer 1993): 12–14; *Star,* 4 Jan. 1998.

53 *Globe,* 12 Oct. 1993.

54 For an overview and references see the special issue of *Orbit* 24, 1 (March 1993). See also Livingstone et al., *The Tenth OISE Survey, 1994,* 25; *Orbit* 25, 3 (1994); 'A Curriculum Pullout: The Safe School,' [OSSTF] *Education Forum,* Spring 1992.

55 See e.g. W. Gordon West, 'Escalating Problem or Moral Panic? A Critical Perspective,' *Orbit* 24, 1 (March 1993): 6–7; *Globe,* 5 June 1996 and 27 Oct. 1997; *Star,* 4 July 1996.

56 Quoted in *Star,* 14 Oct. 1993.

57 For a brief introductory survey and pertinent sources see Royal Commission on Learning, *For the Love of Learning,* 4: 90–6. See also John Porter, Marion Porter, and Bernard R. Blishen, *Stations and Callings: Making It Through the School System* (Toronto: Methuen, 1982); Loren Jay Lind, *The Learning Machine: A Hard Look at Toronto Schools* (Toronto: House of Anansi Press, 1974); Peter McLaren, *Cries from the Corridor: The New Suburban Ghettos* (Toronto: Methuen, 1980); Bruce Curtis, D.W. Livingstone, and Harry Smaller, *Stacking the Deck: The Streaming of Working-Class Kids in Ontario Schools* (Toronto: Our Schools / Our Selves Education Foundation, 1992). See also the various studies of streaming and dropouts referred to in chapter 11.

58 For an Ontario perspective on the literature and research up to the early 1980s, see Paul Anisef, Norman Okihiro, and Carl James, *Losers and Winners: The Pursuit of Equality and Social Justice in Higher Education* (Toronto: Butterworths, 1982). Despite the subtitle, the focus is as much on the schools as it is on post-secondary education. For a general overview of the arguments, see the essays by Claude Lessard and Aniko Varpalotai in Ratna Ghosh and Douglas Ray, eds, *Social Change and Education in Canada,* 3rd ed. (Toronto: Harcourt Brace, 1995).

Chapter 10 The Crisis in Finance and Governance

1 These percentages, however, were always disputed by the politicians in power, who argued that if one included capital costs and government contributions to the teachers' pension plan, the figure was more like 54 per cent in the mid-1980s and 45 per cent in 1991.

2 By the early 1990s, 92 per cent of male and 73 per cent of female elementary teachers had degrees. See MOET, *1992–93 Key Statistics.*

3 See Stephen Lawton, Mark Ryall, and Teresa Menzies, *A Study on Costs: Ontario Public Elementary/Secondary Education Costs as Compared to Other Provinces* (MOET, Aug. 1996). A falling PTR, however, did not mean diminishing numbers in regular classrooms. Special classes, restrictions on the PTR in particular grades, and other factors might lead to some quite small classes and many more large classes in regular classrooms. For most teachers, the number of pupils per class probably rose during these years.

4 High school teachers had had preparation time built into their timetables since the early 1970s and the proportions did not change much over 25 years.

5 Lawton et al., *A Study on Costs*; Anne Drolet, 'Education Price Index – Selected Inputs, Elementary and Secondary Levels, 1991,' *Education Quarterly Review*, Prototype 1993, 48–9 (Ontario figures); Canadian Teachers' Federation, *Economic Service Bulletin* no. 1996–3 (Feb. 1996), 1–2, table 1. One qualification to this paragraph is that the research does not take account of the effects of the 'social contract.'

6 *Star*, 23 Sept. 1988.

7 See *Star*, 15 Feb. 1997, 14 Oct. 1992, 15 Apr. and 4 June 1993; *Globe*, 29 Dec. 1994.

8 *Star*, 6 March 1993 (1980–90), and my calculations from MOET, *1993–94 Key Statistics: Elementary and Secondary Education in Ontario.*

9 *Star*, 28 July 1987 (the reference is to the election of 1985).

10 Ibid., 18 Aug. 1987.

11 Ibid., 10 March 1988 and 19 Jan. 1990.

12 *LFP*, 1 Sept. 1990.

13 *Globe*, 29 Jan. 1991.

14 Ibid., 27 Aug. 1987.

15 Ontario, *Report of the Commission on the Financing of Elementary and Secondary Education* [Macdonald Report], December 1985, 56.

16 Ibid., 48, 56.

17 *Star*, 6 May 1987.

18 See Macdonald Report, 35–6, 40.

19 Ibid., 45.

20 Ibid., 48–59.

21 Ibid., 39.

22 For an accessible example of the extremes in the range of disparities, see Royal Commission on Learning, *For the Love of Learning* [hereafter RCOL] (1994), 4: 129.

23 Macdonald Report, 40–1.
24 Ibid., 39–43.
25 *Star*, 19 March and 10 Aug. 1987.
26 Ibid., 19 March 1987.
27 Ibid., 18 Aug. 1987.
28 For the announcement see *Globe* and *Star*, 18 May 1989. The pertinent legislation was passed in the fall of 1989 and the details set out in a news release from the ministry dated 19 Oct. 1989. For the context and more details see Rouleen Wignall, 'Equity in Ontario: The Pooling of Assessment,' in Stephen Lawton and Rouleen Wignall, eds, *Scrimping or Squandering? Financing Canadian Schools* (Toronto: OISE Press, 1989), 140–7.
29 Some, but not all, the way. The details are complex, but for a tolerably clear explanation of why inequities persisted into the 1990s, see RCOL, 4: 130–1.
30 For the background see Thomas Walkom, *Rae Days: The Rise and Follies of the NDP* (Toronto: Key Porter Books, 1994), 203–7.
31 Ontario Fair Tax Commission, *Fair Taxation in a Changing World* (Toronto: University of Toronto Press, 1993), 600. The report offers a very clear, jargon-free introduction to all of the problems and provides those who want to pursue this subject further with a good place to start. See esp. chaps. 27 and 28. For the references and quotations in the rest of this paragraph, see pp. 74–7, 683.
32 *Star*, 23 Jan. 1994.
33 Macdonald Report, 57.
34 *Globe*, 6 May 1994; *1994 Ontario Budget*, 13.
35 See *LFP*, 20 Apr., 31 July 1991; *Globe*, 8 Nov. 1991 (a survey), 14 Nov. 1991.
36 *Globe*, 1 Feb. 1992.
37 Education Relations Commission, *Annual Report* 1991–2, 8–9.
38 See *Globe*, 1 Feb. 1992; *Star*, 23 Jan. and 1 Apr. 1992. For a typical reaction see the president's message in *OPSTF News*, December 1992, 6–7.
39 *Star*, 14 May 1992.
40 Ibid., 12 Apr. 1992.
41 *Globe*, 12 Feb. 1993. The OISE polls paint a much more optimistic picture, suggesting that while there was significant discontent with levels of spending, the majority of Ontarians were prepared to spend more, not less, on education generally, and in both 1990 and 1994 a slight majority even volunteered to pay higher taxes in support of education. Perhaps the discontented were simply a noisy minority. But the OISE poll does not attempt to distinguish between property owners and others, or by level of income. Thus it is perhaps not surprising that in 1994 those aged 18 to 24 were significantly more enthusiastic than others about paying higher taxes, as indeed were students

and the unemployed. Seniors, by contrast, were notably unhappy and industrial workers were evenly divided. See Livingstone et al., *The Tenth OISE Survey, 1994. Public Attitudes towards Education in Ontario* (Toronto: OISE, 1995), 9–14.

42 *Star*, 23 Apr. 1993.

43 See John Barber, 'School Board Jungle,' *Toronto*, February 1988, 28ff.; *Star*, 3 Nov. 1991.

44 *Star*, 29 March 1990.

45 *LFP*, 21 Feb. 1991.

46 *Star*, 29 Aug. 1992.

47 RCOL, 4: 111–12.

48 See e.g. *Star*, 4 Nov. 1991, 23 Jan 1992 (editorial), 7 Sept. and 13 Oct. 1992.

49 Ibid., 13 March 1992.

50 Ibid., 8 March 1992.

51 Ibid., 9 Nov. 1992. Similarly, see ibid., 25 Nov. 1992.

52 Ibid., 18 Feb. 1992. See also ibid., 12 Feb. 1992.

53 *Globe* and *Star*, 8 Apr. 1992.

54 *Star*, 12 Feb. 1992; *Sarnia Observer*, 10 Nov. 1992; *Globe*, 6 Jan. 1993; *Star*, 20 Feb. 1993.

55 See *Star*, 29 Aug. 1992, 20 Jan. 1993.

56 Ibid., 21 Jan. 1993. Compare Silipo's comments in ibid., 6 Nov. 1989.

57 *Star*, 5 Feb. 1993 (Angus Reid, Southam News Survey).

58 See ibid., 12 May 1994 [Environics Poll]; Livingstone et al., *The Tenth OISE Survey, 1994*, 17.

59 Knowledge of developments elsewhere was not the preserve of a handful of educational experts. It was *news*. See e.g. *Star*, 6 Feb. 1993; *LFP*, 13 Feb. 1993; *Globe*, 25 Jan. 1994.

60 In Ontario, the first formal recommendation that each school establish such a council came in the *Report of the Commission on Private Schools* [Shapiro Report] of 1985. The City of Toronto school board was one of several experimenting with greater parental involvement in the late 1980s, and the NDP had endorsed the mandatory establishment of school councils at its annual convention in 1988: see *Star*, 21 Nov. 1987, 16 May 1989, 24 June 1988. For the background and arguments for school councils and site-based management (a related enthusiasm of the 1980s and early 1990s) there are several good places to begin: *Report of the Commission on Private Schools*, 57–9; RCOL, 4: 14; E.S. Muir, 'Summary and Analysis of Recent Literature on Parental Role in Educational Governance,' in *For the Love of Learning. Background Papers for the Royal Commission on Learning* (Toronto, 1995).

61 On Pascal's views see *Star*, 30 Dec. 1996.

62 See *Globe*, 26 June 1993, 25 Jan. 1994; *Star*, 23 Jan. 1994.

63 *LFP*, 21 Jan. 1995.

64 *Star*, 3 June 1993.

65 Ibid., 8 Nov. 1993.

66 RCOL, 4: 114–15.

67 For the announcement see *Globe*, 24 Feb. 1995; *Star*, 25 Feb. 1995. For the full statement of government policy see MOET, *New Foundations for Ontario Education* [Apr. 1995], 30–1.

68 MOET, *New Foundations*, 27–9.

Chapter 11 The 'Pedagogy of Joy' Meets 'Mental Might'

1 Rosemary Speirs, *Out of the Blue: The Fall of the Tory Dynasty in Ontario* (Toronto: Macmillan, 1986), 230.

2 See Rosemary Speirs's comment, *Star*, 24 Jan. 1987.

3 The priorities are outlined, with pertinent dates, in Minister of Education, *Annual Report for 1986–7*, 4–5. They were formally adopted in March 1987.

4 There are two clearly written introductions to the arcane field of assessment. For concise, intelligible summaries and evaluations of the assessment tools I discuss here, see Alan J.C. King and Marjorie J. Peart, *The Numbers Game: A Study of Evaluation and Achievement in Ontario Schools* (Toronto: OSSTF, 1994), esp. 276 ff. The volume also offers an extensive bibliography on the subject. More generally, see Jennifer Lewington and Graham Orpwood, *Overdue Assignment: Taking Responsibility for Canada's Schools* (Toronto: John Wiley and Sons, 1993), chap. 6.

5 But for some insight on what happened, see Dennis Raphael, 'Accountability and Educational Philosophy: Paradigms and Conflict in Ontario Education,' *Canadian Journal of Education* 18, 1 (1993): 35–7.

6 For an accessible overview of these arguments by two enthusiasts, one that was to have much influence in Ontario, see Andy Hargreaves and Lorna Earl, *Rights of Passage: A Review of Selected Research about Schooling in the Transition Years* (Toronto: Ontario MOE, 1990), chap. 5.

7 See e.g. *Star*, 16 March 1988 (OSSTF), 6 July 1988 (FWTAO), 5 Sept. 1989 (associate director, Toronto Board of Education), 7 Dec. 1989 (superintendent of curriculum, Toronto Board of Education). See also Raphael's comment on his experience in the ministry, 'Accountability and Educational Philosophy,' 37.

8 George Radwanski, *Ontario Study of the Relevance of Education, and the Issue of Dropouts* (MOE, 1988), 56.

9 On the polls see D.W. Livingstone, D. Hart, and L.E. Davie, *Public Attitudes*

towards Education in Ontario, 1996: The Eleventh OISE/UT Survey (Toronto: University of Toronto Press, 1997), 25.

10 Legislative Assembly, *Hansard*, Select Committee on Education, 28 July 1988, E11, E-512.

11 Planning was well under way by September 1986, only two months after Shapiro's appointment. See *LFP*, 1 May 1987.

12 *Star*, 1 May 1987; *Globe*, 8 June 1987.

13 Detailed results were, however, provided confidentially to participating boards and through them to schools. By the time King and Peart were writing (*The Numbers Game*), policy had changed somewhat. For an earlier ministry summary of the process see Ann Jones, 'The New Provincial Review Process,' *OPSTF News*, December 1988, 24–5, and esp. 'Provincial Reviews,' 26.

14 Along with King and Peart, see Neil Graham's account of its early development in 'Achieving Province-Wide Consistency without Provincial Examinations,' *OTF/FEO Interaction*, May 1986, 4–5.

15 For a useful historical overview see Roger Palmer and Jim Brackenbury, 'National Testing in Canada,' in Leonard L. Stewin and Stewart J.H. McCann, eds, *Contemporary Educational Issues: The Canadian Mosaic*, 2nd ed. (Mississauga: Copp Clark Pitman, 1993), 467–80.

16 See *Star*, 29 Apr., 4 Nov. 1987; *Globe*, 7 Aug. 1987. During 1987 there was some confusion about the grade-range of these benchmarks. At one point they were to be developed for grades 3, 6, and 8 and for a much wider range of subjects. But between late 1987 and 1990, the proposal came to encompass only literacy and numeracy in grades 3 and 6.

17 For a brief, helpful overview, see King and Peart, *The Numbers Game*, 4, 273–6, 287–9. See also Lewington and Orpwood, *Overdue Assignment*, chap. 6. A special issue of *Orbit* 24, 2 (1993) on benchmarks and standards is also very useful; see esp. the article by Gail Rappolt, pp. 2–5.

18 See Radwanski, *Relevance*, 33–7 and 128–42.

19 See Sylvia Larter, *Benchmarks: The Development of a New Approach to Student Education* (Toronto: Toronto Board of Education, 1991). This detailed study of the Toronto experience is also helpful for context and background.

20 See Christine Suurtamin, 'Surveying the Benchmarks,' *Orbit* 24, 2 (1993).

21 *Star*, 15 Sept. 1988.

22 See MOE, Memorandum, Assessment Activities as of March 22, 1989. For the announcement and reactions see *Star*, 23 and 27 Feb. 1989. The initiative was reaffirmed in the April 1989 Throne Speech.

23 It was one of the priorities he enunciated for the ministry in early 1987. Minister of Education, *Annual Report for 1986–7*, 4–5.

24 *Star*, 10 May 1987. For the context and the research base for this view see 'FWTAO Speaks Out on Primary Class Size Issue,' and Patricia Hileman, 'Too Many Children,' *FWTAO Newsletter*, January 1986, 1–7.

25 *Globe*, 7 Aug. 1987.

26 See ibid., 7 Nov. 1987; *LFP*, 1 Dec. 1987; Rosemary Speirs's acerbic *Star* column of 7 Dec. 1987.

27 MOE, Policy/Program Memorandum no. 107, 2 May 1988.

28 Legislative Assembly, *Hansard*, Select Committee on Education, E-11, E488, 28 July 1988.

29 MOE, *Report of the Early Primary Education Project* (May 1985), 36–9.

30 Radwanski, *Relevance*, 123ff.

31 [Legislative Assembly] *Throne Speech*, 25 Apr. 1989.

32 *Star*, 29 Apr. 1987.

33 [Ken Dryden] *Report of the Ontario Youth Commissioner*, 1986, esp. 14–18, 37–42.

34 K. Leithwood et al., *The Nature and Consequences of Selected Processes for Developing, Implementing and Institutionalizing Major Educational Processes* (Toronto: OISE, 1987).

35 Including A.J.C. King et al., *Improving Student Retention in Ontario Secondary Schools* (Toronto: MOE, 1988); Stephen B. Lawton et al., *Student Retention and Transition in Ontario High Schools: Policies, Practices, and Prospects* (Toronto: MOE, 1988); Ellen Karp, *The Dropout Phenomenon in Ontario Secondary Schools* (Toronto: MOE, 1988).

36 OSSTF, *Present Challenges, New Directions: A Discussion Paper on Future Directions in Secondary School Education*, 1988.

37 See King et al., *Improving Student Retention*, 130; Radwanski, *Relevance*, 78.

38 Lawton et al., *Student Retention and Transition*, vii; *Star*, 14 Sept. 1988 (Secondary School Principals' Association).

39 K.A. Leithwood and J.B. Cousins, 'Fostering Inequality in Ontario Secondary Schools: The Implementation of OSIS,' *OISE Field Development Newsletter* 18, 1 (Jan. 1988).

40 OSSTF, *Present Challenges, New Directions*, 11.

41 Legislative Assembly, Select Committee on Education, *1st Report*, December 1988, 4–8.

42 Radwanski, *Relevance*, 76.

43 Ibid., 161.

44 See Shapiro's comment to Select Committee on Education hearings, Legislative Assembly, *Hansard*, 28 July 1988, E-11, E499; Ontario Premier's Council, *People and Skills in the New Global Economy* (1990), 34–5; Radwanski, *Relevance*, 159–61.

45 See Dryden, *Report*, 17; Radwanski, *Relevance*, 195; OSSTF, *Present Challenges*,

338 Notes to pages 209–11

New Directions, 12–15; Ontario Federation of Labour, Submission to the Select Committee on Education, 11 Oct. 1988, repr. in *Our Schools / Our Selves* 1, 2 (Jan. 1989): 74–7; *Star,* 6 Oct. 1988 (Peel Board of Education and Metropolitan Toronto Separate School Board submissions to the Select Committee on Education).

46 See Lawton et al., *Student Retention and Transition,* ix ff.; King et al., *Improving Student Retention,* 138–40; Radwanski, *Relevance,* 110–11.

47 Radwanski, *Relevance,* 165–73.

48 Radwanski provides a detailed justification for this curriculum; see ibid., 40ff.

49 For example, see the commentary by John Fraser, Director of the Peel Board of Education, and by Duncan Appleford in 'De-Streaming the Ontario Secondary Schools: Dealing with the Concerns,' *Orbit* 21, 1 (Feb. 1990): 2; *LFP,* 16 Feb. 1988 (Directors, London Board of Education and Lambton Board of Education); *Globe,* 17 Feb. 1988 (OPSTA); *Star,* 17 Feb. 1988 (Lloyd Dennis).

50 See Lawton et al., *Student Retention and Transition,* ix.

51 Eric Wood, 'Radwanski and Streaming: Where Is the Evidence?' *Ontario Mathematics Gazette,* September 1990, 7–11.

52 Ontario Federation of Labour, Submission to the Ontario Select Committee, 77.

53 Andy Hargreaves, quoted in *Star,* 29 Oct. 1988. Similarly see King et al., *Improving Student Retention,* 133.

54 For the initial reaction see *Star,* 16 Feb. 1988. For the story of the turnabout see Vida Zalnieriunas, 'Will Destreaming Be Derailed?' [OECTA] *The Reporter,* October 1989, 32–5; and Bob Dixon, 'Ontario's English Catholic Teachers Take on the Streaming System,' *Our Schools / Our Selves* 1, 2 (Jan. 1989): 63–9.

55 OSSTF, *Present Challenges, New Directions;* OISE presentation, Select Committee on Education, Legislative Assembly, *Hansard,* 22 Sept. 1988, E-19, E1003ff.

56 For OSSTF see Abe Theissen, 'The OSSTF Point of View,' *Orbit* 21, 1 (Feb. 1990): 2–6. For FWTAO see Legislative Assembly, *Hansard,* Select Committee on Education, 14 Sept. 1988, E-14, E670.

57 See Livingstone et al., *Public Attitudes ... 1996,* 22 (figures for the decade of the 1980s).

58 King et al., *Improving Student Retention,* 140. See also King's and Shapiro's comments in *Star,* 30 Aug. 1988. For a thoughtful assessment of both sides at the time, see Mark Holmes, 'A Faltering Step in the Right Direction,' *Orbit* 21, 1 (Feb. 1990): 5–6.

59 King et al., *Improving Student Retention,* 140.

60 Cited in Don Gutteridge, *Stubborn Pilgrimage: Resistance and Transformation in*

Ontario English Teaching, 1960–1993, with a teaching unit by Ian Underhill (Toronto: Our Schools / Our Selves, 1994), 228.

61 Legislative Assembly, Select Committee on Education, *1st Report,* 8.

62 Ibid., 8–12.

63 [Legislative Assembly] *Throne Speech,* 25 Apr. 1989.

64 *Star,* 14 Oct. 1988.

65 Ibid., 5 Sept. 1989.

66 See Georgette Gagnon and Dan Rath, *Not Without Cause: David Peterson's Fall from Grace* (Toronto: HarperCollins, 1991), 216–17.

67 Thomas J. Courchene with Colin R. Telmer, *From Heartland to North American Region State: The Social, Fiscal and Federal Evolution of Ontario* (Toronto: Centre for Public Management, Faculty of Management, University of Toronto, 1998), 113 and 74, and generally chap. 5. Randall White, however, is sceptical about this shift. See *Ontario Since 1985* (Toronto: Eastendbooks, 1998), 175–85.

68 See Jim Cummins and Marcel Danesi, *Heritage Languages: The Development and Denial of Canada's Linguistic Resources* (Toronto: Our Schools / Our Selves Education Foundation, 1990), 42–3; see also *Globe* editorial, 19 March 1987; *Star,* 19 Sept. 1987; *LFP,* 27 Oct. 1988; MOE, Policy/Program Memorandum no. 7, 29 June 1990.

69 See Report of the Provincial Advisory Committee on Race Relations, 'The Development of a Policy on Race and Ethnocultural Equity,' September 1987; *Star,* 15 July 1987 (Sandro Contenta), 16 Jan. 1988; *Globe,* 26 Jan. 1989.

70 The most accessible summary is FWTAO, *Affirmative Action / Employment Equity,* Report 1996, 8–9.

71 See Gagnon and Rath, *Not Without Cause,* esp. chap 2.

72 Ibid., 52–3.

73 For the details see MOE, *Action Plan 1989–94.* For a description of the entire project, its scope and intent, see Howat Noble, 'The Restructuring Initiatives in Education: What Are They and How Will They Be Developed?' *Education Today,* March/April 1990, 8–10 and 24–6.

74 MOE, *The Formative Years Consultation Paper: Issues and Options Response Guide and Working Paper,* June 1990; *The Transition Years: Guide to Discussion and Response,* October 1990; *The Specialization Years: Guide to Discussion and Response,* December 1991. On the number of responses see *Star,* 18 March 1992. For the summaries, see e.g. MOE, *What Was Said: A Summary and Analysis of ... Responses to The Transition Years: Guide to Discussion and Response,* December 1991; *What Was Said: A Summary and Analysis of Responses to The Specialization Years,* 1993.

Chapter 12 The NDP and a Royal Commission

1 On teachers in the campaign, see Georgette Gagnon and Dan Rath, *Not Without Cause: David Peterson's Fall from Grace* (Toronto: HarperCollins, 1991), 215–20; George Martell, *A New Education Politics: Bob Rae's Legacy and the Response of the Ontario Secondary School Teachers' Federation* (Toronto: James Lorimer, 1995), 14–20.

2 See the cover letter, Richard Johnston to All New Democrats who expressed an interest in Education Conferences ..., May 1990, and attached, 'A New Democratic Party Philosophy of Elementary and Secondary Education,' 10 pages. By June 1988 there were eight discussion papers.

3 Chuck Rachlis and David Wolfe, 'An Insiders' View of the NDP Government of Ontario ...,' in Graham White, ed., *The Government and Politics of Ontario*, 5th ed. (Toronto: University of Toronto Press, 1997), 350.

4 On Silipo's background see Derek Ferguson's story in *Star*, 16 Oct. 1991.

5 See Aleda O'Connor, 'A New Government, A New Minister,' [OECTA] *The Reporter*, December 1990, 14–16.

6 For the details and a sampling of reactions see *Star*, 2, 3, 7, 9, 11 May 1991; *Globe*, 14 and 15 May, 1 and 12 June 1991.

7 See Dennis Raphael, 'Accountability and Educational Philosophy: Paradigms and Conflict in Ontario Education,' *Canadian Journal of Education* 18, 1 (1993): 38–9.

8 See Martell, *A New Education Politics*, 23, and various issues of *Our Schools / Our Selves*, 1990–2. The latter is especially valuable because one of the authors of editorials was David Clandfield, who would become Silipo's policy adviser during his stint as minister of education.

9 See David Clandfield, 'The NDP and the Corporate Agenda,' *Our Schools / Our Selves*, Oct./Nov. 1993, 8–26; for the phrase 'democratic socialist' see ibid., 10. See also Clandfield, 'Rae Days,' *Our Schools / Our Selves*, March 1995, 106–18. Because it is based in part on interviews with some of the participants, an indispensable source on these matters is Jerry Paquette, 'Cross Purposes and Crossed Wires: Educational Policy-Making on Equity in Ontario during the NDP Years,' unpublished paper 1998.

10 Cited in Western Ontario Regional Curriculum Council, untitled document dated October 1992, p. 14, 'General Context.'

11 Ibid.

12 *Star*, 7 Apr. 1992.

13 Ibid., 7 Dec. 1991.

14 Gérald Hurtubise, 'Improving Student Results in Mathematics,' *Orbit* 24, 2 (1993): 9.

15 *Star* and *Globe*, 6 Feb. 1992.

16 See e.g. Clandfield's comment, *Star*, 16 Sept. 1992.

17 Martell, *A New Education Politics*, 32.

18 See Ron Wideman, 'Overview: The Common Curriculum ... 1995,' *Orbit* 26, 1 (1995): 2–5. What follows is my summary of the 'package' announced in June.

19 MOE, Policy/Program Memorandum no. 115, 15 June 1992.

20 Clandfield, 'The NDP and the Corporate Agenda,' 10.

21 *Star*, 6 Nov. 1992.

22 Liz Barkley, 'Silipo's Destreaming/Delabelling Initiative,' [OSSTF] *Education Forum*, Summer 1992, 9–10; *Star*, 12 Feb. 1992.

23 Barkley, 'Silipo's initiative,' 10; Eleanor Brown, 'Down at the Harbour Castle with OSSTF Past President, Jim Head,' *Our Schools / Our Selves* 4, 1 (Sept. 1992): 73; Martell, *A New Education Politics*, 32.

24 Marriane Clayton, 'Interview with Liz Barkley,' [OSSTF] *Education Forum*, Fall/Winter 1994, 16.

25 *Globe*, 7 and 23 Nov. 1992.

26 Ibid., 9 Sept. 1992; *Star*, 23 Nov. 1992.

27 Clandfield, 'The NDP and the Corporate Agenda,' 10.

28 *Globe*, 18 Jan. 1993.

29 For the policy along with its historical and legislative background, see MOET, Policy/Program Memorandum no. 119, 13 July 1993, 'Development and Implementation of School Board Policies on Antiracism and Ethnocultural Equity.'

30 *Star*, 4 Feb., 25 March, 30 July (Walkom) 1993.

31 For a review of the work of the revisions committee see Wideman, 'Overview.' See also MOET, *In Common* (newsletter published on revisions process, September 1993 through autumn 1994).

32 *Star*, 30 July 1994 (Walkom). The story was broken by a reporter for the *Ottawa Citizen*. MOET, *The Common Curriculum, Grades 1–9, Version for Parents and the General Public, 1993*.

33 MOET, *The Common Curriculum: Policies and Outcomes, Grades 1–9, 1995*. See also ibid., *The Common Curriculum: Provincial Standards, Mathematics, Grades 1–9, 1995*, and *The Common Curriculum: Provincial Standards, Language, Grades 1–9, 1995*.

34 *Star*, 4 Feb. 1993.

35 *Globe*, 27 Feb. 1993, 9 March 1994.

36 Ibid., 3 Apr. 1993.

37 For descriptions see 'Ontario Tests Grade 9 Students' Reading and Writing Ability,' [OECTA] *The Reporter*, October 1993, 28–31; MOET, *The Ontario*

Grade 9 Reading and Writing Test: The Provincial Report of the 1993–94 Test. It was administered again in 1994–5. For an analysis and critique see Dennis Raphael, 'Student Assessment: A Flawed Framework?' in Geoffrey Milburn, ed., *'Ring Some Alarm Bells in Ontario': Reactions to the Report of the Royal Commission on Learning* (London, Ont.: Althouse Press, 1996), 87ff.

38 *Star*, 30 Apr. 1993.

39 See *Globe*, 13 May 1996 (Lewington); *LFP*, 26 Feb. 1994; *Star*, 30 May, 31 May 1994 (editorial); *Globe*, 3 Sept. 1994.

40 See e.g. *Star*, 26 Oct. 1994 (Metro Toronto Separate, York, and East York), 23 Nov. 1994 (York Region), 16 May 1995 (Scarborough); *LFP*, 25 Oct. 1994 (London, Middlesex Separate, Middlesex Public).

41 For a summary article on Lacey and her goals see Andrew Duffy's piece in *Star*, 16 Apr. 1995. See also *Star*, 4 Feb. 1994, 11 March 1995; *Globe*, 12 Apr. 1995 (editorial).

42 MOET, 'Violence-Free Schools Policy,' 1994. Generally for background and debates, see special issues of *Orbit*: 24, 1 (1993) and 25, 3 (1994).

43 Official biographies of all five commissioners can be found in Royal Commission on Learning, *For the Love of Learning* [hereafter RCOL] (1994), 4: appendix G. For Caplan's ties to the Ontario NDP see Patrick Monahan, *Storming the Pink Palace: The NDP in Power: A Cautionary Tale* (Toronto: Lester Publishing, 1995), 4, 27, 59.

44 See RCOL, 1: 11–13.

45 Ibid., 1: 49.

46 Ibid., 2: 2.

47 For the quotations in this paragraph see ibid., 1: 54–6.

48 Ibid., 1: 54.

49 Ibid., 2: 26. There is a detailed description of what each phrase means in ibid., 2: 26–38.

50 Ibid., 'A Short Version,' 5.

51 Ibid., 1: 6. The engines are described in ibid., 1: 6–7.

52 Ibid., 1: 7.

53 Ibid., 2: 19.

54 For this paragraph see ibid., 2: chap. 8 generally and 61, 56.

55 For this and the next two paragraphs see ibid., 2: chap. 9 generally; 74, 77.

56 Ibid., 3: 9. Generally on the teaching corps see vol. 3.

57 The two pertinent chapters are ibid., 2: chap. 11, and 4: chap. 19. For the quotations see 2: 150 and 151.

58 Ibid., 4: 118.

59 For the leak, see *Globe*, 21 Dec. 1994; *Star*, 20 Dec. 1994.

60 *LFP*, 21 Jan. 1995; *Globe*, 27 Jan. 1995; *Star*, 27 Jan. 1995. For an extended OSSTF response see [OSSTF] *Education Forum*, Spring 1995, 4–7.

61 *Star,* 27 Jan. 1995.
62 *Globe,* 28 Jan. 1995.
63 Quoted in ibid., 27 Jan. 1995; but similarly see the editorial in *Star,* 27 Jan. 1995.
64 *Star,* 28 Jan. 1995.
65 Quoted in ibid., 21 Feb. 1995.
66 Ibid., 17 Feb. 1995; *LFP,* 15 Feb. 1995. For more reflective scrutiny and the mixed assessment of the academic community, see special double issue of *Orbit* 26, 2 (1995), in particular the articles by David Livingstone and Kari Dehli; Martell, *A New Education Politics,* part 2, 68ff.; Geoffrey Milburn, ed., *'Ring Some Alarm Bells in Ontario': Reactions to the Report of the Royal Commission on Learning* (London, Ont.: Althouse Press, 1996).
67 MOET, *New Foundations for Ontario Education: A Summary* (1995), 21.
68 See *Globe,* 7 Feb. 1995; *Star,* 9, 17, 21 Feb. 1995; *LFP,* 15 Feb. 1995.
69 MOET, Program/Policy Memorandum no. 122, April 1995; *Secondary School Reform. New Foundations for Ontario Education* [April 1995], establishing the membership and mandate of the 'Secondary School Reform Reference Group.'
70 For the membership and mandate of these groups see MOET, *New Foundations.*
71 My analysis here follows that of Jennifer Lewington, *Globe,* 7 Feb. 1995.
72 See *Star,* 28 Feb., 12 March 1995 (editorial from *Ottawa Citizen*).

Chapter 13 The 'Common Sense' Revolution

1 For context and background the best source is John Ibbitson, *Promised Land: Inside the Mike Harris Revolution* (Scarborough, Ont.: Prentice Hall Canada, 1997). But see also the essays in Sid Noel, ed., *Revolution at Queen's Park: Essays on Governing Ontario* (Toronto: James Lorimer and Co., 1997); the pertinent essays in Graham White, ed., *The Government and Politics of Ontario,* 5th ed. (Toronto: University of Toronto, 1997); and Thomas J. Courchene with Colin R. Telmer, *From Heartland to North American Region State: The Social, Fiscal and Federal Evolution of Ontario* (Toronto: Centre for Public Management, Faculty of Management, University of Toronto, 1998), chap. 7.
2 Ibbitson, *Promised Land,* 63.
3 The *CSR* didn't contain much more detail on education than that. But it referred readers to a much more thorough exposition of Tory policy set out in *New Directions, Volume II: A Blueprint for Learning in Ontario,* a caucus policy paper produced in 1992.
4 See *Globe,* 16 Aug. 1995; *Star,* 13 Sept. 1995; *Globe,* 23 Aug. 1996.
5 See Ibbitson, *Promised Land,* 279.

6 *Star*, 19 July 1995 and 28 Aug. 1996. On Lacey's appointment, see ibid., 10 Nov. 1996.

7 On the idea of a 'second phase,' see Courchene and Telmer, *Heartland*, 170–1, 198ff.

8 *Star*, 9 Sept. 1995; *Globe*, 28 Sept. 1995. Funding, however, was not eliminated but reduced to the grant amounts allocated for any other elementary grade. See *Star*, 8 Aug. 1996 (letter from Snobelen) and Ian Urquhart's review of the issue, *Star*, 2 Sept. 1997.

9 *Globe*, 12 Oct. 1995; *Star*, 18 and 19 Nov. 1995.

10 Bill 31: An Act to Establish the Ontario College of Teachers ... (chap. 12, Statutes of Ontario, 1996). For the structure, powers, and on-going work of the college see *Professionally Speaking*, Newsletter, Sept. 1995–Dec. 1996; Magazine, May 1997–. On teacher opposition, see e.g. *Globe*, 14 Feb., 13 March, 12 Oct. 1995; *Star*, 13 March 1995; *LFP*, 13 Dec. 1995; Brian McGowan, 'Ontario's Crisismeister Talks Up a Storm,' [OECTA] *The Reporter*, June 1996, 32–3.

11 *Star*, 28 Oct. 1995.

12 Bill 30: An Act to Establish the Education Quality and Accountability Office ... (chap. 11, Statutes of Ontario, 1996).

13 MOET, News release and backgrounder, 2 Nov. 1995 (www.edu.gov.on.ca/ eng/document/nr/95.11/sec1.html).

14 I have two drafts that vary somewhat, but the thrust is the same. One is among a packet of documents included in 'Secondary Education Reform: Overview and Action Plan,' presentation to the Secondary Education Reform House Committee at the Annual Meeting of the [OSSTF] Provincial Assembly, March 1996. The other is MOET, 'Ontario Secondary Schools (1997), Validation Draft Document,' n.d. See also *Star*, 4 Apr. 1996; *Globe*, 4 and 24 Apr. 1996.

15 See [OSSTF] 'Secondary Education Reform,' in note 14; *Globe*, 24 Apr. 1996.

16 MOET, News release, '4 year secondary school program to start in September 1998,' 25 July 1996 (www.edu.gov.on.ca/eng/document/nr/96.07/ prog98.html).

17 The entire package consisted of five MOET booklets, all released in September 1997. For my purposes the important ones are the first three: *Excellence in Education: High School Reform. A Discussion Paper* – two and a half million copies of this were sent to homes and schools across the province; its contents were fleshed out in *Ontario Secondary Schools (1998). Detailed Discussion Document*; and *Curriculum for Ontario Secondary Schools*.

18 For a summary, see Jennifer Lewington's story in the *Globe*, 25 Aug. 1997. But see also 'Make High Schools Work for Students: OSSTF's High School Princi-

pals Take on the Government's Approach to Secondary Education Reform,'
[OSSTF] *Education Forum*, Winter 1996, 28–31; *Globe*, 25 Nov. 1996; *LFP*,
12 Nov. 1996 (editorial); *Star*, 28 Nov., 1 and 14 Dec. 1996.

19 This, however, reflected the views only of those who actually responded. See
Globe, 25 Aug. 1997. An OISE opinion poll showed a very different result. See
D.W. Livingstone et al., *Public Attitudes towards Education in Ontario, 1996*
(Toronto: University of Toronto Press, 1997), 21–2.

20 MOET, News release, 'Ontario will stream Grade 9 to promote student
success,' and Backgrounder, 'High School Highlights,' 20 June 1997
(www.edu.gov.on.ca/eng/document/nr/97.06/grade9e.html); News release,
'High School Reform ...,' and Backgrounder, 'Highlights of the New High
School Program,' 9 Jan. 1998 (www.edu.gov.on.ca/eng/document/nr/
98.01/reform.html). Readers are reminded that this was government policy
as of December 1998. As curriculum policy for the high school becomes
more explicit in ensuing months, some of it may well change.

21 See e.g. *LFP*, 24 Apr., 26 July 1996; *Star*, 28 July 1996.

22 Compare Snobelen's comment about no plans to change the curriculum in
grades 7 and 8, quoted in *LFP*, 24 Apr. 1996, with MOET, *Curriculum for
Ontario Secondary Schools*, September 1997, 7.

23 On the making of the science curriculum see Graham Orpwood and
Marietta Bloch, 'New Grades 1–8 Science and Technology Is a Teachers'
Curriculum,' [Ontario College of Teachers] *Professionally Speaking*, September 1998, 17–19.

24 For a good example see the study of Norfolk County by Helene A. High,
'Policy to Restructure Grade 9: An Analysis of Implementation,' unpublished
MEd. Directed Research Project, Faculty of Education, University of Western
Ontario, 1997.

25 As far as I can see, the first specific reference turns up in [MOET] 'Measures
to Address the $400 Million Reduction in the General Legislative Grants,'
confidential, 9 Jan. 1996. This document was made public by the NDP at the
end of the month; see *Star*, 30 Jan. 1996. The figure, however, was clearly
emergent before January since this particular document was 'in process' in
late 1995. On this point see *Star*, 21 Jan. 1996 (on OPSBA proposals).

26 *Globe*, 30 Nov. 1995.

27 This is the ministry's own figure, in 'Measures to Address the $400 Million
Reduction.'

28 *Globe*, 30 Nov. 1995; Ontario, *1995 Fiscal Overview and Spending Cuts* (Toronto:
Queen's Printer, 1995), 19.

29 See Ibbitson, *Promised Land*, 135; *LFP*, 5 Dec. 1995; *Globe*, 23 Nov. 1995.

30 MOET, 'Measures to Address the $400 Million Reduction.'

31 *Ontario School Board Reduction Task Force. Final Report* [Sweeney Report], 1996, 48–55.

32 Ibbitson, *Promised Land*, 228–9.

33 The phrase is Robert Sheppard's: *Globe*, 25 Sept. 1996.

34 Bill 34: An Act to Amend the Education Act (chap. 13, Statutes of Ontario, 1996). This bill also formally repealed the provision for the introduction of mandatory junior kindergarten.

35 For a summary report covering several boards, see *Star*, 10 March 1996. Labour law required that notices be given six months before they were to take effect.

36 For the figures see MOET, News release, 22 Aug. 1996 (www.edu.gov.on.ca/eng/document/nr/96.08/lawton.html); MOET, 'Report on School Board Taxes, 1996. School Board Tax Changes Compared with Changes in Provincial Grants, Aug. 1996' (www.edu.gov.on.ca/eng/document/reports/reports.html).

37 MOET, *Report to the Minister. The Working Group on Education Finance Reform*, June 1996.

38 *Star*, 11 June 1996.

39 See the comment by Virginia Galt, *Globe*, 17 Feb. 1996; see also *LFP*, 14 Feb. 1996.

40 On the timing, and board responses to the tool kit as a cause, see *Star*, 11 May 1996; *Globe*, 8 May 1996; *LFP*, 24 March 1997; *Macleans*, 10 Nov. 1997, 15.

41 Joel Rumy in *Star*, 30 Oct. 1997 [italics in original]. For the reports, see Stephen Lawton, Mark Ryall, and Teresa Menzies, *A Study on Costs: Ontario Public Elementary/Secondary Education Costs as Compared to Other Provinces*, MOET, August 1996; MOET, 'Report on School Board Taxes, 1996,' August 1996; Ernst and Young, Chartered Accountants, *Ministry of Education and Training Analysis of School Board Spending Patterns*, January 1997.

42 The quotations are from only one of many Tory expositions of their case. See MOET, *Excellence in Education: Student-Focused Funding for Ontario. A Guide Book*, May 1997.

43 See MOET, 'Report on School Board Taxes, 1996,' Aug. 1996.

44 On Snobelen's assessment, see Ibbitson, *Promised Land*, 228.

45 For the figures and the consequences see the column by John Spears, *Star*, 7 May 1996.

46 See *Globe*, 4 Apr. 1998.

47 Ibbitson, *Promised Land*, 232–40, 271–3. For a brief account see also Sid Noel, 'Ontario's Tory Revolution,' in Noel, ed., *Revolution at Queen's Park*, 6–10.

48 The criticism of the boards typical of the first half of the 1990s continued through 1995 and 1996, and an Environics poll indicated that public disenchantment with the boards had increased substantially between 1994 and

1996. See *Star*, 29 Apr. 1996. See also Jennifer Lewington's summary article, *Globe*, 26 Sept. 1996.

49 *Star*, 12 and 18 Oct. 1996; *LFP*, 12 Oct. 1996; Ibbitson, *Promised Land*, 231–2.

50 Bill 104: Fewer School Boards Act (chap. 3, Statutes of Ontario, 1997).

51 The bill also included some egregious clauses giving the government and the EIC exceptional regulatory powers over extant boards. For a discussion of these see Greg M. Dickinson, 'Case Comment. Court Refuses to Ground Ontario's Supersonic Educational Reforms,' *Education & Law Journal* 8, 3 (1998): 347–56.

52 The bill itself reduced the major school boards to 66, not 72; in response to complaints and on the advice of the Education Improvement Commission, Snobelen agreed in May 1997 to increase the number of northern boards by six. See MOET, News release, 9 May 1997 (www.edu.gov.on.ca/eng/document/nr/97.05/northere.html), and *Star*, 10 May 1997. Thirty-seven existing 'isolate' and hospital [school] boards were retained and renamed 'school authorities.'

53 Bill 160: An Act to reform the education system, protect classroom funding, and enhance accountability ... (chap. 31, Statutes of Ontario, 1997). For a summary, see MOET, *Education Quality Improvement Act, 1997. Compendium* [Sept. 1997]. The best brief overview is Barrie W. Earle et al., 'Restructuring Education in Ontario,' *Education Law News*, Winter 1998. My thanks to Maurice Green and Brian Kelsey for help in clarifying some issues relating to the bill.

54 MOET, 'Meeting Students' Needs. What does Ontario's Education Funding Model Need to Include?' 19 Sept. 1996 (www.edu.gov.on.ca/eng/document/discussi/meeting1.html).

55 MOET, *Student-Focused Funding*. Cf. MOET, Backgrounder, 'An Overview of Student-focused Funding,' 25 March 1998 (www.edu.gov.on.ca/eng/document/nr/98.03/overbg.html).

56 But by March 1998 there were several additional grant categories beyond the foundation and nine 'special-purpose' grants.

57 For the changes compare MOET, *Student-Focused Funding*, May 1997, and MOET, Backgrounder, 'Classroom Spending Defined, Protected,' 25 March 1998 (www.edu.gov.on.ca/eng/document/nr/98.03/cspendbg. html).

58 See MOET, News release, 'Snobelen seeks technical advice ...,' 21 May 1997 (www.edu.gov.on.ca/eng/document/nr/97.05/may21.html). The EIC recommendations are in *The Road Ahead: A Report on Learning Time, Class Size and Staffing. The First Report of the Education Improvement Commission*, August 1997.

59 It also included another $1 billion in government contributions to the

Teachers' Pension Plan. All the other quotations in this paragraph are taken from the following: MOET, 'Speaking notes for ... Dave Johnson regarding ... Ontario's new student-focused ... funding ...,' 25 March 1998, or from the backgrounders and fact sheets released at the same time (www.edu.gov.on.ca/eng/document/nr/98.03/speak.html). The entire package runs to 30 pages and includes the dollar amounts.

60 See *Star*, 21 Oct. 1995, 12 Oct. 1996, 12 Jan. 1997.

61 The best introduction to the constitutional issues and political developments are MOET, *Report of the French Language Education Governance Advisory Group* [Cousineau Report], September 1991, esp. 14–48 (for the significant Manitoba court decision after Cousineau, see *Globe*, 5 March 1993); Royal Commission on Learning, *For the Love of Learning* (1994), 4: 66–9; Michael Hines, 'French-Language Governance: The Mahe Case,' *Education Today*, Sept./Oct. 1991, 13–14. On post–Bill 75 Liberal initiatives, see MOET, *Consultation Paper on Franco-Ontarian Governance*, 1990. The NDP decision is included in the terms of reference of the Sweeney Committee, *Ontario School Board Reduction Task Force. Final Report*, 1996, 1–2.

62 On these points see Affidavit of Robert Dixon, in Ontario Court of Justice (General Division), Court file nos. 97-CV-137668 and 98-CV-139317, *OECTA et al. v. Attorney General of Ontario*, Responding Record of the Intervenor, Ontario Catholic School Trustees' Association, vol. 2, pp. 86–92; Affidavit of Nancy Naylor, in ibid., *OECTA et al. v. Attorney General of Ontario*, and *Ontario Public School Boards' Association et al. v. Attorney General of Ontario*, Respondent's Application Record, vol. I, paras. 221–4.

63 *Globe*, 1 Dec. 1997.

64 Affidavit of Robert Dixon, p. 107; Cross-examination of Nancy Naylor, in Ontario Court of Justice (General Division), Court file nos. 97-CV-137668 and 98-CV-139317, *OECTA et al. v. Attorney General of Ontario* and *Ontario Public School Boards' Association et al. v. Attorney General of Ontario*, vol. II, questions 510 and 511.

65 On these two points see the important story broken by Jennifer Lewington, *Globe*, 1 Dec. 1997, and Cross-examination of Nancy Naylor, vol. II, questions 511–20.

66 *Star*, 22 Nov. 1997. See also the political support offered by the OSSTA president, Patrick Daly, for the funding model: ibid., 26 March 1998.

Chapter 14   Disarray

1 Between 1992 and 1997, operating grants fell by just over $1 billion. No more than half of this was attributable to the Tories. See EIC, *The Road Ahead:*

A Report on Learning Time, Class Size and Staffing. The First Report of the Education Improvement Commission, August 1997, 18–19.

2 For the figures 1991–5, see OSSTF, OSSTF Issues, 'Boards Cut Teaching, Administrative and Support Staff,' n.d. (www.osstf.on.ca/www/issues/edfi/boardcut.html).

3 See Stephen Lawton, Mark Ryall, and Teresa Menzies, *A Study on Costs: Ontario Public Elementary/Secondary Education Costs as Compared to Other Provinces,* MOET, August 1996.

4 *Ontario School Board Reduction Task Force. Final Report,* 61–3.

5 Leon Paroian, *Review of the School Boards'/Teachers' Collective Negotiations Process in Ontario,* [MOET] 1996.

6 On the anti-Harris protests see John Ibbitson, *Promised Land: Inside the Mike Harris Revolution* (Scarborough, Ont.: Prentice Hall Canada, 1997), 99, 128, 206ff. In January 1996, to protest the cuts of the previous November, OECTA sponsored the largest anti-government rally to that point: see *Star,* 14 Jan. 1996; Aleda O'Connor, 'That's Us in the Front Row,' [OECTA] *The Reporter,* June 1996, 34–40. As many as half the demonstrators in the march to Queen's Park held as part of the Metro Days of Action in late October 1996 may have been teachers: see Ibbitson, *Promised Land,* 216–17.

7 See e.g. *Globe,* 6 Apr. 1996; Doug Little, 'Ontario Teachers Try Their Luck with the Class Struggle,' *Our Schools / Our Selves,* May/June 1996, 17–23. On community outreach see e.g. materials prepared by OSSTF and two other unions for 'Community Forums on Public Education, November 18 and 20,' 1996, in Waterloo County.

8 The various union journals and web sites give accounts of these efforts. Of particular importance was the attack on the study by Lawton et al. See [OSSTF Provincial Office, Library] 'Queen's Park, 17 Oct. 1996. Informetrica, CTF Studies Critical of Ministry Cost of Education Document,' and attached: Informetrica Ltd., 'A Study on Costs, by Lawton, Ryall and Menzies, A Review,' 10 Oct. 1996, and Memorandum, Wilf Brown, Canadian Teachers' Federation, to OECTA, 'Ontario Ministry of Education Study on Cost of Education,' 30 Sept. 1996.

9 See *OTF Interaction,* March 1997; *OPSTF News,* Apr. 1997, 32; *Star,* 10 March [OECTA], 11 Apr., 25 May, 6 June 1997. Though the vote coincided with announcements about Bill 136, it was initiated by resolutions at the annual meeting in March. See OSSTF Media release, 'OSSTF members fed up – Thumbs down to the Government,' 5 June 1997 (www.osstf.on.ca/www/pub/pressrel/_sept97/ju0597-1.html).

10 On Bill 136 see Ibbitson, *Promised Land,* 275–7.

11 *Star,* 19 Sept. 1997.

12 OSSTF, OSSTF Issues, 'OTF Affiliate Presidents' and General Secretaries' Meeting with Government Representatives regarding Pending Legislation, 27 Aug. 1997' (www.osstf.on.ca/www/issues/teacher1/pndleg.html). Though this critical document comes from union sources only, its contents were reported in the press (*Star*, 5 Sept. 1997) and were never challenged by the government. Thus I take it to be a fair summary of the meeting.

13 Quoted in Ibbitson, *Promised Land*, 276.

14 EIC, *The Road Ahead.*

15 See *Star*, 12 Sept. 1997.

16 Ibid., 28 Oct. 1997.

17 The opinion poll was released four months later. See Richard Mackie's story in the *Globe*, 31 Dec. 1997.

18 *Globe*, 20 Sept. 1997; OSSTF, OSSTF Bulletins, Bulletin #3-978: 'Bill 136 and the Teacher Legislation,' 19 Sept. 1997 (www.osstf.on.ca/www/pub/bulletin/se1997-1.html).

19 MOET, News release, 'Snobelen details further plans for education reform,' 24 Sept. 1997 (www.edu.gov.on.ca/eng/document/nr/97.09/addref_e.html); *Star*, 25 and 26 Sept. 1997. See also reporter Peter Small's useful backgrounder on prep time in the *Star*, 27 Sept. 1997.

20 For examples, see *Globe*, 11 and 22 Jan. 1996; *Star*, 23 Jan. 1996.

21 *Star*, 7 Sept. 1997. For the OSSTF stand see OSSTF, OSSTF Bulletins, 'An Open Letter to OSSTF Members,' 8 Sept. 1997 (www.osstf.on.ca/www/pub/bulletin/se0897-1.html).

22 *Star*, 26 Sept. 1997.

23 See e.g. ibid., 7 Oct. 1997.

24 Ibid., 8 Oct. 1997.

25 Ibid., 7 Oct. 1997.

26 Ibid., 7 Oct. 1997.

27 Ibid., 1 Oct. 1997.

28 See ibid., 7 Oct. 1997; *Globe*, 7 Oct. 1997.

29 On Johnson see Ibbitson, *Promised Land*, 110, 161; *Globe*, 11 Oct. 1997.

30 OSSTF, OSSTF Issues, Teacher Legislation, 'Submission of the OTF and the Affiliates to the Hon. David Johnson ... on Bill 160 ...,' 20 Oct. 1997 (www.osstf.on.ca/www/issues/teacher1/b160eqi.html).

31 *Star*, 22 Oct. 1997.

32 This was largely due to intervention by the Ontario College of Teachers during the previous week. For an account see Ontario College of Teachers, *Professionally Speaking*, December 1997, 10–12, 33–4; March 1998, 6.

33 *Star*, 21 and 22 Oct. 1997.

34 *Globe*, 25 Oct. 1997.

35 The account of the strike that follows and the quotations are drawn from the *Globe* and *Star*, 23 Oct.–10 Nov. 1997.

36 For an example see *Star*, 1 Oct. 1997.

37 Ibid., 25 Oct. 1997.

38 *LFP*, 31 Jan., 12 Feb. 1997.

39 *Globe*, 7 Jan. 1997 (Harris); MOET, 'Speaking Notes for ... John Snobelen announcement of education restructuring,' 13 Jan. 1997, 2 (www.edu.gov.on.ca/eng/document/nr/97.01/res-spe.html).

40 For good examples see Gord Henderson's column published in the *Windsor Star* and reprinted in the *LFP*, 27 Jan. 1996; and the *Star* editorials of 15 Feb. and 28 Aug. 1996.

41 Including even Bob Rae. See his *Globe* column, 1 Oct. 1997.

42 On the polls see *LFP*, 24 Oct. 1997; *Maclean's*, 10 Nov. 1997, 14. For sophisticated assessments of the play of public opinion just before the walkout, see Susan Delacourt's review in the *Globe*, 25 Oct. 1997, and Ian Urquhart in the *Star*, 23 Oct. 1997. For contrary assessments, however, see *Globe*, 31 Oct. and 1 Nov. 1997; OECTA, Press release, 'Public trusts teachers most, not Harris government, survey shows,' 23 Oct. 1997 (www.oecta.on.ca/files/news-frame.html).

43 Michael Marzolini, quoted in *Maclean's*, 10 Nov. 1997, 14.

44 On the polls and the link to the Lacey contract, see *Maclean's*, 17 Nov. 1997, 23; *Globe*, 3 Nov. 1997; *Star*, 2 Nov. 1997.

45 For the court decision see *Globe*, 19 March 1998. For more details on the case see Jerry Paquette, 'Reengineering Ontario Education: The Process and Substance of the Harris Reforms in Education in Ontario,' *Education & Law Journal* 9, 1 (1998).

46 OSSTF, Media release, 'We will never forget ... OSSTF President ... gives a rallying call to delegates at the OSSTF Annual Meeting' [14 March 1998] (www.osstf.on.ca/www/pub/pressrel/sept97_sept98/mr1498-1.html). For press coverage see *LFP*, 16 March 1998.

47 OECTA, *Seize the Day*. The text is also available at the OECTA web site (www.oecta.on.ca/files/seize-frame.html).

48 This issue, about whether or not there should be a province-wide uniform business tax rate to match the uniform residential rate established by Bill 160, became more inflamed when the new assessment rates were released in early 1998. There is a helpful overview of the problems by Royston James in the *Star*, 5 Apr. 1998. See also *Star*, 12 Feb. 1998 (Urquhart); *Globe*, 16 Feb. (Rusk), and 25 Feb. 1998 (Monahan).

49 See *Star*, 22 Jan. 1998 (editorial); *LFP*, 11 Feb. 1998.

50 *Star*, 28 Jan., 14 Feb. 1998.

51 Quoted in *LFP*, 10 March 1998.
52 *Globe*, 26 Feb. 1998; OSSTF, OSSTF Update, 'The First Hit. 1870 Pink Slips in Ottawa-Carleton,' 2 March 1998 (www.osstf.on.ca/www/pub/update/vol25/1mr/1mraott.html). For the other problems see e.g. *LFP*, 14 Jan. and 11 Feb. 1998; *Globe*, 20 Feb. 1998.
53 See *Star*, 3 Nov., 3 Dec. 1997; 25 Jan. 1998; *LFP*, 21 Jan., 9 and 18 March 1998.
54 *Globe*, 14 March 1998, and MOET, News release and backgrounder, 'Limiting class size to ensure quality education,' 13 March 1998 (www.edu.gov.on.ca/eng/document/nr/98.03/classnre.html).
55 *LFP*, 24 Feb. 1998.
56 *Globe*, 6 March 1998.
57 *Globe*, 9 March 1998; *LFP*, 9 March 1998.
58 *Star*, 10 March 1998.
59 *Star*, 24 March 1998 ('friend,' A7). There were only small differences between these 'drafts' and the final version. See OSSTF, OSSTF Issues, 'Analysis of the 1998 Ontario Education Funding Model,' 27 March 1998 (www.osstf.on.ca/www/issues/edfi/funding/newmodct.html).
60 *Star*, 26 March 1998.
61 Quoted by Ian Urquhart in a good column on the Tory turnabout, *Star*, 24 March 1998.
62 *Star*, 27 March 1998.
63 See e.g. *Star*, 18, 26 Apr., 1, 2, 4, 26 May, 3 June 1998.
64 See Cross-examination of Nancy Naylor, in Ontario Court of Justice (General Division), Court file nos. 97-CV-137668 and 98-CV-139317, *OECTA et al. v. Attorney General of Ontario* and *Ontario Public School Boards' Association et al. v. Attorney General of Ontario*, vol. I, question 193; MOET, *Student-Focused Funding. Technical Paper, June 18, 1998 (Revision of March 31, 1998)*.
65 Throne Speech: *Star*, 24 Apr. 1998; budget: *Star*, 6 May 1998; June announcement: *Globe*, 16 June 1998; *LFP*, 16 June 1998.
66 *Star*, 21 Apr. 1998.
67 The judge's decision was widely covered in relatively brief accounts and the *Star* printed the pertinent sections on the funding model; but there was very little beyond that in the press and no 'investigative reporting,' either during or immediately after the hearings, on the large body of court records the case threw up. When, in autumn 1998, someone else did the hard analytical work on these sources, reporters implied that somehow they had been inaccessible. In fact, they were available at the time of the hearings and accessible to anyone from the press who cared to ask for them. Cf. Hugh Mackenzie, Ontario Budget Working Group, Technical paper no. 5, 'Education Funding in Ontario,' October 1998, and *Globe*, 26 Oct. 1998 (Richard Mackie).

68　This, of course, is my summary of hundreds of pages of evidence. Mainly see Joint Submissions of the Applicants, in Ontario Court of Justice (General Division), Court file nos. 97-CV-137668 and 98-CV-139317, *OECTA et al. v. Attorney General of Ontario* and *Ontario Public School Boards' Association et al. v. Attorney General of Ontario,* vol. I, and Cross-examination of Nancy Naylor.

69　Cross-examination of Nancy Naylor, vol. I, questions 244–7.

70　Italics added.

71　For a summary of the government's case, see Factum of the Respondent and the Intervenors, in Ontario Court of Justice (General Division), Court file nos. 97-CV-137668 and 98-CV-139317, *OECTA et al. v. Attorney General of Ontario* and *Ontario Public School Boards' Association et al. v. Attorney General of Ontario,* paras. 6–31. For more detail see ibid., part III B, paras. 269–521. The quotations in this and the preceding paragraphs are taken from paras. 16, 15, 97, and 266. See also Affidavit of Nancy Naylor in ibid., Respondent's Application Record, vol. I.

72　Cumming J., Reasons for Judgment (released 22 July 1998), in Ontario Court of Justice (General Division), Court file nos. 97-CV-137668 and 98-CV-139317, *OECTA et al. v. Attorney General of Ontario* and *Ontario Public School Boards' Association et al. v. Attorney General of Ontario,* p. 18. The summary and quotations that follow are to be found between pp. 10 and 21.

73　The questions, and a summary of the arguments on both sides, are to be found in the decision itself. But for more detail see Ontario Court of Justice (General Division), ibid., Reply Submissions on Behalf of OECTA et al.; Joint Submissions of the Applicants, vols. II and III; Factum of the Respondent and the Intervenors. I want to express my thanks to all those lawyers, especially Brian Kelsey and Maurice Green, who provided me with so many of the court records submitted in the case; and my particular gratitude goes to Elizabeth Sandals, president, and to Maggie McFadzen, executive co-ordinator, of OPSBA, who made available hundreds of pages of cross-examination transcripts and other related material. Without the help of all these people, this section of the book could not have been written.

74　Cumming J., Reasons for Judgment, p. 48.

75　MOET, 'Remarks by ... David Johnson on the court challenge ...,' 22 July 1998 (www.edu.gov.on.ca/eng/document/nr/98.07/ruling.html).

76　*Star,* 14 Aug. 1998. The case was heard during November 1998 by the Court of Appeal for Ontario. A judgment would be forthcoming in early 1999.

77　The labour conflicts were closely followed in newspapers such as the *Globe, Star,* and *LFP* throughout the summer and fall of 1998. The numbers of pupils out of school in September bounced around as one or another conflict was settled or commenced.

78 On the latter point see the opinion poll reported in the *Globe*, 24 Aug. 1998.
79 See *Star*, 29 and 30 Oct. 1998, and subsequent November issues. For examples outside Toronto see *LFP*, 10 and 15 Sept. 1998; *Star*, 23 Sept., 6 and 15 Oct., 13 Nov. 1998; *Globe*, 24 Sept., 1 Oct. 1998.
80 See *Star*, 6 Sept. 1998; *Globe* and *LFP*, 10 Sept. 1998.
81 Cf. *Globe*, 15 and 25 Sept. 1998. For the details of the legislation see MOET, News release, fact sheet, 'Back to School Act 1998' [28 Sept. 1998] (www.edu.gov.on.ca/eng/document/nr/98.09/backsch.html).
82 See *LFP* and *Star*, 7 Nov. 1998; MOET, News release, Office of the Premier, 6 Nov. 1998 (www.edu.gov.on.ca/eng/document/nr/98.11/preme.html); MOET, News release and related fact sheets, 13 Nov. 1998 (www.edu.gov.on.ca/eng/document/nr/98.11/deadline.html).

Chapter 15 Retrospect

1 *Report to the Minister. The Working Group on Education Finance Reform*, 12.
2 Quoted in *Star*, 30 Dec. 1996.
3 For an accessible review of changes in the United States, see 'Robin Hood Rides Again,' *The Economist*, 12 Dec. 1998, 28–9. As I've already suggested, Canadian courts were pressing in this direction for Franco-Ontarian education, while in Ontario in the mid-1990s, Roman Catholic leaders were contemplating a legal challenge unless an equitable funding model was put in place. On the latter point see Affidavit of Robert Dixon, in Ontario Court of Justice (General Division), Court file nos. 97-CV-137668 and 98-CV-139317, *OECTA et al. v. Attorney General of Ontario*, Responding Record of the Intervenor, Ontario Catholic School Trustees' Association, vol. II, p. 109.
4 Ontario Fair Tax Commission, *Fair Taxation in a Changing World: Report of the Ontario Fair Tax Commission* (Toronto: University of Toronto Press, 1993), 683.
5 In the 1992 *Blueprint for Education*.
6 EIC, *The Road Ahead, II. A Report on the Role of School Boards and Trustees*, 2nd report of the EIC, December 1997, 3. See also Ian Urquhart's perceptive review of the issue, 'Is There a Hidden Agenda?' *Star*, 19 Sept. 1998.
7 On this subject, the rhetoric of 'privatization' is endemic amongst the opponents of even the most modest experiments in refashioning *public* education. Yet in the world beyond Ontario's borders there is no shortage of variations, nor is there a paucity of thoughtful alternative scenarios by people doggedly devoted to the cause of public education. For accessible examples of both, see Lois Sweet, *God in the Classroom: The Controversial Issue of Religion in Canada's Schools* (Toronto: McClelland and Stewart, 1997), esp. 125–36, 241–4;

and *The Report of the Commission on Private Schools in Ontario* [Shapiro Report], October 1985.

8 'Interview with Jim Head. High School Teacher Politics in Ontario,' *Our Schools / Our Selves* 3, 3 (Dec. 1991): 146.

9 On this point see the commentary in OSSTF, *Present Challenges, New Directions: A Discussion Paper on Future Directions in Secondary School Education* (1988), 5, and its reference to similar complaints in *At What Cost? A Study of the Role of the Secondary School in Ontario* (Toronto: OSSTF, 1976). Similarly see Royal Commission on Learning, *For the Love of Learning* (1994), 4: 118–19.

10 In 1997–8 I contributed affidavits to two constitutional challenges, one against Bill 104 and the other against Bill 160, launched by a consortium of public school boards, the trustees' association, and teachers' unions.

11 For an extended discussion of the nature of the late-nineteenth-century high school in Ontario, see R.D. Gidney and W.P.J. Millar, *Inventing Secondary Education: The Rise of the High School in Nineteenth-Century Ontario* (Montreal and Kingston: McGill-Queen's University Press, 1990), chaps. 12–15. On the entrance exam in particular see p. 284. The figures presented here are calculated from the 1901 statistics in Minister of Education, *Annual Report for 1902*.

12 For a summary of the research, see Mark Holmes, *The Reformation of Canada's Schools: Breaking the Barriers to Parental Choice* (Montreal and Kingston: McGill-Queen's University Press, 1998), chap. 4: esp. 156–62.

13 For the most recent confirmation see Lewington's summary of a York University study, *Globe*, 27 Jan. 1997.

14 See *Globe*, 18 Apr. 1997.

15 Alan J.C. King et al., *Improving Student Retention in Ontario Secondary Schools* (Toronto: MOE, 1988), 129–30.

16 Ray Marshall and Marc Tucker, *Thinking for a Living: Education and the Wealth of Nations* (New York: Basic Books, 1992), 66–7.

17 Chuck Rachlis and David Wolfe, 'An Insider's View of the NDP Government of Ontario ... ,' in Graham White, ed., *The Government and Politics of Ontario*, 5th ed. (Toronto: University of Toronto Press, 1997), 333. The internal quotations are from studies identified in their endnotes. More recently, see Bruce Little's analysis, *Globe*, 9 and 23 March 1998.

18 Bob Davis, 'Mentally Skilled but Mindless,' [OSSTF] *Education Forum*, Fall-Winter 1993, 18–21, 36–8.

19 Peter C. Emberley and Waller R. Newell, *Bankrupt Education: The Decline of Liberal Education in Canada* (Toronto: University of Toronto Press, 1994), 8. Some readers may be inclined to dismiss such views as backward-looking nostalgia, or even worse, as merely a neo-conservative rant, in which case it is perhaps worth pointing out that thoughtful critics of a variety of political

hues have reached similar conclusions. There may be a need to reinterpret, for our own times, the meaning of a liberal education, as other generations have also done, but that doesn't undermine the thrust of the argument. See e.g. George Martell, *A New Education Politics: Bob Rae's Legacy and the Response of the Ontario Secondary School Teachers' Federation* (Toronto: James Lorimer, 1995), esp. 292ff.; Ken Osborne, *Educating Citizens: A Democratic Socialist Agenda for Canadian Education* (Toronto: Our Schools / Our Selves, 1988).

20 Yale Report of 1828, cited in Richard Hofstadter and Wilson Smith, eds, *American Higher Education: A Documentary History* (Chicago: University of Chicago Press, 1961), 1: 278.

Index